New Testament Commentary

From the Aramaic and the Ancient Eastern Customs

Other Books by George M. Lamsa

THE HOLY BIBLE
(From Ancient Eastern Manuscripts)

THE NEW TESTAMENT
(From Ancient Eastern Manuscripts)

GOSPEL LIGHT
(A Commentary on the Gospels)

OLD TESTAMENT LIGHT
(A Scriptural Commentary Based on the
Aramaic Version of the Ancient Peshitta Text)

IDIOMS IN THE BIBLE EXPLAINED
(A Key to the Holy Scriptures)

New Testament Commentary
FROM THE ARAMAIC
AND
THE ANCIENT EASTERN CUSTOMS

by George M. Lamsa, B.A., F.R.S.A.

HOLMAN • NASHVILLE

Twelfth Printing, 1982
Copyright © 1945 by Holman
Copyright © Renewed 1973 by Holman
All Rights Reserved
All Foreign Rights Reserved
No Parts To Be Reprinted Without Permission
Holman, Nashville, Tennessee 37234
Printed in U.S.A.
ISBN 0 87981 049 1

This volume
is sincerely, and gratefully
dedicated to
Margaret Hall Outerbridge

CONTENTS

FOREWORD BY JOSEPH FORT NEWTON	ix
PREFACE BY AUTHOR	xi
INTRODUCTION NEW TESTAMENT	xiii
THE ACTS OF THE APOSTLES	1
ROMANS	175
I CORINTHIANS	277
II CORINTHIANS	293
GALATIANS	319
EPHESIANS	343
PHILIPPIANS	357
COLOSSIANS	369
I THESSALONIANS	385
II THESSALONIANS	397
I TIMOTHY	403
II TIMOTHY	429
TITUS	439
PHILEMON	447
HEBREWS	451
JAMES	487
I PETER	501

CONTENTS

II PETER	509
I JOHN	519
II JOHN	527
III JOHN	531
JUDE	535
THE REVELATION	539
INDEX	617

FOREWORD

The people of our time, even church folk, are almost without knowledge concerning the Bible. They know certain passages which they have read or heard read but the Book as a whole is a closed mystery. It is a book apart, unlike any other book; and yet it must be read as we read any other book if we are to know how unlike any other book it is.

Anyone who helps people to read and understand the Bible renders a great service to the spiritual life. For many the stately version of King James remains the classic and standard. The author of this book has given us "The New Testament, According to the Eastern Text, Translated from Original Aramaic Sources"; no mean achievement and most helpful to all Bible readers.

Also, he has followed his translation from the Aramaic with an interpretation of the Gospels, entitled "Gospel Light," showing how the old text and the unchanged customs of the East, where he was born, throw new light upon the teachings of Jesus. It is a valuable book, rich in insight and companionable in spirit, helping the Bible student. Often a single word in its Aramaic meaning, or some custom unfamiliar to the West, is like a candle set down alongside a text, lighting up its real meaning. It is not a verse by verse commentary but a spotlight, so to speak, moving to and fro, making dark passages light and making the path plainer and the task of the reader easier.

In this new volume he undertakes the same ministry for the Acts, the Epistles and the Book of Revelation. This book is most welcome and it will add to our obligation to the author but even he cannot make the book of Revelation, in spite of its title, other than a sealed book to most of its readers. It is my honor to speak a foreword to a book which will be highly prized by many who want to best know the Book most worth knowing.

JOSEPH FORT NEWTON.

PREFACE

Since the publication of *Gospel Light*, a commentary on the Four Gospels, hundreds of letters have requested further Comments on the New Testament. This volume, like the former work, aims to throw light on the obscure and difficult passages of the New Testament. The Scriptures are the inspired Word of God which was revealed to the prophets and the apostles who, in turn, recorded them first for the people of their own country and then to the world.

The writers were Easterners, therefore, they wrote in the vernacular which was understood by the simple and unlearned people. Moreover, the Authors of this sacred literature, to make clear their points, used idioms, similes and metaphors which were in common use and which are still in use today.

Eastern customs and manners also played an important part in transmitting and recording the Word of God. The Hebrew prophets, as well as Jesus and his apostles, illustrated their sayings with parables. Most of these Eastern customs are alien to Western thought and speech. This is the reason some of the simple expressions in the New Testament are the subject of theological arguments. The people of the Semitic race with their cultural background understood the language including the parables of the writers and they understood their teaching. On the other hand the converts from other races whose customs and habits of life were different, could not easily penetrate the Eastern mind and the subtlety of Semitic thought. The difficulty in transmitting thought from one language into another is conceded by all biblical scholars. This is especially true of Semitic languages which have a limited vocabulary and words having divers meanings and thoughts and ideas expressed in figures of speech.

Today educators and scholars throughout the world are

cognizant of the important part which Semitic languages played in the Bible. This is also true of other important books and documents. It is difficult to transmit thought from one tongue into another without loss of meaning.

I believe God preserved the ancient and pure biblical culture and language for a purpose. Great empires and splendor went down and have become nothing but history but God's truth has remained.

My humble attempt in this work is to elucidate the difficult and obscure passages so that those who are seeking guidance and comfort from the Bible may more easily understand its message. This I have done with diligence and the best of my knowledge of Aramaic and other Semitic languages. My main objective in this work has been to explain Eastern customs and manners which play an important part in the Scriptures. I have tried to avoid as much as possible theological and controversial passages which to me are destructive rather than constructive.

May this work be helpful to all those who sincerely seek to understand the teaching of our Lord.

GEORGE M. LAMSA.

INTRODUCTION

The New Testament writings like those of the Old Testament were handed down in scrolls. Portions of these were in the possession of churches and individuals for many years. For instance, the gospel of Matthew was originally written on several scrolls, probably five or six. Years later those scrolls were arranged and compiled into a single narrative which came to be known as the Gospel according to St. Matthew. The compilation of the Scriptures began in the second century, but writing on scrolls never ceased. Even today in the Near East, one can find portions of the Bible on scrolls. In the East, few complete texts of the Old or New Testament have been found compiled together.

The Four Gospels were handed down in single volumes. The Pauline epistles were grouped and bound together. The book of Acts was circulated in a single document. There were, however, some texts in which the Four Gospels and the rest of the New Testament books, with the exception of the book of the Revelation and a few minor epistles, were bound together.

The Four Gospels contain the teachings of Jesus. The book of Acts is the history of the growth and expansion of the Christian church. The epistles and other writings are all based on the teachings of Jesus. In other words, they are commentaries and expositions on the teachings of Jesus.

The reader or student therefore must distinguish between the teaching of our Lord and that of his disciples and their disciples and followers. The difference is this: The teaching of Jesus is authoritative. That is, it is based on his infinite understanding of God. Jesus spoke with authority. His teaching was not of men, but of God. In his sermons and discourses he touched on the law and the prophets to some extent in order to explain them to the

Jews. In some instances what he said was written in the book of the prophets. Jesus had the power and authority to interpret the Scriptures, to reveal the mysteries which they contained, and to write a new and higher law —a law to be written in men's hearts.

Jesus' mind was free from complicated doctrines and traditions which hampered the truth and closed the door of the kingdom of God. His teaching was based on divine inspiration. The Jews marveled when they heard him preach and debate with the Pharisees and Sadducees. "And the Jews marvelled saying, How does this man know reading, when he has not been instructed? Jesus answered and said, My teaching is not mine, but his who sent me" (John 7 : 15–16).

The apostles and their disciples on the other hand, were born and reared in Judaism. They were influenced by the Jewish religion, traditions, customs and laws. For a long time they were unable to understand the teaching of their Master. They could not divorce themselves completely from the religion which had nurtured them. In other words, they were human; subject to human weaknesses and temptations.

This is why the apostles in their writing and preaching so often fell back on the Old Testament, Jewish history, Mosaic laws and ordinances. Jesus in his preaching never told his followers whether to circumcise or not. He never recommended the Jewish Temple ceremonies, the system of priesthood, food laws and many other things, some of which became the center of controversies during the apostolic age. Jesus never claimed ties with any royal family, because he did not have to. The apostles and their converts for many years remained loyally in the bosom of Judaism. They prayed in the Temple, fasted, observed the Sabbath Day, made vows and shaved in the Temple, and abstained from eating certain meats and blood.

The New Testament in its present form is what survived from the apostolic writings. Some portions of the Scriptures were lost, and others perished during the persecution which began in the first century after Christ and lasted to the fourth century. Some were rejected when the New Testament canon was formed after the Nicene Council in A.D. 325. Evidently some of these writings were forged; others probably were contrary to the new doctrines and dogmas.

No doubt many manuscripts containing the writings of other apostles were lost. Thaddeus (Matt. 10 : 3), Thomas and Peter were the evangelizers of Mesopotamia, Persia and India, and founders of the ancient Church of the East. Millions of Christians in Malabar, India, bear St. Thomas' name. Thaddeus is the founder of the Church of the East. And Simon Peter preached in Babylon (I Pet. 5 : 13). In our New Testament canon we have only the writings of four apostles who had been with Jesus: Matthew, John, James and Peter.

The epistles were pastoral letters addressed to congregations in various parts of the Roman Empire. Their purpose was to admonish, teach and strengthen the converts. The writers probably never thought that their writings would survive and become sacred literature, and many of these were lost or destroyed. It is a divine miracle that so many of them have survived to the present day.

Dates

Not one of the books of the New Testament was dated by the apostles or scribes. Therefore, dates are all conjectural.

In the olden days, documents, birth records, contracts and legal papers were dated from the years of kings, wars, famines and other important events. This is still the custom in many Eastern countries where birth and death records are not kept. For example, the birth of a certain prominent man is based on the year in which a certain king ascended the throne, but in some instances we have no accurate way to ascertain the year. Moreover, in those days, each nation had its own way of reckoning time. Calendars were known, but not universally adopted. Thus all the scribes could do when dating their writings was to mention the year of the reigning king. Some of the scribes did not take the trouble even to do this. This is because the Scriptures were primarily written for instruction, discipline and consolation. Both writers and readers were interested only in the message and the person of Jesus.

Thus, our Christian era has no positive starting point. It is commonly calculated from a wrong starting point. It begins with the reign of Herod who is supposed to have been made king of Judea in the year 40 B.C. and died in the thirty-seventh year of his reign. The birth of Jesus is supposed to have occurred in 4 B.C.

The practice of dating from the year of our Lord started in the sixth century, when Dionysius Exiguus made the year of the birth of our Lord correspond to the Roman year 754. However, the Easterners dated some of their manuscripts from the Greek conquest of Asia. That is 311 B.C. This practice continued until the sixteenth century, as is seen from Aramaic manuscripts.

It makes little difference what year Jesus was born, or how old he was when he died on the cross. It is important, however, to have plausible reckoning of time and events starting from the ascension of our Lord. This will throw light on the growth and expansion of the Christian church and the period in which the New Testament was written.

The student must realize that considerable periods of time elapsed between Jesus' death, the establishment of churches in Judea and Syria, and the conversion of Paul. These churches were not organized over night. It took many years before the Christians separated themselves from the Jewish synagogue and started to organize and establish congregations of their own. In the book of Acts we are told that Paul persecuted the churches in Judea and Syria (Acts 9 : 1–4).

Paul, Mark and Luke had never seen Jesus. When they were converted only a few of the apostles were living. Had they seen Jesus, they would have made mention of it. Paul in all of his writings never makes any mention that he had seen Jesus before his death. Yet Paul was a learned Jew, a member of the Jewish council. Had he been living at the time of Jesus, he would have seen him and would have mentioned something about Jesus' arrest, trial, and the opposition of the Sanhedrin. Paul would have had access to the Jewish documents and other information concerning Jesus' death. But the event had occurred so long before, that the Jewish records concerning Jesus had perished. Paul throughout his missionary journeys preached the Gospel of Jesus Christ (Rom. 15 : 19).

When Paul was a young man, Christianity was already an organized church rivaling Judaism. When Stephen was stoned, Paul was guarding the clothes of men who participated in his murder (Acts 7 : 58). Thus there is a long period of time between Jesus and Paul, and between Jewish and Gentile Christianity.

In this volume, whenever necessary, I have quoted important passages from the Old Testament and the Four Gospels in order to facilitate the work of the student. The apostles' references to the Old Testament are often too brief to reveal the nature of their arguments. Their writings are pastoral letters addressed to Christian congregations. This is because the people to whom they wrote were familiar with the Bible and the issues. These quotations throw considerable light on the questions and help the student to grasp the meaning.

My purpose in this work, just as in *Gospel Light,* is to throw light on the idioms, customs and manners, and to explain some of the difficult and obscure passages in the light of the Aramaic language and Eastern customs.

NEW TESTAMENT COMMENTARY

THE ACTS OF THE APOSTLES

The book of Acts is an account of the Christian church, beginning with the ascension, the descent of the Holy Spirit and the ministry of the apostles. At Pentecost the disciples and followers of Christ organized the Christian movement in Jerusalem, and started their world-wide missionary work.

The book gives an account of the church in Judea, the persecution of the apostles and their followers, the murder of James, son of Zebedee, the conversion of Saul, and the first church council in Jerusalem. A large portion of the book is devoted to the work of Paul, his missionary journeys in Judea, Asia Minor, Greece and Rome, and the expansion of Christianity from Palestine to other parts of the world. Antioch replaced Jerusalem as the center of Christendom and it became the greatest evangelizing center.

The author of the book is Luke who is also the author of the Third Gospel which bears his name. Luke accompanied Paul on many of his missionary journeys. (Note: When he is not with Paul he uses "them" and "they" and when he is with him, "we." The author keeps himself in the background. He does not disclose any of his own activities, but he does record most of the important events.) Eusebius tells us that Luke was a Syrian from Antioch.

The date of the book, like that of the Gospels, is not

exactly known. It probably was written in about the year 70. Be that as it may, the first part of the book of Acts was written prior to the conversion of Paul. Luke gathered some of his material from the apostles and eyewitnesses, since he himself was a later convert.

THE AUTHOR

The former treatise have I made, O Theophilus, of all that Jesus began both to do and teach. Acts 1 : 1.

Luke is supposed to be the author of the Third Gospel. The Gospel of Luke, however, is entitled "According to the preaching of Luke." That implies that a later scribe has edited the work and added other material based on the preaching of Luke.

Luke's attempt was to set in order the teachings and works of Jesus and the narratives which were familiar to the eyewitnesses. Luke was not a disciple of Christ. Nor was he one of the twelve apostles, but a later convert who became a companion of Paul on several of his missionary journeys. The Third Gospel, therefore, is based on documentary evidence, plus the information which Luke had gathered from eyewitnesses. The story of the birth of Jesus, the coming of the magi and the genealogy had to be told by men and women who had known Jesus, the Virgin Mary and Joseph. Jesus had said nothing about his human ancestry or his birth.

The author of the Third Gospel apparently was asked by Theophilus to write an account of the works of the apostles and the conversion of the Gentiles. In his first treatise Luke undertook to compile and write the story of Jesus from his birth to his ascension. Now he begins where he had left off.

FORTY DAYS

To whom also he shewed himself alive after his passion by many infallible proofs, being seen of them forty days, and speaking of the things pertaining to the kingdom of God: Acts 1 : 3.

Forty is a number frequently used in the Scriptures. Some people call it a sacred number. When the number is divided by ten, the result is four. That suggests the four corners of the earth, the four winds, the Four Gospels. Numbers forty and twelve are closely associated with the calendar and sacred customs. Moses was forty years old when he fled from Egypt. He spent forty years in the desert as a shepherd. He fasted forty days and forty nights in Mount Sinai (Ex. 24 : 18). The flood lasted forty days and forty nights (Gen. 7 : 4). Moses spent forty years in the desert, and forty years traveling with the Israelites. He fasted forty days when he went to the mountain. Jesus fasted forty days and forty nights (Matt. 4 : 2). Elijah fasted forty days. Jewish women purified themselves forty days after they had given birth to a child (Luke 2 : 22). Forty is symbolical of completeness and is frequently used in the Bible.

The risen Christ spent forty days preaching to his disciples and followers concerning the kingdom of God. The dreams of a political kingdom had been shattered on the cross, and so his disciples had to be taught a new meaning of the Messianic kingdom. They now were able to grasp the meaning of spiritual things. In their eyes Jesus' political mission had failed, but Jesus, through his resurrection, had triumphed over evil forces and death. The disciples now were convinced of Jesus' spiritual mission and the unseen kingdom which was soon to become a reality.

Some of his disciples nevertheless were still thinking of the Davidic kingdom and were hoping for another attempt to restore it. But Jesus told them that it was not for them to know the times or the seasons (Acts 1 : 7).

He dismissed the question just as he had done on other occasions previous to his death (Mark 13 : 32).

Forty days were needed to confirm his disciples' faith and explain to them the things which they had misunderstood. They had expected the restoration of the kingdom during his life on the earth (Luke 24 : 21). Jesus had to prove to them that the Messiah had to suffer in order to enter into his glory (Acts 24 : 26). It took forty years for the Israelites to forget Egypt. It took forty days for the disciples to forget the political kingdom and learn to think in terms of a spiritual Messianic realm —the realm of truth. Jesus during these forty days appeared eleven times to his disciples and followers, and strengthened their faith in the gospel which he had entrusted unto them.

ISRAEL'S RESTORATION

When they therefore were come together, they asked of him, saying, Lord, wilt thou at this time restore again the kingdom to Israel?   Acts 1 : 6.

This was one of the questions which Jesus had refused to answer. Before his death his disciples had asked him concerning the restoration of the Davidic kingdom and the fulfillment of the Messianic prophecies as interpreted by the Pharisees and the doctors of the law. "But of that day and hour knoweth no man, no, not the angels of heaven, but my Father only" (Matt. 24 : 36). Jesus during those forty days had opened their eyes to the Messianic kingdom, that is, the kingdom of God, and the coming of the Holy Spirit, but did not set a time for his second coming. His reply to this question, as always, indicated the suddenness of his coming, as the thief that comes in the night. God is the only one to set the time. Jesus had warned his disciples to beware of false prophets who would try to deceive the faithful through false predictions of his second coming. "Then if any man shall say unto you, Lo, here is Christ, or there; believe it not."

Jesus predicts the course of events which were to take place between his ascension and his second coming. The gospel of the kingdom has to be preached throughout the world before his return.

SAMARIA

But ye shall receive power, after that the Holy Ghost is come upon you: and ye shall be witnesses unto me both in Jerusalem, and in all Judœa, and in Samaria, and unto the uttermost part of the earth. Acts 1 : 8.

The Eastern text reads *Beth shamraye,* "The Samaritan territory," and not Samaria. The latter was the capital of the Northern Kingdom which included all the ten tribes of Israel. The word *Shamrin,* "Samaria," sometimes is used for the City of Samaria and, on other occasions, for the whole state, as we speak of New York, and New York State. For instance, "Washington backs England," does not mean Washington, D.C., but the United States. And Babylon is used in the Bible when referring to the Chaldean Empire. In olden days countries were often referred to by the names of their capitals.

Samaritan territory in this case means a district which was restricted to Samaritan people, just as Utah was, some years ago, restricted to the Mormons. Such territories are to be found in many parts of the East, where members of rival sects live in seclusion, practice their religion, maintain their traditions, and work and trade among themselves. For instance, until the country of the "devil worshipers" near Mosul was occupied by Great Britain, no other people were found to be dwelling among them. They did not permit strangers to enter their territory, fearing interference with their faith. Even now one can hardly find followers of other faiths in their villages. This is also true of many districts in Kurdistan, Arabia, Persia, and some parts of China. The territory is restricted to the members of the respective faiths alone.

And today the holy cities of Mecca and Medina are forbidden to non-Moslems.

During the time of our Lord, Palestine was divided into several provinces which were governed by Tetrarchs (governors). The Samaritans were given a territory in the province of Samaria. The people of Galilee, even though racially different from the Jews, adhered to the Jewish faith. But the Jews questioned their sincerity as true members of the Jewish religion (Ezra 4 : 1–4). On the other hand, the Galileans, though racially akin to the Samaritans, were religiously closer to the Jews. Therefore, the Samaritans hated them.

Jesus was not allowed to pass through the Samaritan territory, but his disciples later were to succeed in converting the Samaritans, who were the enemies of both Galileans and Jews. Christianity was to break down racial and religious barriers, and to plant love in place of hatred, truth in place of traditions. The God of Israel was no longer to be worshiped in Mount Gerizim, nor in Jerusalem, but in the hearts of men. (See *Gospel Light*, page 349.)

TAKEN UP

And when he had spoken these things, while they beheld, he was taken up; and a cloud received him out of their sight. Acts 1 : 9.

Nomadic tribes who live in seclusion still believe that clouds are living creatures commissioned by God to perform certain duties, such as taking care of crops, supplying streams and rivers, and carrying people up and down. This belief is largely due to the fact that in the desert and other dry regions the clouds in motion appear to be engaged in some purposeful activity. When white clouds are seen moving from dry areas toward the sea, the people say: "The clouds are going to the sea after water." On their way to the sea they look white and pale, and on their return they appear dark and heavy, as if they were heavily loaded with water.

When there was a drouth in Israel, during the reign of Ahab, Elijah prayed from the summit of Mt. Carmel for rain. And when he saw a cloud coming from the sea, he immediately heralded the coming of rain, and instructed Ahab to rush to shelter from the impending downpour (I Kings 18 : 44).

Then again in the desert, owing to the relative position of the sky to the land, heaven seems a very short distance from the earth, and only a little above the clouds. In those days it was customary to go up on the high places to pray and to offer sacrifices, because the people thought that these places were nearer to the throne of God, and the worshipers could more readily get His ear when making their petitions and supplications. In Kurdistan and other parts of the East some of the people still pray at the sacred shrines of the ancients on the tops of high mountains.

This concept made it easier for the early Christians to believe in the ascension of their Lord. This is because on the Mount of Transfiguration Moses and Elijah had been seen with Jesus and had been taken up in a cloud. The writers of the Synoptic Gospels in their account of the transfiguration of Jesus, all refer to an enveloping cloud about him which filled the three witnesses with awe.

The ascension of Jesus was a spiritual transformation. Jesus rose up from death and was taken up into the heavenly realm in a spiritual body, freed from all physical limitation. He was seen alive and ascending to heaven only by those whose spiritual vision had been strengthened by faith in him.

AN ANGEL

And while they looked stedfastly toward heaven as he went up, behold, two men stood by them in white apparel;
Acts 1 : 10.

The Aramaic word for angel is *malakha,* which means "messenger." Angels are pictured as symbols of purity and holiness, free from all human faults and imperfections. Eastern Christians bury their dead in white garments, symbolic of angelic perfection. No other color is permissible.

The Eastern concept of an angel is a tall, white-bearded, elderly man clad in flowing robes of dazzling white. The reason for this idea is the fact that priests and other church dignitaries are generally old men wearing white mantles while performing their religious duties. Conversation about angels, their rank and activities, is so prevalent that some men and women claim to have seen and conversed with them. According to an old belief, everyone has a guardian angel resting on his right arm to guide him, and a devil on his left arm to lead him astray.

The Hebrew *melakh,* "angel," like the Aramaic word, also means "messenger." Both words are closely related to *milka* (council) and *malka* (king). Kings act as counselors to their people. Our English word "angel" is derived from the Greek *angellos,* also meaning messenger. According to the Bible, angels are sent on divine errands, conveying word from God to men. They are also called "Sons of God." In Numbers 22 : 23 an angel is pictured as wearing a sword, and in Daniel 10 : 5 an angel is seen clothed in linen. Jesus told his disciples that after the resurrection men will be like angels, free from physical weakness. The knowledge of angels is supposed to be limited (I Pet. 1 : 12). Angels may be present in the person of human beings (Heb. 13 : 2). Angels are mentioned throughout the Scriptures. Belief in angels and spirits came to be a doctrine during and after the captivity.

The usual concept of God among some of the Eastern peoples is that of an Oriental monarch dressed in costly robes adorned with jewels, and seated on a golden throne surrounded by counselors whose advice he seemed to need (I Kings 22 : 19–23). Some of these agents are represented as executing his good purposes, and some are engaged in punishing men for their sins, just as an earthly king might do.

The doctrine of angelology and demonology, to which so many references are found in the Scriptures, is still prevalent among both primitive and advanced peoples, especially among the Mohammedans.

GALILEANS

Which also said, Ye men of Galilee, why stand ye gazing up into heaven? this same Jesus, which is taken up from you into heaven, shall so come in like manner as ye have seen him go into heaven. Acts 1 : 11.

The disciples of Jesus, with the exception of Judas of Iscariot, were Galileans, and his followers were recruited chiefly from the region of Galilee. No doubt Jesus had some sympathizers and followers in Judea and Syria, but the center of his movement was the group of towns around the Lake of Galilee. Some of his disciples deserted him. Others were afraid to identify themselves with the new teaching.

Jesus himself was a Galilean, and he did most of his teaching and healing in Galilee. He made some journeys into Judea where he gained a number of converts, but the Jewish officials opposed him. "After these things Jesus walked in Galilee: for he would not walk in Jewry, because the Jews sought to kill him" (John 7 : 1). The work in Judea was much harder. Jerusalem was the center of the Jewish religion and culture. The Jews were opposed to any reformers, especially to those coming from Galilee. They were expecting a Messiah who would be in the order of David. That is, a political and economic

Messiah who was to restore the kingdom of David and the reign of prosperity. Jesus disclaimed any political power. His kingdom was not of this earth. Hence the Jewish priests and scribes rejected him and delivered him into the hands of Pilate. But many of his Galilean followers stood by him to the last.

The Christian movement had become strong in Galilee and the number of the faithful steadily increased. The work in Jerusalem became stronger only after Pentecost. Even then all the leaders of the Christian movement were Galileans. Until the year 50, when the followers of Jesus in Antioch in Syria assumed the title of *Meshikhaye* Christians, they were either called Galileans or Nazarenes. The Jews also, when referring to Jesus and his followers, called them Galileans (John 7 : 52; Acts 2 : 7).

A SABBATH DAY'S JOURNEY

Then returned they unto Jerusalem from the mount called Olivet, which is from Jerusalem a sabbath day's journey.   Acts 1 : 12.

*B*ethzeithey means "home of olives," that is, a place where olives grow abundantly. The Mount of Olives is just outside of Jerusalem. From it one can see many parts of Palestine, Jericho, the Jordan Valley, and the desert.

The Eastern text reads, "separated from the city by seven furlongs." In this case, a Sabbath journey means a short distance, because the Jews walked only short distances on the Sabbath Day. The distance was determined by authorities so that the Sabbath might not be broken. Walking is considered a leisurely act, and is not regarded as work when one does not go on an errand on the Sabbath Day. Thus on the Sabbath Day the Jews ceased all their activities and spent the day resting at home and praying in the synagogue.

Even today one may see the Jews taking a short walk

in the late afternoon. In the olden days, walking on the Sabbath Day was prohibited beyond the limits of the tabernacle. During the time of Jesus the length of walk was from the Temple grounds to the valley of Kedron.

UPPER ROOM

And when they were come in, they went up into an upper room, where abode both Peter, and James, and John, and Andrew, Philip, and Thomas, Bartholomew, and Matthew, James the son of Alphœus, and Simon Zelotes, and Judas the brother of James. Acts 1 : 13.

Most of the houses in Palestine are one-story buildings, square in shape like a box. There are, however, some houses with an upper room which is used for guests, meetings and a place of rest. This room is called *balakhana*. Inns generally have one or more *balakhanas* (upper rooms) with doors and windows facing the courtyard. These rooms are generally rented to strangers, or used as banquet places. Donkeys, horses and mules are tied up in the courtyard and the lower rooms are occupied by guests of the poorer class. Some of the ancient inns are still to be found in Palestine and Syria and other parts of the East.

This upper room was the place where Jesus and his disciples ate the Last Supper (Mark 14 : 15). After the resurrection Jesus appeared unto them at the same place. His disciples had been there on other occasions. They had no other place to gather. The inn was patronized by strangers who had no relatives or friends in Jerusalem. On the other hand, inns are a good place for meeting people, receiving news and doing business. The disciples no doubt met merchant men and converts who came down from Galilee. Then again, there were a number of men and women followers of Jesus, together with Mary, his mother, and probably other relatives. Jesus had instructed them to remain in Jerusalem until the Pentecost (Acts

1 : 4). The members of this peculiar group would have been unwelcome in the homes of people who had seen their leader die on the cross.

PRICE OF SIN

Now this man purchased a field with the reward of iniquity; and falling headlong, he burst asunder in the midst, and all his bowels gushed out.   Acts 1 : 18.

The Eastern text reads: "He is the one who earned for himself a field with the price of sin; and falling headlong, he burst open in the midst, and all his bowels gushed out." That is to say the field was called Judas' field, because it was purchased with the sinful money for which he sold his Master. In the East such properties are named for the person who had been responsible for the money by which they were purchased.

Judas repented and hanged himself. The Jews could not use blood money for Temple purposes, so they bought with it a burying ground for strangers. In the East, strangers, especially members of rival faiths, are buried by themselves.

It is more likely that the rope with which Judas had hanged himself broke and that he fell to the ground. This happens often when heavy people are hanged. Judas did not purchase the field. When he was aware of his sinful act, he turned the money over to the priests before he hanged himself (Matt. 27 : 5).

FIELD OF BLOOD

And it was known unto all the dwellers at Jerusalem; insomuch as that field is called in their proper tongue, Aceldama, that is to say, The field of blood. Acts 1 : 19.

The Eastern text reads: *"khakal-dema,* which is to say *koriath-dem"*—"the field of blood." In his address, Peter renders the name of the field from one Aramaic dialect into another. That is, the Aramaic dialect spoken in the south and that spoken in the north. There were many Jews and Galileans who spoke both dialects among the people who had come to Jerusalem on the day of Pentecost. However, there were some who spoke their native dialect only. Peter spoke several Aramaic dialects. He had traveled for three years with Jesus in Judea, Syria and other parts of Palestine.

The name of the field is called the field of blood because it was purchased with "blood money." Most of the Easterners refuse to receive money paid as compensation for the murder of a relative. It is called "blood money."

VACANCIES

For it is written in the book of Psalms, Let his habitation be desolate, and let no man dwell therein: and his bishoprick let another take. Acts 1 : 20.

The Aramaic word *tishmishty* means "duty" or "ministry." The term "bishopric" was used later. A bishop is an overseer, one who looks after ministers and their congregations. Judas was a disciple and not an overseer. While traveling with Jesus he looked after the money. In other words he was the greedy purser who later sold his Master for thirty pieces of silver. When Mary of Magdala anointed Jesus' head with precious oil, Judas was enraged. He thought that the oil had been wasted. He wanted it sold for cash, perhaps in order that he could steal the money (John 12 : 6).

The above passage is quoted from Psalm 109 : 8. When a disciple or servant is dismissed, his duty is given to another. Judas was chosen by Jesus to a high office, but he proved to be unworthy. The vacancy created through his betrayal had to be filled by one who would be worthy of the high office of apostleship, so that he might become one of the shepherds of the great flock and a witness of the risen Christ who lives forever.

This is the only time on record that a vacant place in the ranks of the apostles was filled. Other vacancies created through death and martyrdom might have been likewise filled, and the record thereof lost.

LOTS

And they gave forth their lots; and the lot fell upon Matthias; and he was numbered with the eleven apostles.
Acts 1 : 26.

Casting of lots is an ancient Eastern custom which is still in use in Palestine, the Arabian Desert and Mesopotamia. Land, sheep, fish, and other things are divided by casting of lots. This method is considered the most honest way by which property can be divided and men elected to offices, because it avoids the possibility of bribery, discrimination, or intimidation.

Casting lots was used by the Israelites. When Saul was selected as king of Israel, Samuel ordered lots to be cast first on the tribes, then on the families. Saul was taken (I Sam. 10 : 20, 21). The soldiers also cast lots on Jesus' garments (Matt. 27 : 35).

When articles are to be divided each person selects and marks a small stone or a piece of wood. Then a boy or a stranger is called to place one of the stones on each article or group of articles. The same method is used for dividing land and electing men to high offices. When the casting of lots is finished everyone is satisfied with his lot and there are no complaints. Easterners believe God intervenes and decides the issue.

The apostles appointed two men who had seen Jesus and heard him preach: Joseph, called Barsabas, who was surnamed Justus; and Matthias. The latter was chosen and elected as a successor of Judas of Iscariot and was numbered among the apostles. Twelve, like seven and forty, was a sacred number and the apostles wished to preserve the original number of their ranks.

PENTECOST

And when the day of Pentecost was fully come, they were all with one accord in one place. Acts 2 : 1.

The Feast of Pentecost is one of the seven important Jewish feasts which God commanded Moses and the children of Israel to observe. They are called feasts of the Lord. "And the Lord spake unto Moses, saying, Speak unto the children of Israel, and say unto them concerning the feasts of the Lord, which ye shall proclaim to be holy convocations . . ." (Lev. 23 : 1–44).

These feasts were: the Feast of the Passover, the Unleavened Bread, the First Fruits, the Wave Offering, the Day of Atonement, the Feast of Tabernacles, and the Feast of Pentecost. "Even unto the morrow after the seventh sabbath shall ye number fifty days; and ye shall offer a new offering unto the Lord" (Lev. 23 : 16). The Feast of Pentecost falls during the harvest season. It was celebrated in commemoration of God's revelation to Moses on the Mount of Sinai.

Jesus told his disciples to wait in Jerusalem for the promise of the Father's gift of the Holy Spirit which was to come on all of them. Hitherto the spirit came only on those whom the disciples had laid hands. But when the promise should be fulfilled, the Holy Spirit would come on the whole body of the church and especially on the disciples. "Ye shall be baptized with the Holy Ghost not many days hence" (Acts 1 : 5). While on earth Jesus had promised to send them the Holy Spirit to abide with them and guide them in all matters. But the Comforter was to come only after Jesus had ascended into heaven (John 14 : 16–17).

Until the day of Pentecost the scope of the Christian gospel was limited to the Israelites, but thereafter the church was to become a world-wide movement, moved by the Spirit of God and embracing people of every race and color.

JEWISH CHRISTIANS

And there were dwelling at Jerusalem Jews, devout men, out of every nation under heaven. Acts 2 : 5.

The first followers of Jesus were all of the Jewish faith. They were mostly Galileans, Jews from Judea, Samaritans, and Syrian Jews. To these people Christianity was the fulfillment of Judaism. Christians worshiped in Jewish temple and synagogues, observed the Jewish customs and traditions, and kept the Mosaic law.

These Jewish converts to Christianity came from many foreign countries to the feast of the Passover and to worship at the Temple, which was the national shrine and center of the Jewish faith.

For many centuries the Church in Jerusalem and other parts of Palestine remained close to Judaism. The Christians were looked upon as dissatisfied Jews. They abstained from eating blood, pork and other food which the Jewish law prohibited. Then again, many Jewish feasts, ceremonies and traditions were observed and some of them are still observed by the members of the ancient churches in the East. On the other hand, at this early stage Christianity was a new movement within Judaism. It did not concern the Gentile world. The fifteen first bishops of Jerusalem were all Semites. Gentiles were not elected to high office until the third century, when the Roman Empire recognized Christianity as the state religion and the emperor exercised great influence in electing the officials.

What happened to the Jewish Christians? The answer is, they were assimilated by the Syrian (Aramean) and other Christians of the Semitic race. Jewish converts were a small minority when compared to Christians in Syria and Mesopotamia. Moreover, Christians were expelled from Judea (Acts 8 : 1).

SPEAKING IN TONGUES

Now when this was noised abroad, the multitude came together, and were confounded, because that every man heard them speak in his own language. Acts 2 : 6.

Semites, more than other races, are gifted in the acquiring of other languages. Shepherds, fishermen, farmers and even unlettered people generally, are able to speak two, three or four languages and several dialects. In the East, a dialect is often considered as a distinct language, not so much because of fundamental differences in words, but because of the differences in pronunciation and the idioms. This has come about because of the lack of printing, and of general intercourse between the tribes. In some regions, a few miles distance between two towns causes a distinct difference in pronunciation. Some learned men speak as many as twelve or more dialects and languages. To learn a dialect or a foreign tongue is one of the highest aspirations of the young men. This is because biblical lands have been conquered and ruled by other races. And since one language is used at court, another for commercial transactions, and still another for social intercourse, this ability has a very real practical value.

Then again, Easterners are clannish, and strongly dominated by their respective religions, traditions and customs, so that intermarriage and social activities between members of rival faiths are discouraged. Even today one can still find three or four languages spoken in a town or city. Each racial group clings to its own tongue and cultural background.

The people who were assembled on the day of Pentecost were Galilean residents of Jerusalem, and other Galileans, and members of the Ten Tribes, and the foreign Jews who had come to the feast. The ancestors of the Galileans had been brought from various parts of the East and settled in Galilee by Assyrian kings in the eighth century B.C. They spoke several Aramaic dialects, and had preserved the customs of the countries from whence they had come. There were also there Hebrew Christians, members of the ancient Ten Tribes who had been converted by Jesus and the seventy disciples whom he sent out to "the lost sheep of Israel," some of whom were settled only a few days' journey from Galilee. There were also Syrians from Tyre and Sidon, all of whom had close racial ties and spoke various Aramaic and other languages.

The disciples were inspired by the Holy Spirit. Some of them had traveled in Mesopotamia and Asia Minor. Quite naturally, the multitude, unused to such a spectacle, found it hard to comprehend what had taken place. They thought that the apostles were drunk. The Holy Spirit had empowered them to speak so that they could be understood by all those who were willing to accept the truth of Christ.

GALILEAN DISCIPLES

And they were all amazed and marvelled, saying one to another, Behold, are not all these which speak Galilæans?
Acts 2 : 7.

All the disciples of Jesus with the exception of Judas of Iscariot were Galileans. Jesus began preaching and teaching in Galilee. He himself was a Galilean. Most of the three years of his preaching were spent in towns around the Sea of Galilee, and in Syria. Jesus made several journeys into Judea but he was not well received there. Even though he made some converts and had some sympathizers in Jerusalem and other towns in Judea, the Jews rejected him, especially the scribes, Pharisees and the upper classes. They would not accept a prophet from Galilee. They said, when Christ comes he will be born in Bethlehem of Judea (John 7 : 41–42). "Out of Galilee ariseth no prophet" (John 7 : 53).

Since the days of the first captivity, Galilee had been known as the land of the Gentiles. When the king of Assyria removed the Ten Tribes he settled in their place Assyrians, Babylonians and people of other races which were brought from the other side of the river Euphrates (II Kings 17). Isaiah called the inhabitants of this region Gentiles, that is to say, foreigners (Isa. 9 : 1, 2).

The apostles who were the leaders of the Christian movement were all Galileans. (See article on the Galilean in *Gospel Light*.)

DRUNK WITH WINE

Others mocking said, These men are full of new wine.
Acts 2 : 13.

The Eastern text reads *meritha*, "the dregs of new wine." The *meritha* settles to the bottom of the jar when wine is purified. These dregs are generally given away to the poor and strangers to be drunk, and the pure wine is kept in containers or earthen jars to mellow.

The disciples were not drunk with new wine, but they were filled with the Holy Spirit and inspired with confidence in their Lord and his teaching. Jesus' resurrection and his victory over death were confirmed by the new miracles of healing which the apostles themselves were able to perform, and by the election of a new disciple who filled Judas' place. Their hearts were fired with fervent zeal. They were ready to spread the gospel of their Lord regardless of difficulties and hazards which they were to meet. The truth had opened their eyes so they understood things spiritually. Hitherto they had been students who had understood things partially, but now they were able to know the meaning of the prophecies and the hidden secrets of the Jewish religion.

The change in the disciples was so sudden that it was very difficult for the common people to comprehend or grasp the situation. They knew that the disciples were simple Galilean fishermen and peasants. So they were amazed to see them conversing with Jews, Galileans, Syrians, Assyrians and members of the Ten Tribes who had come to the Passover from every part of the world. As they could not understand the real cause of this unusual change, they thought these men might have drunk new wine. Then again, in the East it is often said, "He is drunk," which means he is overcome.

The disciples were inspired by the Holy Spirit which gave them the power to speak, teach and preach. Jesus had promised them that the Holy Spirit would teach them and guide them in all matters.

APOSTLES TESTIFYING

But Peter, standing up with the eleven, lifted up his voice, and said unto them, Ye men of Judœa, and all ye that dwell at Jerusalem, be this known unto you, and hearken to my words: Acts 2 : 14.

The other disciples stood up to prove that they were not drunk, as the people had supposed they were.

In the East, during banquets and festivals a speaker may stand or sit as he addresses the people. It depends on the size of the congregation and the place. Peter stood up so that the people might see him. The crowd was very large. We are told that 3,000 of them were converted and baptized. There were others who did not believe and who were not converted.

Peter did not announce his subject at the outset. In the East, good preachers and speakers at first try to prepare the minds of the people and acquaint them with what they intend to say. That is, the subject of the sermon and the most debatable portions thereof are left for the last. This is done to avoid quarrels and breaking up of the meetings which are very common on such occasions.

Many Jews who were gathered there and were not converts or sympathizers would have been offended, and would have walked out if Peter had started to preach his sermon about the Messianic claims of Jesus, his resurrection and his ascension. Some of the men would have started a riot because to them these words would have sounded like blasphemy. Therefore, Peter started his sermon with Jewish history, quoting from the prophets and proving that Jesus of Nazareth whom the Jews had rejected was the very promised Messiah which was foretold by the prophets. Then he announced his subject. "Jesus of Nazareth, a man approved of God among you by miracles and wonders and signs, which God did by him in the midst of you, as ye yourselves also know." Many of the Jews who were present had seen Jesus and witnessed some of his miracles and wonders. The words of Peter recalled these things to their minds, so they began to think about Jesus, the things which he had done, and the peaceful way in which he went to the cross. They were won.

The subject of the sermon was this: "Therefore let all the house of Israel know assuredly, that God had made that same Jesus whom ye have crucified, both Lord and Christ."

Stephen also preached in this manner. He announced the subject of his sermons at the end of his talk (Acts 7 : 56). He began with Abraham and gave an outline of the Jewish history proving that Jesus was the Messiah (Acts 7 : 1). But the Jews were not moved by his plea. They stoned him.

Paul likewise used this method in his letters and during his trials in Jerusalem and in Caesarea. But on some occasions, as soon as Paul made known his subject there was a riot which led to his stoning or arrest.

THREE O'CLOCK

For these are not drunken, as ye suppose, seeing it is but the third hour of the day. Acts 2 : 15.

Three o'clock by our time in America is nine o'clock A.M. in the East, where time is reckoned on the basis of sunset to sunset. There a new day begins at sunset, 6 P.M., and morning breaks at 6 A.M.

In countries where clocks were and still are unknown, time is measured by the falling shadows and by the sunbeams coming through the chimney in the center of the roof, and by crowing roosters. Some Easterners can tell time by instinct. Shepherds rely upon the stars during the night, and during the day they reckon by the shadows of the trees and cliffs. Where there are no cliffs or trees, time is measured by man's own shadow.

Peter did not consult a timepiece to convince the crowd that he was not intoxicated when he said: "It is but the third hour of the day." What he meant was that it was too early to indulge in drinking. In the East, wine is drunk only at meals, and, as Easterners seldom eat breakfast, wine is never used in the morning.

The disciples were inspired with a new enthusiasm and zeal; in other words, they were drunk with success, and with hope for the early triumph of the new faith. Easterners frequently make the remark: "He is drunk with wealth, or drunk with power," meaning that he is too enthusiastic or too extreme. The people were amazed to see these unlearned disciples preaching and expounding theology and religion, and interpreting what to the priests was a mystery. Hitherto they had thought and reasoned materially; now they saw everything from a spiritual point of view. It was no wonder that it made a great stir, and that outsiders were at a loss to account for it.

PREDESTINED

Him, being delivered by the determinate counsel and foreknowledge of God, ye have taken, and by wicked hands have crucified and slain: Acts 2 : 23.

The Eastern text reads: "The very one who was chosen for this purpose from the very beginning of knowledge and will of God, you have delivered into the hands of wicked men, and you have crucified and murdered him."

Peter's charge against the Jews is very strong. He explained that Jesus, even though he died the death of a malefactor, was not a sinner, as his accusers had thought him to be, but that he was chosen by God for this purpose from the very beginning of the knowledge and will of God. That is, God foresaw the fall of man and provided a means of salvation through Jesus Christ. God created man in his image and likeness, but he knew that man would fall from grace and nothing but the death of Jesus on the cross would restore him to his original self and the image of his creator. Through Jesus' death God was to reveal his abundant and infinite love for his children.

Therefore the death of Jesus on the cross was inevitable because it was the divine will of God. God had sent prophets to preach righteousness and bring man to the truth, but some of them were denounced and rejected, and others were slain. God knew that Jesus also would meet the same fate.

Jesus on many occasions predicted his rejection and suffering and told his disciples that he would be crucified. He expounded all the Scriptures, beginning with Moses and the prophets, to prove to them that Christ was destined to die on the cross (Luke 24 : 26, 27). Then again, the angels told the women ". . . Remember how he spake unto you when he was yet in Galilee, saying, The Son of Man must be delivered into the hands of sinful men, and be crucified and the third day rise again" (Luke 24 : 6, 7).

Jesus was chosen from the very beginning to be the Saviour of men. The Jews in rejecting him played an important part in this great drama. Their act brought salvation and blessings to all mankind. Therefore the Christians should not hate them, but, instead, love them, for their part was inevitable.

BREAKING BREAD

And they continued stedfastly in the apostles' doctrine and fellowship, and in breaking of bread, and in prayers.
Acts 2 : 42.

In the East, bread is broken by hand before it is eaten. Table knives and forks are unknown. Customarily it is considered a sin to cut bread with a knife.

Bread is baked thin and round. A loaf is about seven inches in diameter. Before the people begin to eat, a prayer is said by a religious man, if one happens to be present, or by an elderly person. Generally before breaking bread people make a sign of the cross on the forehead and say "in the name of God."

At times when bread is scarce, loaves are broken and

divided evenly among those sitting at the table. When a religious man or a high official is present, people wait until he starts to eat (I Sam. 9 : 13).

The apostles and their followers met on the first day of the week for prayer and religious instruction. They ate bread together as a token of fellowship and as a memorial of their Lord. The apostles composed certain prayers which were recited before the people started to eat. This was done because the Christians at that time did not know how to pray. An ancient liturgy called the Liturgy of the Apostles was compiled in the first century and is still used by the ancient Church of the East.

Bread was brought by the people who came for instruction. Paul admonished some of the members of the congregation to eat at their own homes and to eat and drink less in the meeting. Some of the men came just to eat and drink.

This ancient custom is still observed by Assyrian Christians. Baskets of fresh baked bread and food are distributed by one or several elderly women, who stand at the rear of the church or at the entrance. This is because some of the men and women travel long distances to attend the service. Moreover, Easterners when visiting one another break bread together.

The breaking of bread and participation in the eating thereof was the beginning of the communion service. The Jews also ate food offered at the Temple, especially on the Passover Day when every Jew participated in the eating of unleavened bread and the meat of the lamb.

COMMUNAL LIFE

And all that believed were together, and had all things common;   Acts 2 : 44.

Easterners are noted for their generosity and hospitality. They share food and clothing, and shelter the strangers and the needy; and members of the same faith call one another "brother" and stand by each other in time of danger and need.

"In common" should not be confused with communism. Jesus in his teaching never introduced communistic ideas as we know them today. He warned his followers against the mammon (wealth) of this world, and required those who became his disciples and followers to divest themselves of their earthly possessions, which in those days consisted chiefly of sheep and cattle. Jesus, however, encouraged his disciples and followers to be generous.

"In common" in this case means everyone was generous and ready to help, even to the extent of selling his sheep and field. In the East, even today, sheep, money, lands, and even lives, are sacrificed for the cause of religion when necessary. The disciples by no means were encouraging every convert to sell his field and sheep. This would have created extreme poverty and idleness among the Christians. There were cases, however, when men and women who had no children turned their property over to the apostles, as in the case of Ananias and his wife Sapphira (Acts 5 : 1). We do not know how many converts did this; but we know that such acts were done voluntarily. Paul in his epistles solicited funds from Christians in Asia Minor and Macedonia for the relief of the saints in Jerusalem. In his epistles he admonishes the Christians to give according to their ability. He does not ask them to sell their cattle or fields. "So let every man give according to what he has decided in his mind: not grudgingly, or of necessity: for God loves a cheerful giver" (II Cor. 9 : 7, Eastern text).

The Christians in these early days looked upon one another as brothers. They were persecuted, hated and looked upon as a peculiar people. They had to stand by one another and support those who were in need. Charity is one of the highest examples of Christian life. How can one say that he loves his brother when he sees him hungry and naked, but passes by him (James 2 : 14–20).

BREAD—HOSPITALITY

And they, continuing daily with one accord in the temple, and breaking bread from house to house, did eat their meat with gladness and singleness of heart, Acts 2 : 46.

Easterners when visiting one another's house, eat bread together. When a neighbor or a stranger enters the house, while members of the household are eating, he is invited to sit and eat with them. If he should enter after or before the meal, he is asked if he has eaten or if he would like to eat. Most of the guests and visitors eat when they are asked. Some, however, decline, expecting to be urged by the host. Customarily a host begs the guest seven times to eat.

On the other hand when priests and prominent men enter a house, the women immediately start to cook and set the table for them. When Jesus entered the house of Martha and Mary, Martha started cooking and making preparations (Luke 10 : 39–41). This hospitality is shown as a token of honor. Whether the visitor is hungry or not, he must eat something, for the family's feelings would be hurt if he refused. The only time Easterners refuse to eat bread in the homes of others is when they have bad intentions against them. Once they break bread together they refrain from doing any harm to each other.

This passage should not be interpreted as referring to the breaking of bread at the church (Acts 2 : 42). When the disciples visited the homes of Christian converts, they ate bread with them, not because they were hungry, but because it was the custom. During feasts a person may visit ten to fifteen houses within a couple of hours and must eat something in all of them.

The term bread in Aramaic means food. When a host asks a guest if he has eaten, he says: "Have you eaten bread?" which means, have you had your lunch or supper? When a family is impoverished, it is said "they have no bread." This is largely due to the fact that in the East bread is the main article of food and no meal is complete without it. The people consume a large quantity of bread at each meal.

The converts were glad to set the table before the apostles. The latter had no homes, but were maintained by the generous and pious Christian men and women who thought that the sharing of their food with the apostles would receive God's blessing.

The Temple

The disciples of Jesus and their followers prayed in the Jewish Temple and in the synagogues for many years. Their Lord had told them that he had not come to destroy the law but to fulfill it. Jesus did not start a new religion based on teachings alien to the Jewish prophets and the holy Scriptures. He simply attempted to restore the true teachings of the prophets which had been supplanted by the traditions of the elders and conflicting commentaries. For years the Jews permitted the followers of Jesus to worship in the Temple. For a time they did not suspect them of being the leaders of a new movement which was growing very rapidly. The Christians kept the Sabbath, circumcised, abstained from the worship of images and the eating of blood, and observed the Jewish feasts. Indeed, for the time being, they were identified with the Jewish faith.

LAME HEALED

Then Peter said, Silver and gold have I none; but such as I have give I thee: In the name of Jesus Christ of Nazareth rise up and walk. Acts 3 : 6.

Customarily, Easterners give food, lodging and clothing to the poor and to beggars. Money is so scarce that few men would think of handing over a silver or a gold coin to a beggar. Until recent years, only a few people carried money with them when at home. Gold coins are so scarce that in many places the people have only heard of them, but have never seen them. Persons who do possess gold and silver generally bury it in the ground, or carry it in a small bag or in the girdle. Copper coins are more plentiful and are freely carried about and at times given to beggars.

Begging is usually done on street corners or at holy places, where there are likely to be tourists, strangers, and men and women who have taken vows and have come to pray. Such persons are good prospects, for they usually have some silver or gold with them, and because vows and sincere prayers tend to make one more benevolently inclined. An expert beggar, therefore, would not waste time on townspeople who knew him and saw him every day, but would keep an eye out for pilgrims, whom he could easily recognize by their attire. He always hoped that some wealthy person with plenty of gold or silver might be softened to the point of tossing him a piece.

Peter and John had come from Galilee. They were strangers in Jerusalem. The lame beggar at the gate did not expect bread or clothing from them, but he supposed that they must have some money with them for the purchase of food, lodging and other necessities. So he begged strongly for help, expecting a silver or gold coin. Peter said, "Just take a look at us." He wanted the beggar to note that they were almost as poor as he. "We have no money to give you; but we do have the power to heal, which is far better. In the name of Jesus of Nazareth, you can walk."

Hearing their words, the beggar believed and immediately rose and walked; then, leaping and rejoicing, he went into the Temple to give thanks. The genuineness of his ailment is attested by this act, for had he not been really lame, he would have cursed Peter and John for not giving him money, and would certainly not have gone in and wasted time in the Temple and taken a chance of missing a wealthy "customer."

The apostles gave him something which money cannot buy. His faith in the apostles had healed him, and the sincere words uttered by the apostles opened his eyes unto a new world where sickness, sin and poverty are unknown.

When we believe in those who have power and inner understanding of God, we receive health, happiness and prosperity.

MESSIANIC PROPHECIES

Whom the heaven must receive until the times of restitution of all things, which God hath spoken by the mouth of all his holy prophets since the world began. Acts 3 : 21.

The Aramaic reads: "Whom the heaven must receive until all the things which God had spoken by the mouth of his holy prophets, since the world began, should be fulfilled." The reference here is to the Messianic prophecies. The Aramaic word *molaya* means "fulfillment." The prophets had predicted the coming of Christ, his suffering, his death and his resurrection. And these divine prophecies had to be fulfilled. The death of Jesus was a means of salvation which was pre-ordained by the determined counsel and foreknowledge of God (Acts 2 : 23; Luke 24 : 7, 25, 28).

Isaiah had predicted that the Messiah was to suffer. Moses also foretold his coming (Deut. 18 : 15). Other prophets from Samuel down to John had testified concerning the coming of Christ.

Peter's tone is meek. He tries to prove to the Jews that these things had been prophesied and therefore had to come to pass. He further states that those who had rejected Christ still had an opportunity to repent. In other words, Peter does not condemn the Jews for the death of Jesus, but urges them to repent and receive the blessings which God had prepared for them.

Christ would remain in heaven, he explains, until everything concerning his second coming and his gospel is fulfilled. The prophecies which foretold his coming and crucifixion had already come true, he declared, but those of his second coming are to be fulfilled only in the fullness of time, that is, when the reign of God will be established permanently on earth.

The Jews expected a sudden restoration of the kingdom of Israel, to be followed by the eternal presence of the Messiah, who would conquer and rule forever. On the other hand, Jesus told his disciples that the kingdom was not to come suddenly but in the process of time. It would come slowly, like the working of leaven, which takes considerable time to ferment the dough.

The Messiah has already come and his kingdom is among us, but it will be a long time before the whole world will see the true meaning of his teaching and commands. As the world is gradually converted to Christ and his teaching becomes a reality in the hearts of men, his coming is hastened. People will feel his presence. They will see him just as those who believed in him saw him after his resurrection. He will guide them just as he guided his original disciples and followers. He assured them that he would not leave them alone but would remain with them until the end of the world. And so Christ is here today for those who know him and believe in him. His spirit has been a guiding influence from one generation to another, his words are light and life to those who receive them.

BUILDERS

This is the stone which was set at nought of you builders, which is become the head of the corner.   Acts 4 : 11.

This quotation is taken from Psalm 118 : 22. Jesus while debating with the Jews made reference to this passage: "The stone which the builders rejected, the same is become the head of the corner" (Matt. 21 : 42). The Eastern text reads: "The cornerstone."

In the East a man who wants a new house must furnish stones, beams and other materials necessary for building. The contractor is at liberty to reject certain stones and beams if he should find them hard to be hewn or unsuitable for the building. This is generally done because large stones are hard to place in the wall and must be lifted by hand. However, when stones are too big for the wall they are used as cornerstones. Smaller stones are placed over them and the defects are hidden. At times the builder and the owner of the house may argue as to whether large stones should be rejected. Peter called this stone "rock of offense" because the builders were offended (I Pet. 2 : 8).

Jesus was rejected as Messiah on the ground that he was a Galilean and not of the House of David. The Jews insisted that when the Messiah comes he will be born in Bethlehem and will be a descendant of David. "Others said, This is the Christ. But some said, Shall Christ come out of Galilee? Hath not the scripture said, That Christ cometh of the seed of David, and out of the town of Bethlehem, where David was?" (John 7 : 41–42).

The builders, who were the Jewish priests and elders, found it difficult to accept Jesus' teachings and therefore they rejected him. So he became the cornerstone upon whom a larger church was built. Paul called him the chief cornerstone. That is, the largest stone in the building (Eph. 2 : 20–21).

Jesus Christ, the stone which the builders rejected, has become the cornerstone of the Christian church. He is the image and likeness of the spiritual man and the standard of Christian morality and conduct.

UNLEARNED AND IGNORANT

Now when they saw the boldness of Peter and John, and perceived that they were unlearned and ignorant men, they marvelled; and they took knowledge of them, that they had been with Jesus. Acts 4 : 13.

All the disciples of Jesus, with the exception of Matthew, were illiterate and unlearned. Most of them were fishermen from the little towns around the Lake of Galilee. In the Near East, fishermen, farmers and shepherds seldom acquire education. They believe education is a waste of time. These men are assigned in their youth to occupations which they are to take up when they grow older. That is to say, they work with older men as helpers and assistants in farming, fishing and tending sheep and cattle. Only boys who are destined to be employed in government service or to become ministers of religion are educated.

Matthew was educated to become an employee of the government. In his career as a collector of taxes and customs duties, he succeeded to the high office of the chief publican, a high position in Eastern countries (Luke 19 : 2). The other disciples were disciplined in their own homes and later by Jesus, who taught them how to talk, answer questions, and how to act during feasts and banquets. They spent three years with him and heard him talk to the people, debating with priests and lawyers and preaching in the synagogue and to groups outdoors. They remembered many of his words given in answer to the questions asked by the scribes and Pharisees. When confronted with such questions themselves, the disciples replied with similar answers. That is why the high priests and the council were astonished when they heard them preaching, debating, and quoting the Scriptures. They realized that these men had been with Jesus. In that part of the world education and knowledge are largely transmitted by word of mouth. Some of the most learned and capable men in the East cannot read and write, but they know the law and are good speakers and advisers. The same is true even of some wise men and kings.

The apostles' minds were free from complicated doctrines and traditions of men. They were trained by Jesus and inspired by the Holy Spirit. Their faith in Jesus enabled them to meet every situation and solve any problem. But, the council, feeling that the disciples were ignorant and misled, let them go, hoping they would stop preaching and return to their old occupations.

THINGS IN COMMON

And the multitude of them that believed were of one heart and of one soul: neither said any of them that ought of the things which he possessed was his own; but they had all things common. Acts 4 : 32.

Isolated religious communities are still to be found in many parts of the Near East, especially in Mesopotamia, Syria and the Arabian Desert. People of peculiar beliefs and strange customs prefer to live with others of their own faith, and as far away as possible from their enemies and people of other faiths. This is because their religious doctrines and some of their customs are resented by members of other religions, who predominate in large towns and cities.

Such a religious community or sect is governed usually by a hereditary chief who exercises both spiritual and temporal authority over them. In many instances he is patriarch, judge, lawmaker and treasurer of the tribe. The people are strongly united by the sacred tribal bonds and by means of marriage among their own kin. They are always ready to help, or even to fight and die for one another. Indeed, this unity is necessary to the safety and welfare of a community or tribe which is surrounded by natural enemies and by members of rival faiths.

In some cases, food and money are entrusted to the chief of the tribe. He also cares for surplus supplies of food and clothing, and in time of need he distributes them

THE ACTS OF THE APOSTLES 35

among his people. Then again, members of the community wear one another's clothes and shoes, and borrow oxen to plow with, at times without asking permission.

For example, the Sabians in Iraq, who are known as the people of St. John, live very close to each other and never associate with or eat with others. To some extent this is also true of another people who live in northern Mesopotamia known as Devil Worshipers. They also live a communal life working in the interest of one another. There are also Jewish and Assyrian communities in Turkey whose racial ties are very strong and who share and help each other. One can never find them in want or begging.

The early Christians were living a similar life. Money and material things were given and taken freely. The members were like a family.

The Aramaic reads, "Everything they had was in common." This saying should not be taken literally. It does not mean that everything they had was put together. There were several thousand Christians in the Holy City and such a radical way of living would have aroused suspicion among the Jews and the Roman authorities. Cities are not logical places for communities of this type. What happened was this. The apostles had designated certain places in the inns as places for the poor. These places were supported by such converts who had business or occupations. Then again, food and clothing were distributed among converts who had shelter but were poverty stricken.

Fields were sold because people wanted to leave the city on account of fear of persecutions and property confiscations. Christianity was outlawed from the very beginning; its doctrines and teachings were declared to be contrary to both the Jewish and the Roman institutions. The authorities at the outset did not take cognizance of the importance of the movement, but when they saw the growth of the church they took steps immediately. The Christians were expelled from Palestine and some of them murdered. But not all the Christians sold their fields and homes at this time. Perhaps it was only those who had no children or other responsibility and could go to live with their brethren. But, at any rate, they did it of their own accord (Acts 5 : 4). And the apostles acted as treasurers and overseers.

True religion abolished racial and geographical barriers. Christians of all races are united with a sacred bond. The true believers in Christ are members of the same family. Through Christ they are the children of God. This brotherhood, peace and understanding are more important than money, fields and other material things.

BARNABAS

And Joses, who by the apostles was surnamed Barnabas, (which is, being interpreted, The son of consolation,) a Levite, and of the country of Cyprus, Acts 4 : 36.

Barnabas was a Jewish convert from Cyprus. He was selected by the Holy Spirit to work with Paul among the Gentiles (Acts 13 : 2-4). He went with Paul to Cyprus where they preached in Jewish synagogues. Paul and Barnabas were working among the Jewish communities which were scattered through Syria, Asia Minor and Greece. Most of these people were descendants of the Ten Tribes that had been exiled from Palestine by the Assyrians. During the Persian conquest of Asia Minor and Greece, many of them settled in these regions. Other Jews from Palestine were also scattered throughout the civilized world of that time.

Jesus instructed his disciples to go first to no one but the descendants of the Ten Tribes, who were scattered through Syria, Asia Minor, Cyprus and other parts of the Roman Empire. These people were friendly to Paul and Barnabas and helped them in their work. But the Jews from Palestine, who often invited them to speak in the synagogue, turned against them when they found out that they were teaching doctrines contrary to their established faith.

Barnabas was a missionary among the Jews, but little is known about him outside of his travels with Paul. It seems that there were some differences between him and Paul over the Gentile question. Probably that was the reason that he left Paul. Barnabas went with Paul to present the case of the Gentile before the apostle (Acts 15 : 2ff). Then he was sent with Paul to Antioch (Acts 15 : 22). He was an early convert to Christianity and a Jewish Christian disciple who, like Paul, labored faithfully in the interests of Christianity.

AT THE FEET

Having land, sold it, and brought the money, and laid it at the apostles' feet. Acts 4 : 37.

Laying the money down "at the apostles' feet" does not mean that it was literally placed there, but that it was put at their disposal. "At their feet" is an Aramaic idiom meaning "given without any strings to it." The idiom also means "at their care or mercy," the particular sense being determined by the context. It is often said: "He threw himself at the governor's feet," meaning that he placed himself under the governor's care or mercy. "I put all my house and my wealth at your feet" means that they are yours, to do anything you please with them.

In the East it often happens that married men and women or childless couples, or even unmarried persons, turn over all their property to certain religious men or institutions and are supported henceforth by them. Some of them live and work with priests, bishops and other holy men of distinction. They devote most of their time to prayer and other religious activities connected with the sanctuary, cooking, waiting on tables and other household work, and are supported by the offerings brought by the people to shrines and religious men. Thus it is common even today, among Assyrians, Kurds and Arabs, to find men and women who have left or sold their properties, and are living in the households of religious men.

Cases like this were rare among the early Christians, however. Only a few men among them ever sold their fields. Indeed, no remodeling of the economic order after a communistic pattern was ever contemplated by the apostles, nor did Jesus entertain any such idea. But some of his converts gave up their wealth and went to preach the gospel. Their property consisted usually of sheep and cattle, just as it does today. Of course it would be necessary to relieve themselves of these responsibilities in order to be free to travel and preach.

Apparently, incidents similar to those of Ananias and Sapphira occurred only in Jerusalem and a few other places in Palestine where opposition to the new teaching had forced Christian converts to unite and stand one by another. There were no such examples in Asia Minor, Macedonia, or other countries. Paul appealed to Christians in Asia Minor and Greece to give contributions to the elders in Jerusalem, but he never asked them to sell all of their property and become paupers. Jesus enjoined his followers to practice liberality, but he put no premium on poverty as an expression of piety.

Barnabas was called by the Holy Spirit to become a companion of Paul and to preach the gospel of Christ in Asia Minor, Cyprus and Syria. He sold his field and turned the money over to the apostles to be used for the cause of the Christian gospel. Barnabas had pledged his life. And so it was easy for him to donate the price of his field for the work of the gospel which had opened his eyes and given him a new life. Sincere and pious religious men in the East give everything for the cause of their faith and are ready to die for it. They do this that they may have a treasure in heaven.

TRIBAL MIGRATION

And said unto him, Get thee out of thy country, and from thy kindred, and come into the land which I shall shew thee. Acts 7 : 3.

Tribal migration has always been very common in Arabia, Syria and Western Persia. Chiefs and elders of the tribes meet together to discuss tribal affairs, water supply, pasturage, migration and tribal security being among the chief topics of discussion. Nomadic people are almost constantly on the move. They cannot stay at one place. They have the urge to move and find new pastures. The sustaining of their flocks and herds is dependent upon so many changing conditions. When the wells become exhausted and dry out, a move is inevitable.

Migration from cities and inhabited regions is not due to the growth of the population, but to rapid increase of flocks and cattle, which comes about usually during periods of peace. Semites live chiefly on milk, cheese, butter and other allied products. So sheep and cattle are seldom killed for food; they are the most valuable possessions of the tribe. The increase is amazing; a family with twenty-five sheep may in a decade become very rich, possessing flocks of many hundreds.

Owing to the increase of flocks and the consequent scarcity of pasture lands and water, brothers often divide their sheep and cattle, one remaining in town in charge of land and other immovable family possessions, while the other leaves the country in search of better grazing lands and greater prosperity.

Such migrations are very slow and difficult. It might take almost a decade for a migrating tribe to reach their chosen destination. It is difficult to meet the needs of a large company of people made up of several brothers and their families, a retinue of servants, and numerous flocks and herds, especially with pastures to find, wells to be dug, and wars to be fought with contesting tribes along the way. And the birth of young calves and lambs naturally makes travel anything but speedy. Occasionally, tribes settle and remain in a favorable location for a considerable period of time, some of them even building houses and planting crops, and living more like peasants than nomads.

Terah, the father of Abraham, required many years to travel from Ur, in Chaldea, to Haran, in Syria. He had brought with him many of his kinsmen, with their servants and flocks. They marched westward, halting in some places several years, on their way to Haran. Their destination seemed to be Palestine, but the migration was interrupted by Terah's death. Years later Abraham took Lot, his nephew, with his family and his servants, and resumed the journey to the promised land.

Kharan (Haran) today is called *Hauran,* and is inhabited by Druses and a few Maronites. In biblical times this country was known as the kingdom of *Soba,* and its people were called Arameans. Damascus was the capital. It was conquered by David, but afterward revolted, and became the chief adversary of Israel. This kingdom was one of those overthrown during the Assyrian conquest of Syria and Northern Palestine in 722 B.C., when the Ten Tribes were carried away as captives to Assyria.

MEN OF GOD FEARED

And Ananias hearing these words fell down, and gave up the ghost: and great fear came on all them that heard these things. Acts 5 : 5.

People in ancient lands fear and revere religious men, especially those who are recognized as men of God, and they seek blessings and healing from them. On the other hand, the people are afraid of curses or rebukes uttered by such men. For, just as the people believe that a holy man possesses certain powers from God by which he heals the sick and restores the insane, they believe also that he has power to curse. As a matter of fact, some persons guilty of crimes were suddenly stricken after being cursed by a holy man. Therefore, when persons charged with crimes are brought before a man of God, they fear his power and tremble before him. Criminals who successfully defend themselves during their trials in court, confess their crimes and plead guilty when they are brought in the presence of a holy man.

Ananias and his wife had sold their field. They were probably too old to take care of their land. They wanted to turn over a portion of money to the apostles and keep some for themselves for emergencies. They had decided to join a group of pious Christians and live with them. Of course, the field was theirs, and no one had forced them to sell it. After it was sold, the price thereof was also theirs, and no one could have taken it away from them. Therefore, there was no reason to lie about the money which they had received as the price of the field.

What made Peter angry was that they lied about the price, and not that they had withheld a portion of the money. They were not obliged to give all the money they had. Matthew (Zachaeus) gave only half of his wealth when he was converted by Jesus (Luke 19 : 8). They did it of their own accord.

What happened is this. As Peter looked into their faces and asked them the price of the field, their expression changed and Peter noticed that something was wrong, and he suspected that they were not honest and could not be trusted. The Lord did not want such corrupt persons in the church, which is the household of God.

Ananias and his wife were stricken, and they died of fear, realizing that they had lied against the Holy Spirit. Just as truth gives courage and life, lies cause fear and death. Lies are not only a sin against man but also a sin against God. Lies result in sin and sin results in death.

HEALING POWER

There came also a multitude out of the cities round about unto Jerusalem, bringing sick folks, and them which were vexed with unclean spirits: and they were healed every one.   Acts 5 : 16.

The apostles from the very beginning of their ministry tried to follow in the footsteps of their Master. They preached the gospel, taught, baptized, and healed the sick. Jesus had commissioned them to preach the gospel and heal the sick. The first case of healing at their hands created considerable interest among the people and helped to confirm their faith. Both the believers and the unbelievers saw that the disciples were endowed with powers similar to those of their Master.

The lame man they had healed was a witness to this secret power, possessed by no one besides Jesus and his disciples since the days of prophets (Acts 3 : 6). Naturally the news of the works of healing would spread faster than that of preaching, for persons who are healed were eager to spread the Word of God and to help the healer.

"Unclean spirits" in Aramaic refers to insane people. Prior to the development of medical science the causes of insanity were unknown. Insanity was attributed to demons and devils. Even today bishops and healers in the Near East often rebuke an unclean spirit and some insane men are restored in this manner. Good destroys evil and truth corrects error. And faith in Jesus Christ can restore souls and heal bodies.

TEMPLE GROUNDS

Go, stand and speak in the temple to the people all the words of this life.
And when they heard that, they entered into the temple early in the morning, and taught. But the high priest came, and they that were with him, and called the council together, and all the senate of the children of Israel, and sent to the prison to have them brought. Acts 5 : 20–21.

The Temple in Jerusalem was divided into several parts—the inner and outer courts (I Kings 7 : 12; Ezek. 8 : 16), the holy of holies, the place of worship, and the treasury (where the women stood during the prayer). The outer court was used by the Gentiles, who were not permitted to enter the holy grounds (Rev. 11 : 1–2). The Temple compound was enclosed by a stone wall.

The apostles, like their Master, preached to the people whom they found gathered at the court of the Gentiles, the outer court. The Jews did not permit unbelievers to enter the Temple proper. They would not permit even their own people, if they were not consecrated, to address the congregation in the Temple. The high priest was the only person who, once a year, entered into the holy of holies to offer an offering for the sins of the people. The pattern of the Temple and the rituals used were very similar to those of the ancient tabernacle.

The place where the people gathered for prayer and religious discussions was something like a common, such as Boston Common, or Hyde Park in London. Anyone can address the people on such grounds, but certainly not from the pulpits of great cathedrals or churches.

In the East, temple grounds are used for public meetings. One often sees people gathered at the church courtyard, debating, discussing town affairs and resting. Others pray standing close to the church wall. Such grounds at times prove very useful for strangers who wish to contact the people and to preach to them.

DOCTORS

Then stood there up one in the council, a Pharisee, named Gamaliel, a doctor of the law, had in reputation among all the people, and commanded to put the apostles forth a little space; Acts 5 : 34.

The Aramaic word for doctor of religion is *malpana,* which means "teacher." This was the term used by the Jews when they referred to learned men. At that time the usual studies were limited to five books of Moses and the prophets. In most cases the title of *malpana* was given by the people to an outstanding rabbi who was engaged in teaching. The title generally given to preachers is rabbi, which means "great." Jesus was called *malpana tava,* meaning good or wonderful teacher (Matt. 19 : 17).

The learned scribes also were called *malpaney,* "teachers." Some of these were copyists; others had made a deep study of the Scriptures and therefore were recognized as *malpaney,* teachers or doctors. Some of these men taught in the Temple and sat in the councils. "And it came to pass, that after three days they found him in the Temple, sitting in the midst of the doctors, both hearing them, and asking them questions" (Luke 2 : 46). (See also Mark 12 : 28–35 and I Tim. 1: 7.)

The Romans had taken from the Jews most of their political and economic freedom; but they allowed them complete jurisdiction in religious and social matters. The Mosaic law was still the law of the land. Matters of property division, marriage, divorce and all religious matters were handled by learned Jews. Scribes and teachers of the law rendered decisions in all such cases. Moreover, these men represented the Jews in Roman courts and pleaded the cause of the Jewish faith before the Roman governors and other officials, as in the case of the trials of Jesus and Paul.

BEATEN

And to him they agreed: and when they had called the apostles, and beaten them, they commanded that they should not speak in the name of Jesus, and let them go.
Acts 5 : 40.

In the East, when people are rebuked for minor religious or civil offenses they are beaten on their cheeks or backs. The beating is administered either by soldiers or their servants. Major offenses, however, are more severely punished. The guilty person is stripped of his clothing and laid on the ground, face down; then two men stand, one on either side, and beat him with straps or a stick until his body is blue and bleeding.

The apostles may have been lightly punished by a few slaps on their cheeks, or more severely punished with straps. Whatever the punishment was, they took it with joy. They had done no wrong, but their Master had told them that they would be thrown into prison and beaten for the sake of his gospel (Matt. 10 : 17).

Christians must take their cross under all conditions. Punishment and imprisonment should not be permitted to hamper the preaching of the Gospel of Christ. Throughout Christian history martyrs have served as the highest examples of devotion to Christ. Their suffering and death strengthened the faith of the believers, brought others into the fold of Christ, and helped to spread the gospel. All those who have preached the truth and stood for justice and righteousness have suffered in one way or another.

HELLENISTIC JEWS

And in those days, when the number of the disciples was multiplied, there arose a murmuring of the Grecians against the Hebrews, because their widows were neglected in the daily ministration. Acts 6 : 1.

The term "Grecians" here means "Hellenists," that is, Jews who were unorthodox, having been Westernized under Roman rule. The Revised Version more correctly calls them "Grecian Jews." Some of them may have been Jews from Greece, Egypt, Alexandria and Cyprus, who had returned to Palestine, just as American, Polish and German Jews return to Palestine in modern times, and are still known by the name of the country from which they come. Be that as it may, these Christians were Jews by race, but Gentiles in customs and manners.

Easterners are often identified by the name of the party or sect to which they belong. For instance, some years ago, members of the Young Turk Party were called *Alleman,* "Germans," because they were pro-German. Other Turks were known as "French" and "English," for the same reason. Then again, Armenians who have joined the Presbyterian and the Congregational churches are called "Americans," and Syrians who are members of the Greek church are called "Greeks." The Assyrians who belong to the Roman Catholic Church are known as "French."

Discrimination against members of rival faiths is characteristic of Eastern people. Members of the same race who belong to various sects complain against and mistrust one another, especially in the case of relief. Missionaries and relief workers find this to be as true today as it was in the time of the apostles. This is because the leaders of every sect are eager to help their own people, and the members of one sect mistrust the leaders of the others, no matter how honest they may be.

The Christian Orthodox Jews hated and discriminated against the Hellenized Jewish Christians, just as the Orthodox Jew of today despises the Reformed Jew who broke the Mosaic law and the Jews who have given up their faith. In the East, when such issues arise, headmen from every race and faith or sect are selected to look after each group. Racial customs and traditions have always been a barrier between the various members of the Christian religion and at times have split the church into many denominations. This is a departure from the teaching of Jesus, who taught unity and equality. Christians of all races and color are united in a sacred bond. In Christ there is neither Jew nor Gentile.

STEPHEN STONED

And the saying pleased the whole multitude: and they chose Stephen, a man full of faith and of the Holy Ghost, and Philip, and Prochorus, and Nicanor, and Timon, and Parmenas, and Nicolas a proselyte of Antioch. Acts 6 : 5.

Stephen was a Jew who had become a Christian. In Acts 7 : 2 he addresses the Jewish assembly in these words: "Men, brethren, and fathers, hearken; The God of glory appeared unto our father Abraham . . ."

Stephen, like many other Jews, had assumed a Greek name. This was a common practice, especially among those Jews who did not adhere strictly to the Jewish law and the traditions of the elders. These men adopted foreign names wherever they lived. In Russia, America, Spain and other countries today, liberal Jews use foreign names.

Had Stephen been a Greek, the Jews could not have stoned him. The charge against him would have been referred to the Roman authorities who had sole jurisdiction over all people not of the Jewish race. In similar fashion today in many parts of Asia, European people maintain extra-territorial rights. That is, they have the right to be tried by European consuls or courts. The Jews had authority to stone only people of the Jewish faith who were accused, and tried by the council, and convicted for blasphemy or other violations of the Jewish law and its ordinances. This authority was restricted to the Province of Judea. No Gentile Roman citizen could have been put to death for blasphemy against the Mosaic law. The Jewish council tried and convicted Jesus but, because he was a Galilean, they could not enforce the death sentence called for by their law (John 19 : 7). So they delivered him to the Roman governor who, as a representative of the emperor, had authority over all the people in Palestine. Jesus was crucified by Gentile soldiers.

LAYING ON OF HANDS

Whom they set before the apostles: and when they had prayed, they laid their hands on them. Acts 6 : 6.

The laying on of hands indicates approval, appointment and consecration. Figuratively, the hand is symbolical of divine power. In the East when people select a lamb to be sacrificed at a shrine, they lay hands on it, which means it has been devoted or donated to God. When a girl is engaged, it is said "they have put hands on her," which means that she is pledged to marry. Jewish priests and leaders were consecrated by the laying on of hands. "And the Lord said unto Moses, take thee Joshua the son of Nun, a man in whom is the spirit, and lay thine hand upon him" (Num. 27 : 18). The people also laid their hands on the animals which they sacrificed for the sin offering. "And Aaron shall lay both his hands upon the head of the live goat, . . . And the goat shall bear upon him all their iniquities . . ." (Lev. 16 : 21–22).

By laying on of hands, Eastern people believe, the Holy Spirit is imparted from one person to another. Therefore all consecrations for such ministry are done by the bishops and other higher authorities by the laying on of hands.

Jesus had laid his hands on his disciples when he sent them to preach the gospel, and they in turn laid hands on the believers after they were baptized, thus confirming them in the faith of Christ. This ancient Hebrew custom was practiced by the apostles and their converts, and is still practiced by many Christian churches throughout the world.

The seven deacons selected were ordained to help the apostles in the ministration of relief and other minor duties. They acted as assistants to the apostles, teachers and preachers. The office of the deacon in Aramaic is called *meshamshana,* "minister." The *kahna,* "priest," cannot celebrate communion without one or two deacons.

CONVERTS

And the word of God increased; and the number of the disciples multiplied in Jerusalem greatly; and a great company of the priests were obedient to the faith.
Acts 6 : 7.

"Priests" here is a mistranslation. The Eastern text does not make reference to priests. It reads: ". . . And many people of Jewish faith became converts." There is no evidence that a single Jewish priest was converted at this particular time. The priests, scribes and Pharisees had been hostile to the new teaching from the very beginning. Most of the converts to Christianity were recruited from the illiterate and lower classes. "Then answered them the Pharisees, Are ye also deceived? Have any of the rulers or of the Pharisees believed on him? But this people who knoweth not the law are cursed" (John 7 : 47–49).

Priests and learned men always have been the last to change their beliefs. As religious leaders, they generally depend upon the doctrines and traditions of their faith, whether these be right or wrong. Truths are more readily revealed to simple men whose minds, like those of little children, are free from complicated theologies. This is why Jesus told his followers to become like little children in order to enter into the kingdom of heaven.

BLASPHEMY

Then they suborned men, which said, We have heard him speak blasphemous words against Moses, and against God.   Acts 6 : 11.

According to the Jewish law, blasphemy against God and his holy Temple, was a criminal offense and the person thus convicted was to be stoned. "And thou shalt speak unto the children of Israel, saying, Whosoever curseth God shall bear his sin" (Lev. 24 : 15).

When King Ahab was unable to purchase Naboth's vineyard, he sought two false witnesses who said that they had heard Naboth blaspheme God and the king. Then they took him out and stoned him (I Kings 21 : 10). It was against the law to revile God or the ruler of the people (Exod. 22 : 28).

The accusations against Jesus were similar to those made against Stephen. At the outset he was charged with blaspheming "the temple of God" (Matt. 26 : 60–62).

The charge against Stephen was that he had blasphemed God, Moses (the law of Moses), and the Temple. The false witnesses testified that they had heard him say that Jesus of Nazareth would destroy the Temple and change the law and the customs of the people. (Verses 13–14.)

Stephen was a Jew who had become a Christian convert. The Jewish council in Jerusalem had the power to put him to death if found guilty of violating the Jewish laws. The Romans had granted the Jews some authority in religious matters. Had the charge against Stephen been political, they would have accused him before the Roman governor, as it was in the case of Jesus, but the charge was a religious one. Roman authorities were unfamiliar with the Mosaic law and its ordinances. On the other hand, like the British and the French, they were careful and preferred not to interfere with the laws and customs of the land, especially the religious laws and ordinances.

The Mosaic law and Jewish customs were respected and kept by the Jewish Christians and all converts of the

Semitic race. Jesus had told his disciples that he had not come to destroy the law but to fulfill it. Therefore it is obvious that Stephen did not actually blaspheme against the law. He was misunderstood, just as Jesus was misunderstood when he spoke about the kingdom of God.

MESOPOTAMIA

And he said, Men, brethren, and fathers, hearken; The God of glory appeared unto our father Abraham, when he was in Mesopotamia, before he dwelt in Charran.
Acts 7 : 2.

Mesopotamia" is the Greek term for Iraq. During the time of Abraham the land was called *Beth Nahrin*, "the house between the rivers." Mesopotamia also means "between the rivers." The rivers referred to are the Tigris on the east and the Euphrates on the west. Iraq is almost like an island between these two historic rivers. The land is also called Assyria. Ur of the Chaldees (Chaldea) is near Babylon, in the southern part of Mesopotamia. This is the place from which Abraham migrated to Palestine (Gen. 11 : 31).

Haran now is called *Hauran*. The region is northeast of Galilee, close to the border of Syria. The country is at present inhabited by the Druses. In Aramaic the name of the place is *Aram-Padan*. Abraham and the people who were with him dwelt here for many years; from thence he journeyed into Palestine. But some of his kindred did not follow him; they chose to remain in Haran. Abraham was a Chaldean, but his early descendants were known as Arameans; later they were called Hebrews, which means "the people who crossed the river."

Abraham in his last days made his servant promise to go to Haran to his relatives and bring a wife to his son Isaac. He did not want Isaac to marry outside of his own kinsmen (Gen. 24 : 1–4ff). Jacob also, when he fled from Esau, went to Haran to the home of his Uncle Laban, where he stayed twenty-one years, and married two of his uncle's daughters and their maids and returned with considerable wealth to Palestine (Gen. 29 : 1).

Stephen in his address gave a résumé of the Hebrew history, their migrations and struggles, which lead to the Messianic promises and the old covenant. He was proving to them that Jesus, whom their fathers had rejected, was the very Messiah who had been predicted by the Hebrew prophets, and that Abraham had been called by God to leave his land and his people and go to Palestine for this very purpose.

ANCIENT STUDIES

And Moses was learned in all the wisdom of the Egyptians, and was mighty in words and in deeds. Acts 7 : 22.

When scientific studies such as economics, medicine, engineering, and navigation were in their infancy, magic was considered a science and an art, and was favored over other studies. In some countries magic was the principle subject of study and almost the only means of education. Many ancient manuscripts containing magical formulas and studies have come down from the past. Some of these works still survive in Eastern countries and are still taught to students who desire to become magicians. On the other hand, in the East, any person who is in possession of such rare documents of magic is looked upon as a magician and is often consulted by the people for advice and help.

When men lose some of their sheep or cattle on the mountains, they rush to a magician or a priest who is in possession of the book of magic and beg him to tie up the mouth of the wolf and the bear so that they may not attack the lost animals. The magician opens a knife and prays and leaves it open until the animals are found. It is supposed then that whenever the wild animals see the sheep, their mouths will not close and therefore they will not harm them. When this act is performed by a religious man, through faith in the power of God and prayer, it usually works, and the stranded animals are found safe.

Centuries ago even chemistry and astronomy were considered as magic. Moses had studied these things when he was in Egypt, not because he wanted to become a magician, but because these were the usual studies offered in those days. This is why he acted as a magician when he appeared before Pharaoh. His work surpassed that of the state magicians. He also studied Egyptian law, which consisted of administration, religion and ethics. In those days, state laws and religious laws were all the same. Moses did not make two sets of laws, one for religion and another for the state; he wrote a single code which embodied both. Indeed, Moses was familiar with both Babylonian and Egyptian laws and sciences.

REVERENCE TO GOD

Then said the Lord to him, Put off thy shoes from thy feet: for the place where thou standest is holy ground.
Acts 7 : 33.

Eastern Christians and Mohammedans always remove their shoes when they enter a church or a house. To sit down uninvited when in the presence of a ruler or a high government official is a breach of etiquette. But to enter a church, synagogue or mosque with shoes on is considered sacrilegious. Therefore it is not permitted. This is because the people believe that in church they are standing in the presence of God.

Moses was born and reared in Egypt. He was educated in the knowledge of all Egyptian sciences and religion. When at the palace, he had sat in the presence of Pharaoh, attended national ceremonies, and worshiped at the Egyptian shrines and temples. Moses had seen men taking their shoes off and bowing before the emperor and before the images in the shrines.

During the time of Abraham, the Hebrews were unaware of any such pomp or ceremony. They were a sheep-raising people, living a simple life, in tents, furnished with a few small blankets made of lamb's wool, which were used for bedding, and a few large, flat stones for chairs. There was no need to take their shoes off, nor do the people do it today in Palestine and in the Arabian Desert. When God appeared to Abraham and conversed with him, Abraham received him in a simple way, as an Arab chief would welcome an Oriental king today. Abraham, in his vision, washed God's feet and set bread before him (Genesis 18 : 1-9).

Reverence to God is man's highest expression of respect. God does not want man to bow and beg, but it is proper to revere God and to enter into his house and before his presence clean, both inwardly and outwardly. To remove the shoes is symbolical of the removal of the earthly things and readiness to accept things of the spirit.

JOSHUA

Which also our fathers that came after brought in with Jesus into the possession of the Gentiles, whom God drave out before the face of our fathers, unto the days of David;
Acts 7 : 45.

Jesus is the name of Joshua, who in Aramaic is called *Eshoo Barnun,* which means "Jesus the son of Nun." *Yashua* in Hebrew means "saviour." Joshua lead the Hebrews into Palestine about 1400 B.C.

The tabernacle of the congregation which was used as a place of worship in the desert, was brought into the Holy Land by Joshua. It was kept as a holy relic until the time of King Solomon (II Chron. 5 : 5, 6). It remained, together with the ark and its sacred contents, in Jerusalem until the city was taken and the Temple burned by the Chaldean army in the year 586 B.C. Nothing was heard about it thereafter.

The tabernacle was a large portable tent furnished with costly curtains and adorned with fine gold and precious stones. It was covered with sheepskins. Whenever the people moved, the tabernacle was dismantled and the ark of the covenant and the holy relics were carried by the priests and the Levites.

The sheepskins and the fabric (made of hair of goats) were probably worn out and became difficult to preserve long before the Temple was built. These materials could not have been kept for a period of four hundred years. The other parts which were made of gold, silver and shetim were no doubt preserved and later kept in the Temple together with other sacred national relics. The Hebrews also preserved the staff of Aaron, the tablets, a pot of manna, and a few other holy relics. These were kept in the ark (Deut. 10 : 5; 31 : 26).

AT THE RIGHT HAND OF GOD

And said, Behold, I see the heavens opened, and the Son of man standing on the right hand of God.
Then they cried out with a loud voice, and stopped their ears, and ran upon him with one accord, Acts 7 : 56–57.

Standing on the right hand of God" is an Aramaic idiom which means "having authority and power." (Compare Matt. 26 : 64.) In earthly realms this place is given to the queen or other high state dignitaries. During the state ceremonies and other functions the queen sits on the right hand of the king. When the queen is not present, the most important official of the government occupies this place of honor. In Oriental countries, where kings and emperors were worshiped as deities, ministers of state always stand when in the presence of the monarch. In olden days monarchs were inaccessible to their people; not even their wives could come into their presence without being called (Esther 4 : 11). The Jewish conception of God was similar to the Eastern conception of a great monarch.

According to the Jewish theocratic conception of deity, no one could come close to God or see his face. For a man to stand at the right hand of God was a blasphemy or a contradiction of the Mosaic law. God was so holy that he could not be approached by mortals (Exod. 19 : 21–24). Not even great prophets like Moses and Elijah could see his face.

Jesus, in Jewish eyes, died the death of a malefactor. His statement that he saw the son of man standing at the right hand of God, was a blasphemy, according to the Jews.

It is likely that Stephen quoted the words of Jesus (Matt. 26 : 64; Luke 22 : 69). Such an assertion was proving that Jesus was the promised Messiah and that the Jews were wrong in rejecting him. On the other hand, the Jews believed that the Messiah was yet to come and that when he comes he will be invested with great powers. They had repudiated Jesus' claims to this high office, and therefore Stephen's address only made them angry.

GUARDING GARMENTS

And cast him out of the city, and stoned him: and the witnesses laid down their clothes at a young man's feet, whose name was Saul.   Acts 7 : 58.

"At a young man's feet" is an idiom which means "in his charge or care." The young man to whom the garments were entrusted agreed to guard them until their owners returned. The clothes are on the ground beside him.

In the East, when men do hard work or any sort of physical exercise, they remove their flowing outer garments to avoid soiling them and to permit free use of their arms and legs. The garments are taken off and placed in separate piles at a distance in the care of boys who keep an eye on them so they will not be stolen or exchanged. As clothes and shoes are made by hand, they are scarce, and their owners are afraid to lose them. Even during the hour of prayer the worshipers are anxious about their shoes which are left outside the church or mosque. It often happens that men with worn-out shoes cut their prayers short and hasten to leave in order to pick up a better pair. During the hour of prayer, many Mohammedans bring their little sons to watch their shoes while they are praying. Some mosques have shoe-guardians whose job is to see that every person gets his own shoes. They look at each person and his shoes as he enters. They are trained to remember the faces of the worshipers and their shoes.

Paul at this time was too young to throw stones and participate in the murder of Stephen. But he performed his duty by guarding the garments of the men who were stoning Stephen. And thus he showed his zeal and devotion to the Jewish religion by taking part in the stoning.

When a man is stoned he is taken to a vacant place outside the city. Then he is placed in the midst and the men throw stones at him from a short distance. At times the victim tries to escape and in trying to stop him the men may get their garments stained with his blood. The stones are thrown from all sides so rapidly that the man is almost buried under them. Easterners would consider themselves defiled if stained with the blood of a person who has been condemned for blasphemy (Acts 8 : 1; 22 : 20).

EVIL SPIRITS

For unclean spirits, crying with loud voice, came out of many that were possessed with them: and many taken with palsies, and that were lame, were healed. Acts 8 : 7.

"Unclean spirits" is an Aramaic term used to describe lunatics. The Eastern text reads: "Many, who were mentally afflicted, cried with loud voices and were restored." The Aramaic word *Akhidan-way,* means possessed with insanity or the power of the devil.

In olden days medical terms and the causes of diseases were unknown. Most illness, especially insanity, was attributed to evil spirits or demons. The Aramaic text refers to sick men and women, some mentally afflicted and others paralytic or lame, who were healed by the apostle Philip. It was these who cried with loud voices and gave thanks, and not the evil spirits. When the sick are healed they shout praises and offer thanks to God and to the healer.

Compare Mark 1 : 34 in *Gospel Light*.

MAGIC

And when Simon saw that through laying on of the apostles' hands the Holy Ghost was given, he offered them money.   Acts 8 : 18.

Magic is taught and learned like other arts. Eastern magicians, fortunetellers and witchcraft workers often exchange information with one another. The secrets of the art are bought and sold. New secrets are disclosed and new practices taught to disciples or to strangers who wish to acquire the much coveted art of magic and witchcraft.

Noted magicians are besought by apprentices and less prominent magicians. Magic is handed down from father to son and the secrets are not disclosed without some remuneration. Students of magic often pay large sums of money to acquire the secrets and the confidence of the masters whose popularity is well known and whose reputation is established. The money and time are considered well spent because the art of magic is very popular in the East, and those who practice it are prosperous.

As theaters and moving pictures are not known, magic is used as a sort of entertainment at banquets, weddings and special occasions. Some wise men are also magicians. This is why Herod expected that Jesus would perform some signs when Pilate sent Jesus to him.

Magicians, fortunetellers and astrologers are known to

kings and wealthy men and are highly respected and honored by them. They enter freely into palaces and the homes of noblemen to perform their acts. They are honored, well received, and highly paid. They also ask for favors for their friends from rulers, governors and other officials (Acts 13 : 6–9). This is why Moses and Aaron had little trouble in getting permission to appear before the presence of Pharoah. Had they not been recognized as noted magicians they would have been drafted into the army of slave laborers and sent to make bricks like the other Hebrews.

Simon, the magician, had heard of Peter and John performing miracles and wonders in the name of Jesus. Jesus' fame had spread throughout Palestine and Syria, and the miracles and wonders which he had performed were remembered by the people, especially by the magicians, who thought that Jesus must have certain secrets and written formulas. Many magicians were eager to find out these secrets. The Jews, on many occasions, asked Jesus to show them a sign.

Simon was very eager to meet Peter in order to get such information. He thought that he would have no trouble in purchasing this power. He had acquired his own magical knowledge by means of money. He thought he could purchase more knowledge with the money he had made. He did not know that what Peter and John had could not be purchased with silver and gold, but could be acquired only through faith in Jesus. When he faced the disciples he not only failed to acquire healing powers, but his magical knowledge was destroyed and he was stricken with blindness. Truth destroyed the error and the hypnotic power which Simon had wrongly acquired.

VISIONS

And the angel of the Lord spake unto Philip, saying, Arise, and go toward the south unto the way that goeth down from Jerusalem unto Gaza, which is desert.
Acts 8 : 26.

In countries where telephone, telegraph and other means of communication are unknown and illiteracy dominates, many people rely on dreams and visions for communicating with friends and relatives. The popular belief in divine communication by such means is so firm that most people follow the instructions given to them in a vision without any hesitancy or doubt. When Joseph was told in a dream to flee to Egypt, he obeyed the divine command immediately. The Magi were also warned in a dream not to return to Herod, but to return to their country by another way. They obeyed the command (Matt. 2 : 12). When God appeared in a dream to Abraham and told him to leave his land and go to a country which he was going to show him, he departed without question. There are many instances in the Bible where God spoke to his prophets through visions and in later times he communed with Peter, Philip, Paul and other apostles, instructing and guiding them in their preaching and work. Many books in our Bible are based solely upon visions which men of God saw.

God has always revealed himself to those who seek him, through visions and divine communication. The epistle to the Hebrews speaks of "God, who at sundry times and in divers manners spake in time past unto the fathers by the prophets" (Heb. 1 : 1). Today, as of yore, God speaks through the gospel of Jesus Christ. He calls men and women and sends them to preach his word and directs and guides them in their work.

EUNUCH

And he arose and went: and, behold, a man of Ethiopia, an eunuch of great authority under Candace queen of the Ethiopians, who had the charge of all her treasure, and had come to Jerusalem for to worship. Acts 8 : 27.

A eunuch is a slave attendant in an Oriental harem or in the household of a rich man or a high government official. The custom of making eunuchs is as old as the Bible.

A eunuch cannot marry. Therefore he is assigned to certain duties in a harem or the household of a rich man. Some rulers employ a great many eunuchs. Some of the eunuchs are so trustworthy that they are highly honored by their masters, and are elevated to high government offices. Others become confidential advisers on social and political matters. On the other hand, some eunuchs are badly treated and may even be murdered.

Queen Esther, before she was brought before Ahasuerus, King of Persia, was placed under the care of Hegai, the king's chamberlain who took care of the women. Hegai was a chief eunuch in charge of harems (Esther 2 : 8).

Prior to World War I the Turkish and Persian kings, who had large harems, kept many eunuchs. At present some of the Arabian rulers who maintain harems employ eunuchs as guardians of women and children.

Jesus, when discussing marriage and divorce, spoke of eunuchs. He said: "For there are some eunuchs, which were so born from their mother's womb; and there are some eunuchs, which were made eunuchs of men; and there be eunuchs, which have made themselves eunuchs for the kingdom of heaven's sake" (Matt. 19 : 12).

There are several classes of eunuchs. Those who are captured and made eunuchs by force, those who are born eunuchs, and those who willingly make themselves eunuchs for the sake of the kingdom of heaven. This ancient practice still prevails in Africa and a few isolated and primitive countries in Asia.

The Ethiopian government was accused by the Italians of continuing this practice. The League of Nations appointed a committee to see that this custom was discontinued. The present emperor has done everything within his power to abolish this ancient custom of slavery and reform the people.

Many Ethiopians were believers in the Jewish God and adhered to the Jewish customs and manners. It is said that one of their great queens, the Queen of Sheba, came to see Solomon, and later married him. Historians say that the Queen of Sheba abolished pagan worship and accepted the Hebrew religion. On the other hand, there were many Jews in Ethiopia who had fled to Africa after the fall of Jerusalem in the year 586 B.C. Many of them came to the Holy City for worship and instruction in the Jewish law.

FOLLOWING THE CHARIOT

Then the Spirit said unto Philip, Go near, and join thyself to this chariot.   Acts 8 : 29.

The Aramaic word *kap* means both "to join" and "to follow," but in this case it more correctly reads "follow." In Palestine, strangers would not attempt to sit in the chariot of a distinguished person without being formally invited. Even when they are invited they must decline at first.

In a caravan a great many people travel together. Social etiquette is forgotten, so travelers mingle and converse in a friendly fashion. The caravan moves slowly, so that the footmen can keep up with the chariots. The poor travel on foot, and follow close behind the noblemen who ride on horses or sit in chariots. They listen to conversations, especially when the person traveling is a wise man or a government official. Customarily a person riding in a chariot is either a prominent man or a government official. He is surrounded on all sides by his servants for protection and as a token of honor. When on a long journey,

Easterners easily get acquainted with one another and acquire the confidence and friendship of prominent travelers. Friendly conversations are engaged in. Religious and racial barriers are forgotten in order to make the long and weary journey easy and pleasant.

This eunuch was a Jew by faith but Ethiopian by nationality. Even today there are about 300,000 Jews in Ethiopia. They probably were settled there after the conquest of Jerusalem by the Chaldeans in 586 B.C.

This minister of finance had come to worship at the Temple in Jerusalem, which was the central and most sacred shrine to all followers of the Jewish faith throughout the world. Easterners come from great distances to offer sacrifices and pray together at holy places. Some people travel more than a thousand miles. Today Mohammedans from the Philippine Islands, India, China and other far-off countries go to Mecca to pray. The Jews from Europe and the United States travel to Jerusalem for prayer and to visit holy places. This is equally true of Christians, who travel from Russia, Poland, and other parts of the world to worship at the holy sepulcher.

Orthodox Jews generally pray in their ancient Aramaic and Hebrew tongues. The people, with the exception of religious leaders, do not understand the meaning of the prayers they recite. Some people can read, but cannot understand the ancient languages.

This Ethiopian eunuch could read Hebrew and Aramaic, but could not understand the portions of the Scriptures which he was reading. He spoke Amharic, a language akin to Hebrew and Aramaic. He needed someone to explain to him the meaning of the prophecy. Philip was led by the Spirit to give him the inner meaning of the Scripture passages which he was reading. Philip followed close to the chariot, but when he began to converse with the eunuch, the latter invited him to ride with him. The friendly conversation led to the conversion and baptism of the Ethiopian minister of finance. Philip was led by God who opened the eyes of the eunuch to the faith of Jesus Christ.

PRAYING ON A JOURNEY

And Philip ran thither to him, and heard him read the prophet Esaias, and said, Understandest thou what thou readest?

And he said, How can I, except some man should guide me? And he desired Philip that he would come up and sit with him. Acts 8 : 30–31.

In countries where prayer is a habit, and adherence to religion a duty, most people are content with the mere recital of a few oral or written prayers. This is true of some of the unlearned members of ancient religions; they read the Scriptures, but made no effort to understand their inner meaning. Most of the sacred books were written in classical languages, which to some extent differ from the vernacular speech. Therefore, difficult words and phrases are explained by the priests and learned men.

In some countries the language of one race is adopted as the sacred tongue by another race. For instance, Mohammedanism originated in Arabia and the Koran was written in Arabic; hence Arabic became the sacred language of Moslems, Hindus, Persians, Turks, Egyptians, Chinese and many other races whose members have embraced the Moslem faith. Many of these people can read Arabic but cannot understand the meaning of what they read. This is true even today. Even priests and learned men cannot come to an agreement about the meaning of certain words, because the parables, allegories and idioms in one language cannot be transmitted into another language without loss of meaning.

This Ethiopian eunuch was no doubt reading from a scroll in Hebrew, or Aramaic, but he was unable to grasp the meaning. He appears to have been a Hebrew who had risen to the position of the minister of finance. Many Ethiopian tribes had become Jewish proselytes before Christianity was introduced into Ethiopia in the first century. The prophet Jeremiah mentions an Ethiopian eunuch at the court of King Zedekiah, named Ebed-melech (Jer. 38 : 7).

SUFFERING MESSIAH

In his humiliation his judgment was taken away: and who shall declare his generation? for his life is taken from the earth. Acts 8 : 33.

The Eastern text reads: "In his humiliation he suffered imprisonment and judgment: none can tell his struggles," which means that no one can fully relate the facts and hardships.

The Aramaic word *dara* means struggle, conflict, trial, or war. The letter *heh* which is equivalent to "h" is added to the word to indicate possessive case, *dareh,* his struggles. The letter *resh* (r) is doubled in pronunciation. Thus *dara* becomes *darra.* When the same word is used to mean a generation or period of time, the letter "r" is not doubled. This is why the translators were unable to see the difference. This word is rarely used to mean "war" or "generation." There are other words used in both cases which appear in Aramaic literature frequently.

The reference here is to the conflict which Jesus fought against evil forces, his struggles, trial, judgment and suffering on the cross. These were predicted by the prophet Isaiah: "He was oppressed, and he was afflicted, yet he opened not his mouth: he is brought as a lamb to the slaughter, and as a sheep before her shearers is dumb, so he openeth not his mouth" (Isa. 53 : 7).

Jesus during his trial said very little. He refused to reply to the accusations which were brought against him. He bore his cross, prayed for his enemies, and at last entrusted his soul to God his Father with the assurance of triumph and ultimate victory.

CAUGHT BY THE SPIRIT

And when they were come up out of the water, the Spirit of the Lord caught away Philip, that the eunuch saw him no more: and he went on his way rejoicing.
But Philip was found at Azotus: and passing through he preached in all the cities, till he came to Cæsarea.
Acts 8 : 39–40.

To be caught away by the spirit has several meanings. Literally it could mean, taken by the spirit from one place and put into another. When there is need, God can do anything. In Aramaic, it is often said, "He has been seized by the spirit," which means he has been driven to act promptly, or "the wind has entered into him," which means he is very hasty. The Aramaic word *rockha* means both "spirit" and "wind."

In the Gospel of Matthew we are told that Jesus was led of the spirit. "Then was Jesus led up of the spirit into the wilderness to be tempted of the devil" (Matt. 4 : 1). This means that the spirit prompted him to go to the desert. The place where he was baptized was close to the desert. Moreover, when good things are done, people often say it is the spirit that is doing them or making someone do them. At times the spirit prevented the disciples from going to certain places. When Paul and Silas wanted to visit Bithynia, the spirit suffered them not to go (Acts 16 : 7). In the Gospel of Luke we are told that Simeon "came by the Spirit into the temple," which means he was led by the spirit (Luke 2 : 27).

After the baptism of the Ethiopian eunuch, Philip was "caught away" by the Spirit of the Lord, to preach the gospel in other cities, toward which he had started to go before he met the eunuch on the road. He was found later at Azotus. The high Ethiopian official had been converted and baptized, and there was no reason for further delay. No doubt the eunuch was accompanied by a retinue of servants and other companions. Being occupied for a time, he suddenly found that Philip had left him.

Jesus, prior to his resurrection, always walked from one

place to another. His disciples did likewise. There is no mention in the Gospels that the disciples of Jesus were carried by the spirit from one place to another, or used any other means of travel. Jesus, after his resurrection, appeared to his disciples and disappeared suddenly. This was done after his physical body had been spiritualized, so that he could even enter when a door was locked.

When one is engaged in God's work, the doors are opened to him, he meets people of prominence, and the spirit of the Lord leads and guides him in all matters. He reaches his destination promptly and safely.

THE PRICKS

And he said, Who art thou, Lord? And the Lord said, I am Jesus whom thou persecutest: it is hard for thee to kick against the pricks. Acts 9 : 5.

"It is hard for thee to kick against the pricks" is an Aramaic saying, meaning that while you strike another man, you may hurt yourself. In the Holy Land, hornets, mosquitoes, and other insects, are often killed by clapping one's hands together or by hitting one's hand against the wall. When the hornet is struck, the sting may stick in the hand and cause inflammation. Some of these insects when disturbed try to sting people. It is often said, "You have made them like hornets," which means you have antagonized them or made them bitter.

Paul, prior to his conversion, looked upon the Jews who were embracing Christianity as thorns, hornets and bees which annoy men. The Christian Jews were a great annoyance to the high priest, the Pharisees, and the Jews who were zealous about their religion and traditions and who opposed all changes and reforms. The sooner Paul got rid of them, he thought, the better it would be. But he did not realize what the consequences would be. The killing of the Christian martyrs was creating more interest in Jesus and was actually spreading his teachings. It was also arousing the people's hatred toward the established faith which Paul was representing. The converts, when accused, stood before judges and governors and told about the teaching of their Lord and exposed the religious authorities. On the other hand, the law of compensation and divine punishment was at work. Those who take sword and use force will perish by the sword, as Jesus said.

Paul here was being warned by Jesus that his violent acts against the Christians would react against him and make things difficult for him. He began to see that persecution could not get rid of the followers of Jesus. Indeed, Paul's task was not an easy one. Zealous as he was, he regretted his actions, and his false testimonies against Christian converts whom he heard suffering and dying but praising God and confessing Jesus' name. These things made Paul think things over.

JESUS WARNED PAUL

And the men which journeyed with him stood speechless, hearing a voice, but seeing no man. Acts 9 : 7.

The Aramaic word *kala* means "sound," "voice," or "noise." The Aramaic word for speech is *mamla*. In this verse (Acts 9 : 7) the author says that the men who were with Paul saw the light and heard the voice, when Jesus spoke to Paul. But in Acts 22 : 9 he quotes Paul as saying, "they heard not the voice."

These two statements are not contradictory, as some people think they are. That is to say, both Paul and his companions heard the voice of Jesus and fell on the ground, but his companions, being innocent and frightened, did not recognize or understand the voice. To them it may have sounded like a clap of thunder. The other men could not grasp the meaning of the sound, but Paul, having a guilty conscience, understood what Jesus said to him. No doubt a few minutes before he heard the voice, he had been thinking things over. He had seen and heard

Stephen delivering his wonderful speech (in which he proved that Jesus was the promised Messiah) and had seen Stephen die a horrible death but with a prayer on his lips. No doubt the scene had made a great impression on him. Paul had arrested and persecuted many men and women and had been impressed with their great faith and loyalty to their Lord Jesus.

Now Paul had come to himself. He had discovered that he was wrong in persecuting the church of God. The words uttered by Jesus were meant for him only. That is why the other people did not understand what was said.

SPIRITUAL BLINDNESS

And he was three days without sight, and neither did eat nor drink. Acts 9 : 9.

Travelers in the Arabian Desert, the Sudan and other hot countries are often blinded or stricken by the sun's rays. Today, Englishmen and other Europeans when traveling in these countries wear dark glasses to protect their eyes. In olden days glasses were unknown and people suffered greatly from the sun, and even now Arabs and other native travelers are often stricken by the sun during the hot summer months. The heat is intense and the sun's rays are so bright that one cannot raise one's face.

Some people say Paul was stricken by the sun's rays. Arabian historians relate similar cases of people being blinded by the sun. But in the third verse of this chapter we are told that "suddenly there shone round about him a light out of heaven." Paul was blinded in a mysterious way; no one knows what happened but himself.

For years he had been blind to the truth of the gospel of Jesus Christ. He had been instrumental in persecuting the Christians, attacking their churches, burning their books, and bringing men and women to trial. Now he was temporarily stricken blind so that he might open his eyes to a new world. The old vision, derived from the traditions of the elders, was completely destroyed. Hitherto Paul had seen nothing but the theologies and arguments which he had been taught in his youth. Now he was to see the truth with a new vision.

Men are often blinded by their own physical and material desires. Nevertheless, some of them in due time come to themselves. Their eyes are opened and they see things differently. There are men, however, whose eyes are perfect, but at times cannot see the things around them. For instance, when Hagar was thirsty she could not see the well, though it was near by. No doubt she was bitter against Sarah her mistress. When she prayed and her spiritual sight was restored, she saw the well and both she and her son were saved (Gen. 21 : 19).

PAUL GIVEN AUTHORITY

And here he hath authority from the chief priests to bind all that call on thy name. Acts 9 : 14.

The Jewish high priest had no temporal jurisdiction over Syria, but, as a spiritual leader he exercised religious authority over the Jews throughout the Roman Empire and other parts of the world. His political authority was limited to the Province of Judea.

Syria at this time was under a governor-general whose seat was at Antioch. Syria was occupied by the Romans during their conquest of the Near East, about 67 B.C. This region was of military importance, being close to the borders of the Parthian Empire.

The high priest, as an ethnarch, that is, the head of the Jewish race, could appeal to the Roman authorities in Syria through the procurator at Jerusalem who, in turn, would consult the governor-general at Antioch or other high Roman officials stationed at Caesarea. The Romans did everything possible to please the Jews in order to collect their taxes. Without Roman approval Paul could not have gone to Damascus on such a mission.

A similar situation exists today. Leaders of minority groups in Syria and Iraq hold positions similar to that which the Jewish high priest held under the Romans, and they exercise religious jurisdiction over their people who live under separate mandates. At times they obtain letters from one governor-general to another.

Paul's authority was limited to the Jews who lived in Damascus. Paul had no power to interfere with people of other races who had embraced Christianity. Having obtained authority from the Romans and a supplementary document from the Jewish high priest, he could close up Christian churches and arrest the Jews who had become Christians, and bring them back to Jerusalem to be tried before the council (the Sanhedrin).

SCALES

And immediately there fell from his eyes as it had been scales: and he received sight forthwith, and arose, and was baptized. Acts 9 : 18.

"Scales"—Aramaic *kalpey*—means "a thin layer of skin." We do not know in what manner Paul became blind, but we are sure that he could not see until Ananias laid his hands on him and restored his eyesight.

A man who is full of hatred and revenge is often called blind. Spiritual blindness sometimes causes physical blindness. Aramaic-speaking people often say, "his eyes have darkened so that he cannot see," which means that he is misled by false ideas, hatred and anger.

Paul's blindness was symbolic of the doubt in which he had wandered for many years. He had been searching for truth, but his eyes were closed by false pride, literalism, and traditions which hung as a veil over his eyes and blinded him. On his way to Damascus his blindness became more intense until finally he lost his vision completely and had to be helped by the men who journeyed with him.

The scales which fell from off his eyes are symbolical

of traditions and dogmas which had closed his eyes to the real truth, and led him to take revenge upon the followers of Jesus. Now his physical sight was restored and his eyes were opened for the first time to understand the meaning of religion. Jewish doctrine and dogma vanished from his mind and had no longer a hold on him. They disappeared before the real truth, like a shadow which disappears before the light. The physical blindness was temporal, intended to awaken Paul's consciousness to the real truth and make him a loyal follower of Jesus.

LET DOWN FROM THE WALL

Then the disciples took him by night, and let him down by the wall in a basket. Acts 9 : 25.

The houses in Damascus and other ancient towns and cities in Syria and Palestine are generally one-story buildings. Large houses have an inner courtyard and stairs which lead to the roof. In that part of the world housetops are used for drying vegetables and wheat, as playgrounds for children, and as meeting places for men. Jesus often spoke about housetops. "And let him that is on the housetop not go down into the house" (Mark 13 : 15–16). On another occasion he told his disciples that what he told them secretly they should preach from the housetops.

Some houses are built close to the city gate. Others adjoin the city wall. Rahab, the harlot, concealed Hebrew spies under the stalks of flax that she was drying on the housetop, which adjoined the city wall (Joshua 2 : 6). Then she let them down by a cord (Joshua 2 : 15). David was likewise let down through a window when he escaped from Saul (I Sam. 19 : 12). Paul refers to his escape in the second epistle to the Corinthians: "And through a window in a basket was I let down by the wall, and escaped his hands" (II Cor. 11 : 33).

GRECIAN JEWS

And he spake boldly in the name of the Lord Jesus, and disputed against the Grecians: but they went about to slay him. — Acts 9 : 29.

The Eastern text reads: "And he spoke openly in the name of Jesus, and debated with the Jews who understood Greek." The term "Grecians" is wrongly used. The Aramaic word for Greeks is *Yonaye*. *Yonaaith* is a verbal noun with an adverbial form, which refers to the language of the people, that is, the Greek language.

Josephus, the famous Jewish historian of that day (44 A.D.), in his book of Jewish wars, states that Greek was not spoken in Palestine and that there were only a few men who had tried to learn this language (*Antiquities* xx, xi, 2). Nevertheless, there were Jews from Alexandria, Greece and Rome who came every year to Palestine to worship. These Jews were liberal in their religious concepts and they could speak Greek. Foreign Jews often spoke several languages in addition to their own tongue.

Paul was educated as a Pharisee and brought up from boyhood in Jerusalem. The Pharisees were opposed to reforms, strange customs and foreign languages, especially Greek. Paul, like Josephus, knew some Greek. Nevertheless, speaking a foreign tongue and being able to write it are two different things. For example, it is easier to learn to speak a language than it is to read and write it.

TABITHA RAISED

But Peter put them all forth, and kneeled down, and prayed; and turning him to the body said, Tabitha, arise. And she opened her eyes: and when she saw Peter, she sat up. Acts 9 : 40.

In most of the houses in biblical lands there is little or no privacy. A small house, fourteen by twenty-four feet, is often occupied by two, three or more families. This makes it very difficult for any who are sick or who seek quietness and peace. When a member of a family is sick, the house becomes crowded with relatives, neighbors and other visitors from the town and from near-by villages. On such occasions, friends, relatives and even enemies come to see the sick person whom they fear may die. The patient is never left at peace; every visitor expresses his sorrow, weeps copiously and lectures to the patient, thus worsening his condition and frightening him. The house is constantly filled with noise and confusion, and when the patient is dying he is removed to a closet in the corner, where the mourners and professional singers gather around his remains. The younger people and children are asked to leave the house and stay out. When a person dies late in the afternoon, the corpse is put in a little room or is taken to the church for the night. It is considered unclean to leave the body in the house. In any case, the burial takes place the next day.

Peter ordered the professional mourners and the visitors out of the room. On such occasions, healers throw themselves down beside the bed and pray aloud with tears. Some healers touch the body of the person to see whether he is really dead. Elijah stretched himself over the body of the widow's son, as he prayed for his restoration to life. Such an act cannot be performed before a crowd, especially in the case of a woman.

Peter kneeled down and prayed, then he used some Aramaic expressions similar to those which Jesus used when he raised the daughter of Jairus: *"Talita comi,"* which means "Little girl, arise." Peter called her by her maiden name *"Tvita"* (Gazelle). She arose and sat down. The disciples were endowed with power to raise the dead, to restore the insane and to cleanse the lepers. There are other cases like this, where apostles and men of God brought the dead back to life.

CONVERSION OF CORNELIUS

There was a certain man in Cæsarea called Cornelius, a centurion of the band called the Italian band, Acts 10 : 1.

Cornelius was a Roman captain of the regiment called "The Italian." The Romans had several Italian regiments stationed in Syria and Asia Minor, and small garrisons in Palestine. The rest of the Roman army which maintained order in the Eastern provinces was composed of native soldiers and mercenaries.

Prior to World War II, Great Britain had a few regiments of her army scattered in various parts of the Near East. These were divided into companies and stationed, together with native soldiers, at strategic places in Iraq and Egypt. The British, however, did not interfere with the native government and its civil functions. British officers often enter Christian churches to pray, especially in cities, where there are no churches of their own denomination. This is also true of Russian soldiers when stationed in Persia.

Cornelius had spent considerable time in Palestine. He lived among the Jews. He was married and had children to bring up, but no place of worship of his own. That is to say, the Romans had no temples, and did not have army chaplains as we do today. The soldiers and their officers were free to do whatever they pleased in regard to matters of faith and worship.

It seems probable that Cornelius was a proselyte who had been a regular attendant of the local Jewish synagogue, but who was seeking something deeper than Judaism. Cornelius had heard about Jesus and his teachings and miracles. He had also seen some of the great works which his disciples and followers were doing. God revealed to him the true way, the Christian faith. This was done by means of the vision while Cornelius was praying, and earnestly seeking God's direction and guidance.

DREAMS AND VISIONS

He saw in a vision evidently about the ninth hour of the day an angel of God coming in to him, and saying unto him, Cornelius.   Acts 10 : 3.

In Arabia messages are carried by word of mouth and by carriers whose task is to take written news from one town to another. This ancient medium of communication still prevails, but it is inadequate. At times friends and relatives living a short distance from each other cannot easily communicate with one another. They therefore constantly think of the welfare of each other and rely on dreams and visions for information concerning each other's welfare. Many men and women claim to have seen angels and to have conversed with them.

The belief in visions and angelic visitations is so firmly established that people do not hesitate to carry out instructions which are revealed to them in visions. Everything is taken at its face value. Warnings and bad omens often prevent caravans from leaving a town, or even discourage men and women from buying and selling. It often happens that as two persons are thinking of each other, both of them see a vision on the same day or night.

Cornelius was anxious to receive the gospel of Jesus Christ. He was a member of the Jewish faith but had not found satisfaction in that religion. He had heard about Jesus, his healing power and his teachings. He did not know how to get in touch with those who were in possession of his gospel to ask them to share it with his household; being a Gentile and an army officer, his task was difficult and peculiar. The government was deliberately trying to stamp out Christianity. This made it difficult for him to approach the disciples of Jesus whom he thought might suspect his sincerity.

At last Cornelius was guided and directed by God in his effort to contact Peter, who at this time was staying at the house of Simon, the tanner, at Joppa. The Lord had revealed to Peter through a vision in the daytime that he should not be afraid and refuse to go to Caesarea to convert Cornelius and his household, because the Gentiles were also to be given an opportunity to share in the new gospel. Peter was convinced and obeyed the divine call. He immediately came down from the roof and was met by the messengers who had been sent by Cornelius. They told him of the vision which Cornelius had seen. Peter then departed with them and went to Caesarea (see Acts 8 : 26).

TRANCE

On the morrow, as they went on their journey, and drew nigh unto the city, Peter went up upon the housetop to pray about the sixth hour:
And he became very hungry, and would have eaten: but while they made ready, he fell into a trance,
Acts 10 : 9–10.

Modern canning, refrigeration, and other scientific methods of preserving food were unknown in Palestine until recent years, and are still unknown in most parts of the Near East. Even in ancient times these people knew how to preserve certain vegetables and fruits by sun-drying. But where modern methods have not been introduced, bread and other foods are prepared fresh daily, even though cooking is a difficult task, and the family supply is often insufficient from day to day.

Bread and other foods are baked in an earthen oven dug in the ground floor of the house. Most Eastern houses consist of one large room which is used for kitchen, living room, bedroom and guest room, and in some regions it is shared by animals and chickens.

An elderly woman rises early, mixes the dough and leaves it to leaven. Then she fires the oven with grass, manure, or wood. Other women rise and light their ovens, and soon every house becomes an inferno, filled with heat and smoke. The other occupants of the house are wakened and rise quickly and leave the house, the little children cry and everything is in confusion until the cooking and baking are over.

In the East it is not unusual for people to wait five or six hours before dining. Generally the family supply of bread has been exhausted during the evening meal. Sometimes this is caused by the arrival of unexpected guests late at night. Then again, when an important guest is entertained, many townspeople gather in the house of his host, and they are fed also. On the other hand, Easterners eat very little in the morning. Half of a loaf of bread, a slice of cheese, or a bowl of curds (buttermilk) is sufficient for a breakfast. When other food is scarce, nothing but bread can be served, and the guests and members of the family must wait until the bread is baked.

While the women are baking bread and preparing the meal, the men impatiently wait on the housetop to escape the smoke and to pass the time. In the East the housetops serve as the playgrounds and meeting places for men and children. Hungry persons every once in a while look down the chimney in the center of the roof to see if the women are through cooking and the table ready. The long waiting, and the aroma of the bread or other fresh food coming up with the smoke, increases their hunger. Every minute seems like an hour, especially to guests who have arrived late and have had no supper or breakfast. Religious men, while waiting on the roof, say their prayers when the hour for prayer comes. Pious men pray four or five times a day.

Peter had been staying at Simon's house as a guest. His host had evidently received other guests so that he was short of bread. Peter was so hungry that he fainted, and while in an ecstatic state he beheld a large sheet being let down from the sky, full of animals and all sorts of creeping things. The vision was an answer to the prayer of Cornelius, and to the Gentile questions. The vision revealed that all men were equal in the sight of God and that the Gentiles were also invited to enter into the kingdom of God.

UNCLEAN FOOD

And saw heaven opened, and a certain vessel descending unto him, as it had been a great sheet knit at the four corners, and let down to the earth: Acts 10 : 11.

The Aramaic word *shmaya*, may mean "heaven," "universe" or "sky." In this instance, it means "sky."

The Aramaic word *mana*, "vessel," in this case describes a peculiar object, that is to say, something of unfamiliar quality, form and size. The Eastern text reads: "And he saw the sky open and something fastened at the four corners, resembling a large linen cloth. . . ."

Poor families who cannot afford to own a copper tray, serve their food in a piece of cotton cloth about a yard square. The cloth is spread on the floor before the seated guests. The dishes containing the food and loaves of bread are set upon it. The cloth is called *supra*, or *patora.*

When Peter fell into a trance, he was hungry and was expecting to be called at any minute to go down to eat. In the trance he saw a heavenly vision—a large tablecloth hanging from the sky, full of all kinds of beasts and reptiles, unholy in the sight of a devout member of Jewish faith. He was mystified by the awful sight, and he did not know the meaning of it until the messengers who had been sent by Cornelius arrived and told him about the vision of Cornelius. Then Peter was directed to proceed straightway to Caesarea, the capital of Roman Palestine.

Peter was a Galilean, but a Jew by faith. The Jews were not only prohibited from eating certain animals which the Gentiles ate, but also they had no social dealings with pagans, especially with the Romans and Greeks. At the outset Peter hesitated to preach to the Gentiles, especially to the Romans. Both he and Cornelius were divinely guided to meet for a common purpose.

The Jews had declared many animals, birds and certain kinds of fish unclean. The Gentiles made no such discrimination. By means of Peter's vision, what man had declared unclean was shown to be clean in the sight of God, who has created everything for a good purpose. The four-footed beasts were symbolic of the Gentiles, whom the Jews regarded as unclean. But they too were clean in the sight of God.

The four corners of the cloth denote the four corners of the earth. Hitherto the gospel of Christ had reached only Galileans and the Jews, but now it was to be preached to the people of all races and colors throughout the world. Jesus had told them that his gospel should be preached among all nations, beginning at Jerusalem (Luke 24 : 47).

GENTILES INVITED

But Peter said, Not so, Lord; for I have never eaten any thing that is common or unclean.　　Acts 10 : 14.

The Mosaic law prohibited the eating of the meat of certain animals, birds and other creeping things. For instance, animals whose hoofs were not split, or animals whose hoofs were parted but who did not chew their food, were declared unclean. Nevertheless some animals who chewed their food but whose hoofs were not divided, were lawful to be eaten, as in the case of camels. On the other hand, swine, whose hoofs are divided but who do not chew their food, were declared unlawful (Lev. 11 : 1–7). Moreover, all creeping things crawling on four feet were declared unclean (Lev. 11 : 20). The law specified in detail what the Jews were to eat and what they were not to eat. Eastern Christians and Mohammedans still keep the Mosaic law. They refrain from eating the meat of animals which are forbidden by the law.

Peter was a strict follower of the Mosaic law. He had never eaten anything that had been declared unlawful. It was hard for him to depart from the customs and traditions of his people.

The unclean creatures that Peter saw in the vision symbolized the Gentiles, with whom the Jews refused to associate (Acts 10 : 28). But now they were declared clean. The old covenant had been given to the Jews in order to prepare them for God's mission. The new covenant was given for all the world. From the very beginning God had not discriminated against the Gentiles, for they too were his children (Acts 10 : 34-35).

SYMBOLOGY

Now while Peter doubted in himself what this vision which he had seen should mean, behold, the men which were sent from Cornelius had made enquiry for Simon's house, and stood before the gate. Acts 10 : 17.

In some visions the message is imparted by word of mouth. That is to say, the person hears a voice and may even hold a conversation. Other visions are revealed by means of symbols, like Jacob's vision of the ladder (Gen. 28 : 12), Joseph's dream of the sheaves of wheat, the stars, the moon and the sun (Gen. 37 : 5-11), and Pharaoh's dream of seven fat cows and seven lean ones (Gen. 41 : 1-5). Many such visions occur in Isaiah, Ezekiel, Daniel and other books in the Bible. Some of these dreams are difficult to decipher and understand. One has to know the meaning of the symbols to be able to interpret them. That is why people sought the aid of wise men and dream interpreters, and at times were doubtful about the meaning of a dream until they could have it explained. Pharoah and Nebuchadnezzar did not rest until they found wise men to interpret their dreams. The Egyptian and Chaldean wise men often were unable to decipher the meaning of the symbols, but Joseph and Daniel were divinely enabled to decode them. At times one dream reveals the meaning of the other. For instance, when Daniel was unable to understand certain symbols, he prayed, and the secret was disclosed in a second vision (Dan. 8 : 15ff).

Peter doubted the value of his vision because he was unable to understand its meaning. When the men who were sent by Cornelius arrived, however, Peter was convinced that God had called him to preach the gospel of Christ to the Gentiles.

CHRISTIANITY BEGAN IN GALILEE

That word, I say, ye know, which was published throughout all Judœa, and began from Galilee, after the baptism which John preached; Acts 10 : 37.

Christianity started in Galilee. It began after the baptism of Jesus in the river Jordan in the wilderness of Judea. Jesus came down from Nazareth in Galilee and was baptized by John. After his baptism he went into the Arabian Desert where he fasted forty days and forty nights (Matt. 4 : 1). From thence he returned to Galilee where he immediately began to preach and recruit disciples.

Most of the three years of Jesus' ministry were spent in the towns by the Lake of Galilee and in Syria. His disciples and his first converts were all Galileans. Jesus made several visits to the Holy City, where he preached in the courtyard of the Temple, in the market places, and in the homes of the people, but his starting point was Galilee, to which he always returned. He was not welcome in Judea.

Peter gave Cornelius a brief résumé of the history of the Christian faith, the life of its founder, the miracles and wonders he had performed and the tragic death he had met. Peter was proving to Cornelius that Jesus was the promised Messiah who had been rejected by the Jews and who now had opened the door for the Gentiles to enter into the kingdom of God. Cornelius had heard of Jesus and the many miracles and wonders he had wrought. He wanted to hear some news at first hand from a man who had been with Jesus from the beginning of his ministry and who was an authority.

CROSS

And we are witnesses of all things which he did both in the land of the Jews, and in Jerusalem; whom they slew and hanged on a tree: Acts 10 : 39.

The Aramaic word *kessa* means "a piece of wood." The Aramaic word for "tree" is *elana*. *Kessa,* "dry wood," is the word used in this instance. According to the Eastern text, what Peter means here is that Christ was crucified on the cross. When a man is crucified he is stretched out on the cross, and his hands and feet are fastened with nails. Jesus was not hanged on a tree or to a piece of wood, as he has been wrongly depicted by some European writers and artists. He was crucified; both his hands and feet were nailed to the cross. "And he bore all our sins, and lifted them with his body on the cross" (I Pet. 2 : 24). The Aramaic word used by Peter in this instance is *sliva,* which means "cross." *Kessa* is a general term and is used in some cases (Acts 5 : 30). *Sliva,* "cross," is generally used in Aramaic when the form of the cross is described.

EATING WITH GENTILES

Saying, Thou wentest in to men uncircumcised, and didst eat with them. Acts 11 : 3.

In the East, members of rival religions never associate with one another even when they live under the same roof; they never eat meat and certain other foods with each other. Every faith has its own ordinances, customs and food laws. The people in this respect are governed by traditions and the dictates of their hearts. The state seldom interferes in religious matters.

For instance, a Mohammedan never eats meat if the animal has been slaughtered by a Jew or Christian. The Christians do not eat bread baked by the Jews. On the other hand, the Jew is prohibited from eating cheese or meat in the home of a Christian. This is because the Jews do not eat the meat of animals which have not been killed by a Jew.

Peter was upraided by the Jewish Christians for eating with the Gentiles. Note that even though Paul is accredited with being the apostle to the Gentiles, Peter was the first apostle to admit Gentiles into the church and to eat with them.

Jesus had healed and converted Gentiles, but he instructed his disciples to limit their activities, for the time being, to the Jews, the Galileans and the members of the Ten Tribes who had been scattered abroad. He did not want to offend the Jews by breaking their laws. He told the disciples to go to no one but the lost sheep of the house of Israel (Matt. 10 : 6). Jesus ate with publicans and sinners, followers of the Jewish religion, but there is no evidence that he ever ate with Gentiles.

The seed of the Christian gospel was to take root first among the Jewish people, then to spread throughout the Gentile world.

At last the Holy Spirit had come to the Gentiles, who were invited to enter into the kingdom of God. Thereafter there would be neither Jew nor Gentile but only brethren and believers in Jesus Christ. Doctrines and teachings concerning the truth of God which had been hidden in the Jewish faith were to be unveiled and shared with the Gentile world.

CHRISTIAN MISSIONS

Now they which were scattered abroad upon the persecution that arose about Stephen travelled as far as Phenice, and Cyprus, and Antioch, preaching the word to none but unto the Jews only.   Acts 11 : 19.

The refusal to preach among non-Semitic people was based on an early Christian doctrine, derived from Jesus' own command, "Go rather to the lost sheep of the house of Israel" (Matt. 10 : 6). Many descendants of the Ten Tribes and the Jews of the tribe of Judah were scattered in Syria, Cilicia, Cyprus and Asia Minor. Christianity was to be firmly established among them first, then among the Arameans and other people who were racially and geographically close to the Jews and Galileans. They all spoke Aramaic dialects, and their customs and cultural backgrounds were very similar. This made it easier for the early missionaries to spread the gospel and establish Christian centers in Antioch, Damascus, Edessa, Babylon and Rome. The apostles and their disciples were usually welcomed to speak in synagogues and homes. This was the experience of Paul during his journeys in Asia Minor and Greece. The people were friendly. Jesus once had preached in the vicinity of Tyre and Sidon in Syria.

Christianity was first introduced into Syria by Jesus and his disciples. Jesus had visited several Syrian cities, and his fame had spread throughout that country. But the church in Antioch was founded by the Christian Jews who had fled from severe persecution in Palestine. Later Barnabas visited the city and was much encouraged by the progress the church was making. After having met

Paul at Tarsus he brought Paul with him to Antioch where both of them taught the people.

The disciples were first called *Meshikhaye,* "Christians," at Antioch. Before that they had been known as *Nasroye,* that is, "the followers of Jesus of Nazareth" (Acts 11 : 26).

The work among the Greeks in Macedonia and Greece was very early indeed, but the gospel was not introduced into these countries by the disciples themselves (the twelve), but by their converts, such as Paul, Luke, Barnabas and others. Then again, Christian soldiers, prisoners, slaves and merchants did their part. Paul on his journeys met many Christians.

A similar situation exists in the East today. Moslems and Christians never finance mission projects. They leave the work for their converts to do. Acts 11 : 20 clearly explains that certain converts from Cyprus and Cyrene went to Asia Minor and preached among the Arameans, Greeks and other pagans. In those early days every believer in Christ was a full-fledged missionary ready to sacrifice everything, even his life, for the sake of his faith. This zeal and sincere devotion was strongly manifested during the period of widespread persecution.

ANTIOCH IN SYRIA

And when he had found him, he brought him unto Antioch. And it came to pass, that a whole year they assembled themselves with the church, and taught much people. And the disciples were called Christians first in Antioch.
Acts 11 : 26.

After the death of Alexander the Great, about 323 B.C., his kingdom was divided among his four generals. Antioch became the capital of what in the second century B.C. was known as the Syrian kingdom. The kings of the Syrian kingdom persecuted the Jews, forced some of them to eat swine, and defiled the Temple of Jerusalem. Under their rule, the Jews revolted and gained their freedom. The struggle between the Syrian kingdom and the new Jewish commonwealth under the Hasmonean dynasty continued until both Syria and Palestine were conquered by the Romans about 65 B.C.

Antioch in the days of its glory was a rival of Alexandria, Athens, Seleucia and other great cities in the East and West. The city was famed for its magnificent temple of Jupiter, theater and other beautiful buildings. It was a center of art and culture and a gateway to the East. During Roman occupation, Antioch became the seat of the Roman governor-general. The city was important both from a commercial and military point of view. The Romans had large garrisons and military supplies stored in the province of Antioch for their campaigns against Persia. The city for nearly five centuries remained the spearhead of the Roman armies and a base of operation.

(Antioch in Syria, where the followers of Jesus were first called Christians, should not be confused with Antioch in Pisidia.)

After the martyrdom of Stephen many Christians fled to Antioch. The Christian church there prospered under the Romans. Thus Antioch became an important Christian center and the headquarters of the apostles. It was at Antioch that certain prophets and teachers laid hands on Paul and Barnabas and sent them on their missionary journey. For many centuries Antioch remained a strong evangelizing center. It sent missionaries both eastward into Persia and westward into the Roman Empire.

At the present time the city is called *Antakia*. It has once more come under the Turkish rule. The city is the capital of the Sanjak of Alexandretta.

HEROD AGRIPPA

Now about that time Herod the king stretched forth his hands to vex certain of the church. Acts 12 : 1.

Herod Agrippa was the grandson of Herod the Great, who was the son of Antipater, the founder of the Herodian dynasty. Antipater was an Idumaean who held an office under the Hasmonean kings. When the Romans conquered Syria and were exerting influence over the Jewish kingdom in Palestine, Antipater conspired against his master and as a reward was appointed procurator of Judea by Julius Caesar, in 47 B.C.

Herod, his son, was made King of Judea by an act of the Roman senate. This Herod in the New Testament, was known as Herod the Great. To win the favor of the Jews and to establish his rule over them, he erected the magnificent Temple in Jerusalem which became the center of worship until it was destroyed by Titus. Herod's descendants ruled for many years after his death.

The king referred to in this verse was known as Agrippa I. He was a strict Jew and very crafty like his grandfather. He did everything possible to please the Jews. He was the father of King Agrippa II, by whom Paul was tried before he was sent to Rome.

Agrippa I was the first king to persecute the Christian church. He beheaded James, the son of Zebedee, who at the time was the leader of the apostles.

THE MURDER OF JAMES

And he killed James the brother of John with the sword.
Acts 12 : 2.

This James should not be confused with James, the son of Alpheus, and James, the brother of our Lord, the latter playing an important part in the Christian ministry. This James is the son of Zebedee, one of the twelve disciples and the author of the epistle which bears his name. He is known to have been one of the disciples closest to Jesus. James and his brother John were among the first disciples. Jesus often took James, John and Peter with him. They were together on the Mount of Transfiguration (Matt. 17 : 1). At the Last Supper Jesus confided to John the name of the disciple who would betray him. James and his brother John were related to Jesus.

After the resurrection James the son of Zebedee and Peter were looked upon as the leaders of the Christian movement. In other words, they succeeded Jesus. James, as a relative of Jesus, was consulted on church matters. Both the government authorities and the Jews looked upon him as the leader of the new sect, known at the time as the Galileans. This is why Herod Agrippa put him to death.

James, the brother of Jesus, was not a disciple. That is to say he did not travel with Jesus during his lifetime. He became identified with the Christian movement after the resurrection and was honored as an apostle and respected and revered by the Christians. At times he seems to have been looked upon as the leader of the Christian movement and the successor of James, the son of Zebedee (Gal. 1 : 19; 2 : 9–12; I Cor. 9 : 5).

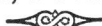

PRISONS

> *And when Herod would have brought him forth, the same night Peter was sleeping between two soldiers, bound with two chains: and the keepers before the door kept the prison.*
> *And, behold, the angel of the Lord came upon him, and a light shined in the prison: and he smote Peter on the side, and raised him up, saying, Arise up quickly. And his chains fell off from his hands.*
> *And the angel said unto him, Gird thyself, and bind on thy sandals. And so he did. And he saith unto him, Cast thy garment about thee, and follow me.*   Acts 12 : 6–8.

Prisons in the Near East are different from those of the Western world. Modern methods of sanitation are unknown; prisoners sleep in a row close to each other, their feet in fetters, and long chains hanging from their necks. During the day their hands also are chained. Those who are charged with grave offenses are securely chained and heavily guarded to prevent escape.

Prison buildings are not fortified. Prisoners who succeed in breaking their chains can easily escape. The buildings are generally very old, their walls tottering and their roofs leaking. Some of the stones in the walls can be removed easily to make a passage for escape. That is why the prisoners are constantly chained and heavily guarded. In many Eastern countries when prisoners make a successful escape, the prison-keeper and the guards are either severely punished or put to death, for they are suspected of taking bribes. Prison guards receive no salary. They live on bribes and gifts of money, food and clothing which the prisoners offer in exchange for favors. At night when the prisoners sleep, they remove their upper garments or cloaks (overcoats) and shoes. They lie on the ground with the rest of their clothes on. Their upper garments and shoes are used as pillows, and to prevent the guards from stealing them.

Peter Freed by the Angel

The angel of the Lord touched Peter on his side to awaken him. As he rose, the chains fell off his hands.

Peter then put his upper garment on and fastened his sandals on his feet, not knowing what was happening, but thinking he saw a vision. The doors of the large room where he was confined and the outer door, that is, the door of the courtyard, opened seemingly of their own accord.

Some men ascribe this miracle to an earthquake or some other natural phenomenon. No matter what happened, it was the mighty hand of the Lord that freed Peter. Even if the doors were opened by means of an earthquake, that would not minimize the importance of the miracle. The chains also were broken. They could not have been broken by an earthquake. If there was an earthquake, the fact that it occurred at a time when Peter's life was in danger is in itself a miracle. When Paul and Silas were delivered from the prison at Philippi, an earthquake shook the prison to its foundation. The doors were opened and their bonds loosened. (Acts 16 : 26, 27). No doubt, something beyond our comprehension occurred in the prison. Jesus had promised his disciples that he would be with them always. He had assured them of divine guidance and protection.

GUARDIAN ANGEL

And they said unto her, Thou art mad. But she constantly affirmed that it was even so. Then said they, It is his angel. Acts 12 : 15.

The Aramaic word *malakha*, "angel," also may mean "messenger" or "minister." Easterners believe that every person has a guardian angel. Everyone is entrusted by the Lord to the care of an angel who advises and guides him in spiritual matters and cautions him against evil thoughts and actions.

Jesus warned his followers not to despise little children, because their angels stand in the presence of God. "For I say unto you, that in heaven their angels do always behold the face of my Father which is in heaven" (Matt. 18 : 10). In other words, the guardian angels act in heaven as representatives of men. The angels are spirits, that is, messengers from God, "who maketh his angels spirits; his ministers a flaming fire" (Psalms 104 : 4).

The word for "angel" as it is used in this passage may mean "messenger." The people in the house thought that Peter might have sent them a message from the prison. In the East, messengers are permitted to see the prisoner and take him food. On the other hand, the prisoner can send word through a messenger to friends, asking for money, food and other things he needs. John the Baptist had sent messengers to Jesus to ask him if he was the Christ or whether they should expect someone else.

The people in the house knew that Peter had been securely bound and heavily guarded. They doubted that he could have been released at such an early hour or that he could have escaped. That is why they did not believe the girl.

JAMES, BROTHER OF JESUS

But he, beckoning unto them with the hand to hold their peace, declared unto them how the Lord had brought him out of the prison. And he said, Go shew these things unto James, and to the brethren. And he departed, and went into another place. Acts 12 : 17.

This James is the brother of our Lord. James the disciple, the son of Zebedee and brother of John, was beheaded by Herod Agrippa I (Acts 12 : 2). It seems that James, the brother of Jesus, was chosen to fill the vacancy made by his death, just as the apostles chose Matthias to replace Judas Iscariot (Acts 1 : 2–26). James thereafter played an important role in the Christian ministry. Jesus had three other step-brothers who are known as Joses, Judas and Simon (Matt. 13 : 55; Mark 6 : 3).

When the dispute arose over the circumcision, the matter was referred to the apostles in Jerusalem. Both

Paul and Barnabas spoke before the apostles in defense of the Gentiles. When they were through talking, James rose and spoke confirming what Peter had said in his address (Acts 15 : 13). Both James and Peter were honored as leaders. When Paul returned from his missionary journey in Asia Minor and Macedonia, he was received by James (Acts 21 : 18). Paul in his epistle to the Galatians states that when he went to Jerusalem, he saw only two apostles there, Simon Peter and James, the brother of our Lord (Gal. 1 : 18, 19).

Paul also relates how when the men who were sent by James arrived in Antioch Peter separated himself from the Gentiles because he feared the criticism of the Jewish Christians (Gal. 2 : 12). See the comment on Acts 12 : 2 and the introduction to the epistle of James.

SMITTEN BY AN ANGEL

And immediately the angel of the Lord smote him, because he gave not God the glory: and he was eaten of worms, and gave up the ghost. Acts 12 : 23.

"Smitten by an angel" is a frequently used expression in the East which means "to become paralyzed." In pronouncing a curse upon an enemy a man may say, "May the angel smite you." When a person has been stricken by paralysis, people often report, "He has been attacked by an angel." During the night, when people must cross a brook or a river, they call on the name of the Lord, fearing that they may be smitten by an angel.

"Eaten by worms" suggests that Herod suffered from a serious cancer. Easterners do not know the names of diseases and germs. When they speak of a certain malady, they use terms that describe vividly its nature.

Herod had been persecuting the Church. He had murdered one of the apostles. Now he who had done so much evil to others, himself fell the victim of evil.

SELEUCIA IN SYRIA

So they, being sent forth by the Holy Ghost, departed unto Seleucia; and from thence they sailed to Cyprus.
Acts 13 : 4.

There are two cities that bear the same name: Seleucia in Mesopotamia and Seleucia in Syria. Both of these cities were named after Seleucus, one of the generals of Alexander the Great.

After the death of Alexander in 323 B.C., his kingdom was divided among his generals. Seleucus held much of the Eastern portion of the empire, which embraced countries from India to Syria and Asia Minor. Seleucia in Mesopotamia was made the capital of the Eastern empire. The city is situated on the bend of the river Euphrates in lower Mesopotamia. In the middle of the third century after Christ Seleucia became the capital of the Sasanid dynasty and remained an important center of education and government until the seventh century, when the Arabs occupied it. Seleucia was also the seat of the ancient Church of the East, and a great center of missionary enterprise. From there many missionaries went to Georgia, Turkistan, India and China.

The other Seleucia is not well known. It was a small city of much less importance, situated in Syria not far from Alexandretta and Antioch.

PREACHING IN SYNAGOGUES

And when they were at Salamis, they preached the word of God in the synagogues of the Jews: and they had also John to their minister.
Acts 13 : 5.

From the very beginning of his missionary journey, Paul preached to the Jews in the synagogues. The people of other races who inhabited the island of Cyprus had not heard of Christianity. They were interested in

THE ACTS OF THE APOSTLES

their own religion. On the other hand, Christianity was looked upon as a Jewish movement which had its origin in the Jewish church in Palestine. The Jews were well informed of political and religious changes that took place in their native land. They had heard of the teachings of Jesus and of his death on the cross. Moreover, Jewish synagogues were very liberal and sympathetic to Jewish travelers regardless of sectarian beliefs. They invited strangers of their own race to speak, especially if they happened to have come from Jerusalem (Acts 13 : 15).

Therefore, it was easier for Paul and his companions to preach among the people of their own race, language and cultural background. When Paul succeeded in converting some of them, the converts shared the gospel with their Gentile neighbors. "And as Paul and Barnabas were leaving them, the people besought them to speak these things to them the next sabbath" (Acts 13 : 42).

John as a Minister

John, who was also called Mark (Acts 12 : 25), ministered to Paul and Barnabas in their missionary work. His duties were to carry the bag which contained books and food supplies for the journey, look for lodging places, run errands, write letters and so on. However, while ministering to Paul and Barnabas, John Mark was preparing himself to become a preacher. At that time theological schools were unknown. Younger men received their education and discipline from the older ones. This custom still prevails among the Assyrian Christians. Priests train laymen. On a missionary journey, the younger men minister to the older. John's position was similar to that of a deacon in the Church of the East.

BAR-JESUS

And when they had gone through the isle unto Paphos, they found a certain sorcerer, a false prophet, a Jew, whose name was Bar-jesus:
Which was with the deputy of the country, Sergius Paulus, a prudent man; who called for Barnabas and Saul, and desired to hear the word of God. Acts 13 : 6–7.

Sorcerers, magicians and astrologers are very popular in Eastern countries. Their company and advice is sought by kings, princes and governors. Some of them sit in the councils of state and are closely associated with the ruler, over whom they exert tremendous influence. They advise on political and religious matters, predict periods of peace and prosperity, and warn the people of impending disasters.

Pharaoh consulted his magicians on state matters. Nebuchadnezzar looked to his soothsayers and fortune-tellers for an explanation of his sinister vision.

Bar-Jesus means "Son of Jesus." In the Eastern text he is called *Barshuma*. He was a false prophet who had exerted tremendous influence over the governor of the island and his people. Bar-Jesus no doubt debated with Paul and tried to prevent the governor from accepting Paul's teaching. He felt the power of Paul, but he wanted to save his position.

Paul rebuked him bitterly. The rebuke caused him to lose his sight. His blindness to the truth resulted in physical blindness. Paul said to him, "Thou shalt be blind, not seeing the sun for a season," which implies that he was only temporarily blinded. Barshuma, like Simon (Aramaic, *Seemon*), was a false prophet (Acts 8 : 18–24).

Opposition to the truth often obscures the vision and causes temporary blindness.

PREACHING TO THE JEWS

Then Paul and Barnabas waxed bold, and said, It was necessary that the word of God should first have been spoken to you: but seeing ye put it from you, and judge yourselves unworthy of everlasting life, lo, we turn to the Gentiles. Acts 13 : 46.

The first objective of Paul and Barnabas was to spread the word of God among the people of their own race. The apostles had been instructed by their Lord to preach first to the tribes of Israel. Thus the conversion of the Jews was their primary effort. The Jews in those regions so far from Palestine were not thoroughly acquainted with the religious situation.

When the Jews invited Paul and Barnabas to speak, they were not aware of the purpose of their mission, nor did they expect them to preach concerning Jesus. What the Jews wanted was a brief talk on Jewish history and some news about the Jews in Syria, Palestine and other regions where they had traveled. When they realized that Paul and Barnabas were preaching a new doctrine contrary to Judaism, were seeking converts, and had already made an impression on many of their people, they were infuriated. When Paul began his address, the Jews held their peace, but now they rose up against him and tried to contradict him. Nevertheless Paul's address was successful.

A number of Jews and many of the Gentiles were converted to Christianity, but Paul and Barnabas were thrown out of the city.

SYNAGOGUE

> *And it came to pass in Iconium, that they went both together into the synagogue of the Jews, and so spake, that a great multitude both of the Jews and also of the Greeks believed.* Acts 14 : 1.

The Jews adopted the synagogue as a place of assembly for worship and education during the Babylonian captivity. Before the destruction of the Temple by the Chaldeans in 586 B.C. the Jews worshiped at holy shrines and in the tabernacle designed by Moses according to the instructions given him by God.

In the year 967 B.C. King Solomon built the Temple in Jerusalem and instituted a Jewish form of worship similar to that of the tabernacle (I Kings 6 : 1–38). The Temple became a national shrine both for prayer and the offering of sacrifices. Consequently religion was centralized in Judea. After the conquest of Judea by the Chaldeans, sacrifices were discontinued, but the people maintained their religion and worshiped in synagogues, houses and other available places.

About the year 450 the Jews returned from Babylon. Zorobabel, with the help of the Persian kings, built the Second Temple on the site of the old, beginning about 515 B.C. Later, Herod the Great restored the Temple to its former glory. Nevertheless the Jews in villages, country places and especially in foreign countries continued to worship in the synagogues. Every large village had a synagogue in which men and women assembled on the Sabbath Day to worship. During the feasts and other important occasions, however, they went to Jerusalem to worship and make offerings in the Temple (Luke 2 : 22–42).

The synagogue resembled the Temple in many respects. It had a similar candlestick and scrolls containing the books of the law and the prophets. The rabbis occupied the place of the priests, and the elders the place of the Levites. The lessons were read from the books of the law and the prophets by a learned layman, or a teacher

(Luke 4 : 16). (This custom is still observed by the Church of the East. The lessons from the Old Testament are read by a layman, the epistle by a deacon, and the gospel by the priest.) The sermon, based on the text, was preached by the rabbi or a learned layman, and then discussed by any scribes and learned men who happened to be present.

Then again, the portions of the Scriptures which were in Hebrew were interpreted in Aramaic. On a certain occasion Jesus read the lesson and commented on it. "And he began to say unto them, This day is this scripture fulfilled in your ears" (Luke 4 : 21). The synagogue was a simple place of worship, void of images and statues.

Adherents of the Jewish faith, whether strangers or members of the local congregation, were invited to speak after the Scriptures were read. Distant and isolated Jewish communities were always eager to hear from Jerusalem. This is one reason why Paul was permitted to speak in so many Jewish synagogues on his journeys in Asia Minor and Greece. It is true that some of the Jews in Asia Minor and Greece were not aware of Paul's commission as a preacher of the gospel when they invited him to preach to them. "And after the reading of the law and the prophets the rulers of the synagogue sent unto them, saying, Ye men and brethren, if ye have any word of exhortation for the people, say on" (Acts 13 : 15). The Jews were very liberal and tolerant in the matter of worship. They let laymen and even strangers debate and express their opinions on different scriptural passages, because the synagogue was an educational center as well as a place of worship.

GREEKS

In this instance the reference to the Greeks is correctly translated. The Aramaic word *Yonaye* means "Greeks." But the Aramaic word *Ammey* means "Gentiles"; that is, kindred people in Palestine and Syria, like the Ammonites, Idumeans, Moabites and other peoples of Semitic origin but not of the Jewish race. The Jews had synagogues in nearly all the large cities of Syria and Asia Minor.

There was a Jewish synagogue at Iconium. Paul was invited to address the people. The Jews in this area were not conservative like the Jews in Palestine. Some of them were descendants of the Ten Tribes; others were generally discontent with the Jewish authorities. Still others held liberal views concerning the Gentiles. That is why Paul was always welcome to speak there on the Sabbath. Such privileges were never granted in the synagogues of Palestine.

Apparently, a number of Greeks in Asia Minor like Syrians had accepted the Jewish faith, some as a result of intermarriage, some because of honest convictions, and some for other reasons. Many of these Greeks had become members of synagogues.

This is one of the few instances where the Greeks are mentioned in the New Testament. These Greeks became converts to Christianity in the first century, but most of them had been converted to Judaism before accepting Christianity. Christianity spread among the pagan Greeks in the second and third centuries.

HUMAN GODS

And they called Barnabas, Jupiter; and Paul, Mercurius, because he was the chief speaker. Acts 14 : 12.

The Eastern text reads *Marey Alahey,* "the Lord of gods," that is, the chief god. Both Arameans and Greeks were idolators in their religious concept and worship. Each tribe had its own gods. Gods of the more powerful tribes were given higher places in the temples and shrines. This was especially true of the gods of conquering races. At times the emperors declared themselves gods and their images were venerated.

Jupiter is the Latin for the Greek *Zeus,* the god of the land, whose image was revered both by the Greeks and other pagans in Asia Minor.

Images and idols represented the heavenly bodies, which were worshiped by most of the pagan world. Prior to Hebrew monotheism, the sun, moon and stars were universally worshiped as deities. The images were made originally as a token of honor to heavenly bodies, but centuries later the pure idea was lost and the images became the gods of the pagans.

Hebrews also venerated and worshiped images on many occasions. It took the Hebrew prophets many centuries to rid the land of idols of clay, stone, silver and gold. Gideon broke the image which belonged to his father, and destroyed the altar (Judges 6 : 25). Elijah slew the prophets of Baal and destroyed their places of worship (I Kings 18 : 40).

Barnabas was called Jupiter, and Paul, being the chief speaker, was called Mercurius. Paul was a great thinker but not a fluent speaker. On one occasion Greek philosophers called him a chooser of words. Paul was trained in Jerusalem. He was well versed in the Scriptures and the law.

PAGAN

Then the priest of Jupiter, which was before their city, brought oxen and garlands unto the gates, and would have done sacrifice with the people. Acts 14 : 13.

The offering of animals and food before the shrines and to holy men is still common in many parts of the East. When sheiks, noblemen and other high secular and ecclesiastical officials travel, they are greeted by the people with offerings of animals, food and expensive garments as tokens of welcome, loyalty, and submission. As the distinguished visitor draws near a town, the reception party kills an ox or a number of sheep in his honor. The meat is then eaten by the servants and hungry travelers and distributed among the poor. Then again, on the arrival of some of these honored guests, a lamb or sheep is slaughtered at the entrance of the house. Live sheep, oxen and horses are also given as gifts to distinguished guests. This is largely because Easterners have plenty of animals but little cash. Some religious men and government officials return home from a journey with many sheep, oxen, horses and other gifts.

To offer an animal before an honored guest, especially a religious man, is the highest token of loyalty and welcome. To entertain the guest and his many servants with plenty of meat and bread is a general and ancient custom. When God appeared to Abraham, the latter killed a calf and prepared food as a token of welcome (Gen. 18 : 6–7).

TEARING GARMENTS

> Which *when the apostles, Barnabas and Paul, heard of, they rent their clothes, and ran in among the people, crying out,*   Acts 14 : 14.

Tearing the clothes and cutting the hair in mourning is very common among Semitic people. When they receive sad news, as of the death of relatives, men tear their clothes and women cut their hair as a token of mourning and grief. This custom still prevails among the Arabs, Jews, Assyrians, and Kurds. Likewise when a man is accused of treason, he tears his garments, in order to prove his innocence and as a protest. In such cases the tearing of garments indicates humiliation. When a person is humbled and severely punished, he is stripped of all or part of his clothes. When governors, noblemen and officials are demoted or dismissed on charges of treason and disloyalty, the royal robes, rings and other tokens of authority are taken from them. In some instances, the giver of the garment takes it from the body of the person who has been accused and tears it in pieces.

On the other hand, insane persons nearly always walk about naked. Mourners and accused men often become very violent and act insane. In most cases, the garment is ripped open in front from the neck down. Noblemen and kings tear only a small part of their garment. David and all the men who were with him tore their garments when they were informed of the death of Saul and Jonathan (Sam. 1 : 11). At times mourners are prevented by friends from tearing their garments. Some mourners therefore wait until their friends arrive before they try to tear their garments.

Paul and Barnabas tore their garments as a protest against those who proclaimed them gods. By tearing their garments, they emphatically declined the honor of being gods, proving that they were men. Gods have no garments to tear, nor do they act like crazy men. Paul and Barnabas wanted to show that they were human beings like everyone else. Had they not done this, they would have been charged with treason by both the state and religious authorities for posing as gods. Paul knew the temper of the Eastern people. He knew that such acts would not be tolerated by the priests and people in general. The crowd was moved by his speech, but the enthusiasm would not last long. On the other hand, Paul and Barnabas were preaching about the God of heaven and earth; they could not have accepted any honor that was contrary to the gospel of Christ.

ELDERS AND TEACHERS

And when they had ordained them elders in every church, and had prayed with fasting, they commended them to the Lord, on whom they believed. Acts 14 : 23.

The Eastern text reads, "They appointed them *kashishey* (elders) in every congregation (church)." *Sam,* (ordain), is not used in this passage, nor is there any mention of the laying of hands on the elders. The Aramaic word used here is *akimo,* (they appointed). Probably the elders were ordained as ministers later.

The appointing of elders was an old Hebrew custom, inaugurated in the wilderness (Exod. 18 : 21). It acquired a new meaning during the Babylonian captivity and thereafter. At that time the synagogue took the place of the Temple; the Aaronic priesthood came to an end, and a new system of priesthood was established with different functions from that of the old. This change occurred because the Temple had been destroyed, most of the rituals discontinued and animal sacrifices abolished. The people now were seeking spiritual truth in the Scriptures rather than mere literalism. Elders were elected just like vestrymen in modern churches. The elders in turn elected a rabbi, who acted as preacher and instructor in religious matters. Nevertheless some of the elders participated in services as they do even today in many ancient churches and synagogues in the East.

They read the lessons and taught the people. When the rabbi was absent, one of the elders delivered an address.

In the East, elders devote most of their time to prayer and fasting. Some of them act as judges and arbitrators in religious and legal disputes. The people look up to them for guidance in many matters, spiritual and political.

Paul and Barnabas appointed elders to take charge of small congregations, to guide them and to teach them the true religion of Christianity (Acts 20 : 17). At this time converts were very few, books were rare, and false teachers of religion abounded. Elders were not needed especially to take charge of ritual and ceremonial practices, but to guard the congregation against false teachings, soothsayers and deceptive missionaries who followed in the footsteps of the apostles. In Heb. 13 : 17 the elders are referred to as leaders. In I Timothy and Titus, their office becomes more important; they are ordained by the laying on of hands. They must be qualified in order to become teachers and guardians of the faith (I Tim. 3 : 1ff; Tit. 1 : 6).

NEW CHRISTIAN SEE

And thence sailed to Antioch, from whence they had been recommended to the grace of God for the work which they fulfilled. Acts 14 : 26.

About A.D. 50 Antioch in Syria became the new center of the Church and of its missionary activities in Syria, the Persian empire, Asia Minor and other parts of the world. The martyrdom of Stephen and later that of James, the brother of John, sealed the fate of Jerusalem as the seat of Christianity (Acts 7 : 60; 12 : 1, 2).

Antioch offered many advantages. Its geographical position made it a central place from which to spread the Gospel of Jesus Christ in Syria, Mesopotamia and Asia Minor. On the other hand, Jerusalem was far south, its people were hostile to the new teaching, and the Jewish authorities had some political power and influence in the province of Judea (Acts 9 : 1).

Both the Jews and the Arameans in Antioch, Damascus and other Syrian cities were friendly to the Christians. Many of the Jews in Syria were descendants of the Ten Tribes. They were unfriendly to the Jews in the south. Then again, Antioch, because it was the seat of the Roman government in Syria, offered protection to the Christians. The Christians in Antioch were free to worship, teach and make converts. In Jerusalem the Christians were still identified with the Jewish faith. They observed the Jewish law, ate Jewish food and dressed like the Jews. The Jewish Christians demanded that the converts from among the Gentiles should be circumcised and keep the law of Moses (Acts 15 : 5). The Jews looked upon the new movement with suspicion. They felt it was a menace to Judaism.

Thus Antioch became the center of the Christian church throughout the world. From Antioch, Christian missionaries went both into the East and the West, Christianizing the people of both the Persian and Roman empires. For many centuries Antioch remained the chief center of Christianity. By the fourth century Antioch was noted for its theological schools and other institutions of learning. Today the city is still the seat of the Malkites, one of the branches of the ancient Church of the East.

CONVERSION OF GENTILES

That the residue of men might seek after the Lord, and all the Gentiles, upon whom my name is called, saith the Lord, who doeth all these things. Acts 15 : 17.

The Hebrew prophets had predicted the conversion of the Gentiles. Both Amos and Isaiah recognized God's rule over the Gentile world. Isaiah prophesied that the Gentiles in Galilee would see a great light. ("Light" in the Semitic language means "truth.") He states that the people who dwelt in darkness (ignorance) will see a great light (Isaiah 9 : 2).

The prophet Amos speaks of the Gentiles who are called by the name of God. These were to be invited into the kingdom, when the tabernacle of David would be mended and set up once more. This was to be a spiritual tabernacle and a spiritual kingdom. The old tabernacle was symbolical of the things to come. The Jews were not to possess the Gentiles politically and materially, but spiritually. The Jews were to share with them the truth of God by which they themselves had been blessed, and set aside. "That they may possess the remnant of Edom, and of all the heathen, which are called by my name, saith the Lord that doeth this" (Amos 9 : 12).

James quotes from Amos. He is proving that God from the very beginning has been mindful of the Gentile world, and that the Gentiles need not be compelled to observe certain Jewish laws which were enacted solely for the Jewish people at a time when they were living in the desert. The Gentiles were saved by the grace of God and therefore were exempt from the observance of Jewish traditions.

STRANGLED

But that we write unto them, that they abstain from pollutions of idols, and from fornication, and from things strangled, and from blood. Acts 15 : 20.

Easterners never eat the meat of strangled animals. Even the touching of the dead bodies is considered an abomination. The meat of sheep and cattle that are killed by a boulder or other accidental means is given to dogs (Lev. 22 : 8).

These observances date back to the Mosaic law. The Jews were prohibited from eating the meat and the blood of strangled animals.

The Gentile Christians ate all kinds of meats. Therefore, the Jewish Christians found it difficult to have any dealings with them. In the eyes of the Jews, the Gentiles were unclean. The Jewish Christians, at this time in the majority, were in control of the Church. The apostles and missionaries were all of the Jewish faith; therefore the observance of the Mosaic law was necessary.

Both Christians and Mohammedans still adhere to biblical ordinances concerning food and the eating of blood. Gentiles were instructed to observe these ordinances in order that they would not offend the Jews (Rom. 14 : 15).

Jesus observed the laws of the Jewish religion. As to the question of food, he told his disciples that what enters into a man cannot defile him; only the evil that comes out can defile him. However, the early Christians were required to observe some of the Jewish restrictions.

BOOKS OF MOSES

For Moses of old time hath in every city them that preach him, being read in the synagogues every sabbath day. Acts 15 : 21.

Prior to the Babylonian captivity and the destruction of the Temple in Jerusalem in 586 B.C., the books of Moses constituted the only sacred literature of the Hebrews. Most of the other books in the Bible had not yet been written; those which may have been written were not recognized as sacred. Priests were opposed to the prophets. Many of the latter were persecuted and put to death.

The five books of Moses made the *Torah,* the Hebrew word for "law." They contain laws and ordinances given to Moses on Mount Sinai. Portions of the Scriptures were read on the Sabbath, and during national festivals portions of books (scrolls) were used in many parts of the country. They were studied by priests and Levites and taught to the people. On the other hand, books that contained laws were in the possession of judges, elders and kings. They were also read at gatherings. "And he took the book of the covenant, and read in the audience of the people . . ." (Exod. 24 : 7). The law demanded that the king must have a copy of the law, taken from that in the possession of the priests and Levites (Deut. 17 : 18, 19).

"Moses" in Acts 15 : 21 means the books of Moses, or the first five books in the Bible. This does not imply that Moses wrote all of them, but that they contain an account of the words and works of Moses. Moses' death and burial are recorded in some of them. In the East, books are called by the name of the person about whom they are written. The author or compiler does not mention his own name. For example, according to the Eastern style, a book written by Abraham Lincoln about George Washington would be entitled "Washington." Lincoln's name would not appear in it. Of course, Moses probably did write the laws and ordinances. He was well educated, and employed scribes.

The books of the prophets were adopted later and read in the synagogue. In the worship service the law was read first and the prophets afterward (Acts 13 : 15).

WRITING

And they wrote letters by them after this manner; The apostles and elders and brethren send greeting unto the brethren which are of the Gentiles in Antioch and Syria and Cilicia: Acts 15 : 23.

This is the first evidence in the Scriptures that the apostles employed writing to keep in touch with the churches about matters of doctrine. In places where letter writing is not common, and post offices unheard of, most messages are transmitted orally. The message is dictated to a messenger who is to repeat it word by word. Only official documents and important church and government decrees are written. In some cases where writers are not to be found, people are informed of such decrees by word of mouth.

Writing was common in Palestine. The alphabet had been in use there from the eighth or ninth centuries B.C. In the time of the apostles the whole of the Bible (the Old Testament) was in written form. Commentaries on the Bible, doctrines of great Jewish rabbis, and Jewish traditions were also in writing. Then again, when a man divorced his wife, he gave her a written paper (Matt. 5 : 31, 32; 19 : 7; Mark 10 : 4).

It is evident that the apostles had recorded all the teaching of Jesus and most of their official business. The Gospel of Matthew was in circulation and in the possession of missionaries who were heralding the glad tidings. Like the Jewish authorities, the Christians had scribes who attended to the official business of the church. This is how Luke had access to events which had taken place years before his conversion.

A written official document would carry more weight among the Christians in Antioch than an oral message delivered by Paul, who, a few years before, had been persecuting the church of Christ.

This epistle was written to Jewish and Syrian converts in their own language, Aramaic, which was also the language of the apostles and the official language of the church. Similar letters were written to other congregations. "And as they went through the cities, they delivered them the decrees for to keep, that were ordained by the apostles and elders which were in Jerusalem" (Acts 16 : 4).

The Gentile Christians were admonished to abstain from the eating of blood, the worship of idols, fornication and eating the meat of strangled animals. These instructions were in accordance with the Mosaic law, which prohibited fornication and the eating of blood and unclean meats. The Gentile converts were not aware of these ordinances. They were not under the law of Moses. They ate blood and the meat of strangled animals. This created a disturbance among the Jewish converts who were strict followers of the Mosaic law. They could not understand how a Gentile could become a Christian without first pledging his loyalty to the Jewish law.

The apostles, in order to avoid a breach between the Jewish Christians and the Gentiles, ordered the latter to conform to the law of Moses. The Jewish Christians at this time were in the majority. They looked upon Christianity as the fulfillment of Judaism.

The instructions were given in writing so that nothing could be added or omitted from what the Holy Spirit had revealed to the apostles. In the East, ordinances and laws pertaining to matters of faith are delivered in writing. Even the Mosaic law was given in writing at a time when writing was very new. Unfortunately, this epistle to the Christians in Antioch is lost. Luke touches only on the important decrees. The other material it contained is not mentioned.

KOSHER

That ye abstain from meats offered to idols, and from blood, and from things strangled, and from fornication: from which if ye keep yourselves, ye shall do well. Fare ye well. Acts 15 : 29.

The law of Moses prohibited the eating of the blood or flesh of dead animals and animals strangled or torn by wild beasts (Gen. 9 : 4; Lev. 22 : 8). The Orthodox Jews, to the present day, eat only kosher meat; that is, meat approved by their religious authorities. The animal's head must be severed and the body left to bleed until every drop of blood is gone. Both Mohammedans and Eastern Christians still observe this biblical law. They do not eat the meat of an animal whose head is not severed. They also keep other Jewish religious ordinances relative to food.

The first Christians were adherents to the Jewish faith. Many of them were brought up strictly according to the law of Moses and the traditions of the elders. Jesus had revealed the inner meaning of the law and the prophets, but had not recommended a change in the law. He had come to fulfill the law and not to destroy it. Therefore the apostles and their followers observed all of the Mosaic law, but rejected some of the traditions of the elders.

The Christians in Antioch were asked to observe these laws, to encourage the Jewish Christians and other Jews who might become converts. They were told especially to abstain from eating the things offered to idols and from fornication (I Cor. 8 : 10).

Exemplary conduct was required of the Christians in order to carry on the work of spreading the gospel. Christians were to live in purity and sincerity in order that their light might shine among the Jews and the pagans.

SYRIA

And he went through Syria and Cilicia, confirming the churches.   Acts 15 : 41.

Syria is the name of that country west of the Euphrates river, between Palestine and Asia Minor. Tyre, Sidon and Beyrouth are the important seaports, serving Transjordania, Mesopotamia and parts of Arabia. The largest cities are Damascus (the capital), Antioch and Aleppo. Most of these cities are located on commercial routes between Europe and the Near East. The country is rather poor. For a living its inhabitants depend upon caravans and the transfer of merchandise through its ports.

During the time of Paul, Syria was a Roman province to which Palestine was subordinate. "And this taxing was first made when Cyrenius was governor of Syria" (Luke 2 : 2).

Syria should not be confused with Assyria, nor Syrians with Assyrians. The countries adjoin each other, and their names are similar in English but not in Aramaic, which once was the language of both countries. In Aramaic, Assyria is called *Athor* and Syria *Sur*. The name of Syria is derived from the province of Suria, which the

Greeks nicknamed Tyre. The city of Tyre was famed for its shipbuilding and trading and its dye works. Syrians were the builders of one of the greatest civilizations of the world. They had a large merchant marine and were accomplished in working steel, iron and brass.

Syria still has a large Christian population. A part of the country, called Lebanon, is governed separately from the rest of Syria. The inhabitants of this region are Aramean in their origin and Maronites in religion. (The Maronites are a Christian sect under Rome.)

TIMOTHEUS

Then came he to Derbe and Lystra: and, behold, a certain disciple was there, named Timotheus, the son of a certain woman, which was a Jewess, and believed; but his father was a Greek: Acts 16 : 1.

Timotheus' father was an Aramean (Syrian) and his mother a Jewess, according to the Eastern text. As Syria borders on Palestine, a great many Syrians had married Jewish women. The children from such marriages were generally brought up in the Jewish faith. Jewish women often won the favor of their husbands and succeeded in converting them to their religion. This was also true of Titus. His father was an Aramean and his mother a Jewess.

Religion in Syria was dying out, so that many Syrians had become interested in the Jewish faith. They attended the synagogue and observed some of the Jewish customs, but did not practice circumcision.

Many of these men were glad to accept the Christian religion in preference to Judaism, because the Jews demanded strict adherence to the Jewish traditions and racial customs.

Paul was preaching among the Jews, and the Gentiles who had been interested in the Jewish worship. He took Timotheus and circumcised him for fear of the Jews. The

Jews would not have permitted Paul to preach to them, if he had had in his company an uncircumcised Aramean.

Timotheus became an earnest preacher of the gospel of Christ and a faithful companion of Paul. Years later Paul appointed him overseer (bishop) of the churches in Cyprus.

GUIDED BY SPIRIT

After they were come to Mysia, they assayed to go into Bithynia: but the Spirit suffered them not. Acts 16 : 7.

"The spirit suffered them not," is an Aramaic saying. It means that they were warned through a vision or a divine communication not to go into Bithynia.

The Semites believe in visions and prophecies and inquire of holy men about them. The Hebrew kings consulted their prophets before they went to war. Saul consulted Samuel when he warred against the Palestinians. Ahab sought the advice of the prophets when he wanted to declare war on Syria (I Kings 22 : 6-7).

When the faithful are warned by a man of God or through a vision, they obey. Paul was so sure that he was being guided by the spirit of God that he postponed his departure. On other occasions he received instructions by means of revelations and he complied with them (Gal. 2 : 2; Acts 16 : 9-10). Those who rely on God are guided and directed.

WE AND THEY

And after he had seen the vision, immediately we endeavoured to go into Macedonia, assuredly gathering that the Lord had called us for to preach the gospel unto them.
Acts 16 : 10.

The first person plural is used here to include Luke, the author of the Acts, who accompanied Paul to Macedonia. When the writer is with Paul, he uses the first person plural, "we." It is evident from the style of the book of Acts that Luke acted as a reporter. On some occasions, for certain reasons, he is not with Paul. It seems reasonable to suppose that Paul left some of his co-workers behind to look after the converts and take charge of the work. In this instance, Paul's departure was rather sudden. He was told in a vision to go to Macedonia (II Cor. 2 : 13). When the author is not with Paul, he relies on the information given to him by Paul and his other companions.

Paul, like other people in the East, believed in visions and was guided by them. He even foresaw the difficulties and the imprisonment he would experience at Jerusalem (Acts 21 : 11). Peter also was sent on an important mission to Caesarea by means of a vision that came to him at Joppa (Acts 10 : 17). Luke was very modest; he kept himself in the background.

PAGAN SHRINES

> *And from thence to Philippi, which is the chief city of that part of Macedonia, and a colony: and we were in that city abiding certain days.*
> *And on the sabbath we went out of the city by a river side, where prayer was wont to be made; and we sat down, and spake unto the women which resorted thither.*
> Acts 16 : 12–13.

The Eastern text reads: "And on the sabbath day we went outside the city gate to the river side because a house of prayer was seen there, and when we were seated, we spoke to the women who had gathered there."

In olden days, temples, shrines and houses of prayer were erected outside the city walls, far away from business places, bathing houses and other public places. In the East, places of worship are set aside and the ground around them is considered sacred. Today one finds ancient churches and shrines outside the towns and cities. Some of them are from half a mile to two miles away; others are at far-off places. They are visited by the people for prayer.

"A house of prayer" does not necessarily mean that this was a church with chairs, lamps, books and a caretaker. Most of these houses of prayer are desolate places. Some of them are ancient abandoned churches, but the ruins are still venerated. Others are small shrines with four walls and a small door, some of them covered, others open. For instance, the Kurdish people generally worship at such places. They have no churches. They call them *Misgaud;* that is, "the place of worship." Some of these shrines are near streams and brooks. This is because Easterners wash their hands before they enter into a church or shrine to pray. The Mohammedans wash both their hands and feet.

It seems that there was no Jewish synagogue at Philippi. The Jews went outside the city to pray in the out-of-doors, as the people do today in the towns where churches, mosques and synagogues are not to be found.

This is true especially of small colonies which cannot afford to build a place of worship. They pray in houses, at the ruins of ancient temples and in the open air. Each person prays by himself, some standing, others kneeling.

During holidays, the shrines and places of prayer are visited by a great many people. Some come to worship, others to meet friends, and still others out of curiosity. The vendors also seek purchasers for their dry-goods, food, perfume and other merchandise. These places serve as common grounds until the sun goes down; then they are deserted until the next holiday.

This was a Jewish holiday, the Sabbath. The Jews ceased all kinds of work and spent their time leisurely walking.

WOMAN MERCHANT CONVERTED

And when she was baptized, and her household, she besought us, saying, If ye have judged me to be faithful to the Lord, come into my house, and abide there. And she constrained us. Acts 16 : 15.

The Aramaic text reads: . . . "If you are sincerely convinced that I believe in our Lord" . . . Business men and merchants are not readily trusted. This is because business is carried on by bargaining, taking of oaths, and lying, so that what a merchant says is not always taken seriously. Moreover, merchants generally do not quarrel over religion and theology while they are bargaining with a prospective customer. Both merchant and buyer agree on many disputed and hair-splitting doctrines until the deal is terminated. Some of the salesmen would not hesitate to pretend to be of the same faith as the prospective buyer. When the bargaining fails, then the customer and merchant reveal the identity of their faith, and each curses the religion of the other.

This woman was a small silk merchant, or a peddler. She was not quite convinced that Paul believed her to be a sincere convert. This was because missionaries and strangers often doubted a merchant's sincerity. To prove that she was a real convert, she invited Paul to her house to break bread with her household. This is one of the highest tokens that a person can bestow upon his friends, because members of one faith never have social dealings with those of other faiths. This woman convert wanted to demonstrate her sincere faith in the gospel of Jesus Christ through her hospitality. Paul and his companions were strangers in the city. They needed a place to lodge.

SOOTHSAYER

And it came to pass, as we went to prayer, a certain damsel possessed with a spirit of divination met us, which brought her masters much gain by soothsaying:
Acts 16 : 16.

The Aramaic word *kisma*, "soothsaying" (or fortune-telling), is derived from *kasam*, "to deliver an oracle." *Kasoma* is the deliverer of messages and interpreter of past and future events. The medium is a type of astrologer who tries to trace the causes of sickness, accidents and other misfortunes and to prescribe remedies. The stars and so-called unseen spirits are blamed for all misfortunes. This is because no one can examine the stars or converse with spirits to verify the facts. Thus the soothsayer is a sole authority in this field, and he is never challenged nor disputed by his followers and those who seek his aid.

In diagnosing cases of disease, the astrologer opens an old manuscript which contains many complicated formulas. The consultant puts his hand on a certain letter referring to a certain passage in the book, which describes the causes of the illness, and prescribes a remedy. Such documents are very rare and jealously guarded.

Another form of witchcraft is called *zakorey*. In this

case the medium goes into a trance and tries to get in touch with the spirits of the departed. Some of the soothsayers use a small copper or silver bowl which they fill with water before they begin to converse with the spirits. Then the medium claims to describe the person with whom he has talked.

The practice of witchcraft is a prosperous vocation. Students of the art become rich quickly. Large sums of money are paid by a credulous public. Even governors, princes and kings have become victims of these men and women. Compare with them the witch of Endor who claimed to talk with the spirit of Samuel (I Sam. 28 : 7–14).

When the medium is a woman, a male guardian always attends her. This is because it is not considered proper for a strange man to enter into the presence of a woman medium. The message is delivered by the guardian or protector, who is also the master of the fortuneteller. Sometimes a man who seeks an interview with a woman medium, will dress like a woman in order to come into her presence, but he is very likely to be detected. For instance, Saul changed his garments when he consulted the witch of Endor, but she recognized him at once (I Sam. 28 : 8, 12).

Most of these women are unmarried and free to be hired by men who take them to cities where their vocation is profitable, and where there is no competition. Women mediums in Paul's day often were bought and sold. The owner of this medium probably had paid a large sum for her and expected good returns from her work. When Paul restored her to sanity, her master's hopes were shattered. This is why he took immediate action against Paul.

WITCH

And this did she many days. But Paul, being grieved, turned and said to the spirit, I command thee in the name of Jesus Christ to come out of her. And he came out the same hour. Acts 16 : 18.

The word "spirit" here refers to the spirit of false prophecy; that is, divining and fortunetelling. There are many persons in the Near East who claim to possess mysterious powers to tell fortunes, advise, heal, and practice black magic. They are often consulted by people in distress.

During the time of the judges, men and women "with familiar spirits" (witches) were numerous. Samuel sought to exterminate them. King Saul sought the help of the witch of Endor (I Sam. 28 : 7–14). The person with a familiar spirit is a sort of mystic. The work is done by intense concentration. After a long period of concentration and chanting, the medium portrays a picture of the person with whom contact is desired and delivers messages. The mystified inquirer may even see a mental image of the person.

This girl recognized that Paul was endowed with powers superior to her own. In studying him she discovered how wrong she had been and realized that her power was not real and permanent. Therefore, she followed Paul and sought his help to free her. She was ashamed of her practice of witchcraft. Paul rebuked the spirit (power) in her, and she became normal. This act displeased her masters, who seized Paul and Silas, brought them before the court, and had them beaten.

Just as the rays of the sun cause the snow to melt, so does the light of truth destroy error.

STRIPPED

And the multitude rose up together against them: and the magistrates rent off their clothes, and commanded to beat them. Acts 16 : 22.

The Eastern text reads, "Then the soldiers stripped them of their clothes and gave command to scourge them." Scourging is still common in many parts of the East, especially among primitive people. The prisoners are stripped of their outer garments, laid on the ground, then beaten by two men who stand one on each side. In some cases, all the clothes are removed and the victims beaten until they are unconscious.

According to the Aramaic text, Paul and Silas were brought before the soldiers and the city magistrates. (The soldiers were Romans, but the magistrates were natives.) Paul and Silas were accused of preaching and teaching customs alien to those of the place. In other words, they were charged with having incited the people. The soldiers stripped Paul and Silas of their clothes and ordered them to be scourged. The city was under the Roman authorities. Native officials and judges had authority in local matters only. Paul and Silas were strangers from countries which were also under Roman rule.

ROMAN CITIZENS

But Paul said unto them, They have beaten us openly uncondemned, being Romans, and have cast us into prison; and now do they thrust us out privily? nay verily; but let them come themselves and fetch us out. Acts 16 : 37.

Romans," in this case, means Roman citizens and not merely natives of Rome or other parts of Italy. Paul was a Hebrew by race, a member of the tribe of Benjamin, a Jew by religion, and a Roman citizen by nationality. He was born in Tarsus, a city in Cilicia, not far from Syria. This part of Asia Minor was made a Roman province. Hence its citizens were considered Romans. Other regions such as Palestine, Transjordania and some parts of Syria, were ruled by native princes who were appointed by the Roman emperors or the Senate. Since the inhabitants of these countries had some kind of home rule, they were subject to the laws of their land. Roman citizens, on the other hand, were treated with high respect and the utmost care. When charged with crimes they were tried before Roman officials.

This is true of Britishers in Egypt, Iraq, Transjordania and Palestine today. A British subject in these countries cannot be tried or punished by a native court. He is tried by a British tribunal or a consul. On the other hand, these countries have been mandated by the British. British officials and military authorities can arrest, try and punish natives, but they usually must refer a case to the native court, with whom they act jointly. Roman citizens had extraterritorial rights.

CHRIST MUST SUFFER

Opening and alleging, that Christ must needs have suffered, and risen again from the dead; and that this Jesus, whom I preached unto you, is Christ. Acts 17 : 3.

Paul here is confirming what Jesus had said concerning his suffering, death and resurrection. Jesus, prior to his suffering and death, had told his disciples many times that he was to be crucified and that he would rise again. "The Son of man must be delivered into the hands of sinful men, and be crucified, and the third day rise again." Even after his resurrection he told some of his disciples that they should have known that Christ was to suffer and that the Scriptures which predicted his death must be fulfilled. "Then he said unto them, O fools, and slow of heart to believe all that the prophets have spoken:

THE ACTS OF THE APOSTLES 123

ought not Christ to have suffered these things, and to enter into his glory?" (Luke 24 : 25–26).

The Jews were expecting the coming of another Christ, the Messiah who was to restore the kingdom of David and establish a political rule over the world. Paul here is proving that there is no other Messiah and that Jesus is the promised Messiah who was to suffer and rise in glory.

It was difficult for the Jewish people to reconcile the Messiah on the cross with the Messiah predicted by the early Hebrew prophets. To them the Messiah was the messenger of God empowered to rule throughout the world and to live forever. They did not deny the miracles and wonders that Jesus had done and the manifest interest in his gospel, but they could not believe in a defeated Messiah. To them the Messiah was the everlasting ruler who would restore Israel (Luke 24 : 21).

GREEK CONVERTS

And some of them believed, and consorted with Paul and Silas; and of the devout Greeks a great multitude, and of the chief women not a few. Acts 17 : 4.

This is one of the few references to the Greek people in the New Testament according to the Eastern text. The Aramaic word used here is *Yonaye,* which means Greeks. In many other instances the term "Greek" in the English Bible is a mistranslation. The Aramaic word is *Aramaye,* "Arameans" or "Syrians." The translators, for some unknown reason, changed it like many other passages to *Helenos,* "Greeks."

Indeed, Greeks in Asia Minor, Macedonia and Greece were among the first converts to Christianity. They inhabited countries bordering on Syria. Moreover, Greeks are closer to the Semitic people than any other European race. Some of their customs and manners are very similar. Greeks are hospitable and religiously inclined.

These early Greek converts were somewhat influenced

by Hebrew thought. The Hebrews believed in one God and despised image worship. Greeks had the power of reasoning. They were easily convinced that the images were not God's, but the works of men. Some of the Greeks had joined the Jewish synagogues. They worshiped the God of heaven and were devout in every respect.

IMAGE WORSHIP

Now while Paul waited for them at Athens, his spirit was stirred in him, when he saw the city wholly given to idolatry. Acts 17 : 16.

Idolatry was prohibited by the Jewish law. The Mosaic law decreed against the veneration of idols, the worship of images, and any other man-made things. The Jews were instructed not to worship any God but Jahveh (Jehovah), the living God (Exod. 20 : 1–5).

The Hebrew prophets, from Moses down to Elijah, warred against the veneration of idols. In those days this type of worship was called "baal worship." Most of the books in the Old Testament condemn the making and the adoration of images. They are called deaf and dumb gods, who had ears but could not hear, eyes but could not see, and mouths but could not speak. "For all the gods of the nations are idols: but the Lord made the heavens (Psalms 96 : 5).

Image worship prevailed among the Hebrews for many centuries, but finally was completely destroyed.

The Greeks, like other pagans, worshiped images of mysterious deities, kings and great heroes. Paul was a strict Jew who had become a convert and a preacher of the gospel of Jesus Christ. He was displeased by the sight of so many images and by the manner in which they were venerated. Paul had changed his mind about some of the Jewish traditions relative to ceremonies and customs, but he revered and kept God's commandments. The scene at Athens displayed a flagrant violation of the first and second commandments. Therefore, Paul was provoked in his spirit to see the Greeks and their philosophers worship the work of their own hands.

Man is the child of God and his likeness. Man should not bow down to things which were created for him. "We ought not to think that the Godhead is like unto gold, or silver, or stone, graven by art and man's device" (Acts 17 : 29).

AREOPAGUS

For all the Athenians and strangers which were there spent their time in nothing else, but either to tell, or to hear some new thing. Acts 17 : 21.

Areopagus was a large courthouse with several courtyards and halls. Idle persons and strangers to Athens often gathered outside the court to hear philosophers expound their theories and orators deliver addresses and debate on subjects of current interest. In other words, Areopagus was something like Hyde Park, in London, or Columbus Circle, in New York.

According to the Eastern text, Paul was arrested or compelled to be brought to the courthouse at the Areopagus to explain his teachings, which were strange and disturbing to the Greeks. Paul succeeded in converting a number of the people, among them Dionysius, one of the judges of the Areopagus. Other listeners mocked Paul; the rest were indifferent.

IMAGE WORSHIP

Then Paul stood in the midst of Mars' hill, and said, Ye men of Athens, I perceive that in all things ye are too superstitious. Acts 17 : 22.

Deglat shedey in Aramaic refers to image worship and its ritual. Statues and images were venerated by the pagans with pomp and ceremony, including the burning of candles and incense. The statues and images were at the center of the highly organized pagan worship. *Shedey* means a demoniac. Pagan images and idols were false, and the worship of them was insanity in the sight of the Jews. The Hebrew prophets condemned the images and called them devilish, deaf and dumb (Ps. 115 : 5).

Paul, according to the Eastern text, told the Athenians: "You are excellent (the Aramaic *yaterin*), or rich, in your image-worship and its ritual." Paul had seen many images which had been donated by worshipers. One of these images had been erected to a forgotten god, whose worship had been neglected, probably because all of its supporters either had died or become poor.

In the East, no one would attempt to reproach in the slightest degree the worship or the sacred shrines of the adherents of a rival faith, especially at the place of worship. Such an act would lead to quarrels and bloodshed. No matter how much Easterners may disagree on their theology and religion, when visiting the churches and the shrines of one another, they always make a few complimentary remarks about the buildings, the images and the ritual. For instance, a Moslem will praise a Christian image in a church, if he happens to be present on some state occasion, although in his heart he may curse it and ask God's forgiveness for having even beheld such a despised object.

Paul was not interested in Greek worship, and its ritual. His casual complimentary remarks were intended as bait, to gain for him the interest and good will of the Greeks. Eastern missionaries always try to get the confidence of the people among whom they are to work by stressing something they have in common. Like his Master, Paul disregarded the established Jewish customs and was friendly toward pagans. What concerned him most was how to win them to Christ.

PAGAN SANCTUARY

For as I passed by, and beheld your devotions, I found an altar with this inscription, TO THE UNKNOWN GOD. Whom therefore ye ignorantly worship, him declare I unto you. Acts 17 : 23.

The Aramaic word *ilatha* means "sanctuary." The Aramaic for "altar" is *madebkha* (a place to offer gifts or burn offerings) (Matt. 5 : 23–24). In the Christian churches, the altar is used for communion. In Assyrian churches, altars are situated in the sanctuaries, the most holy place in the temple. The Eastern text reads, "I found a sanctuary (or an image) with an inscription on it: 'This is of the unknown god,' whom you know not, but whom you worship."

In ancient days, sanctuaries and images were generally built through gifts of rich and noble persons. Idols were donated by tribes as memorials in the temples for tribal patron saints, around whom tribal history and traditions were built. The sanctuaries were visited during the feast days, and costly gifts, foods and animals were offered before them. This custom still prevails among some Christians and Moslems in the Near East who patronize and care for particular sanctuaries, graves of saints, and ancient shrines.

When a tribe was destroyed, its idols were either thrown out or incorporated into the faith of the conquering tribe, under a different name. Consequently the worship of these idols was neglected and their tradition forgotten. In other words, these shrines, bereft of their worshipers and supporters, in due time, became lost in obscurity.

The sanctuary to which Paul called attention was one of the oldest objects in the temple. Its name and tradition had been forgotten. The inscription, "The sanctuary of the unknown god," which Paul saw, had been made in recent years. The other shrines and images still bore the original inscriptions containing the names of the donors. The worshipers were thus advised concerning their history and traditions.

Paul made reference to this mysterious sanctuary, so that he might explain better his God who also was not known, and whose nature was a mystery to pagans accustomed to worshiping idols. Pagan cults in Greece had been imported from Babylon, Persia and Egypt and were in their infancy. *Yahveh* (the Hebrew God) was also worshiped by means of images and statues in the beginning. Abraham's father is said to have destroyed the images which had caused so much dispute and trouble in his country, and in so doing, he discovered the true God. Mohammed likewise, after his victory over pagan Arabia, destroyed several hundred tribal idols (gods) at Mecca. In those days gods were responsible for many quarrels. Their respective worshipers disagreed and fought one another on their account.

RACIAL EQUALITY

And hath made of one blood all nations of men for to dwell on all the face of the earth, and hath determined the times before appointed, and the bounds of their habitation; Acts 17 : 26.

The latter part of this verse in Aramaic reads, "And he has appointed seasons by his command, and has set limits to the age of men." The quotation is from the book of Psalms.

Paul is explaining to the Athenians the universality of God, who is the sole Creator and Ruler of heaven and earth, and who has made of one blood all the nations.

The Hebrews believed in one God, maker of heaven and earth and all that is therein. "The heavens declare the glory of God; and the firmament sheweth his handywork" (Ps. 19 : 1). The Greeks, on the other hand, were idolators. They believed in many gods with diverse interests. The gods of one race had nothing to do with the people of another race. The doctrine of the existence of many gods had been upheld by the Hebrews prior to the eighth century B.C. They had believed in the gods of the Gentiles, but confessed the supremacy of Yahveh (Jehovah). The Hebrew concept of monotheism was crystallized later.

The Semitic people believe in predestination, that is, they maintain that every event is ordained by God and that man's life is governed and guided by him. However, they believe that man is endowed with the free will to distinguish between right and wrong, and to follow the true path of life; that God knows what is in a man's heart, but does not interfere with his free will. And they believe that God is as much interested in the Gentiles as he is in the Jews.

SADDLE-MAKERS

And because he was of the same craft, he abode with them, and wrought: for by their occupation they were tentmakers. Acts 18 : 3.

The Aramaic more accurately reads *"lawlarey,"* "saddle-makers," and not "tentmakers" as translated in the King James Version.

Saddle-making is an art, and in the East saddles always were and still are made by highly skilled artisans of this trade. Boys from the age of ten, or even younger, are employed as apprentices for from four to five years to learn the trade. On the other hand, in Arabia and Palestine, tentmaking was never an art nor a business. Tents are never made for sale. Tents are made from the hair of goats, and the material is spun and woven by women. Each family makes its own tents and repairs them when they wear out. But saddle-making is a man's occupation. Only the embroidered cloth on the saddle and a few minor parts are made by women, and even this work and leather parts are designed by skilled male artisans.

Saddles are still sold and bought in Oriental markets, and saddle-making is a thriving business, especially in large cities. The townspeople buy their saddles in these markets, and expert artisans travel to far-off places where saddle-makers are not available. They make special saddles for the chiefs of tribes. The trade as a whole is very prosperous.

Paul had learned this trade as an occupation. In the East, scribes and doctors of religion, in order to earn a livelihood, often work as saddle-makers, coppersmiths, engravers, silversmiths, or shoemakers. These trades are considered honorable occupations, from which educated and religious people may earn a livelihood. In the East, missionaries and religious men have always supported themselves by the work of their hands. Salaries were unknown until they were recently introduced by Occidental missionaries, who pay native workers. The unpaid missionaries work from eight to ten hours and lecture in the afternoons and nights, when working people are at leisure. Jesus did most of his preaching and healing during the evening hours because most of the people were working in the fields during the day. But he addressed the artisans and shop-keepers while they were at work in the market place. This custom prevails even at the present time. Moslem religious men and missionaries preach in the market places where artisans and business men are engaged in their work.

Paul worked hard at his trade in order that he might not burden financially the Christian converts. In those early days, Christian teaching met everywhere with opposition, and most of the converts were poor. Paul, under no obligation to anyone, could be bold in his teaching and admonitions.

PAUL OPPOSED

And when Silas and Timotheus were come from Macedonia, Paul was pressed in the spirit, and testified to the Jews that Jesus was Christ. Acts 18 : 5.

The Eastern text reads, "Paul felt he was not free to speak, because the Jews opposed him and blasphemed as he testified that Jesus is the Christ." The Aramaic word *aliss* means "pressed," or "suppressed."

Paul was prevented by circumstances from preaching to the Jews. He was eager to convert them, but they blasphemed and did everything possible to interfere with his preaching.

Note:—Hitherto the Jews had been friendly to Paul and his companions. In every city where there was a Jewish synagogue they had asked Paul to speak to them. But now the Jews became wise. They received warnings from Judea and other places that Paul had left Judaism and that he was converting Jews to Christianity. At the beginning of Paul's mission, most of the Jews in Asia Minor and Greece were ignorant of the things that had taken place in Palestine, and some of them were indifferent. Now, however, the Jews were determined to do away with Paul. They sent their agents to the cities where he went, and they stirred up the people against him (Acts 17 : 13; 18 : 12).

SHAKING OF CLOTHES

And when they opposed themselves, and blasphemed, he shook his raiment, and said unto them, Your blood be upon your own heads; I am clean: from henceforth I will go unto the Gentiles. Acts 18 : 6.

Shaking the raiment and throwing dust and ashes on the head is a general custom among Easterners. When men wish to renounce or repudiate certain people or ideas or deeds, they shake off the outer robe from the front.

This signifies that they are through. This custom is similar to the shaking of dust from the sandals. Some men take a little dust or a stone and throw it away, stating, "I have no part in it." Where there are no sandals nor stones to be found, people shake off their outer garments as proof of repudiation. Moreover, when people relinquish certain responsibilities or disagree on important matters, they generally shake their garments, to signify that they will have nothing further to do with the matter in question.

Paul hitherto had obeyed the command of his Lord and the apostles. From the outset he preached first to the Jews. But when he saw that the Jews were stubborn, he changed his plans and warned them that he would begin to preach to the Gentiles, that is, Arameans, Greeks and Romans. Hitherto, Paul had been sincerely seeking the Jews and the descendants of the Ten Tribes, preaching to them in the synagogue and in the homes of the converts. Even as a prisoner in Rome he first preached to the Jews in their synagogue. Paul was zealous to help his people to understand and accept the truth of Jesus' gospel. Like Jesus, he sought his own, but they rejected him.

TITUS JUSTUS

And he departed thence, and entered into a certain man's house, named Justus, one that worshipped God, whose house joined hard to the synagogue. Acts 18 : 7.

The Eastern text reads, "His household were members of the synagogue," and not, "His house joined hard to the synagogue." Justus is not mentioned in the Eastern text.

Missionaries and travelers always seek lodging in the homes of their co-religionists and converts. On their arrival in a town they inquire about other followers of their faith, and if there are none to be found, they lodge in a *khan,* an inn. This is true of missionaries who are unwelcome in places where the feeling between believers of rival faiths is bitter.

On the other hand, churches, synagogues and mosques are always built at some distance from other buildings and dwellings, and are generally surrounded by a courtyard about twenty to thirty feet out from the walls. This courtyard is enclosed by a stone or mud fence, thus setting the place apart from the rest of the town. Both the building and courtyard are considered sacred, and no animals are allowed to enter there. Mohammedans even forbid unbelievers to trespass on the sacred grounds. Christians often use the grounds for the burial of holy men.

The Aramaic word *betey*, refers to his household, or his family. *Bnibetey* means "the members of his household." People often say to each other, *"Beti,* You are my house," which means, "You are a member of my family." Titus' father was an Aramean and his mother a Jewess. He was a member of the Jewish synagogue, but later was converted to Christianity. Hotels and public lodging places were scarce in those days. Travelers and missionaries were entertained by friends and converts, just as they are today.

Titus accompanied Paul on his last journey to Jerusalem (Gal. 2 : 2–3). Paul mentions him in his other epistles.

A VOW

And Paul after this tarried there yet a good while, and then took his leave of the brethren, and sailed thence into Syria, and with him Priscilla and Aquila; having shorn his head in Cenchrea: for he had a vow. Acts 18 : 18.

The making of vows is an ancient Semitic custom which is still practiced in Bible lands. A vow is a pledge to serve God, make an offering, and give alms to the poor, as a token of thanksgiving for God's mercies and favors. When a man is to go on a long and hazardous journey or to undertake a hard task, he makes a vow. On his return from a journey he offers a gift at a shrine or kills a sheep and distributes its meat among the people.

When Jacob fled from Esau, he made a vow in which he

pledged to God a tenth of all that God would give him. "And Jacob vowed a vow, saying, If God will be with me, and will keep me in this way that I go, . . . so that I come again to my father's house in peace; then shall the Lord be my God: . . . and of all that thou shalt give me I will surely give the tenth unto thee" (Gen. 28 : 20–22).

Then again, men or women who were dedicated to God, took vows upon themselves. They were not to touch a dead person. They would not drink wine nor eat moist or dried grapes. Men would not shave until the days of the vow had been fulfilled. Such were the biblical laws governing the statutes of the Nazirites (Num. 6 : 2–20). At the end of the vow the Nazirite was to shave his head at the door of the tabernacle of the congregation. The hair was thrown into a fire (Num. 6 : 18).

When Samson was conceived, the angel of the Lord told his mother not to drink wine or unclean things (Judges 13 : 7). Samson let his hair grow long and was known as a Nazirite.

The long hair serves as a reminder to the man of his vow and of the divine promises. When Samson's hair was shaved, he lost his strength. His power was not in the hair itself, but in the divine promises that the long hair symbolized. Samson did not follow the instructions given to his mother by the angel of the Lord. He made his vow, but when he broke it, he lost his strength.

Then again, women made a vow when they prayed for a male child. Samuel's mother prayed to God for a male child and vowed to give the child to the Lord (I Sam. 1 : 11).

Paul had vowed. He had not cut his hair for a certain length of time. When the days were fulfilled he shaved his head while he was in Cenchrea. Now he was on his way to Jerusalem to attend the feast as was his custom (Acts 18 : 21). God had helped and guided him in every way. God had saved him from his enemies. His preaching mission had been fruitful. Upon his arrival at Jerusalem, Paul went to the Temple with other men who, like himself, had taken vows (Acts 21 : 23–34).

FOLLOWERS OF JOHN THE BAPTIST

This man was instructed in the way of the Lord; and being fervent in the spirit, he spake and taught diligently the things of the Lord, knowing only the baptism of John.
Acts 18 : 25.

The Aramaic text reads, "He spoke and taught very fully concerning Jesus." The Aramaic word for "the Lord" is *Mariah,* which appears in the first part of the verse. The name used in the latter part of the verse is *Eshoo,* "Jesus."

Apollos was an Alexandrian Jew. He was a believer in Jesus, but not a disciple. He belonged to a sect which still held to the baptism and the teaching of John the Baptist. Although many of John's followers believed in Jesus, they were still identified as the followers of John. And some of them, even though friendly, were not converts to Christianity. In other words, they had not received the Holy Spirit, which comes only at baptism.

At present there are about ten thousand of these people in Iraq. They are called "the people of St. John" and are also known as Sabians. They believe in Jesus, but baptize according to John's baptism. They know nothing of the baptism of the spirit. A man is baptized many times. To them, baptism is like taking a bath. They knew nothing about the Holy Spirit. Some of Apollos' followers in Ephesus were baptized by Paul. They received the Holy Spirit (Acts 19 : 6). Hitherto they had lacked this power. This is why Paul, in the outset, did not recognize them as the followers of Christ.

DESCENDANTS OF TEN TRIBES

But when divers were hardened, and believed not, but spake evil of that way before the multitude, he departed from them, and separated the disciples, disputing daily in the school of one Tyrannus. Acts 19 : 9.

The Jews in this part of Asia Minor were largely descendants of the Ten Tribes. Some of them already had been baptized with the baptism of John the Baptist, and were friendly to Paul. These Jews were followers of the Jewish faith but they did not adhere very strictly to the law of Moses and support the Jewish institutions. Like the Galileans, they neglected to observe some of the Jewish traditions.

There were also certain Palestinian Jews from Judea who were bitter against Paul and who disputed his teaching concerning Jesus, whom their co-religionists in Judea had condemned and delivered to the Romans.

In the beginning they had welcomed Paul and invited him to speak to them and bring them news from Palestine. They were not fully aware of his teachings and mission until they heard him preach about Jesus of Nazareth. In the East, it takes a long time for news to travel. The news of Paul's conversion was not known in Asia Minor. The Jews who were living among the Gentiles were not well informed of what was going on in Jerusalem.

HANDKERCHIEFS OF HEALING

So that from his body were brought unto the sick handkerchiefs or aprons, and the diseases departed from them, and the evil spirits went out of them. Acts 19 : 12.

The Aramaic word *rookiatha* refers to pieces of old garments which are used for mending clothes. Men never wear aprons, nor can they afford to give such garments away. In countries where cloth is woven by hand and scarce, people mend their clothes. Even rich men and women refuse to give their garments away when they are worn out. They mend them with new or old pieces of cloth. The mending of clothes is so common that no one is embarrassed or disturbed, no matter how many patches of different colors and materials he may have on his trousers. Some clothes are so mended that at times it is difficult to tell what the original cloth was. On the other hand, when a garment is so worn out that it cannot be mended, it is cut up and used for mending other garments. On one occasion, Jesus illustrated his teaching by referring to the use of new cloth to mend an old garment (Matt. 9 : 16; Mark 2 : 21; Luke 5 : 36).

When Peter walked by, the people brought the sick out of the houses and laid them on the ground so that his shadow might fall on them (Acts 5 : 15).

Paul, like the apostles, had the gift of healing. On his journeys he performed a number of miracles. His fame as a healer had spread so widely that people who could not come to him were satisfied to have a small piece from one of his old garments. But it was their faith in Jesus Christ that healed them, and not the cloth.

Garments of certain noted bishops and religious men who practice healing are considered sacred. And pieces of garments and portions of the Scriptures written on parchment or paper are carried great distances for healing purposes. People have such strong faith in the healer that they believe that even a piece from his garments or a prayer written down by him will heal the sick and restore the insane. They understand that the piece of garment is nothing but a material object. What helps them is their faith in the healer and the thoughts concerning his power that are aroused by the piece of cloth. Indeed, this token helps to establish the contact that strengthens the faith of the sick in the healer and his healing power.

Some healers living in far-off and isolated places, bless water so that the sick person may wash the afflicted parts of his body with it. The sacred water is mixed with other water and used for bathing the sick. This also serves to strengthen their faith.

The shrines and even the graves of certain holy men

138   NEW TESTAMENT COMMENTARY

are constantly visited for healing purposes. Easterners believe that the power to heal does not die with the healer but remains forever.

This practice of visiting the healer undoubtedly became established because of the difficulty of traveling. In the East, holy men are always prey to the attacks of bandits and members of rival religions, and thus cannot travel to see all the sick, in person. The sick then must travel to see the holy men. The strong faith manifested by the believers that enables them to persevere through the difficulties and hardships of travel no doubt contributes much toward their cure. Some healers just speak a word of comfort and assure the sick of quick results. Some afflicted men travel more than a thousand miles to reach a healer or a shrine. Since traveling is not customary, the journey is probably the first in their lives. The change as well as the faith required to make the journey, quickens the healing power which exists in every individual but which sometimes is dormant.

Paul was sought by many men and women who needed his help spiritually, mentally and physically, but he could not be present everywhere at once. At times, he could not travel at all because of lack of money and the danger to his life. This is why he allowed the people to have a piece of his tattered garments. He felt compelled to do something, if only in a small way, for those who besought him to relieve their suffering.

TALISMEN

Then certain of the vagabond Jews, exorcists, took upon them to call over them which had evil spirits the name of the Lord Jesus, saying, We adjure you by Jesus whom Paul preacheth.   Acts 19 : 13.

In many parts of the East diseases are attributed to evil spirits who at some time have suffered injuries from the diseased person. Those who practice witchcraft, magic and sorcery claim that evil spirits have babies which, after dusk, they leave on the streets purposely so that men may step on them and injure them. Some people believe that men who carry written charms issued by a healer are immune from attacks by evil forces but that the evil spirits injured by these men avenge themselves upon persons who possess no means of protection. Many mothers rush to the healers to get charms, written on parchment, which they sew in the garments of their children for fear of disease.

When a sick person is brought before a medium, the latter opens a book and tells the patient that he has injured a certain baby belonging to a tribe of evil spirits and that the only thing to appease the evil spirit is to sacrifice a sheep, distribute some of the meat to the poor, and give the hide and a part of the meat to the medium. The sick one is also asked to repeat certain complicated formulas and to take oaths many times, mentioning the names of certain spirits and pledging that he will never again cause injury to their babies. The doctrine of *jins* (evil spirits) is prevalent among Mohammedans, especially in Arabia and Persia.

These are some of the ancient and deep-rooted pagan beliefs still held by many simple and credulous men and women.

FAKE HEALERS

And the evil spirit answered and said, Jesus I know, and Paul I know; but who are ye?   Acts 19 : 15.

In the East, ministers and other religious men are commonly recognized as healers of the insane and those afflicted with mental diseases. Their authority and reputation in this field is well established. In many cases, the services of some distinguished healer in one locality are sought by the people of other places. His fame spreads so rapidly and widely that the sick and those afflicted with insanity are brought from distant places and countries to seek healing and health from his hands. Prior to the visit, the insane are told all about the healer and the powers he possesses. Their minds are prepared before they are brought into his presence.

On the other hand, the insane, so easily annoyed, are always suspicious and afraid of fake healers who pose as men of God, prescribing tortures to drive out insanity. As this sort of healing is a form of witchcraft performed through physical means, including bodily tortures, its effectiveness is doubted by those who are mentally afflicted and who seek divine healing and comfort.

Thus the insane may scream and become violent when approached by fake healers, but they are usually calm in the presence of true men of God.

The sons of this high priest were not true healers but magicians and witchcraft workers. The insane man recognized them and knew that they were fake healers. When approached by them he became violent and cried out saying, "I recognize Jesus and Paul, but who are you?" He knew Paul was a true healer and preacher of the gospel of Christ of which he had heard, and he had been anxious to receive healing and comfort through his hands. Therefore, the insane man jumped to his feet and tore the garments of the fake healers. It was the demoniac who talked and acted and not the spirit or demon, as stated in the King James Version.

BURN THEIR BOOKS

Many of them also which used curious arts brought their books together, and burned them before all men: *and they counted the price of them, and found* it *fifty thousand* pieces *of silver.* Acts 19 : 19.

Easterners revere their sacred literature and look upon it as the basis of their religion. The authority and authenticity of the Scriptures is never questioned. Therefore, members of every faith live according to the beliefs, practices and doctrines as contained in their sacred writings. Nevertheless, when members of one faith decide to change their religion and become converts to another religion, they burn all of their sacred literature and renounce their faith, traditions and customs. Some of them destroy their shrines and places of worship, and even change their names to conform with the new faith which they have adopted. When theological differences between the two sects are of a minor nature, the converts preserve their literature, but forge the points of difference. Then again, during wars and persecutions, churches and sacred literature are destroyed.

Converts to a new religion destroy their sacred writings and other symbols of their former faith as a token of their loyalty to the new faith and its teachings. Easterners on such occasions try to show their utmost loyalty and sincerity both inwardly and outwardly, in order to help forget the old practices and theologies and learn the new ones. On the other hand, some of the fanatical religious authorities demand these things from their converts. For instance, when a Christian becomes a Mohammedan he has to destroy his wine and any swine he may own, because Mohammedans never drink wine nor eat pork.

IMAGES OF DIANA

So that not only this our craft is in danger to be set at nought; but also that the temple of the great goddess Diana should be despised, and her magnificence should be destroyed, whom all Asia and the world worshippeth.
Acts 19 : 27.

The worship of Diana (Artemis), like that of other Babylonian cults that had been adopted by the people of the Eastern Mediterranean, was declining. The goddess, which supposedly had come down from heaven, was gradually losing its influence over the people. Rivalry among the priests of some of these cults created doubt in the minds of the people. There were other contributing factors. The number of Jewish settlers in this part of Asia Minor was increasing and new religions and philosophies were introduced. The Jewish religion exerted no little influence on the lives of the pagans. Some of the Gentiles, not being content with their own faiths, had openly joined the synagogues, as in the case of Titus (Acts 18 : 7). The Gentiles were searching for something tangible and deeper. The Roman law and good government had brought peace and freedom into Asia Minor, and the people were largely free to join any religion which they deemed to be the best.

The religion of Diana had degenerated into witchcraft and become purely commercial. The priests and artisans derived comfortable incomes from countless silver images which they made and sold to the people who came from all parts of Asia Minor to worship in the shrine of the goddess. The number of silversmiths employed in this art was so large that they had formed a league to protect their business interests. Some of the beautiful images they made were exported; others were offered as gifts at the temple of the goddess. (Some of these were discovered by an Englishman, Sir Woods, about 60 years ago.)

Paul denounced the images of the goddess Diana. He persuaded the people not to believe in them. The craftsmen saw the danger of losing all of their business. They started a riot and brought Paul and his companions before the city magistrates.

The silversmiths and Ephesians valued their goddess and the image business more than the truth. Like the people of Gadara, they were afraid that Christianity would destroy their means of support (Matt. 8 : 33, 34).

The sale of images is still common among pagans and even some Christian sects. Millions of images of the Virgin Mary, Jesus, Joseph, the apostles and saints are sold in various parts of the world. Even today the Palestinian artisans manufacture and sell many religious objects in Bethlehem and Jerusalem. Tons of beads and other relics, some of which are imported from Czechoslovakia, are blessed and sold to foreign tourists. The Mohammedans are strongly opposed to this ancient practice and like Paul despise image vendors.

GODDESS DIANA

But when they knew that he was a Jew, all with one voice about the space of two hours cried out, Great is Diana of the Ephesians.

And when the townclerk had appeased the people, he said, Ye men of Ephesus, what man is there that knoweth not how that the city of the Ephesians is a worshipper of the great goddess Diana, and of the image *which fell down from Jupiter?* Acts 19 : 34–35.

Diana, the great Ephesian goddess, was venerated throughout Asia Minor. In the Eastern text she is spoken of as "Great Artemis," whose image had fallen from heaven.

In older days, when people were living in ignorance and darkness, legends of gods and goddesses who had come down from heaven were common. Every god and idol had a legend, especially those which were imported from Babylon and Egypt.

In early times the Hebrews were often deceived by these legends and worshiped images of the gods of other nations. For instance, King Solomon, with all his wisdom, was misled by the worship of *Ashtoreth,* the Syrian goddess (I Kings 11 : 5). Jeremiah admonished the Jews who had forsaken God and were worshiping and burning incense unto the queen of heaven (Jer. 44 : 17). This is *Ashtoreth,* the goddess of the Sidonians in Syria. She was worshiped by the Jews in Egypt and Pathros. Syrians were great merchants, their ships sailed all the known seas. Wherever they went they introduced their culture and religion. Rachael, Jacob's wife, stole some of her father's images of Syrian (Aramean) gods and brought them to Palestine (Gen. 31 : 34).

Assuredly, religion and civilization of the Orient exerted

a steady influence upon the life of the people who inhabited regions around the Mediterranean. The worship of Diana was one among many other influences from the East which were spreading westward.

All the pagan gods were supposed either to have come from heaven or to be the representatives of heavenly bodies. An old Mohammedan legend upheld by the millions of followers of Islam states that the block of stone at Kaba, in the city of Mecca, came down from heaven during the time of Abraham. The stone is worshiped by thousands of pilgrims who visit the holy shrine every year. Some of these men claim that the stone is hanged between heaven and earth. As no Christians are permitted to visit the city of Mecca, this story cannot be verified. Some people say the stone is a portion of a meteor. Be that as it may, legends of this kind are still found in many other parts of the world.

EUTYCHUS INJURED

And upon the first day of the week, when the disciples came together to break bread, Paul preached unto them, ready to depart on the morrow; and continued his speech until midnight. Acts 20 : 7.

In Cilicia and some other parts of Asia Minor, two- or three-story houses are very common. One-story dwellings are more usual in Mesopotamia, Palestine and Arabia, where Western civilization has not penetrated. Some of these three-story houses are built against a slope or a rock, so that young men can easily ascend to the roof, and watch from the little window in the center of the roof, or from the side window constructed in the front wall. In the East, social and business conversations are often carried on through the chimney or the window; and many meetings are held on the roof (I Sam. 9 : 26). When a wedding, a public meeting or some entertainment is going on in the house, curious young men watch through the chimney or the front window. At times they slip or fall off and are badly injured.

Eutychus, while asleep, lost his balance and fell to the ground and was mortally injured. Paul rushed to help him. And after he had embraced him, he told the people that the young man was alive.

"Dead," in this case, means "unconscious." As in the case of Paul (Acts 14 : 19), when a man is seriously injured or very sick, he is described as being dead. Some men when summoning a healer or doctor in order to hurry him, say, "The patient is dead, do not trouble to come." Eastern doctors and healers are never alarmed or in a hurry. They know that Easterners are frightened when a member of the family is injured or seriously ill. If the man were actually dead, they would not send for a doctor. In the East, no death certificate is required.

The people at the gathering thought that Eutychus was dead, but Paul, according to the Eastern text, told them not to get excited, for "his life is in him." Paul healed him from the injuries he had sustained. Paul had the power to raise him from the dead, but he did not claim to have done so. The young man evidently was not dead.

LAMPS

And there were many lights in the upper chamber, where they were gathered together. Acts 20 : 8.

Earthen lamps are still in use in many countries where kerosene and electricity are unknown. Nomad tribesmen in Kurdistan and the Arabian Desert light their tents by burning wood or grass. The glow is only sufficient to light the central part of the tent where the people sit in divans, conversing and once in a while looking at each other between the tiny pillars of smoke.

During public meetings and weddings, candles made of wax, or of cloth covered with fat, are burning in the rooms. These lights are placed on the walls. On such occasions the house must be lighted as brightly as possible. Large tents and houses require several lamps or candles.

The house where this meeting was held no doubt was large. Paul's fame had spread in these regions and consequently many men and women wanted to see him and hear him. The house was well lighted so that the people might see the speaker.

UPPER ROOM

And there sat in a window a certain young man named Eutychus, being fallen into a deep sleep: and as Paul was long preaching, he sunk down with sleep, and fell down from the third loft, and was taken up dead. Acts 20 : 9.

An upper room is generally built over another room, or on one end of the roof of a house. Its roof is even with those of adjoining houses. There are, however, some upper rooms built one over another in Western style.

The room in which this meeting took place was in a three-story building; that is, two upper rooms built over a house adjoining another house or a slope. Young men could climb, lean and look into the room from one of the front windows or from the window on the roof.

Paul was preaching a long sermon, but it was interesting to Christian converts who were eager to learn all they could about Jesus. Then again, Paul visited these cities only once in several years, and he had many things to tell them. On the other hand, Easterners never tire of listening to long sermons. Missionaries and preachers who speak for several hours are admired and looked upon as learned men. Preachers who are brief lose their reputation.

PAUL WARNS JEWS AND ARAMEANS

Testifying both to the Jews, and also to the Greeks, repentance toward God, and faith toward our Lord Jesus Christ. Acts 20 : 21.

The Eastern text reads: "Testifying both to the Jews, and also to the Arameans (Syrians), . . ."

The majority of the early Christians in Asia Minor were Jews and Arameans (Syrians). Paul always spoke at Jewish synagogues. Many Syrians were members of the Jewish faith; others were married to Jewish women, as in the case of Timotheus, whose father was an Aramean and whose mother was a Jewess (Acts 16 : 1).

Paul warned them to repent. The Aramaic word *tiavotha,* "repentance," is a biblical term, and is well understood by the Jews. Hebrew prophets called on the people to repent and return to God. John the Baptist used this word in his warning to the Pharisees and Sadducees: "Repent ye: for the kingdom of heaven is at hand" (Matt. 3 : 2). Jesus also used this term when addressing the people (John 12 : 40).

The Jews in this region were bitter against Paul and at times caused him considerable suffering and persecution. Paul bids them to repent—that is, to change and accept Jesus Christ as the promised Messiah.

To repent also means to repudiate evil ways and return from pagan worship to the worship of God, the Supreme Ruler of heaven and earth.

WARNED BY THE SPIRIT

And now, behold, I go bound in the spirit unto Jerusalem, not knowing the things that shall befall me there: Save that the Holy Ghost witnesseth in every city, saying that bonds and afflictions abide me. Acts 20 : 22–23.

In times of persecution or danger, Easterners consult religious men, seers and wise men before starting on a journey. On such occasions they pray, meditate and seek God's counsel and guidance. Their prayers are often answered through visions and predictions of men who have prophetic gifts. Jewish kings inquired of the men of God when they wanted to go to war against their enemies and when their land was being invaded. Saul inquired of Samuel and was told that he would be slain (I Sam. 28 : 15–20). The Hebrew kings also inquired of the Lord by means of dreams and by urim and thummim, holy relics possessed by high priests (I Sam. 28 : 6).

Paul throughout his last missionary journey had seen the handwriting on the wall. He had been warned by the Holy Spirit as well as by Christian converts not to go to Jerusalem. The Jews throughout Asia Minor and Macedonia were seeking his life, and were spying on him (Gal. 2 : 3–4). But regardless of these warnings Paul was determined to be at the Holy City on the day of Pentecost (verse 16). He was bound in the spirit. Paul knew that it was dangerous to go to Jerusalem on a feast day. He knew that hundreds of Jews from Asia Minor would be there also. In the East, holy places are not a safe place to visit on feast days. On such occasions many people do not come to the feast to worship, but for other reasons; some bring merchandise to sell, others come to buy things they need; but still others come to seek their enemies. Men are often murdered during the feast days.

When Palestine was under the Turks, Turkish soldiers patroled the streets of Jerusalem and kept strict vigilance over the holy places. Riots often broke out between the Orthodox and the Roman Catholic Christians.

Jesus was also warned not to go to Jerusalem to the

feast of the tabernacles. But after his brethren and followers had gone, he went secretly. "Then the Jews sought him at the feast, and said, Where is he?" (John 7 : 10-11.) Jesus was arrested during the Feast of Passover.

Paul, like Jesus, set his face toward Jerusalem entrusting his life in the hands of God. He was carrying with him the gifts which the Christians in Macedonia and Asia Minor had collected for the relief of the saints in Jerusalem (Rom. 15 : 25-26). Like Jesus, he predicted his own arrest and imprisonment. He told some of his followers that they would never see his face again.

BLOOD OF JESUS

Take heed therefore unto yourselves, and to all the flock, over the which the Holy Ghost hath made you overseers, to feed the church of God, which he hath purchased with his own blood. Acts 20 : 28.

The Eastern text reads: "The church of Christ which he has purchased with his blood." A later Monophysitic Aramaic text known as Peshito agrees with both the Greek and the King James versions, and uses the word "God" instead of "Christ." This text was slightly revised by Rabulah, bishop of Edessa, and other Monophysitic bishops who sought union with the Byzantine church in the fifth and sixth centuries A.D.

Jesus was not called God in those early days. The term generally used by his disciples and their followers was *Maran,* "our Lord," and *Eshoo,* "Jesus." Peter, on the day of Pentecost, called him "Jesus of Nazareth, a man approved of God among you by miracles and wonders and signs" . . . (Acts 2 : 22).

Jewish Christians could not have used the term God, because in their eyes God is spirit, and spirit has no flesh and blood. The term "God" was adopted later when the question of Jesus' divinity and humanity had become the subject of discussion and debate and Christians took sides on the issue of Christology. It was Jesus of Nazareth who shed his blood on the cross for us, and not God.

The Church is often called "the bride of Christ." This is because in the East men pay large dowries for their beloved brides. Jesus paid with his own blood. In the book of the Revelation the Church is spoken of as the wife of the Lamb (Christ). (Rev. 19 : 7; 21 : 9.)

Jesus died on the cross as a man. His divinity neither suffered nor died. This is because his divinity (the Christ in him) was not subject to natural laws. Christ existed from the very beginning. He was neither born, nor did he die, but he lives forever. This belief is still held by Christians in the East.

NO SALARIES

I have coveted no man's silver, or gold, or apparel.
Acts 20 : 33.

Ministers and missionaries of the churches in the Near East receive no fixed salaries for their work. Most of them work in the fields and tend sheep. Some of them, however, are supported by the contributions of their people. Others regularly receive a portion of the gifts which are offered to the church, consisting of butter, bread, cheese, lambs, milk and cloth.

Some ministers and missionaries, however, receive small gifts of money from pious men and women. Generally when a priest, bishop or other high church dignitary is entertained, the host presents him with a small sum of money consisting of silver or gold coins, or a good garment. These gifts, no matter how small they may be, are accepted with gratitude, and the giver and his family are blessed. Some bishops and priests refuse to accept money, especially if they believe the gift is offered for ulterior reasons. When Simon offered Peter a gift of money, the latter declined it and rebuked the giver for his wrong intentions.

Paul earned his livelihood by the work of his own hands. He was a saddle-maker (Acts 18 : 3, Eastern text). Nevertheless, on some occasions Paul did receive money from the Christians in Macedonia, especially when he was in prison in Rome. But as a whole, Paul did not burden the congregations which he had organized. He was independent and above reproach in money matters. There were many false teachers and "evangelists" who preyed on the faithful, and against whom Paul issued warnings (I Tim. 3 : 3; Titus 1 : 7–11). However, the apostles and the gospel workers were entitled to receive generous support from the congregations unto whom they ministered, for the worker is worth his daily bread.

LOST DOCUMENTS

I have shewed you all things, how that so labouring ye ought to support the weak, and to remember the words of the Lord Jesus, how he said, It is more blessed to give than to receive. Acts 20 : 35.

This saying of Jesus is not found in the Four Gospels. It is very likely that Paul quoted from other written sources existing in his time but since lost or destroyed. Some of these documents were destroyed during the persecutions that began under the reign of Nero in A.D. 64 and lasted until the time of Constantine I in A.D. 318. We must not overlook the fact that many documents containing the teaching of Jesus were rejected when the New Testament Cannon was set up many years after Paul's death. Others were destroyed by rival church factions, and a great many scrolls were excluded for certain reasons.

During the apostolic age, writing in Aramaic was common. The apostles sent pastoral letters to Christians in Antioch and Asia Minor. "And they wrote letters by them after this manner . . ." (Acts 15 : 23). "As for the believers among the Gentiles, we have written that they should abstain from the things sacrificed to the idols and from fornication, and from what is strangled, and from blood" (Acts 21 : 25). These letters and many other documents written by the apostles are now lost. Even Paul had other epistles and writings, some of which perished during the persecutions; others were lost. Considering the difficulties of those times, it is a miracle that any of the sacred literature survived and was handed down from one generation to another.

This verse points out that both the giver and the receiver are blessed. The former is blessed spiritually; and the latter receives material blessing. His prayers are answered and his needs met.

PHOENICIA

And finding a ship sailing over unto Phenicia, we went aboard, and set forth.   Acts 21 : 2.

Phoenicia is the Greek name for *Sur*, "Tyre," an important port in Syria, not very far from Galilee. This city was famous for its dyes, especially purple. The Phoenicians were noted for the manufacture of cloth, steel and brass. They supplied the markets with the best cloth and other goods.

The name of the city is derived from the occupation of its people. Syrians were famous for building ships, temples and palaces. They were also noted for the hard steel which they made. Damascus swords were sought by European monarchs when the steel industry was unknown in Europe.

TYRE

And when we had finished our course from Tyre, we came to Ptolemais, and saluted the brethren, and abode with them one day. Acts 21 : 7.

Tyre is one of the most important Syrian seaports on the Mediterranean sea. The city is close to Palestine. In ancient times Tyre, then called *Sur*, was the capital of Syria. During the reign of King Hiram, the little kingdom co-operated with King Solomon in his great enterprise, when he undertook to build the Temple at Jerusalem (I Kings 5 : 4–5). The city for many centuries was a dyeing center.

Jesus had preached in the vicinity of Tyre and Sidon. And these cities were visited by Christian missionaries from Damascus and Jerusalem. The people of this region spoke Aramaic. Undoubtedly there were a great many Christian converts in Syria. The country was a connecting link between the East and the West. The caravans from Egypt and Mesopotamia passed through it, and Christians from various parts of Asia Minor and Egypt met there. Paul, being a native of Cilicia, in Northern Syria, was at home in this region.

WE

And the next day we that were of Paul's company departed, and came unto Cæsarea: and we entered into the house of Philip the evangelist, which was one of the seven; and abode with him. Acts 21 : 8.

"We" in this case means the author of the book of Acts, Luke. He uses "they" and "them" in referring to Paul and his companions when he is not with them. He uses "we" and "us" when he is with them.

There were times when Luke could not be with Paul. Persecutions, expense and emergencies made it impossible for Paul to have all of his co-workers with him. At times he sent some of them to visit congregations and look after important matters for him.

When Luke wrote about events that happened when he was not present with Paul, he obtained his information later from Paul and others who were with him.

VIRGINS

And the same man had four daughters, virgins, which did prophesy.   Acts 21 : 9.

The Aramaic word *petolatha,* "virgins," in this case means maidens, that is, unmarried women.

It is rather unusual for a man to have four daughters who had vowed to remain unmarried. In families where the number of children is large, one of the girls may take a vow and remain unmarried for the rest of her life. In some cases the pledge is made with the father's consent. (Compare I Cor. 7 : 36–38.)

The four maidens might have been too young to be married. On the other hand, Philip was an evangelist; his daughters may have been engaged in teaching and preaching, and may have had the gift of prophesying. They taught and warned the people of forthcoming events.

PREPARATIONS FOR JOURNEY

And after those days we took up our carriages, and went up to Jerusalem.   Acts 21 : 15.

The Eastern text has *ettayaven,* "We made our preparation." "Carriages" in this case refers not to vehicles, but luggage. The Greek word used here is *aposkeuasameni,* "having packed the baggage."

Travelers in the East cannot travel at their will, they

must wait until a caravan is going to the city which they want to visit. This is because it is dangerous to travel alone or even with a few companions. Then again, before beginning a journey, travelers hire animals for transport, change their money, and bake bread.

Paul and his companions had only a little baggage with them, which consisted of sacred scrolls and bread. Jesus had told them not to carry luggage (Matt. 10 : 10, Eastern text). Easterners do not carry suitcases, extra pairs of shoes, shaving kits and other things which Occidentals carry when on a journey. Travelers in the East carry from thirty to fifty specially baked loaves of bread, several pounds of cheese, baked and dried fish, and other articles of food. These are necessary and must be obtained before they start. Sometimes it takes several days to make preparations.

Paul was carrying with him the money that had been donated by Christians in Asia Minor and Macedonia for the Christians in Judea. He had to be careful of bandits. Jerusalem is six to seven days journey distant from Tyre.

SHAVING VOW

Do therefore this that we say to thee: We have four men which have a vow on them; Acts 21 : 23.

People often make vows when they are far away from their homes and sacred shrines. Sometimes they make vows to abstain from certain things until they worship at a certain shrine. Then again, they may fast and make a vow when they pray for the recovery of a sick person, the birth of a child, or for victory over enemies, or when returning from a long journey.

"And Jephthah vowed a vow unto the Lord, and said, If thou shalt without fail deliver the children of Ammon into my hands, then it shall be, that whatsoever cometh forth of the doors of my house to meet me, when I return in peace from the children of Ammon, shall surely be the

Lord's, and I will offer it up for a burnt offering" (Judges 11 : 30–31). His daughter came out to meet him and she was sacrificed by her father (Judges 11 : 39).

On some occasions people vow with a curse, so that no one would dare to break it. Saul put a curse on anyone who ate food before evening (I Sam. 14 : 24). His son Jonathan broke the vow, but he was forgiven (I Sam. 14 : 45).

All Hebrew Nazirites vowed vows. They had to abstain from strong drink and from shaving their hair (Num. 6: 3–5; Judg. 12 : 7–14).

Growing of hair was a reminder of the vow. The Nazirites were distinguished from other people by their long hair. When Samson lost his hair, he also lost his strength. The loss of the strength was caused by the breaking of the vow. Samson believed in the vow and trusted that his strength was in his hair. When the hair was gone, the divine promises were broken and Samson's power was lost (Judg. 16 : 19).

These four men had vowed not to shave their heads until a certain time. They may have just arrived from far-off countries to worship in the Temple at Jerusalem (Num. 6 : 13–14). Paul was instructed by the apostles to pay the expenses of their purification and hair-cutting. This was done to show that Paul was not against the Mosaic law or the Jewish customs. Reports had been circulated that Paul had been preaching to the Jews in Asia Minor in opposition to the law of Moses and other Jewish religious customs (Acts 21 : 21). The apostles wanted to avoid any serious break between the Christian Jews and Paul. This was also a warning to Paul to be careful in his attacks upon Jewish theology, for Paul personally had no use for some of the Jewish traditions and ordinances (Col. 2 : 16–17).

PAUL IN THE TEMPLE

Then Paul took the men, and the next day purifying himself with them entered into the temple, to signify the accomplishment of the days of purification, until that an offering should be offered for every one of them.
Acts 21 : 26.

Most of the Jewish feasts lasted a week. Jewish rituals were long and the ceremonials and ordinances were many. Visitors had to change their money for Temple money, buy sacrifices, purify themselves before presenting their offerings, and perform various other duties according to the law. Those who had made vows were required to shave and then burn the hair in the fire under the sacrifice. The priest took a portion of the sacrifice and other gifts, placed them in the hands of the person who had vowed, and then offered it to the Lord (Num. 6 : 18–19). Such were the laws of the Nazirites and their vows.

Paul also had made a vow. But the days of his vow were fulfilled when he was at Cenchrea (Acts 18 : 18). Now he was sent by the apostle James to accompany four converts who had made vows. He was told to do this to silence the rumors that were being circulated against him by Jewish Christians (Acts 21 : 20–21). But his visit to the Temple and his subsequent participation in the ceremonies led to his arrest and imprisonment.

PAUL MISTAKEN

And as Paul was to be led into the castle, he said unto the chief captain, May I speak unto thee? Who said, Canst thou speak Greek? Acts 21 : 37.

After the revolt under Ishmael, about 585 B.C., a large number of Jews fled to Egypt because of fear of the Chaldeans. These Jews remained in Egypt during the period of the Babylonian and Persian empires.

After the fall of the Persian empire in the latter part of the fourth century B.C., the Greeks conquered Egypt. They built new cities and tried to develop the country. As a result, the Jews in Egypt increased and prospered during this period. Being a small minority, they clung together and succeeded in preserving their religion and racial customs, but they lost their language. The Hebrew tongue in Alexandria and other large commercial centers was replaced with Greek. It was during the Greek rule over Egypt that the Septuagint was made. This was a translation of the Bible into Greek for the Jews who spoke Greek. But the work was condemned by the Palestinian Jews, who declared a day of mourning as protest against the new version branding it unreliable and inaccurate.

The Roman captain mistook Paul for an Egyptian Jew. That is why he asked him if he could speak Greek. "Art not thou that Egyptian, which before these days madest an uproar, and leddest out into the wilderness four thousand men that were murderers?" (Acts 21 : 38.)

The Jews in Palestine and Syria did not speak Greek. Josephus in his book, *The Wars of the Jews,* tells us that Greek was not spoken in Palestine and that only a few men who tried to learn it were rewarded for their efforts. The Jews in Judea spoke a Chaldean dialect, or southern Aramaic, and the Galileans spoke northern Aramaic. Paul, being a learned man, could speak both.

HEBREW TONGUE

And when he had given him licence, Paul stood on the stairs, and beckoned with the hand unto the people. And when there was made a great silence, he spake unto them in the Hebrew tongue, saying, Acts 21 : 40.

"Hebrew" here means "Aramaic"; that is, the Aramaic language spoken by the Jews, who are known as members of the Hebrew race.

Aramaic replaced Hebrew during the Babylonian captivity in the sixth century B.C. The Jews remained in Babylon about seventy years and gradually lost their native tongue. This linguistic change was inevitable because Hebrew and Aramaic were so closely related. Aramaic was the language which Abraham, Isaac, Jacob and his children spoke before the Hebrew language came into existence. Aramaic was spoken in Palestine prior to the fourth century B.C. The early Hebrews were called Arameans (Deut. 26 : 5).

After the return from Babylon the Jews spoke Aramaic. For more than one thousand years Aramaic remained the language of the Jewish people. Aramaic in Palestine was replaced by another Semitic tongue, Arabic, in the ninth century. When Jesus spoke to Paul on his way to Damascus, he spoke in Aramaic, which was Paul's mother tongue. Many portions of the Scriptures were written in Aramaic. Jewish prayers and theologies were also written and circulated in Aramaic. Today many prayers in Aramaic are found in the Jewish Prayer Book.

Paul was a scholar. He had studied at Jerusalem under the great scholar, Gamaliel, and had become a member of the Jewish Sanhedrin. When he addressed the people in his own defense, he spoke in their language. His address dealt with his conversion, Jewish history, and theological matters which anyone can best express in his native tongue. No doubt Paul knew some Greek. Some Jews speak several languages; they need to know them for business and traveling purposes; but they would not be familiar with theological and legalistic terms in those languages. On the other hand, Roman officials always spoke the native languages. And today English and French officials in Palestine and Syria are able to converse in the language of the people over whom they rule.

Paul, being in the presence of Roman authorities, might have been expected to speak in Greek. But, though he could speak some Greek, he did not speak it well enough to explain his case. So he spoke in his own language, because he was addressing the people of his own race, telling them of his religious experience and conversion. Roman officers were not interested in religion. They were stationed at the Temple only to keep order.

RACE AND RELIGION

I am verily a man which am a Jew, born in Tarsus, a city in Cilicia, yet brought up in this city at the feet of Gamaliel, and taught according to the perfect manner of the law of the fathers, and was zealous toward God, as ye all are this day. Acts 22 : 3.

"I am a Jew" does not mean that Paul was of the tribe of Judah, but rather a member of the Jewish faith. When Easterners meet each other in business or during social events, the first thing they ask is: "What is your *Din* (religion)?" Business and social activities are carried on according to the treatment which one religion accords to the members of the other. For instance, a Mohammedan cannot lend money at interest to a member of his own faith, but he may lend to a Christian if he desires to do so. Likewise, a treaty or contract between a Moslem and an unbeliever, is not binding. Then again, a Mohammedan would be insulted if a person of another faith saluted in the same way that a Mohammedan salutes him. Only a Moslem is permitted to say to another Moslem, *Salam al-eko*, "peace be with you." The unbelievers cannot use these words because a Mohammedan does not consider himself at peace with them until they accept Mohammedanism.

Paul's race and religion were often in question. At times he declared that he belonged to the sect of the Pharisees. When among Gentiles he acted and lived as one of them in order to win them over and convert them to Christianity. The Jews would not have allowed him to speak in their synagogues, had they known he was not a strict Jew by faith. His race would not have mattered much, because there were many Arameans who had intermarried with the Jews, and whose children had adopted the Jewish faith. Paul showed good judgment. He always waited to disclose his religious connections until the conclusion of his sermons. He always started with the Jewish fathers and Jewish history, climaxing all with Jesus Christ. The Jews then might go into an uproar, but Paul had delivered his message and had gained many converts and supporters. At times, however, he was beaten and imprisoned.

In the East, race and religion are inseparable. No one can be loyal to a race if he tries to weaken its faith and traditions. This is because the race is governed by the justice and morality derived from religion. Therefore, disloyalty to religion would be disloyalty to the race and the state.

Paul was a Hebrew of the tribe of Benjamin. He was a Jew by faith and a member of the sect called *Parishey* (Pharisees). The Pharisees were nationalists. They believed in the Messianic promises and the ultimate restoration of Israel.

UNDER TEACHER'S CARE

I am verily a man which am a Jew, born in Tarsus, a city in Cilicia, yet brought up in this city at the feet of Gamaliel, and taught according to the perfect manner of the law of the fathers, and was zealous toward God, as ye all are this day. Acts 22 : 3.

"At Gamaliel's feet" means "under his care." In the East, when a father entrusts his son to a teacher, he says, "Let him be the servant of your feet." This is because when a teacher enters a house, servants rush to remove his shoes. And during school hours students may take care of their teachers' shoes, go on errands, and do other work for them.

In the East, teaching is one of the highest professions and teachers are highly honored. But desks and chairs are unknown; the teacher sits on a cushion on the ground, with a long stick in his hand, and his pupils sit around him in a circle. When he stretches out his feet he may almost touch some of the students around him. A favorite student always sits directly in front of the teacher. Both teachers and students must remove their shoes during their studies. This is because most of the courses are religious, where Scriptures are read and prayers recited. Easterners always remove their shoes when guests are present.

Apparently, Paul was a favorite student.

PAUL WARNED

And it came to pass, that, when I was come again to Jerusalem, even while I prayed in the temple, I was in a trance;
And saw him saying unto me, Make haste, and get thee quickly out of Jerusalem: for they will not receive thy testimony concerning me. Acts 22 : 17–18.

The phrase "I was in a trance" is not found in Aramaic manuscripts. It is likely that the translators added it. The Aramaic reads, "And while praying in the temple, I saw a vision, saying unto me, . . ."

What the author of the book of Acts means is that Paul while praying was warned in a kind of vision, perhaps similar to that which Peter saw when he prayed on the roof at Joppa (Acts 10 : 10). On other occasions Paul had similar experiences. He often was guided and directed through visions (Acts 23 : 11).

A ROBE

And as they cried out, and cast off their clothes, and threw dust into the air, Acts 22 : 23.

Easterners, when not at work, generally wear expensive and heavy robes. The outer robe or garment usually worn on such occasions is called *abaya*. It is an expensive and heavy garment which many men wore as a token of dignity and not because of necessity. When men enter a house they remove their *abayas*. Likewise, when at church or mosque, the robe and shoes are removed and set aside. Then again, when people quarrel, they throw off their garments to avoid getting them soiled. A man would almost rather have his body stabbed than have his good robe destroyed.

These men cast off their robes as a signal of protest and of readiness to attack Paul, as in the case of the stoning of Stephen.

Dust is symbolic of mourning, or of repudiation of some act wrongly committed. When a man is killed, his relatives throw dust over their heads and garments. Likewise, when some awful deed is committed, Easterners lose their tempers and act almost mad. Paul, in the eyes of the Jews, had defiled the Temple by bringing Gentiles into it. The priests and religious men tried to magnify the seriousness of the incident in order to incite the crowd and bring about the arrest of Paul.

PAUL SCOURGED

The chief captain commanded him to be brought into the castle, and bade that he should be examined by scourging; that he might know wherefore they cried so against him. Acts 22 : 24.

Officials generally scourge the prisoners before the trial. They are beaten at the scene of the crime or on the way to prison. This punishment is administered for two reasons: First, to quiet the mob, and second, to frighten the prisoner and obtain a quick confession from him.

Pilate, hoping to appease the Jews, ordered Jesus to be scourged in the midst of the trial (John 19 : 1–2). Even today, men who are charged with insurrection or other serious crimes are severely punished before they are brought to trial.

Paul was charged with sedition and with being a ringleader of the sect of Nazarenes. He was also accused of having profaned the Temple by bringing into it the uncircumcised Gentiles. Both charges were serious. The first was against the Roman government, and the second against the Jewish religious laws which were respected by the Romans. Not even the Roman authorities could enter the sacred ground of the inner court of the Temple. That area was reserved for the Jews only.

WHITED WALL

Then said Paul unto him, God shall smite thee, thou whited wall: for sittest thou to judge me after the law, and commandest me to be smitten contrary to the law?
Acts 23 : 3.

"Whited wall" is an Aramaic idiom which means "hypocrite." *Astha* is the lower part of the wall, just a little above the foundation. Houses in the East are not generally painted, either within or without. Nevertheless, because of black dirt caused by smoke, the lower part of the wall is often whitened or plastered with white clay to protect the clothing of men and women who may lean against it. Rough and unhewn stones are used for foundations. This incident recalls Jesus' statement concerning "the stone which the builders rejected" and which became the cornerstone.

The wall after being whited looks clean only for a short time, and then it has to be whited again and the dirt covered.

The high priest, whom Paul evidently mistook for an elder, was black within, like the painted wall. He was sitting in judgment to convict others for breaking the law, when he himself was guilty. "Whited wall" was a casual but scornful rebuke on the part of Paul, who, after being struck in the face, was unable to control his anger. The Jewish law prohibited the cursing of priests (Exod. 22 : 28). Jesus likewise was struck in the face when he answered the high priest informally and indifferently, saying, "Why askest thou me?" (John 18 : 21–22.)

Easterners when arguing with one another, still use this phrase, "Oh, you whited wall," which means, "Oh, you're a hypocrite."

PRIESTS MISTAKEN FOR LAYMEN

Then said Paul, I wist not, brethren, that he was the high priest: for it is written, Thou shalt not speak evil of the ruler of thy people. Acts 23 : 5.

Semites do not wear clerical collars or ecclesiastical garments, or possess diplomas when they become rabbis or ministers of religion. Priests, mullahs and rabbis dress simply, and live like ordinary people, except when performing their religious duties; then they dress in ecclesiastical robes and are covered with white mantles. (Some of the Mohammedan religious men are an exception to this.) This makes it difficult to distinguish a rabbi or minister from other men. Learned Mohammedan men generally wear green turbans.

In the East, religious men, in order to make a livelihood, work as farmers, merchants, teachers and artisans. Some of them are supported by tithes and gifts which are given by worshipers. But as the homes of religious men are open to the poor and strangers, they are always impoverished and in want.

Tithes and gifts are not sufficient to maintain religious men who are married. Therefore most priests and ministers of religion live simply and dress like their parishioners. However, in large cities one may occasionally meet a few religious men wearing heavy turbans or some distinguishing garment. But such garments may also be worn by other dignitaries, noblemen, and the rich.

This is why Paul did not recognize this high priest as such, his garments being like those of other people. Paul thought that he must be an elder sitting in judgment. This is the custom in the East; many quarrels and disputes are settled by priests or elders, or any other dignitaries who may be available. Paul called the high priest a hypocrite, but when he saw his mistake, he apologized, stating that he did not recognize him. The Mosaic law prohibits the cursing of priests, because in those days priests were sanctified to God's work, and therefore were unreproachable (Exod. 22 : 28). But in Paul's day, the priesthood could be bought by the highest bidder. Nevertheless, Paul showed his respect and devotion to the Jewish law and the high priest.

To obey and respect the authorities is a Christian doctrine.

ROMAN OFFICIALS

And he wrote a letter after this manner: Claudius Lysias unto the most excellent governor Felix sendeth greeting. Acts 23 : 25-26.

During apostolic times Palestine was divided by the Romans into several small kingdoms which were ruled by native princes appointed by Roman military or provincial authorities, and later confirmed by Caesar. The power of these kings was limited in many respects, especially in regard to crimes and political affairs. The native kings had power to collect taxes, maintain law and order, and perform other duties in civil matters, but political crimes involving capital punishment were tried by the Romans.

High Roman officials called pro-consuls were stationed in Antioch and other strategic cities in Syria near the Persian border. Romans and Persians were constantly at war. Syrian provinces which were in the path of the Persian armies were strongly fortified, and served as spearheads for Roman campaigns in the Euphrates Valley. Therefore Syria, after its occupation by the Romans in 67 B.C., was made a Roman province. High Roman officials resided in Antioch and other important cities which were garrisoned by Roman soldiers and were needed for military operations.

Minor Roman officials, known as procurators (governors) were stationed in Jerusalem and other places to act as advisers to look after native government and see that taxes were collected. The Roman rule was similar to the present-day British rule in Palestine and Transjordania. Great Britain is represented by high commissioners who reside at Jerusalem and Ammon respectively. Other minor civil and military officials with some administrative powers are stationed in smaller places. Native kings and their officials have limited powers, except in religious matters. The countries' foreign policies are determined by the British foreign office. British citizens are tried in special courts under English law.

Felix, the Roman governor of Caesarea, had jurisdiction over Palestine and certain parts of Syria. He was well acquainted with the Jewish laws and customs. His wife was a Jewess. Mandatory powers, not having courts in the mandated countries, try their own people at the Residency (palace). This is why Paul was accorded so much protection. He was entitled to full Roman justice.

Paul was a native of Cilicia in Syria. He was a Roman citizen and therefore entitled to Roman protection. The Romans had extraterritorial rights, enabling them to be tried in special courts under Roman law. The justice in the native courts was perverted, officials were corrupt and judges easily bought. Had Paul been a citizen of Palestine, the Jews could have put him to death by stoning, as in the case of Stephen (Acts 7 : 58–59). Jesus was tried by the Roman governor because he was from Galilee. The Jewish priests and native authorities in Jerusalem had no jurisdiction over Galilee. That region was under Herod (Luke 23 : 6–7).

Roman courts were good, but the authorities often sacrificed justice to please native kings and priests.

KING AGRIPPA II

Especially because I know *thee to be expert in all customs and questions which are among the Jews: wherefore I beseech thee to hear me patiently.* Acts 26 : 3.

King Agrippa II, was a son of Agrippa I, and a great-grandson of Herod the Great. His father, in order to please the Jews, had beheaded James, son of Zebedee, and had tried to kill Peter (Acts 12 : 1–2).

Agrippa II was educated in Rome. He was also well trained in the Jewish law and traditions. Like his father and his great-grandfather, he wanted to win the favor of the Jewish people. But Herod the Great had been hated by the Jews. He was an Idumean by race, but a Jew by faith. His children and grandchildren were brought up according to Jewish law and customs.

King Agrippa, being an Easterner and a member of the Jewish faith, knew that the Jews were divided into several theological schools and that they quarreled over the doctrine of the resurrection of the dead. Paul was a Pharisee and believed in the resurrection of the dead. But the Sadducees denied it. The Pharisees were the largest and strongest party in Palestine and the Jewish kings nearly always sided with the powerful majorities. Agrippa could have released Paul, if he had wanted to do so, but like Pilate he was afraid of losing his position.

Paul appealed to King Agrippa as one who was well versed in Jewish theologies and Scriptures. He proved from the Scriptures that Christ should suffer and that he should be the first to rise from the dead. Agrippa, like other Jews, believed in the coming of a political Messiah, but was not interested in the restoration of the Davidic kingdom. His great-grandfather had exterminated the princes of the Hasmonean dynasty. A Jewish state ruled by a Jewish messiah was contrary to the policy of Herodian dynasty.

CHRISTIAN JEWS

And I punished them oft in every synagogue, and compelled them to blaspheme; and being exceedingly mad against them, I persecuted them even unto strange cities. Whereupon as I went to Damascus with authority and commission from the chief priests, Acts 26 : 11–12.

Christianity was preached first to the Jews and therefore the first Christian converts were Palestinian members of the Jewish faith. Jesus had preached in the Jewish synagogues, and his apostles likewise were permitted to worship and, at times, speak in the synagogues. At the outset Christianity was not regarded as hostile to Judaism and many Jews were sympathetic toward the Christian cause. Years later, however, Christian converts began to establish their own congregations and teach Christian doctrines which were contrary to the traditions of the elders.

Paul was commissioned by the high priest to investigate the Jews who were suspected of being sympathetic toward Christianity and to arrest and punish those found guilty of disloyalty to Judaism. In this early period of the Christian era, the followers of Jesus could hardly be distinguished from the adherents of the Jewish faith. Christians and Jews wore the same style of clothes and ate only kosher food. Their religious practices, customs and manners were the same. They both worshiped in the Temple and attended services in the synagogues. In other words, the followers of Jesus could not be easily distinguished from the Jews, except that they were sympathetic toward the new revelation which, in their eyes, was true Judaism. Jesus had told them that he had not come to destroy the law and prophets, but to fulfill them. Therefore the Christians were friendly toward the Jews.

FASTS USED AS A CALENDAR

Now when much time was spent, and when sailing was now dangerous, because the fast was now already past, Paul admonished them, Acts 27 : 9.

In lands where printed calendars are unknown, fast days and festivals are used to reckon time. Priests, deacons and a few elderly men and women keep track of the days and months, and inform the people of coming feasts and fast days. Of course, some of the people know when feasts and fasts will fall, for they are the most important events of the year, and the people are mindful of them.

Then again, feasts and fasts are used as reminders to pay off debts, transact business, and travel. Fasting is mentioned here simply in order to indicate the season of the year that is dangerous for sailing. This Jewish fast falls on the tenth day of the seventh month and is known as the Day of Atonement. On this day the people rest from all work and devote their time to fasting and prayer. The fast is followed by the Feast of the Tabernacles, observed on the fifteenth day of the seventh month (Lev. 23 : 26–34).

The Eastern text reads: "There we remained for a long time, till also the day of the Jewish fast was over. . . ."

BITTEN BY A VIPER

And when Paul had gathered a bundle of sticks, and laid them on the fire, there came a viper out of the heat, and fastened on his hand. Acts 28 : 3.

Many religious men and women defy the fear of snakes, scorpions, and other poisonous insects, and pick them up in their hands without thought of being harmed by them. Such men are never disturbed by the sight of such poisonous reptiles and insects.

There are some people on whom poison has no harmful effect and therefore are immune from bites. Such persons collect honeycombs from beehives without protecting their faces and hands, and handle snakes and scorpions. Even when they are bitten, the poison does not take effect.

Such persons are always recognized by the public as having some hidden power which protects them. Some are looked upon as men of God and healers. Then again, most religious men are not afraid of snakes, which are often found in church buildings. In some ancient shrines snakes may even crawl among the worshipers, but they will not attack anyone who does not disturb them. Priests and caretakers walk among them and even step on them without being harmed.

According to the Eastern text, Paul was bitten by a viper which hung on his hand. The Aramaic word *nekhtat* is derived from *nak* which means "to strike or bite." The Hebrew is *nakae*. When Paul saw the viper hanging from his hand he was not alarmed. He shook his hand and the viper fell into the fire. The savage islanders and the superstitious immediately recognized him as a healer and a man of God, immune from harm, and so they began to worship him and bring their sick to him to be healed. Jesus had told his disciples that they would be able to handle snakes without being harmed. Paul of course did not know that the viper was among the sticks. He did not handle it just to prove his power. It was accidental; and therefore Paul was divinely protected. The same God who had saved him from the shipwreck saved him from the poisonous viper.

PAUL AS A LEADER

And it came to pass, that the father of Publius lay sick of a fever and of a bloody flux: to whom Paul entered in, and prayed, and laid his hands on him, and healed him.
So when this was done, others also, which had diseases in the island, came, and were healed: Acts 28 : 8–9.

In places where medicines and doctors are unknown, sick persons seek the aid of holy men, and the wise. Today in many parts of the Near East and Asia, American and English missionaries are looked upon as doctors and are frequently consulted by sufferers. Easterners believe that those who can minister to the soul must surely be able to minister to the body. On the other hand, illnesses such as fever and dysentery are easily cured.

Paul, though a prisoner, was the wisest man in the whole group, and his advice was sought by many who were with him on board the ship. He had predicted the disaster, but also had assured the sailors that not one of them would be lost. His unusual power was felt by all who talked to him and sought his help. They were greatly impressed when they found that he had the gift of healing. This power seemed especially wonderful to the simple barbarians, whose faith was almost like that of little children.

CHRISTIANS IN ROME

And from thence, when the brethren heard of us, they came to meet us as far as Appii forum, and The three taverns: whom when Paul saw, he thanked God, and took courage.

And when we came to Rome, the centurion delivered the prisoners to the captain of the guard: but Paul was suffered to dwell by himself with a soldier that kept him.
Acts 28 : 15–16.

Groups of Christian converts were found in many cities in the Roman Empire. The teaching of Christ was spreading through merchants, prisoners, soldiers and travelers.

Jewish Christians were found everywhere. Some of these men were present in Jerusalem on the day of Pentecost (Acts 2 : 10). Jesus' fame had spread to many countries outside of Palestine.

Nevertheless, hitherto the Christian movement had not been well organized in Rome. There were a number of followers and sympathizers among the Jews, Syrians and proselytes, but they had no teachers or places of worship of their own. They still attended the synagogue, and the pagans knew them as Jews. These men had been informed about Paul, his work and his arrest, by Christians who had come from Greece. Paul met them and the chiefs of the Jews, and discussed with them his imprisonment and persecution. Many of the Jews believed and were converted, but others refused to hear him again. Thus the Church in Rome was organized by Paul during the two years of his imprisonment. The little lodging place he had rented was used as a meeting place. Thus, even though bound in chains, Paul was able to add to the number of converts in the Imperial City.

ROMANS

INTRODUCTION

Romans is one of the most important of the Pauline letters. The epistle covers many aspects of Jewish law, ordinances and customs. Its contents are chiefly doctrinal. The epistle embodies many phases of the Old Testament teaching. These are interpreted through the light of the Gospel of Jesus Christ, the gospel of the grace of God and of salvation to both the Jews and the Gentiles.

The epistle was dictated by Paul but written by Tertius, a scribe (Rom. 16 : 22) and sent from Corinth about A.D. 60. Paul had been desirous of visiting the imperial capital and sharing his experiences and the new message of the Christian gospel with the Jewish Christians in Rome, who were still living under the Mosaic laws and ordinances of the flesh.

Paul in his epistle explains that God does not discriminate between the Gentiles and the Jews, but that he is the God of all. The Jews and Gentiles are to be saved by the grace of God and faith in Jesus Christ. Paul argues that no one can fully observe the law, and therefore the Jews and Gentiles are under sin, and can only be saved by the grace of God. The Gentiles were grafted to the broken branches, and are to receive equal grace with the Jews. Christians are to be crucified and die with Christ and rise into a new life.

Paul also admonishes the Roman Christians to be loyal to the government and to show their good works. He also warns them against teachers who are causing divisions and introducing doctrines that are stumbling-blocks to the Jewish Christians. (There were many teachers who were teaching that salvation must be earned by means of the law and its ordinances.) Paul hopes for the salvation of a remnant of Israel, that is, those who have accepted Jesus Christ. The remnant is the spirtual Israel, which is to serve as leaven to ferment the Gentile world.

The epistle, as a whole, is addressed to the Jewish Christians. Paul makes a strong plea on behalf of the Gentiles who, by the grace of God and the death of Jesus, had been made equal with the Jews.

JESUS THE MAN

And declared to be the Son of God with power, according to the spirit of holiness, by the resurrection from the dead: Romans 1 : 4.

For thirty years Jesus was known as an ordinary man. The people of Nazareth had seen him as a child, as a boy, and then as a grown man. No one knew that he was the promised Messiah. When Jesus declared that he was the Messiah, they threw him out of the synagogue and sought to kill him (Luke 4 : 28–30). Peter, while addressing the audience on the day of Pentecost, had spoken of Jesus of Nazareth as "a man approved of God among you by miracles and wonders and signs, which God did by him in the midst of you, as ye yourselves also know" (Acts 2 : 22).

When Jesus began to preach and heal and to raise the dead, he was then declared the Son of God. This sonship was further proven through his resurrection from the dead, which was the greatest of all miracles. Prophets had healed the sick, cleansed the lepers and raised the dead, but none of them had risen from the dead.

Thus, to Paul, resurrection from the dead was the greatest proof of the living Christ, the Messiah, who had been foretold by the prophets. Victory over Sheol and death was the greatest of all. The Jews looked on death as an end and considered Sheol (hades) as unconquerable.

Jesus was a man, but Christ in him was God. The human and the divine were united. This doctrine is still upheld by the Christians in the East.

GOD AS A WITNESS

For God is my witness, whom I serve with my spirit in the gospel of his Son, that without ceasing I make mention of you always in my prayers; Romans 1 : 9.

"God is my witness" is an Aramaic expression which is generally used during debates and important conversations. One often hears people say "God knows" or "God is a witness." "My witness is in heaven." Easterners trust a person when he produces one or two witnesses.

The Jewish law demanded two or three witnesses (Deut. 17 : 6). Jesus also told his followers that if a brother should trespass against them they should get one or two witnesses (Matt. 18 : 16).

When witnesses are not available, people say, "The Lord is my witness." "And the elders of Gilead said unto Jephthah, The Lord be witness between us . . ." (Jud. 11 : 10). Samuel warned the people when they demanded a king, telling them that the Lord was a witness against them (I Sam. 12 : 5).

Jesus used this saying when debating with the Jews. "And the Father himself, which hath sent me, hath borne witness of me" (John 5 : 37).

Paul calls God his witness to prove his sincerity and love toward the Jewish Christians who were in Rome. Most of these Jews were strict adherents to the Jewish laws and customs. They doubted Paul's sincerity. Paul was accused of teaching against the law of Moses and the Jewish customs and the holy Temple. These charges Paul denied very strongly during his trial (Acts 24 : 14). Nevertheless, Paul had no other witnesses to disprove some of the charges made against him and to testify to his loyalty to the people of his race. The only witness he had was the living God.

On the other hand, Paul's work among the Gentiles had caused considerable uneasiness among the Jewish Christians. But Paul is neither ashamed nor afraid because of the gospel which he preached both to the Jews and to the Arameans (Syrians). (Rom. 1 : 16.)

ARAMEAN CHRISTIANS

For I am not ashamed of the gospel of Christ: for it is the power of God unto salvation to every one that believeth; to the Jew first, and also to the Greek.
Romans 1 : 16.

The Eastern text reads: ". . . whether they are Jews first, or Arameans" (Syrians). The term Christians was given to the followers of Jesus in the year 50 and at Antioch in Syria. The Christians in Syria had more freedom than those in Judea who were harassed and persecuted. Syria was a Roman province, and Antioch the seat of the governor-general. Then again, the Jews in Syria were a minority, and were not on friendly terms with Syrians.

After the persecution of the Church in Judea under Agrippa I and the murder of James, the son of Zebedee, the seat of Christianity was transferred from Jerusalem to Antioch, where Christians were enjoying considerable freedom and the Church had prospered. The Church in Damascus had grown to such an extent that the Jewish priests had commissioned Paul and sent him there to persecute the Christians (Acts 9 : 2).

It is interesting to know that some of the first converts to Christianity were Arameans. Jesus had preached in Tyre and Sidon. The seventy disciples were sent out into Syria. Geographical, racial and linguistic factors helped the Christian cause in Syria. Galilee was only a short distance from Tyre and Sidon. Both Galileans and Syrians spoke Aramaic. They were kindred people.

The Arameans were noted for shipbuilding, dyeing of garments, and building of temples and palaces. They were skilled in the use of silver, iron, and other metals. When King Solomon was ready to build the Temple, he hired Arameans to help him in his project (I Kings 7 : 13–14). The Arameans were noted for their wisdom. Their culture was supreme for many centuries and had spread throughout North Africa. The ruins of their magnificent temples and palaces still remain in Carthaginia in Africa, *Balbak* in Syria, and in other parts of the East.

JEWISH CONCEPT OF SALVATION

For as many as have sinned without law shall also perish without law: and as many as have sinned in the law shall be judged by the law; Romans 2 : 12.

The Jews were the chosen people to whom the law and the Scriptures were given. According to the Jewish concept of salvation, only those who were able to live according to the law and its ordinances were to be saved. In other words, God was the God of the Jews and therefore salvation was for the Jews. The Gentiles and pagans were to be lost. This belief was also held by pagan people, whose gods were concerned only with the welfare of their own people.

Paul argues against this Jewish concept. He points out that God from the very beginning has made himself known to his creations so that they might not have an excuse. That is to say, men everywhere felt the power and presence of God. Even those who had no law realized that murder, stealing and lying were wrong. The law was written in their hearts. Therefore, after the resurrection, these people are to be judged according to their works. Many Gentiles who had no law did by nature the good things which were in the law. But those who had committed sin and were not under the law would meet the same fate as those who sinned and were under the law.

The Gentiles who had done good works are to be saved. The guilt of those who had the law and prophets and yet sinned is greater than those who had no law or prophets. Salvation by means of the law was an impossibility, since no one could live up to the precepts of the law. According to Paul, salvation is by means of the grace of God. Both Jews and Gentiles are God's children, and they will be judged without discrimination.

SALVATION BY FAITH

Thou that makest thy boast of the law, through breaking the law dishonourest thou God? Romans 2 : 23.

The Jews boasted of their law. The Ten Commandments given by God to Moses have never been surpassed. The civil and moral ordinances revealed and written by Moses were also superior to the laws of other nations in biblical days.

Thus, the Jews were living under the light of the law and the Scriptures, while most of the Gentiles were ignorant wandering in the darkness. Therefore, the Jew considered himself an instructor of the law, and a guide to the blind. The Jews were a small race in comparison to the Gentiles, but their religion and laws were superior to those of the latter. This is because the Jews worshiped the living God, and the Gentiles worshiped blind, deaf and dumb images. Therefore the Jews boasted of their faith and law which served as a lamp.

Paul upbraided the Jews because they broke the very laws of which they boasted. For in breaking even one of the laws, they sinned. On the other hand, the Gentiles who had no moral law, were not under sin. Sin came into the world by means of the law. Why then should the Jew boast of something that is not able to save him? Salvation is to be attained by means of faith and good works. Faith in Jesus Christ brings salvation by the grace of God. "Christ has redeemed us from the curse of the law . . ." (Gal. 3 : 13). Man cannot earn his salvation by means of the law because no man can live up to the precepts of the law. But he can receive salvation by faith in Jesus Christ (Acts 13 : 38; Heb. 9 : 26).

Sin is the result of transgressing the law, by doing evil instead of good. The law distinguishes between good and evil, but it does not stop people from transgressing it. "But that no man is justified by the law in the sight of God, it is evident: for, The just shall live by faith" (Gal. 3 : 11).

CIRCUMCISION OF CHRIST

But he is a Jew, which is one inwardly; and circumcision is that of the heart, in the spirit, and not in the letter; whose praise is not of men, but of God. Romans 2 : 29.

Circumcision, from the scientific point of view, was performed for sanitary reasons. Religiously, it was a sign by which members of one race or faith were distinguished from those of others.

Just as baptism by water was symbolical of the baptism of the spirit, circumcision also had a symbolic significance. What Paul infers here is the change of heart, which means the change of the whole life. Just as circumcision distinguished the Jews from the Gentiles and made them pledge to live according to the law of God, circumcision of the heart distinguishes the believers and makes them live after the law of Jesus Christ. Good takes the place of evil.

Circumcision, being a racial symbol, lost its primary objective and wrought no effects in the lives of those who believed in it. It became merely a tradition. Its inward meaning and spiritual value were lost.

LAW INADEQUATE

Now we know that what things soever the law saith, it saith to them who are under the law: that every mouth may be stopped, and all the world may become guilty before God. Romans 3 : 19.

In the East, the members of one race are not bound by the laws and traditions of another. Thus, even though the laws of a race which is in power may be forced upon others, the subjected peoples do not consider them to be valid. Therefore, the transgression of the law is not regarded as a sin, even though the violator may be severely punished, according to the law. However, when an individual or a race adopts a new religion, it must also adopt the manners and customs which go with it, and obey the laws and honor the prophet who is the founder of the new faith. For instance, when a Christian embraces Islam, he severs all of his ties with his own race and pledges allegiance to those of Islam.

This was not the case with the Christian religion. Jesus was not out to make converts to the Jewish faith. His mission and that of his disciples was to win Jews and Gentiles alike to a purer and more spiritual religion, which had been revealed by the prophets, but had later been perverted and corrupted by the traditions of men.

Paul here emphasizes the fact that Gentiles cannot hope to find justification through the laws and practices enjoined by the Jewish elders, but only through the grace of God and faith in Jesus Christ. To accept Jesus and then proceed to live by the literal interpretation of the law would indicate that the acceptance of Jesus and his teaching were inadequate for salvation and that the believers were not free from what the Jewish authorities called sin. Paul courageously denounced some of the narrow Jewish precepts and observances, thus inviting Jews and Gentiles alike to forget their differences and emulate the example of the apostles and himself, who had exchanged Judaism for Christianity. He also urges them to give themselves whole-heartedly to the practice of the pure and simple religion of which Jesus was the cornerstone.

SALVATION

Being justified freely by his grace through the redemption that is in Christ Jesus: Romans 3 : 24.

The Aramaic word *porkana* means "salvation" and not "redemption" as translated in the King James Version. *Porkana* is derived from the Aramaic word *prak,* "to save." *Mekhar* and *zban* mean "to purchase," "redeem" or "acquire." Neither of these words occur here.

Paroka in Aramaic means "Saviour," "comforter" or "one who saves a person from drowning," but with no sense of giving his own life or of paying a price. It is often said, "He puts his life in danger in order to save others."

"Redemption" means "to purchase with money" or "to free a slave with the payment of a price." The term "redemption" occurs in other places, but it does not imply that Jesus gave his life as a debt to some other power. The Aramaic phrase *zavnan badmey* means "he gave his life in order to save us." We often say, "He bought us from death," which means "He saved our lives."

The mercy seat was sprinkled with the blood on the day of atonement. The animal was slain against his will for the sins of the people (Lev. 16 : 14).

Jesus, by giving his life willingly, offered a living sacrifice, but paid no debt to anyone. There was no one to accept payment of such a debt. No one has jurisdiction over the world but God, his Father. God neither collects debts nor does he owe anything to anyone.

Jesus' death, through the revelation of God's truth, provided the means of overcoming evil and sin and leading mankind into the true path of life. He gave his life in order that we also may be willing to sacrifice for others. His death destroyed the power of sin and did away with animal sacrifices, superstition, and false doctrines that had kept mankind in darkness and ignorance. Jesus opposed the priestly order, the Jewish sacrificial system and its teachings, which had been openly denounced by the Hebrew prophets. Jesus died as a protest against the evils of that system in order that Jews and Gentiles alike may be freed and led into the way of salvation. A righteous person gave his life to save mankind from evil and ignorance.

EARLY MONOTHEISM

Is he the God of the Jews only? is he *not also of the* Gentiles? Yes, *of the Gentiles also:* Romans 3 : 29.

In ancient days, gods were the property of individuals and tribes. Each tribe had its own deities. The tribal laws and morality did not extend beyond the boundary of the tribe. That is to say, the people considered it a sin to kill and steal from members of the tribe, but lawful to plunder and murder other tribes. The tribal deity was represented in the person of the chief of the tribe, who made laws and ordinances in the name of the deity and led the people into war. This was the first phase of theocracy (Gen. 31 : 30–32). When a man changed his religion he also changed his nationality. And Ruth said: "Thy people shall be my people, and thy God my God" (Ruth 1 : 16). Members of one tribe joined other tribes by means of a blood covenant. This custom still prevails in Arabia.

Jehovah was a tribal god. He was the God of the Hebrews and his jurisdiction did not extend beyond the boundaries of the Hebrew tribes. On the other hand, the Jews at times recognized the deities of the surrounding people, among whom they lived, but they acknowledged the superiority of their God over other gods. At times, when they suffered defeats, they thought that the gods of the Gentiles were stronger than their God. When they were harassed and taken captive by the Assyrian and Babylonian kings, however, they blamed it on their own sins. The powerful Gentile kings were called "God's agents," who were empowered to execute justice.

The chief difference between the Jews and the Gentiles was that the Jews believed in one God and were united; the Gentiles in Palestine and Syria had many gods and as the result they were divided. In other words, the Jews were monotheistic in their worship. They worshiped the unseen God, the Creator of heaven and earth. But they were reluctant to share their true faith with the Gentiles.

Jesus proclaimed the God of heaven and earth as the Father of all people. Racial and religious boundaries were abolished. All nations were made of one flesh and blood. Jesus gave his life as a means of salvation for all people. He instructed his disciples to go to all nations throughout the world. "Go ye into all the world, and preach the gospel to every creature" (Mark 16 : 15).

JUSTIFICATION BY WORKS

For what saith the scripture? Abraham believed God, and it was counted unto him for righteousness.
Romans 4 : 3.

This quotation is from Genesis: "And he believed in the Lord; and he counted it to him for righteousness" (Gen. 15 : 6). What Paul infers here is the works of the law, the traditions and other Jewish observances. According to the Jewish teachers of religion, the observance of the law and the tradition of the elders was the only means by which a man could be declared righteous and earn his salvation.

Abraham proved his faith by his good deeds. He loved Jehovah with all his heart and soul. His God came first, before everything else. Abraham must have possessed many Christian qualities to be called to such a high mission. In referring to the faith of Abraham, Paul does not mean that anyone, regardless of his works, can be justified by faith. Abraham proved his faith by his willingness to sacrifice his son, and by his hospitality, charity and other good works. The one who fears God, does the works of God.

James, the apostle, states: "Ye see then how that by works a man is justified, and not by faith only" (James 2 : 24). James here does not exclude faith as a means of salvation, but states that faith without works is not sufficient. One may have hundreds of good ideas, but what good will they do if he never tries them out? When one is sure of his faith and loves God he is bound to do the works of God.

RIGHTEOUSNESS WITHOUT WORKS

But to him that worketh not, but believeth on him that justifieth the ungodly, his faith is counted for righteousness. Even as David also describeth the blessedness of the man, unto whom God imputeth righteousness without works, Romans 4 : 5–6.

The word "works" should not be confused with the works of charity, visitation of the sick, hospitality and other acts which are known as "good works." The apostle James emphasizes the importance of good works of charity. According to his teaching, faith is dead without works (James 2 : 14–20). The Aramaic word *palakh* means "to serve," that is, both to worship and observe the laws. When people are obedient to religious laws, it is said, "They serve and worship the Lord."

The Jews believed that salvation was attained by means of the strict observance of the law of Moses. There were many other laws and traditions which defined the law of Moses and guided the people in observing it. In other words, the Jews laid too much emphasis on the observance of the law and traditions, more than they did on charity, love and forgiveness. For instance, the law states that people should observe the Sabbath, but it does not say not to extinguish one's house if set afire. In some parts of the East, however, the Jews would rather see their houses burn than break the Sabbath. Even their candles and lamps are lighted by the Gentiles on the Sabbath. Moses did not decree this strict observance of the fourth commandment. What he recommended was that people should cease from all manner of labor. Extinguishing fire is not labor. Healing a sick person is a good work. And lifting up a man who falls under a heavy burden is a work of mercy. But when Jesus healed a paralyzed man, the Jews charged him with having broken the Sabbath.

These observances which were based on the traditions and doctrines of the elders were spoken of as "works." Those who observed them strictly were declared righteous. Paul argues that at the time of Abraham there was no law, and yet Abraham was declared righteous through his faith in God. (Faith also means trust.) That is, Abraham trusted God. He did what God commanded him to do. He proved his faith by good works at a time when there was no law to keep except the law which was written in his heart. Abraham obeyed God and did good works. Jesus said: "Let your light so shine before men, that they may see your good works, and glorify your Father which is in heaven" (Matt. 5 : 16).

ABRAHAM'S FAITH

And he received the sign of circumcision, a seal of the righteousness of the faith which he had yet being uncircumcised: that he might be the father of all them that believe, though they be not circumcised; that righteousness might be imputed unto them also: Romans 4 : 11.

Abraham was called by God many years before circumcision and the law were revealed. His faith in God was counted to him for righteousness. That is to say, that while Abraham himself was a Gentile, he believed in God and did good works which justified his faith. From the day of his calling to his death, Abraham obeyed God and walked in his way.

Circumcision came after Abraham had demonstrated his faith (trust) in God. It was given as a reward for his strong faith in God and as a seal of his call to be the Father of all that believe. On the other hand, the law was revealed four centuries later. Hence Abraham is a father of those who are not of the circumcision, but who, like Abraham, believe in God and do good works.

The Gentiles, like Abraham, were also to be justified

by their faith in Jesus Christ. They did not need to observe the ordinances of the Mosaic law, or to circumcise. Abraham became the father of the believers, not through the law, but through his unwavering faith. The Gentile Christians were the heirs of the faith of Abraham. The law was given at a time when the Hebrew people had gone astray and forgotten the faith of Abraham. The law now was fulfilled in Jesus Christ.

LAW DOES NOT JUSTIFY

Because the law worketh wrath: for where no law is, there is no transgression.   Romans 4 : 15.

The Aramaic text reads: "For the law causes provocation; for where there is no law, there is no transgression." The reference here is to the breaking of the law and the punishment of the guilty. When there was no law, there was no transgression and, therefore, no punishment. The law introduced both sin and punishment. This is because the law distinguished between good and evil.

Thus the law, as a guide, points out the true path of life and its conduct. It opens the eyes of men to see both the good and the evil, but it does not help those whose conduct is weak. On the other hand, when laws are read, understood and deliberately broken, the power of sin and lust is increased. Therefore, salvation is only through understanding of God's truth. For the promise was made to Abraham because of his faith in God. Abraham knew nothing of the Mosaic law, which was revealed centuries after, but he worshiped God in his heart. And as the result of his strong faith in God, he received the promise to be the father of many nations. . . . "For a father of many nations have I made thee" (Gen. 17 : 5). Abraham could not have earned this title by means of the law, for no one can observe the whole of the law. He earned it through his firm faith. Thus the title and the promise were given by the grace of God on account of faith and not because of the works of the law. Paul believes that faith alone can be counted for righteousness before God. The promise was made before the law, so that all those who believe in God may become the heirs of the faith of Abraham and of the promise which is fulfilled in Jesus Christ.

ABRAHAM PROMISED AN HEIR

Who against hope believed in hope, that he might become the father of many nations, according to that which was spoken, So shall thy seed be. Romans 4 : 18.

The Aramaic text reads: "For he who was hopeless trusted in hope." When God appeared to Abraham and told him that Sarah, his wife, would bear a male child, Abraham was one hundred years old and Sarah ninety years of age (Gen. 17 : 15–18). Prior to this, God had assured Abraham of an heir and told him that his seed would be like the countless stars in heaven (Gen. 15 : 5).

Abraham, despite his age and the incapacity of his wife to bear a child, believed in God. Not many years later Abraham begat Isaac, and Isaac begat Esau and Jacob. God had blessed Abraham's seed. His children multiplied and became strong nations.

Today many people in the Near East speak of Abraham as "our father Abraham." And those who are direct descendants of Abraham look to him as their father. This is because of Abraham's faith in God. He was the first to attain righteousness by faith and thus became the father of all the believers.

Faith can work wonders and make the impossible possible. Faith is the pattern of the things which are unseen. Jesus told his disciples that if they had even a little faith, not more than a mustard seed in quantity, they could remove mountains.

CONTROVERSIAL DOCTRINES

Therefore being justified by faith, we have peace with God through our Lord Jesus Christ:
By whom also we have access by faith into this grace wherein we stand, and rejoice in hope of the glory of God.
Romans 5 : 1–2.

People whose religion is based on the observance of the law and traditions find no peace. They quarrel over doctrines and methods by which certain customs and laws are observed. Religious authorities disagree on many controversial points. This results in quarrels, divisions and hatred.

The Jewish biblical authorities wrote vast commentaries on the law, the form of worship and customs, but they disagreed on many theological questions, some of which were fundamental. The Pharisees and Sadducees, always at odds, quarreled over the interpretations of the law and the doctrine of the resurrection of the dead. The rivalry between various schools of thought made people doubtful and restless. They found no peace with God. Not being able to observe the law correctly, they felt God was always angry at them; and therefore they were hopeless.

Jesus, through his death on the cross, did away with the ordinances of the law and reconciled men to God. Through his teaching men began to look upon God as a loving and forgiving Father, who desires to see his children live in peace and harmony and ready to forgive the true repentant.

JESUS DIED TO SAVE SINNERS

For scarcely for a righteous man will one die: yet peradventure for a good man some would even dare to die.
                                                     Romans 5 : 7.

The Aramaic word *rashiaa*, which means "wicked," has been confused with the Aramaic word *zadika*, "righteous." The Eastern text more correctly reads: "Hardly would any man die for the sake of the wicked, but for the sake of the good, one might be willing to die."

Pious Easterners when pleading in behalf of a good man, who is unjustly condemned to die, offer to die for him. During conversations people say to one another: "I will die for you" or "I will give my life for your sake." On the other hand, Mohammedans fast and pray for one another. When a person is unable to fast, he hires another to fast and pray for him. Moreover, some men willingly serve jail sentences for crimes which are committed by others. One may even give his life for the sake of a good man, but no one would offer to die or go to jail for the sake of a notorious criminal or a wicked person.

Jesus died for the wicked. He gave his life so that he might save those who had gone astray. He came to preach the gospel of forgiveness, call the sinners, strengthen the weak, and seek those who were lost.

THE MEANING OF SIN

Wherefore, as by one man sin entered into the world, and death by sin; and so death passed upon all men, for that all have sinned: Romans 5 : 12.

The Hebrew word *saten* means "to turn aside," "to trespass," "to err," or "to miss the mark." In Aramaic, "sin" is called *khatita*. The Aramaic word *sata* means "to mislead," "to go astray," "to slip," or "to miss the mark." *Satana* is a verbal noun denoting the action of the verb *sata*.

Thus "sin" in Semitic languages has many meanings, such as transgression of the law, erring, and walking in the wrong direction; any departure from the truth or breaking of the law is termed sin. When the law is repealed, sin is eradicated.

Nevertheless, the word "sin" is the result of an action or a fault. It has no existence of its own. God cannot be the author of evil, if evil can be overcome with good. And what can be avoided or overcome has no separate existence. For instance, if people were to learn not to make mistakes and do wrong, there would be no need for such a word as sin in our vocabulary or dictionaries. Then again, to some extent, certain sins are more or less a matter of geography. Some things which are considered sin in one country are declared lawful in another. To eat pork or oysters is a sin to Moslems and the Jews, but not to the English and Americans. Stealing and some other practices considered sinful in this country are pious acts in other places. Therefore "sin" is a human term devised to draw a line between things which we call clean and unclean, good and bad. In biblical days, the breaking of the law and the Sabbath were considered greater sins than murder, stealing, false testimony and adultery. The transgressors of the law were stoned.

There are various degrees of sin. Murder and some other sins are directly against God, but the sins which are the result of breaking a man-made law or tradition are not sins in reality; because what the law decrees as sinful today may declare it good tomorrow. For instance, a few decades ago, dancing and some other social activities were regarded as sin by religious people, but now they occasionally take place even in church buildings.

ORIGINAL SIN

Therefore as by the offence of one judgment came upon all men to condemnation; even so by the righteousness of one the free gift came upon all men unto justification of life.
Romans 5 : 18.

In ancient days when a man was found guilty and condemned to death, members of his family and other relatives were also condemned to die with him. This was done so that there should be no one to avenge the blood of the condemned. Easterners never forget crimes or severe punishment inflicted on members of their families. The blood and wrongs must be avenged, even if it takes three or four generations.

When Achan was found guilty of hiding some of the booty which he had taken during the capture of Ai, Joshua ordered him stoned, together with his family (Josh. 7 : 24–25). Even today in many Eastern countries, children are made to pay the debts of their parents and suffer for their crimes. At times all the family and close relations of a criminal, or a person condemned for treason, are put to death.

Paul here refers to the sin of Adam and Eve, which was brought upon all their descendants. He argues that just as by the act of one man entered sin and death, so by the righteousness of one, salvation came to all men. That is to say, we sinned in Adam and were forgiven through Jesus Christ. (Compare verse 15.)

LAW MADE SIN MANIFEST

Moreover the law entered, that the offence might abound. But where sin abounded, grace did much more abound:
Romans 5 : 20.

The Aramaic word *tesgey*, "abound," does not infer that the law is responsible for the increase of sin, but that the law made sin manifest in the world. Before the law was revealed, few things were considered sinful. For instance, men married as many women as they pleased, and divorced them at their will. (This is still done in Arabia, Egypt and some other Near Eastern countries.) Stealing, robbery and crimes committed against the members of other tribes were not considered sin. The law increased sin by regulating men's conduct and denouncing injustices. Breaking of the law resulted in sin. That is to say, sin was made evident by means of the law.

When men discovered that no one can live up to the precepts of the law, because all men are sinners, they began to seek other means of salvation. They appealed to the grace of God and his abundant mercies. "There is none that understandeth, there is none that seeketh after God. They are all gone out of the way, they are together become unprofitable; there is none that doeth good, no, not one" (Psa. 14 : 3; Rom. 3 : 11–12).

Just as sin was made manifest by means of the law, the grace of God abounded through forgiveness and faith in Jesus Christ.

BAPTISM INTO DEATH

Know ye not, that so many of us as were baptized into Jesus Christ were baptized into his death?

Therefore we are buried with him by baptism into death: that like as Christ was raised up from the dead by the glory of the Father, even so we also should walk in newness of life. Romans 6 : 3–4.

Baptism by immersion is still practiced by churches in the East. Infants and adults when baptized are dipped into the water three times.

Baptism by immersion is symbolical of the death and burial of physical bodies and of resurrection into a new life.

Through baptism we become the partakers of Jesus' death and resurrection. We leave the former life and rise with a spiritual body dedicated to God and made the temple of the Spirit. Through baptism we pledge ourselves as members of Christ's Church and supporters of his gospel, not only with money and other material things, but with our lives.

Paul had pledged his life for the new gospel. He was not afraid of imprisonment, hunger and death. The old body, which had been dominated by fear, was dead; the new body was clothed with the armor of truth and was indestructible. (See *Gospel Light,* p. 158.)

SLAVES TO SIN

But God be thanked, that ye were the servants of sin, but ye have obeyed from the heart that form of doctrine which was delivered you. Romans 6 : 17.

"Servants of sin" means "enslaved to sin." The Jewish law was difficult to keep. Breaking of a single ordinance or statute resulted in the breaking of the whole law. Therefore, sin became dominant over men. No matter what they did, they were guilty of breaking the law. Not a single person could attain righteousness by law, for not one could live up to the precepts.

The Christians were free from many of the ordinances of Jewish law. They offered no sacrifices and offerings to seek forgiveness for their sins as they had done in the past. They kept the Ten Commandments and obeyed the law of Christ, but, being divorced from the Jewish ordinances and traditions of the elders, sin had no more power over them. They were servants of God, who had freed them through his grace. Therefore the Christians were to be loyal to the doctrines of Christ and to his commands, just as they had tried to be loyal to the law of Moses and the traditions of the elders.

The Roman Christians were asked to show good works in order to prove that they were worthy of their freedom from the law and the sin which resulted from disobedience to it. In other words, one must live up to the law of Christ, whose yoke is easy and whose burden is light. The law of Christ had the power to free men from fear of the law of Moses and from sin which resulted from breaking the law. Therefore, Christians were no longer servants of the transgressions which the Jews called sin. They were wearing the armor of the truth and were prepared to fight mortal sins, that is, sins that destroy the soul.

LAXITY OF DIVORCE LAW

So then if, while her husband liveth, she be married to another man, she shall be called an adulteress: but if her husband be dead, she is free from that law; so that she is no adulteress, though she be married to another man.
Romans 7 : 3.

The Mosaic law, like the Christian law, granted divorces under certain conditions, such as adultery. Nevertheless, the Mosaic law concerning divorce had many loopholes. Men could divorce their wives with less trouble. Mohammedans divorce their wives if they fail to bear children, and for minor reasons. "But if the priest's daughter be a widow, or divorced, and have no child, and is returned unto her father's house, as in her youth, she shall eat of her father's meat: . . ." (Lev. 22 : 13). The divorced women took vows and observed other ceremonies as described by law (Num. 30 : 9). A woman was given a certificate of divorce which made her separation from her husband legal. The innocent party was free to marry again. Jeremiah likens Israel to a divorced woman who had committed adultery, and had been put away and given a bill of divorce (Jer. 3 : 8).

What Paul refers to here is desertion. The woman who deserted her husband and married another man was considered an adulteress. Jesus condemned the laxity of the Jewish law, because some men put their wives away without reasonable cause. Jesus approved divorce only on the ground of adultery (Matt. 5 : 31–32; 19 : 9).

The law of Moses and the Jewish ordinances had dominion over the people as long as they remained loyal to the Jewish faith. But when they left the Jewish faith they were no longer under the law. A woman is bound to her husband as long as he lives, but when he dies, she is free. The Christians were divorced from the Jewish law. They had come under the law of Christ. Therefore, Jewish ordinances had no power over them. It was a dead law as far as they were concerned.

SIN CAUSES DEATH

For I was alive without the law once: but when the commandment came, sin revived, and I died.
And the commandment, which was ordained *to life, I found* to be *unto death.* Romans 7 : 9–10.

When a man loses his freedom, he is spoken of as dead. A slave does not enjoy real life, his world is limited and his actions and desires are restricted, subject to the will of his master. On the other hand, when a person is free and his actions are governed only by his own will, he is really alive.

"For I was alive without the law" means "I was free to act as I pleased." Before the commandments were given there was no way to determine what was right or wrong, except man's conscience. Therefore man was free from sin. He could not be held responsible for the things which he did not know were sinful. But when the law was given, then man became conscious of sin. He was constantly mindful of the things that he did, fearing he might break the law. In other words, man lost his freedom.

The breaking of the law resulted in sin and death. Those who broke the law were stoned and considered lost forever. Although the law was a good thing, it could not be observed. Thus instead of bringing freedom and joy to men's hearts, it brought sin and fear of death. Whereas the law of Christ gave hope, life and joy, because it contained forgiveness.

The law of Christ is Christian conduct, charity, love and forgiveness. According to Christ's law it is the spirit that counts, not the letter. Those who are under the ordinances of the law are constantly mindful of the things which pertain to the body, and not the things of the spirit. The believers in Christ are no longer under the law of the flesh, but under the grace of God, who is a forgiving Father.

THE LAW OF LIFE

For the law of the Spirit of life in Christ Jesus hath made me free from the law of sin and death. Romans 8 : 2.

When a dynasty is overthrown, its officials and functionaries are replaced by the officials of the new dynasty. As soon as the new king ascends the throne, he introduces new laws and some of the old ones are repealed. This is because in the East governments are autocratic. All political, religious and legal authority is vested in the person of the ruler, who is empowered to repeal old laws and enact new ones. A few decades ago, the state had neither constitution, congress nor senate. Some laws are established precedents, handed down orally. Others are derived from opinions and decisions rendered by previous rulers or kings whose legal reputation is established by wise men.

When a change in dynasties takes place, prisoners are often released. Crimes against individuals and the state are forgiven, and, in some cases, debts are canceled. This is done by the new ruler in order to win the support of the people until he is strong enough to issue his own laws and levy his own system of taxes.

The law of sin became operative when the law was given to Moses. Prior to that time, sin was a matter of instinct and custom. Changes in the law and conduct of the people were regulated by the decisions of the rulers, guilty persons were either punished or forgiven and differences promptly adjusted. In other words, the people were not fully conscious of moral guilt.

The law of the spirit and the truth through Jesus did away with the law of sin, because there was no truth in the old law. Man found no relief through his obedience of the law, and its literal interpretations. In Jesus Christ men felt the spirit of the law. This is because the law of the spirit is not a law of condemnation and punishment, but of forgiveness and release from the bondage of sin. The law of the spirit has power over sin.

ABBA, FATHER

For ye have not received the spirit of bondage again to fear; but ye have received the Spirit of adoption, whereby we cry, Abba, Father. Romans 8 : 15.

Abba (pronounced *ava*) in Aramaic means "father." The letter "b" is aspirated and hence becomes "v."

During conversations and debates Easterners often call one another "my father." Priests and high officials are also addressed as father. Moreover, servants, as a token of sincerity and devotion, call their masters "father." Some men would resent such a remark from a stranger or a servant whose loyalty is in question. Judges and officials, who are noted for their kindness and fairness, are called "father." "I was a father to the poor" (Job 29 : 16).

The Jews in olden days spoke of God as the Father of their race. David admonished Solomon to look on God as his father. "I am a father to Israel, and Ephraim is my firstborn" (Jer. 31 : 9). "A father of the fatherless, and a judge of the widows, is God in his holy habitation" (Psa. 68 : 5). "Thou art my father, my God, . . ." (Psa. 89 : 26).

This old, but beautiful and pure conception of God was lost. The Jews, during the time of Jesus, seldom spoke of God as a father or of men as his children. Their concept of God was deistic. They resented Jesus' remarks when he spoke of himself as the son of God. Jesus reminds them that the Scriptures speak of men as God's children (Gen. 6 : 2).

The Christians, through Jesus, looked on God as a loving father. They had become close to him, as children are close to their parents. Jesus in his prayers called God "Father," or "my Father." He told his disciples and followers that his Father was their Father also.

CALLED

For whom he did foreknow, he also did predestinate to be conformed to the image of his Son, that he might be the firstborn among many brethren.

Moreover whom he did predestinate, them he also called: and whom he called, them he also justified: and whom he justified, them he also glorified.

Romans 8 : 29–30.

The Aramaic word *resham* means "to mark," "set aside," or "separate." Animals to be sacrificed are marked. Sheep and goats which are pledged to God are marked on the ears. Nevertheless, not all the animals which are set aside are offered to God. Some die, others are injured, and others are rejected.

Believers in Christ were preordained, or set aside. God knew those who would accept the gospel. He also knew that some of those who had been called would fall from grace and consequently be rejected. The choice is left to man's own will. God does not force men to be good or bad. According to the Scriptures, he calls certain men and prepares them for certain work. All men are equal in the presence of God and are endowed with the knowledge of right and wrong. Those who follow the true path of life are marked or called: some as preachers of the gospel, some as healers of the sick, and others as ministers of the gospel.

In studying some of the passages which refer to predestination, one must understand the Semitic manner of speech and the Eastern conception of God. Semites believe God knows and chooses a person before his birth. "Thus saith the Lord that made thee, and formed thee from the womb . . . Fear not, O Jacob, my servant; and thou, Jesurun (Israel), whom I have chosen" (Isa. 44 : 2). Then again, Easterners believe that men are called to be agents of God according to their qualifications. For instance, the Scriptures tell us that Pharaoh was called for a purpose . . . "And in very deed for this cause have I raised thee up, for to shew in thee my power" (Exod. 9 : 16; Rom. 9 : 17). This is also true of Nebuchadnezzar, Cyrus and other kings who, according to the Hebrew prophets, were called. Indeed, this is the way God's action and judgments were understood in the old days.

SLAUGHTERED LIKE SHEEP

As it is written, For thy sake we are killed all the day long; we are accounted as sheep for the slaughter.
Romans 8 : 36.

In biblical lands, animals are killed in cities to provide fresh meat daily. Refrigeration and canning were unknown until recently.

Sheep are kept in the fields and on the hills, and are carefully counted. The butchers visit the fold every day to take the sheep to the slaughter, and to decide on those to be killed the next day.

This quotation is from Psalms 44 : 22. The Jews suffered for their religion and their way of life. They were hated, persecuted and slaughtered by their enemies. The early Christians likewise suffered for the truth of the gospel. They were persecuted and murdered like sheep. Jesus had warned his apostles of the hardships and persecutions which they were to face for the sake of his gospel. The Christians were to take their cross and be ready to die for the sake of the truth which he had entrusted to them.

I SAY THE TRUTH

I say the truth in Christ, I lie not, my conscience also bearing me witness in the Holy Ghost, Romans 9 : 1.

"I say the truth in Christ, I lie not . . ." is characteristic of Aramaic speech. Easterners invariably engage in conversation and say things which they do not mean. But when the speaker is really serious he uses such terms as "Verily, verily, I say unto you," or "This is the truth," or "I am not lying."

Jesus used several of these terms when addressing the people. On the other hand, some preachers and teachers are gifted humorists. They speak in figures and parables, some of which they themselves compose during their discourses. They purposely exaggerate some things. Therefore, people do not take seriously everything which is said.

Paul, in writing to the Jews, had to make himself clear and to assure them of his sincerity and his love for them. Since his conversion to Christianity his sincerity was doubted by his people. In the East, when a man renounces his faith and embraces a rival faith, he is no longer trusted by people of his former faith. Paul was constantly engaged in the conversion of Jews to Christianity. He was convinced that the new faith which he had adopted was the very fulfillment of Judaism, and he invited the Jews to follow in his footsteps.

In verse 3, he used even stronger terms of speech, in order to destroy every doubt in the mind of the Jews in Rome. He made an oath, not in the name of God or the holy Temple, as most of the people did, but in the name of truth. He did not hide anything from them.

PECULIAR LANGUAGE

For I could wish that myself were accursed from Christ for my brethren, my kinsmen according to the flesh:
Romans 9 : 3.

Such remarks as "I wish I were accursed" or "I wish I never had been born," are very common in Oriental speech. During heated arguments in market places and on the streets, one often hears people saying to one another: "May I lose my religion," or "I have denied my God for your sake," or "I will give up my religion for your cause," or even "May I become a dog."

Religion is the most important thing to people in the East. When one offers to sacrifice his faith for the sake of another, he sacrifices everything.

These statements are not to be taken literally, of course. Speakers and writers know that the people understand their language and would not be disturbed by such remarks.

What Paul implies here is that he would give his life for the sake of saving his people. He does not mean that he would renounce Christ, but that he would rather lose everything, even his faith, than to fail to bring his people to Christ. In another place Paul stated that not even persecution, famine, distress or sword could separate him from the love of Christ (Rom. 8 : 35). He used strong language in order to persuade his people of his sincere desire to win them to Christ.

DESTINY

For the scripture saith unto Pharaoh, Even for this same purpose have I raised thee up, that I might shew my power in thee, and that my name might be declared throughout all the earth. Romans 9 : 17.

Even for this same purpose have I raised thee up" means "this was your destiny." That is to say, "you were raised to the kingship for this cause."

These words are similar to the words of Jesus before Pilate, when the latter asked him, "Art thou a king then? Jesus answered, Thou sayest that I am a king. To this end was I born, and for this cause came I into the world, that I should bear witness unto the truth . . ." (John 18 : 37). Jesus came into the world not to become a political king, but to die for the truth. His kingdom was not of this world. Jesus, prior to his journey to Jerusalem, had predicted his death. He told his disciples that his death was inevitable and that the Scriptures must be fufilled.

Easterners ascribe everything to God. Blessing, prosperity, victories and defeats are all credited to God. This is because they believe that God permits these things to happen and not that he causes them to occur. God could have made Pharaoh to act the way he wanted him to act, but that would have destroyed his free will. He could have changed the hearts of the Jewish priests and prevented the Roman authorities from crucifying Jesus. But he let things run their natural course, and in both cases the result was good, for the death of Jesus brought blessings on humanity, and the experience of Moses with Pharaoh serves as a good lesson.

Pharaoh's disobedience to God was motivated by his greed for power and wealth. He was unwilling to lose a strong people whom he had enslaved and whom he needed to perform labor. Had Pharaoh not hardened his heart, God's miracles and wonders could not have been wrought in Egypt. The world would have been deprived of some of the portions of the greatest book in the world—the Bible. God knows and sees what is going to happen, but

GENTILES CALLED

> *Even us, whom he hath called, not of the Jews only, but also of the Gentiles?*
> *As he saith also in Osee, I will call them my people, which were not my people; and her beloved, which was not beloved.*
> Romans 9 : 24-25.

The prophet "Osee" referred to here is Hosea. Hosea was one of the first of the Hebrew prophets who foresaw the rejection of Israel and the calling of the Gentiles. He lived in the seventh century B.C. when both Israel and Judah were threatened by Assyria. "And I will say to them which were not my people, Thou art my people; and they shall say, Thou art my God" (Hos. 2 : 23).

Paul argues that the Gentiles were destined to know God and become his people. He admits that the Jews were first. For they were the people with whom God had made a covenant. Paul argues that not all descendants of Abraham were Israelites, but only those to whom the promise was made. The children of Ishmael and Esau were not included in the children of promise. The children of promise were the descendants of Jacob. And not all Israelites were to be saved; only a remnant of them.

The Gentiles in the fullness of time were to call upon God and be invited into his kingdom. Even Moses, the lawgiver, predicted the admission of the Gentile world. "I will provoke you to jealousy by a people that are not my people" (Deut. 32 : 21; Rom. 10 : 19).

THE REMNANT

And as Esaias said before, Except the Lord of Sabaoth had left us a seed, we had been as Sodoma, and been made like unto Gomorrha. Romans 9 : 29.

Sabaoth means "hosts." The reference here is to the angelic orders. The term is used frequently by Isaiah (Isa. 1 : 9–14; 10 : 23). "Seed" in this case means "posterity." The Hebrews had suffered many persecutions and were carried into captivity. But a remnant of the race was always preserved by God. This small remnant preserved the Jewish faith and the holy Scriptures. Compare the condition of Israel during the time of Elijah. Most of the people had begun to practice Baal worship, and Syrian customs and gods were imported on a large scale from Tyre. Elijah thought that he was all alone and that the end had come, but there was still a remnant which survived and became the leaven (I Kings 19 : 14–18; Rom. 11 : 3–4). The remnant of the race was spared because of the Jewish faith and the Messianic promises. God was not any more interested in Israel than he is in any other race, except that he had revealed himself to Israel more completely than he had to other people. This is why Israel is called "the elect" or the "chosen people." They were chosen for a great mission, to convert the world. The race because of its mission and God's revelations, which were entrusted to her, suffered persecutions and privations. Their cities were made like Sodom and Gomorrah by the Gentile rulers. But a remnant has survived to our day. This remnant will survive until the kingdom of God and his reign of justice are established on earth.

STUMBLING BLOCK

As it is written, Behold, I lay in Sion a stumblingstone and rock of offence: and whosoever believeth on him shall not be ashamed.   Romans 9 : 33.

Kepa, "rock," means also "faith" or "teaching." The reference is to Jesus Christ. In the East, a true faith is spoken of as a rock. When Peter said to Jesus, "Thou are the Christ, the Son of the living God," Jesus said to him, "On this rock will I build my church," which means "On this truth (or confession) I will build my church."

The Christian faith was destined to divide the people, create hatred, and result in the persecution of the faithful. Truth is a stumbling block for those who cannot see it or accept it. But the truth always triumphs in the end.

Christians were expected to suffer persecutions and deny themselves the comforts of this life, but they looked forward to a time of great joy after their struggle and suffering.

The followers of Jesus, even though persecuted and hated, were not ashamed of their teaching.

SELF-RIGHTEOUS

For they being ignorant of God's righteousness, and going about to establish their own righteousness, have not submitted themselves unto the righteousness of God.
For Christ is the end of the law for righteousness to every one that believeth.   Romans 10 : 3, 4.

The Aramaic word *kenotha,* "righteousness," which occurs here and in several other places, also means "piousness" or "justness." It is used to describe a person who lives a pure life and respects the rights of others. For instance, Joseph, the husband of Mary, was known as *kena* (Matt. 1 : 19). However, righteousness should not be confused with self-righteousness, which means "being righteous in one's own opinion." A pious man is one who is trustworthy in all his actions and deeds, and reveres and serves God with his whole heart. Abraham was a pious man, and so was Job.

The reference here is to the self-righteousness of some of the Pharisees. They claimed they had attained righteousness through strict adherence to the letter of the law. But at heart they were selfish and proud. In other words, they passed as pious men, but in reality they were ungodly.

Righteousness through Christ is offered to everyone who believes in him and demonstrates his faith through Christian character, love and charity.

LAW OF COMPENSATION

What then? Israel hath not obtained that which he seeketh for; but the election hath obtained it, and the rest were blinded.

(According as it is written, God hath given them the spirit of slumber, eyes that they should not see, and ears that they should not hear;) unto this day.

Romans 11 : 7, 8.

The Hebrews were monotheists. They believed in one God, the Creator of heaven and earth and all that is in them. But they thought of God as an earthly ruler who governs his kingdom as he pleases, favoring and rewarding some, rebuking and punishing others. Nevertheless, this ancient concept of God did not declare him to be the author of evil. On the contrary, everything which God created at first was good. There is no mention of evil and satan among God's creations. This early belief is still held in the East and many other countries.

Indeed, what made the people attribute some of their weaknesses and evil deeds to God, is the fact that they believe that God permits evil. "God had given them the spirit of slumber" means God allowed the condition. "He hardened Pharaoh's heart" simply means that God permitted Pharaoh to resist Moses and Aaron. God knew what was in Pharaoh's heart. He knew that Pharaoh would refuse to let Israel leave Egypt, but he did not interfere.

Some teachers and laymen ask this question: If God hardened Pharaoh's heart, how can God blame him for resisting his will? Paul did not try to answer that question, because to him the answer was obvious. He likens God to a potter who has power over the clay, and who of the same clay makes one vessel to be honored and the other for service (Rom. 9 : 21). Just as the clay cannot question the potter, we cannot question the wisdom of God. We do not know what God has in store for us. His works and wonders bring blessings to all. His long suffering is never exhausted.

The blindness mentioned here is the spiritual blindness which is caused by man's own evil works. God is light, life and truth. He cannot conceive evil or cause injuries to his children. The difficulties and hardships are man's own creation. That is to say, we harvest what we have sown and gather what we have scattered.

TABLE AS A SNARE

And David saith, Let their table be made a snare, and a trap, and a stumblingblock, and a recompence unto them:
Romans 11 : 9.

Easterners never eat from a table. The food is laid on a tray or a cloth which is spread on the ground. The Aramaic word *pathora* means "tray," but at times the term is used in referring to all the food that is spread upon it. If this phrase is translated literally, it would mean "Let your kitchen be a snare."

Easterners are noted for their lavishness in entertaining guests, friends, strangers, and even their enemies. Generous people are especially noted for their abundant food. Friends and enemies discuss men who are hospitable and generous hosts. Some men would rather go to bed hungry than refuse a guest food. This is largely due to their traditional belief in hospitality. "Cast thy bread upon the waters: for thou shalt find it after many days" (Eccl. 11 : 1). Those who receive guests and strangers are always welcome at the homes of others.

There are some, however, who use their tables (food) to make friends so that they may use them against their enemies, or to win favors from government officials and praise from noblemen. On the other hand, conspiracies and seditions are generally conceived and planned while men are at the table eating and drinking. Absalom made a banquet so that he might slay his brother Amnon (II Sam. 13 : 23–31). Thus when ulterior motives are disclosed, the host and his guests may disagree and quarrel at the table. Thus the conspiracy which the host had devised against others is disclosed and his friends turn against him.

The quotation is from the book of Psalms: "Let their table become a snare before them: and that which should have been for their welfare, let it become a trap." That is let them suffer with their own evil devices.

GRAFTING OF TREES

And if some of the branches be broken off, and thou, being a wild olive tree, wert graffed in among them, and with them partakest of the root and fatness of the olive tree;

Boast not against the branches. But if thou boast, thou bearest not the root, but the root three.

Thou wilt say then, The branches were broken off, that I might be graffed in.

Well; because of unbelief they were broken off, and thou standest by faith. Be not highminded, but fear:

For if God spared not the natural branches, take heed lest he also spare not thee. Romans 11 : 17–21.

When cultivated trees are scarce, branches of wild trees are sometimes grafted upon old trees. The wild branches are more prolific than those of the natural tree, but the fruit does not have the same flavor as that produced by the natural branches. It is said that grafting of wild branches to old cultivated trees strengthens their roots. But this kind of grafting is contrary to nature and is rarely done.

Paul likened the Jews to a cultivated olive tree, and the Gentiles to wild branches which were grafted on them. Judaism was like an old tree which needed grafting to strengthen its dying roots.

The analogy is perfect. Just as the branches of wild olive trees are nourished from the roots of the natural trees, the Gentiles received their spiritual food from Judaism. They were blessed through God's promises which were made to the Jews. They were guided by the light of the Scriptures which were revealed to the Jews. Then again, in those early days, Christians worshiped like the Jews. They observed the Ten Commandments and in many respects were identified with the Jews. In other words, they had found the true Judaism of Abraham and the prophets.

Paul warns the Gentiles that they should not boast of being grafted into the Jewish faith, nor hate the Jews from whom they derived their spiritual nourishment. For if God had not spared the Jews because of their unbelief, he might also cast off the Gentiles. There were many disputes between the Jewish and the Gentile Christians, for their customs and ways of life were very different. That explains why Paul's warning was necessary.

PROPHECY

Having then gifts differing according to the grace that it is given to us, whether prophecy, let us prophesy *according to the proportion of faith;* Romans 12 : 6.

The Aramaic word *neviotha,* "prophecy," is derived from the Aramaic word *neba* or *neva,* "to spring forth," "to foretell," or "to give news." Prophecy is a gift of God, by which the recipient can foretell future events and interpret mysteries which are beyond the comprehension of human reason. In the realms of spirit there is no time or space.

Prophesying is a spiritual gift. The mortal mind sees things when they become manifest, but the infinite mind, or the spirit, may see them before they happen.

The prophet communes with God by means of the spirit through visions. On some occasions the message is received in words, as though the prophet were talking face to face with an angel or some important person. On other occasions the prophet actually sees events taking place. Some of the scenes are dramatic and vivid. The prophet sees the future events occurring as though projected on a screen. Compare the visions of Isaiah, Ezekiel, Daniel and other prophets.

Paul warns the Christian prophets not to go to extremes in the interpretation of their visions, and to be sure that their interpretations do not contradict the doctrines of the church. This is because at times interpretations were exaggerated and facts falsified.

Many prophets in biblical days predicted the coming of Christ. The New Testament prophets were to interpret Christ's teaching and his second coming. These were to be in accordance with the gospel, the apostolic teaching and doctrines.

SAINTS

Distributing to the necessity of saints; given to hospitality. Romans 12 : 13.

The Aramaic word *kadishey* (here translated "saints") means "the holy ones," that is, those who had separated themselves from the things of this world and had consecrated their lives to God's work. In the Hebrew religion, all things which were set aside for God were called holy. For instance, vessels, instruments, tithes, priests, prophets and offerings were holy. ". . . But holy men of

God spoke as they were moved by the Holy Ghost" (II Pet. 1 : 21).

Priests, Nazarites and others who minister to the church are supported by gifts and offerings which pious men and women give from time to time.

The term "saints" does not refer to canonized men, but those who were engaged in the preaching of the gospel, ministering, teaching and healing the sick. These men had no incomes. They were supported by members of their congregations. Some of them had devoted all their time to the work of the church and therefore were entitled to some support. Some had sold or lost their homes, fields and other property; others were persecuted and reduced to poverty. Both the imperial and the local governments were trying to stamp out Christianity in Judea.

SHARING OF JOYS AND SORROWS

Rejoice with them that do rejoice, and weep with them that weep. Romans 12 : 15.

Easterners are very emotional. During weddings, banquets and feasts, the people forget their differences and enmities, and eat, drink and rejoice together. A wedding brings joy to all the people in the town. The bridegroom and bride are presented with generous gifts of food in order to make their wedding a success.

When a person dies, the whole town shares in mourning. Friends and enemies lament and weep aloud. Nearly all of the women in the town gather at the house of the dead, to weep and sing songs of lamentation.

Weeping and lamentations are considered as good works. They are looked upon as a token of sincerity and devotion. "Did not I weep for him that was in trouble? Was not my soul grieved for the poor?" (Job 30 : 25.)

Paul admonishes the Jewish Christians to manifest some of their good racial qualities by sharing in joys and sorrows of each other. Partaking of the joys and sorrows of others results in harmony and peace. Christians are united by a sacred bond. They are members of the church of Christ, which is his body.

COALS OF FIRE

Therefore if thine enemy hunger, feed him; if he thirst, give him drink: for in so doing thou shalt heap coals of fire on his head.
Be not overcome of evil, but overcome evil with good.
Romans 12 : 20–21.

One of the most peculiar customs in biblical lands is that of feeding and sheltering one's enemies. Easterners are noted for their hospitality to friends and strangers who visit their homes, but they are equally mindful of their enemies. At times, they are more generous toward the latter than the former. This is because the people believe their bread will protect them and eventually change the attitude of their enemies toward them. One hears people say: "His bread protected him," which means that the enemy did not kill him on account of the bread which he had broken with him. To eat bread with one another is a pledge of peace. When a person refuses to eat bread when invited to do so, he is considered a dangerous enemy. On the other hand, when a person eats another's bread and then does him harm, it is said, "His bread will blind his eyes."

To set the table before one's enemy is an ancient Eastern custom. In Psalm 23 we read these words: "Thou preparest a table before me in the presence of mine enemies," which means that God provided an abundant supply of food for his table when his enemy came to his house, and thus saved him from embarrassment.

Many enemies, after eating bread and drinking water with their hosts, change their attitude toward them. Some of them are so embarrassed with the generosity which is showered on them that they are not ashamed or afraid to confess their wrong motives and seek forgiveness.

The phrase "heap coals of fire on his head" suggests that charity will wake him up and destroy his wrong thoughts. The verse is almost a literal quotation from Proverbs 25 : 21.

Evil cannot be overcome with evil; only good overcomes evil. Good causes one's light to shine on one's enemies, and makes them see the truth and change their hearts.

LOYALTY TO GOVERNMENT

Let every soul be subject unto the higher powers. For there is no power but of God: the powers that be are ordained of God. Romans 13 : 1.

The Jews, more than other races in Palestine and Syria, despised their foreign rulers and officials. They constantly revolted and tried to overthrow the foreign yoke and establish their own theocratic form of government as in former days. Indeed, the Jewish conception of government was different from that of the Gentiles; the state and religion were embodied in one, and the king and the high priest were God's representatives on earth. The Jews, being a religious people and believers in one God, the unseen ruler of heaven and earth, could not sincerely pledge their loyalty to a pagan government whose laws, customs, religion and other institutions were contrary to their own. The Jews could not tolerate heavy taxation and injustices. This resentment resulted in discontent, rebellion and a deadly struggle between the Jews and their alien rulers.

The Christian religion was founded on the teaching of Jesus, who asked his followers not only to respect foreign officials, but even to pray for them. Christian love and good examples of citizenship might be able to change the attitude of pagan rulers and convert many of them to Christianity, whereas opposition to government would only increase the burden of the people and intensify their suffering.

The Christian religion thus exhorts its members not only to obey pagan rulers and respect their laws but to pray for them that they might be guided to justice. They are God's agents, no matter to what faith and race they belong.

GOVERNMENT OFFICIALS

Render therefore to all their dues: tribute to whom tribute is due; custom to whom custom; fear to whom fear; honour to whom honour. Romans 13 : 7.

In many parts of the East, certain government revenues are leased to foreign governments or pledged as collateral for loans. For example, in Persia, the customs receipts were leased to Belgium. Nearly all the high officials in the customhouse were Belgians. Then again, the central government leases certain cities and territories to powerful overlords. These employ their own tax collectors and devise means by which taxes are levied. Thus the method of taxation becomes hard and harsh. This results in hatred toward the officials, especially those who act as agents of the government and are engaged in collecting taxes.

The word "fear" should read "reverence" or "respect." Paul admonishes the Roman Christians to respect and revere government officials and those who were entrusted with collecting taxes and customs. By so doing they would show their loyalty to the government and make their burden lighter and easier to carry. In Judea the collection of taxes was a problem. The Jews resented paying a head tax and hated their countrymen who acted as agents and publicans. This is why publicans were looked upon as sinners, so that the pious and patriotic Jews could not have any dealings with them.

Jesus was often called a "friend of sinners and publicans." He never shunned them on account of their occupation. He sought them and converted them.

WEAK IN REASONING

Him that is weak in the faith receive ye, but not to doubtful disputations.   Romans 14 : 1.

The Eastern text reads: "He who is weak in the faith, assist him, and be consistent in your reasoning."

The weak in faith are those who do not understand the fundamental things in the Christian gospel and are subject to traditions of men, and whose conscience would be offended by eating certain foods.

Some of these people were Jewish converts to Christianity who continued to uphold the traditions of the elders. They did not know that foods cannot defile a man. So Paul admonishes those Christian converts who had a better understanding of the teaching of Jesus, not to offend these men by eating things which were declared unclean by the Mosaic law but rather to assist them.

CALENDAR

One man esteemeth one day above another: another esteemeth every day alike. Let every man be fully persuaded in his own mind.   Romans 14 : 5.

In Palestine and Arabia there is considerable religious rivalry. Members of each faith observe their own calendar, holy days, festivals and other holidays. For instance, the Mohammedans keep Friday, the Jews observe Saturday, and the Christians Sunday. Then again, when members of one Christian sect are celebrating Epiphany, those of the others are preparing for Christmas. For example, Assyrians celebrate Christmas and Easter several weeks before Arameans. This variance is caused by differences in calendars.

There are so many racial and religious holidays that few days are left for work. At times some of the Jews observe Friday as a token of friendliness toward Mohammedans. In towns where the Jews are a majority, business is at a standstill on the Sabbath. On the other hand, some of the Mohammedans observe Friday, Saturday and Sunday, as well as many other Christian and Jewish holidays. This is largely due to the fact that most business is carried on by Jews, Armenians and Syrians, and because some of the Moslems have nothing to do.

During the period immediately following World War I the Turks saw the disadvantage of this old system and its bad effect on the economic life of the people. Therefore, they proclaimed Sunday as the only legal holiday.

Today in countries where the old calendars still exist and national and religious holidays are strictly observed, many complications arise. A Christian working as a servant for a Jew is often forced to work on Sunday. Likewise, a Jewish servant is made to work on Saturday. This practice creates discontent and mistrust and results in quarrels and religious persecutions.

Paul here admonishes the Christian converts who were employed by pagans not to make an issue of feast days and national holidays, and not to quarrel over the traditions and fables of old men, but to demonstrate their faith through their loyalty to their masters, and to serve and obey faithfully.

In the East, a Christian servant working for a non-Christian is forced through circumstances to obey his master and to serve him at all times.

A SERVANT

He that regardeth the day, regardeth it unto the Lord; and he that regardeth not the day, to the Lord he doth not regard it. He that eateth, eateth to the Lord, for he giveth God thanks; and he that eateth not, to the Lord he eateth not, and giveth God thanks. Romans 14 : 6.

The Eastern text correctly reads: "And he who is an embezzler is an embezzler to his master and he confesses to God. And he who is not an embezzler is not an embezzler to his master and he confesses to God."

Akhel is an Aramaic word, derived from *ekhal,* meaning "to eat," but the same word is also used for "embezzling" and "devouring." Thus *akhola,* "eater" (glutton), sometimes is applied to an embezzler. In colloquial speech people often say "he has eaten my money," which means of course that he embezzled it. He had eaten widows' houses and their sheep. Jesus used this expression. "Woe to you scribes and Pharisees, hypocrites; for you embezzle (Aramaic eat) the property of widows" (Matt. 23 : 13; Mark 12 : 38; Luke 20 : 47, Eastern text).

As certificates and letters of recommendation are not known in the East, servants are given verbal recommendations. Unemployment is hardly known in some of the Eastern countries, and servants and laborers are scarce. Only a few servants seek changes. Most of them prefer to work for the same person as long as they can. Therefore, when a servant seeks employment, people begin to gossip about him. They wonder if he had been discharged because of embezzlement or inefficiency. Such rumors make things hard for a servant. When a servant's reputation is bad, he finds difficulty in securing a new position. This is because the new employer is not satisfied with what the servant says about himself until he learns something about his past from former employers.

Generally when a servant leaves his master and seeks a new position, he is praised by his friends and criticized by his enemies. Some people picture him as an embezzler, extravagant and lazy, while others testify to his good character, honesty and efficiency. All of this is done by whispering. When one master refuses to hire a servant, the others would be suspicious of hiring him. Consequently the servant is branded as dishonest and unfaithful. Some people indulge in such gossip concerning servants, not because they are interested in the welfare of the employer, but because it is their habit in which they take some delight.

Paul warns against this kind of destructive gossip and criticism. He bids the Christians to mind their own business and let the masters or employers find out about their servants and laborers. Whatever the servants do, whether good or bad, is known to God, and their acts are only accountable to him. Men are not to judge one another, because they themselves might be guilty of the same acts they condemn in others. Some men in the East, when hiring servants or laborers, say: "I leave it to him and to his God." "God is a witness between us."

QUARRELS ABOUT FOOD

But if thy brother be grieved with thy meat, now walkest thou not charitably. Destroy not him with thy meat, for whom Christ died. Romans 14 : 15.

The Eastern text reads, "But now if you have caused your brother to grieve on account of meat (food), then you are not living in harmony."

Quarrels and disputes over food are common among people who still observe the biblical laws and traditions relative to eating and drinking. They abstain from eating certain meats, such as pork, the meat of strangled animals, blood, oysters, clams, and many other things that Americans and Europeans eat.

When food laws are broken, family relations and friendships may become strained. Dishes used for foods that have been declared unlawful are considered unclean. As a result, a man would refuse to eat with his brother, or stop visiting the house of his friend, simply because he could not eat from dishes or drink from cups that are considered unclean.

"And let us not, because of food, destroy the works of God. All things indeed are pure; but it is wrong for that man who eats with offence" (Rom. 14 : 20, Eastern text).

The breaking of these laws in towns and cities, where several families may live together under the same roof, is serious. Dishes, spoons and utensils, which are often borrowed, may easily become unclean. For example, the Orthodox Jews have two sets of dishes and cups, one for food that contains meat, and the other for food that contains milk. Dishes and cups once used for milk must be purified before being used for meat.

Jesus denounced some of these Jewish customs, which were based on the tradition of the elders. He said, "For you have ignored the commandment of God, and you observe the tradition of men, such as the washing of cups and pots, and a great many other things like these" (Mark 7 : 8, Eastern text).

Some of the Christian Jews in Rome observed the Jewish food laws and traditions. Others lived as the Romans did. Even today some Christians observe the Jewish food laws. They do not eat pork, blood, the meat of strangled animals and other things prohibited by the Mosaic law.

Paul warns against disputes and quarrels about foods. He suggests that for the sake of peace and harmony a man should not offend his brother by breaking the Jewish laws.

JESUS OBEYED THE LAW

Now I say that Jesus Christ was a minister of the circumcision for the truth of God, to confirm the promises made unto the fathers: Romans 15 : 8.

Use of the phrase, "minister of circumcision" indicates that Jesus complied with the law of circumcision. That is to say, Jesus observed the custom which was in accordance with the Jewish law. Circumcision was practiced many centuries before the birth of Moses. Abraham was circumcised many years after God had promised him an heir. Circumcision was the seal of the covenant which God made with Abraham (Gen. 17 : 10).

Jesus was circumcised not because he was under the law, but to fulfill the promises which God had made to Abraham. He was Abraham's spiritual heir, through whom God would fulfill his promises and shower his divine blessings upon his children.

When Jesus was circumcised he was only eight days old

(Luke 2 : 21). Every Jewish male child has to be circumcised at this age. This is because Isaac, the first child of circumcision, was circumcised when he was eight days old (Gen. 21 : 4). The Mohammedans circumcise their children when they are thirteen years old, because Ishmael was thirteen when he was circumcised.

Jesus never advocated circumcision nor did he speak against it. It was an old racial custom. Jesus respected the ancient Jewish laws and customs, but he denounced interpretations of them that were not in harmony with the spirit of the law and the Scriptures.

SERVANT SUFFERING

And again, Esaias saith, There shall be a root of Jesse, and he that shall rise to reign over the Gentiles; in him shall the Gentiles trust. Romans 15 : 12.

"Root," in this case, refers to an offspring or an heir. At times when an old tree dies, a tender stem grows out of its roots.

The quotation is from Isaiah 11 : 10: "And in that day, there shall be a root of Jesse, which shall stand for an ensign of the people; to it shall the Gentiles seek: and his rest shall be glorious."

When the Chaldean army destroyed Jerusalem in 586 B.C., the dynasty of David, son of Jesse, came to an end. The last king, Zedekiah, was carried out of the land as a captive, and his sons were put to death. Only a few men of royal blood escaped the wrath of the Chaldean conquerors.

The rise of the powerful realms of Babylon, Persia, Greece and Rome destroyed all hope for the restoration of the political Israel. Isaiah prophesied the rise of a spiritual kingdom to be ruled by the Messiah, who would gather together the scattered remnant of Israel and bring the Gentiles to the knowledge of God.

In the first part of the book of the prophet Isaiah, the

Messiah is pictured as restoring the kingdom of David and conquering the Gentiles. In the second part of the prophecy, the Messiah is presented as a suffering servant. "For he shall grow up before him as a tender plant (the Aramaic uses the word "child") and as a root out of a dry ground. . . . He is despised and rejected of men; a man of sorrows, and acquainted with grief. . . . Surely he hath borne our griefs, and carried our sorrows. . . . He was oppressed, and he was afflicted, yet he opened not his mouth" (Isaiah 53 : 2–7).

When Isaiah saw that political Israel could not be restored, he understood that the Messianic mission would be spiritual and that the Messiah, like the prophets, would have to suffer for his teaching.

HARD WORKERS

Who have for my life laid down their own necks: unto whom not only I give thanks, but also all the churches of the Gentiles.   Romans 16 : 4.

They "laid down their own necks" is an Aramaic idiom meaning "they were willing to work hard." Easterners bend down when working in fields. Carpenters, blacksmiths, and other artisans work on the ground, bending over their work. Benches are unknown.

When oxen are first harnessed to the yoke, they resist and throw it off. However, after they get used to it, they come under the yoke willingly.

Paul met Aquila and his wife Priscilla in Corinth. They had fled from Italy when Claudius Caesar expelled the Jews from Rome. They, like Paul, were saddle-makers and at times worked together (Acts 18 : 2–4).

Paul expresses his gratitude to Aquila and his wife Priscilla for the help they gave him. Both Aquila and his wife were sincere Jewish converts. They stood by Paul, even risking their own lives for his sake.

COPYING

I Tertius, who wrote this epistle, salute you in the Lord.
Romans 16 : 22.

In the East high ecclesiastical authorities and learned men employ scribes to write down their letters and manuscripts. The author either drafts his document or dictates it orally. Nevertheless some learned men and church authorities whose penmanship is poor hire scribes to take care of their correspondence and copy their works. Most of the scribes are professional. They are employed to write and copy. When a book is copied, the scribe attaches his name to it as though he were its author.

It seems as though Paul prepared the epistle and asked Tertius to copy it. The document is so important and so well written that Paul must have prepared it carefully before it was copied by Tertius. Other copies of this epistle may have been made and sent to other places or kept by Paul.

I CORINTHIANS

INTRODUCTION

Corinth was an old Greek city, rebuilt by the Romans. The city was a prosperous commercial center and therefore had a large foreign population of Romans, Jews and Syrians. The inhabitants of Corinth, like those of other large commercial cities, were careless and corrupt. Immorality was prevalent everywhere.

There was a large Jewish colony in Corinth, and a synagogue. Paul preached first to the Jews in the synagogue. But when he was rejected and persecuted by the Jewish leaders, he began to preach to the pagans and Jewish converts.

It was in Corinth that Paul had met Aquila and his wife Priscilla, Jews who had fled from Rome because of the persecution under Emperor Claudius. Paul spent two years in the city, working with Aquila and Priscilla in making saddles (Acts 18 : 1–3). He continued preaching in the house of Titus, a Syrian member of the Jewish synagogue. When Paul was at Ephesus he was visited by certain members of the church in Corinth, who discussed many important church matters with him and told him of the bad conduct of some of the Corinthian Christians. The epistle is supposed to have been written about A.D. 57 from Ephesus.

In the epistle Paul admonishes the Corinthian Christians to refrain from pagan practices and to live Christian lives according to the gospel of Jesus Christ. The document deals with some of the Jewish ordinances, marriage, the Christian ministry, and the hardships of the apostles. He condemns immorality, sensuality, worship of idols and other vices which were prevalent among the Corinthians.

Paul also speaks of the various spiritual gifts, such as speaking in tongues, healing, prophesying and preaching. He esteems charity and love above all other gifts. The epistle also stresses the resurrection of the dead. Corinthian Christians were living among people who did not believe in the future life and who lived a lost life.

GIFTS

So that ye come behind in no gift; waiting for the coming of our Lord Jesus Christ:
Who shall also confirm you unto the end, that ye may be blameless in the day of our Lord Jesus Christ.
I Cor. 1 : 7–8.

When a high priest, king, or a prominent authority enters a city, he is greeted with gifts. Noblemen and dignitaries prepare the gifts in advance. Some procure fine horses, others rugs and tapestries and others offer gifts of money, according to their wealth and position. Pastoral people bring fruits, lambs and rams, which are offered and sacrificed on the highway as the honorable visitor passes by. Those who lack gifts or are not ready are absent.

In this connection, Jesus had told the parable of the wise and foolish virgins. Five of them, being wise, bought extra oil for their lamps and were ready when the bridegroom and bride entered the house. But the other five, who were foolish, waited too long and at last, not being able to buy oil for their lamps, lost the privilege of greeting the bridegroom and the bride (Matt. 25 : 1–13).

Paul warns the Christians in Rome to be ready for the coming of Christ. They must prove their faith with Christian works, which are the gifts of the spirit, fit to be presented at his second coming.

CROSS

For the preaching of the cross is to them that perish foolishness; but unto us which are saved it is the power of God.   I Cor. 1 : 18.

Death on the cross was considered the severest punishment ever inflicted on a human being, and was dreaded by every Jew. Bandits, insurgents and other malefactors met with this shameful death. The victims' bodies often were left on the crosses for days, so that the bleeding corpses could be seen by the public and serve as an example.

Moreover, crucifixion was a sure way to end any revolutionary movement that might start among the people. It not only removed the leader, with his aspirations for worldly power, but his followers usually dispersed and the movement promptly collapsed. Those who died on the cross were known as accursed ones, cut off from the living God, and lost forever. "For he that is hanged (crucified) is accursed of God" (Deut. 21 : 23).

Some transgressors of the law were stoned. This was the kind of death prescribed by Joshua when Achan was condemned for the stealing of a small portion of war booty. "And all Israel stoned him with stones; . . . And they raised over him a great heap of stones, unto this day" (Josh. 7 : 22–26). Stephen also met with the same kind of death (Acts 7 : 58).

Crucifixion as a form of capital punishment was not a Roman custom. It was an ancient Oriental custom which the Jews had borrowed. But the Romans usually employed native methods of capital punishment. This is true today in countries which are mandated by foreign powers.

Joshua crucified the king of Ai about 1400 B.C. "And the king of Ai he hanged on a tree* until eventide" (Josh. 8 : 29).

The Hebrews may have adopted this custom while they were in Egypt or Babylon. Capital punishment under the Mosaic law was that of stoning.

*Eastern text: "And he crucified him."

Thus, in the eyes of the Jews and pagans, death on the cross represented a political and moral defeat. The crucified persons were accursed ones (Deut. 21 : 23; Gal. 3 : 13). Only those who died in battle were honored. To the Jews, it was blasphemy to speak of men who had been condemned for blasphemy by their religious authorities.

To the Gentiles, however, the cross was meaningless. If a man had failed to accomplish his mission in this life, how could he triumph after death? The Gentiles knew nothing of life hereafter.

But to the Christians, the cross was the seal of Jesus' teaching. Jesus had told his disciples to turn the other cheek, to pray for their enemies, and to go the second mile. This he fulfilled by his death. Indeed, death on the cross was an answer to those who believed and relied on force. It proved that love, justice and meekness will triumph in the end.

The cross revealed God's infinite love and care for his children in letting his beloved Son meet with such a tragic death. "For God so loved the world, that he gave his only begotten son, that whosoever believeth in him should not perish, but have everlasting life" (John 3 : 16).

WISDOM OF MEN

For it is written, I will destroy the wisdom of the wise, and will bring to nothing the understanding of the prudent.
I Cor. 1 : 19.

This quotation is taken from the prophecy of Isaiah against the city of Ariel (Isaiah 29 : 14). The prophets predicted the destruction of the city and confusion of the wise men who acted as counselors to their princes and kings. These wise men gave wrong advice and perverted and hid the truth from their people.

Paul warns against human wisdom in explaining the spiritual things and the message of the gospel of Christ. The gospel is to be understood through the inspiration of the Holy Spirit and not through philosophical arguments which often prove destructive and mislead the people. The truths of the gospel were revealed to the simple-minded and unlearned. The learned, like the scribes and Pharisees, were guided by the letter. They failed to understand the spirit of the gospel and rejected Christ. Human wisdom blinded their eyes to the truth of God. God had chosen the simple men to confound the wise.

SIMPLE GOSPEL

For after that in the wisdom of God the world by wisdom knew not God, it pleased God by the foolishness of preaching to save them that believe. I Cor. 1 : 21.

The reference here is to the simple gospel of Jesus Christ which was preached by unlearned fishermen disciples.

Judaism, during the time of Paul, had lost its simple and direct message. Since the return of the Jews from the Babylonian captivity, the Scriptures were constantly being examined, translated, and their meaning interpreted. Vast commentaries were written in an attempt to explain the law and the prophets. The Jews during the Babylonian captivity lost their own language and adopted Aramaic as their vernacular tongue. The Scriptures, after being read during the services, were interpreted into Aramaic. This resulted in diverse interpretations and exegesis, which in turn gave rise to speculative theology. Therefore, only the learned were permitted to interpret the holy writ. Thus rival schools of thought arose and the scholars were divided into parties.

The Christians in Asia Minor and Greece, owing to diverse interpretations of Jesus' teaching, were divided among themselves, some claiming to belong to Paul, others to Cephas (Peter), and others to Apollos. Paul warned the Corinthian Christians against these divisions which had resulted in strife and were hampering the cause of the

Christian gospel. God had rejected the wise who took more pride in their wisdom than in the truths they tried to explain. Thus salvation was in part to be attained by means of philosophical arguments, but by means of the simple gospel of Jesus Christ. The acceptance of Christ and Christian life were more important than disputes over feasts, foods, ceremonials and other so-called doctrines of the elders.

CROSS A STUMBLING BLOCK

For the Jews require a sign, and the Greeks seek after wisdom:
But we preach Christ crucified, unto the Jews a stumblingblock, and unto the Greeks foolishness;
But unto them which are called, both Jews and Greeks, Christ the power of God, and the wisdom of God.
I Cor. 1 : 22–24.

The Eastern text reads: "Because the Jews want miracles (wonders), and the Arameans (Syrians) want wisdom, but we preach Christ crucified, a stumbling-block to the Jews, and foolishness to the Arameans."

The term "Greeks" here is a mistranslation. At this early time there were no Greek converts. Both Greeks and Romans were hostile to the gospel of Jesus and tried to stamp out Christianity from the Roman Empire. Most of the Gentiles were employed in government service and were hard to approach. The gospel was at first preached among the simple folk in a quiet manner. The disciples often had to flee and take refuge in distant places.

The Jews at this time were still expecting a Messiah to perform great wonders and to establish the Davidic kingdom forever. Thus the preaching of the restoration and salvation through a crucified man, who in the eyes of the Jews had been condemned and sent to the cross as a malefactor, was a stumbling block. Nor was it in harmony with the current Jewish theology and the popular expectation of a Messiah who was to live and rule forever.

On the other hand, the cross was nothing but foolishness to the Arameans. To them, death was the end. When a prophet or a leader died, his mission died with him. In other words, how could one who has not saved his own life and come down from the cross save others? The Arameans were philosophers, scientists, engineers and industrialists. (Solomon sought the help of Hiram, King of Syria, to send him engineers and builders for his great project.) (I Kings 5 : 18.) The Arameans were also great shipbuilders, artists, weavers and dyers. The Greeks called them "Phoenicians"; that is why we have the term Phoenician used in Western biblical texts. The Arameans contributed much toward the spread of knowledge. Their industries in Damascus were not excelled until the rise of the British Empire. Even today their works in brass, steel and silk are renowned. To them a religion that stressed life hereafter and minimized the importance of this life and all wealth, luxury and splendor was nothing but foolishness.

The Syrians were admirers of generals and kings who had won victories and achieved other triumphs in this life. Some such men were worshiped by their followers, and their graves became national shrines. They sought wisdom and the Jews looked for signs and wonders.

Therefore, the cross was meaningless to both Syrians and Jews. It was a stumbling block and the stone which the builders had rejected. No one but Jesus had conceived of victory after death. His death on the cross became the basis of a new doctrine, alien to the Jews and Syrians, but a means of salvation to believers. Jesus, through his suffering and death, removed the curse and made death on the cross a glorious way to salvation. "And he that taketh not his cross, and followeth after me, is not worthy of me."

Paul is here addressing the Jews and Arameans (Syrians) who had been converted to Christianity. To them the meaning of the cross was the power of God, because God had shown his wisdom by means of things that men called foolishness. Jesus had triumphed where other men had failed. He was crowned king after his death.

SIMPLE ONES

But God hath chosen the foolish things of the world to confound the wise; and God hath chosen the weak things of the world to confound the things which are mighty:
I Cor. 1 : 27.

The Aramaic text reads: "But God has chosen the foolish ones of the world to put the wise to shame . . ." The term "foolish" means "simple."

Priests of Jewish and pagan religions were chosen from among the learned and noble. They served as judges, advisers, scientists and counselors to their kings and princes. The people sought their advice in business, legal and religious matters. Thus the priests, being the only learned men in the country, boasted of their knowledge and disagreed among themselves.

On the other hand, Jesus' disciples were chosen from among the unlearned. They were looked upon by Jewish priests as ignorant men (Acts 4 : 13).

God chose simple and sincere men to restore the true religion and preach the gospel of truth. The strength of the gospel was in itself and not in wise words. The unlearned followers of Jesus were easier to be trained than the learned Pharisees and scribes who constantly quarreled over their human knowledge. The priests of the new gospel were simple and sincere, like children. Their minds were open and free from complicated doctrines. They relied on the Spirit of God for wisdom. They were divinely guided in their words and actions. In other words, they were called and ordained by God to preach the gospel of truth and life.

HUMILITY

And I was with you in weakness, and in fear, and in much trembling.   I Cor. 2 : 3.

The Aramaic text reads, "And I was with you with much reverence and in trembling." That is to say, "I conducted myself well and was shy." Wise men often conceal their wisdom and pretend to be ignorant. This is because the people expect too much of them and inquire of them concerning things which are difficult and controversial. Such questions generally result in divisions and strife. Therefore, the wise men do not publicize themselves, they let the people find out. "If any man among you seemeth to be wise in this world, let him become a fool, that he may be wise." That is, let him consider himself as a fool or simple (I Cor. 3 : 18).

Paul acted as if he did not know anything about the world except the story of the cross and its power. He did not let the Jews know that he was versed in the Jewish law and the traditions of the elders in order to preach to them the new gospel and the power of the Spirit which worked through it. This gospel was not based on wisdom and interpretations of the Jewish laws, but was built on faith in Jesus Christ and salvation through his death on the cross. This new way could not be explained through words of wisdom, theological debates, or signs, but only through humility and the demonstration of the power of God. The faith that is built on human wisdom is temporal and changeable, but that which rests on the power of God is revealed through the Spirit of God, and is eternal.

SPIRITUAL GUIDANCE

But as it is written, Eye hath not seen, nor ear heard, neither have entered into the heart of man, the things which God hath prepared for them that love him.
I Cor. 2 : 9.

Reference here is to the things of the Spirit, truths which cannot be seen or grasped by the mind of man, but are revealed through the Spirit of God to those who believe. The mysteries of God cannot be discovered by the wisdom of men, but were revealed to prophets and men of God from the very beginning. These divine truths were eternal and needed not to be supported by words of wisdom. They were revealed and explained by the Holy Spirit, even to the unlearned.

The Holy Spirit was guiding Paul and those who were preaching the new gospels and explaining the ways of God. Men understand the teachings of men, but the things of God cannot be understood or explained without the Spirit of God. Man's wisdom is foolishness when compared with the wisdom of God.

The Scriptures are the inspired Word of God; they must be studied through the divine guidance of the Holy Spirit.

FED WITH MILK

I have fed you with milk, and not with meat: for hitherto ye were not able to bear it, neither yet now are ye able.
I Cor. 3 : 2.

Palestinian and Syrian mothers nurse their babies until they are two or three years old. Mother's milk is considered the best and is the only food which the babe receives until it is able to eat solid food. Meat and other strong foods are seldom given to little children. Easterners never use knives or forks; they cut the meat with their hands and teeth. Thus, until children have strong teeth, they are never given meat. They are given only milk and buttermilk.

Ignorant and unlearned men are called babes. One often hears people say to one another, "You are still a babe fed on milk," which means, "You cannot understand deep things."

Paul, like other teachers in the East, taught the people the elementary things first. He knew they could not understand the deeper theological questions. The Christians in Corinth were not yet free from the things of the flesh, and therefore they could not understand the Christian doctrine of salvation. They first needed to be taught the simple truths concerning the teachings and death of Jesus Christ.

DIVISIONS IN CORINTH

For while one saith, I am of Paul; and another, I am of Apollos; are ye not carnal?
Who then is Paul, and who is Apollos, but ministers by whom ye believed, even as the Lord gave to every man?
I Cor. 3 : 4–5.

Apollos was a learned Alexandrian Jew who had become a follower of John the Baptist. He was well versed in the teaching of the Lord God but at the outset was not familiar with the central truths of the Christian gospel. When Apollos was in Ephesus he met Aquila and his wife Priscilla, who helped him and directed him unto the way of Christ. Later he went out among the Jews, preaching Jesus Christ (Acts 18 : 24–28).

In the East, students are often identified with the teachings of their masters. For instance, the followers of St. John the Baptist, are called "the people of John the Baptist." Christians in the East are called *Nusrani*, "the Nazarenes." That is, the followers of Jesus of Nazareth. Even today the members of various Christian sects are called by the name of their teacher or the founder of their particular faith. This is also true of many sects in Europe and America, which are nicknamed and identified by the name of their founders.

Paul rebukes the Corinthians for assuming other names than that of Christ. He himself does not want any glory for being instrumental in converting them, nor does he want Apollos or any other disciple to be looked upon as the founder of the Church at Corinth. He wants the credit and honor to be given to Jesus Christ, whose teachings had changed the lives of the Corinthian Christians and revealed to them the eternal way of salvation. Paul and Apollos were only instruments in imparting the truth of the gospel.

Jesus had warned his disciples against human pride, worldly honors, and divisions. His followers were told to be meek, humble and in one accord. Christian unity was sadly needed in that disturbed and divided world.

PLANTING AND WATERING

Now he that planteth and he that watereth are one: and every man shall receive his own reward according to his own labour. I Cor. 3 : 8.

In Palestine and Syria plowing, planting and watering are each done by different people. The country is mountainous and fields are difficult to plow, especially in Judea where the fields are merely small terraces on slopes and on the mountain sides.

Plowing is done with oxen. It takes an expert to handle the plow and direct the oxen. Generally this type of work is done by elderly and experienced men. And it is only the older men who know how to scatter the scanty seed and plant the crops. Indeed, this type of work cannot be entrusted to the care of young men.

Watering is not considered a difficult task. It is done by younger men and women. The crops are watered once a week. Planters receive higher wages than those who water the crops. Paul had planted the seed of the Christian gospel in many cities in Asia Minor and Macedonia, and Apollos had watered it. But then the seed was entrusted to God, who guards it and causes it to grow. Paul denounces the idea that he and Apollos and Peter were building on different foundations and that they were at variance with each other. They were entrusted with different tasks, but they were building on the foundation which was laid down by Jesus Christ, who is the builder of the House of God.

CHRIST ONLY FOUNDATION

Now if any man build upon this foundation gold, silver, precious stones, wood, hay, stubble;
Every man's work shall be made manifest: for the day shall declare it, because it shall be revealed by fire; and the fire shall try every man's work of what sort it is.
I Cor. 3 : 12–13.

Ancient temples were built of stones and covered with wood, hay and stubble. The hay was laid over the wood and then covered with soil. Stones, wood and hay were offered as gifts. The structures were built by master builders. The wood work was done by carpenters, and the roof was covered by roof experts. Each group took pride in its own work.

When temples were completed they were adorned with gold, silver and costly stones. In those days, just as today, silver and gold were tested by fire. Impure silver and gold do not withstand the test; they burn. But pure gold and silver stand the test and their donors receive their due reward.

But Paul exhorts the Corinthians to be careful in choosing the builders and the materials to be used. For in due time every man's work is shown. That is, wrong teaching would be exposed and teachers thereof rewarded accordingly. The Church is the holy temple of God. Anyone who destroys this temple will be destroyed. The glory of this living temple belongs to God and not to any builders who received a reward for their work.

FAITHFUL STEWARDS

Moreover it is required in stewards, that a man be found faithful. I Cor. 4 : 2.

In the East, stewards and guardians of church properties are selected from among pious men who are noted for their trustworthiness and sincerity. No books are kept, and an accounting is seldom demanded. Most of these men are elderly and spend considerable time in prayer and fasting. They are hospitable to strangers and to the poor. Banks and trust companies were not known until recent years, and in some regions they are still unknown.

The steward or guardian uses his own discretion and good judgment in all matters. This is also true of stewards who are employed in the service of wealthy men. They are given full power to buy and sell, to transact other business, and to look after the welfare of the family of their master.

Paul in this instance compares himself with a steward of the church of God into whose hands were entrusted the mysteries of God (the teachings). Paul had been a faithful servant in every way. He had collected money from the Christians in Macedonia for the relief of the poor Christians in Palestine. He himself delivered this relief and saw that it was rightfully administered. Nevertheless Paul, like anyone else, had many enemies who tried to make things hard for him. He suffered hunger and privation to help others. "Even unto this present hour we both hunger, and thirst, and are naked, and are buffeted, and have no certain dwellingplace" (I Cor. 4 : 11).

CRITICIZING

Therefore judge nothing before the time, until the Lord come, who both will bring to light the hidden things of darkness, and will make manifest the counsels of the hearts: and then shall every man have praise of God.
I Cor. 4 : 5.

"Judge," in this case, means "criticize." Paul says, "Do not pass judgment on the teachings of the apostles." This is in accordance with the teaching of Jesus. "Judge not, that ye be not judged. . . . And why beholdest thou the mote that is in thy brother's eye, but considerest not the beam that is in thine own eye?" (Matt. 7 : 1–3.)

Paul admonishes the Christians in Corinth to forget their differences and quarrels over the leaders and apostles and refrain from criticizing their teachings. Inevitably there would be some differences between their teachings. But these were largely in wording. Their central ideas were the same. No two teachers can speak and teach alike. And if there were any real differences, these were to be left until the coming of Christ who knows men's hearts and thoughts. The apostles and teachers were all human. They could not pass judgment on the work of one another without weakening the church.

LIVING LIKE KINGS

Now ye are full, now ye are rich, ye have reigned as kings without us: and I would to God ye did reign, that we also might reign with you.
I Cor. 4 : 8.

"Ye have reigned as kings" is an Eastern saying, which means you have been very independent. When people have plenty of food and clothing and are free of care, it is said "they live like kings."

The Corinthians had taken things into their own hands, forgetting the apostles and evangelists who had labored among them and brought them to Christ. They felt that they were grown up and independent children, free from the care of their parents. Paul wished that they were so, but he knew that they were babes who could not eat strong food, but had to be fed with milk (I Cor. 3 : 2). They needed to consult the apostles and seek their guidance in matters which pertained to theological questions. The Corinthians were not yet ready to take full responsibility in spiritual matters. The church was in its infancy and needed to be nursed by the mother church in Antioch.

The apostles were commissioned by the Holy Spirit to preach and teach the gospel of Jesus Christ. They had suffered hunger, thirst, and imprisonment for its sake. They had the right to Christian leadership.

WEAK IN BODY

We are fools for Christ's sake, but ye are wise in Christ; we are weak, but ye are strong; ye are honourable, but we are despised.   I Cor. 4 : 10.

In the East, teachers of new doctrines are suspected, persecuted, belittled and called fanatics, but they take the blame for their teachings and carry the heavy burden, regardless of opposition and suffering. Their followers are looked upon as ignorant men who have been lured and misled. On the other hand, when the authorities decide to take action and suppress the new teaching, they imprison or murder the leaders of the group first. It often happens that while the leaders suffer persecutions and privations, some of their followers enjoy freedom and carry on unsuspected by the authorities.

Paul and the other apostles bore such burdens and suffered many persecutions. They were imprisoned, stoned and beaten. Having been reduced to poverty, they lacked clothing, shelter, food and other comforts of life. Their bodies had been weakened through suffering and hardships. But the Corinthians enjoyed prosperity and were benefited by the Christian teachings. They were blessed with material things and the comforts of life.

IMMORALITY

It is reported commonly that there is fornication among you, and such fornication as is not so much as named among the Gentiles, that one should have his father's wife. I Cor. 5 : 1.

Where polygamy is still practiced, it is not unusual for a son to fall in love with and marry one of his father's wives. Reuben, the son of Jacob, sinned with Bilhah, his father's wife (Gen. 35 : 22). Absalom, son of David, committed adultery with all of his father's concubines, which he had left behind when he fled (II Sam. 16 : 21–22). Moreover, Adonijah sought to marry Abishag, one of his father's wives (I Kings 2 : 17). Fathers sometimes sinned with their sons' wives, as in the case of Judah and his daughter-in-law, Tamar (Gen. 38 : 18). Mohammed married his adopted son's wife. Thus, immorality of this kind was common among primitive people and among the Gentiles in Greece and other pagan countries. But such practices among the Jews were a violation of the law and were severely punished.

Reference here is to the Christians in Corinth. Some of these men had been pagans, and when they had become Christians they had not broken away from the bad influences of their pagan religion and its established customs. There were also some lax Jewish converts to Christianity who behaved like the Gentiles, and were guilty of immorality, which Paul condemns.

The weaknesses of the old law were overcome through the law of Jesus Christ. Christians were admonished to do away with their former practices and to live a true and pure life.

LEAVEN

Purge out therefore the old leaven, that ye may be a new lump, as ye are unleavened. For even Christ our passover is sacrificed for us:
Therefore let us keep the feast, not with old leaven, neither with the leaven of malice and wickedness; but with the unleavened bread of sincerity and truth.
I Cor. 5 : 7–8.

Leaven" is an Aramaic idiom meaning "teaching." This term is often used in conversation when referring to the teaching or the policy of certain men. Good teachings are considered as having a good leaven and bad teaching as having a bad leaven. Just as leaven in dough determines the quality of the bread, so the doctrines a man believes determine the quality of his life.

Jesus warned against the leaven of the Pharisees and Sadducees. "Take heed and beware of the leaven of the Pharisees and of the Sadducees" (Matt. 16 : 6). At times, his disciples took this word literally, thinking that Jesus spoke about bread. But the term "leaven" is generally used in Northern Aramaic speech, and is seldom misunderstood.

Paul, like Jesus, is warning the Christians in Corinth to purge away the old leaven (doctrine) which was corrupt, so that they might become like little children, ready to be trained in the doctrines of Jesus, which is the new leaven. (See *Gospel Light,* page 100.)

ELDERS AS JUDGES

Dare any of you, having a matter against another, go to law before the unjust, and not before the saints?
I Cor. 6 : 1.

In many parts of the Near East, lawsuits, disputes and quarrels are brought before the priests and bishops. Trivial matters are generally settled by pious laymen and elders. Only major crimes are tried in civil courts. At times, even these are arbitrated before high ecclesiastical authorities whose decision is final. The government does not object to this, but instead co-operates with the Church authorities. The people are easily persuaded by priests and elders. They trust them and accept their decisions. It would take the court months to settle what a priest can settle in a few hours.

For instance, matters of property division, inheritance, divorce, default in the payment of loans, and minor offenses are all tried by the Church. This is in accordance with the teaching of Jesus. "Moreover if thy brother shall trespass against thee, go and tell him his fault between thee and him alone: if he shall hear thee, thou hast gained thy brother. But if he will not hear thee, then take with thee one or two more, . . . And if he shall neglect to hear them, tell it unto the church: . . ." (Matt. 18 : 15-17).

Paul is referring here to small matters and disputes which are easily settled by elders and priests. He does not object to civil courts and judges. At times a small matter brought to court becomes a costly affair to both parties. Paul, like Jesus, admonishes the Corinthians to avoid civil courts as much as possible. "Agree with thine adversary quickly, whilst thou art in the way with him; lest at any time the adversary deliver thee to the judge, . . . Verily I say unto thee, Thou shalt by no means come out thence, till thou hast paid the uttermost farthing" (Matt. 5 : 25-26).

Many cases need not go to courts. They can be settled through the offices and good advice of ministers and elders. Men entrust their souls to them; how much more should they trust them with their worldly affairs.

REDEMPTION

For ye are bought with a price: therefore glorify God in your body, and in your spirit, which are God's.
I Cor. 6 : 20.

The Aramaic phrase *ezdventon badmaya* means "you are bought with a price." The Eastern text differentiates clearly between the above phrase and *porkana,* "salvation."

When a person is saved from danger or death, it is said: "You have been bought with a price," which means that another person has exposed himself to danger in order to save your life. Many men in trying to save others from fire, or water, lay down their own lives. Thus the person saved is bought with the life of him who saved him. Then again, kidnaped persons are redeemed with a ransom. In the ancient liturgies of the churches in the East one finds many passages where the term "redemption" is used. "The church is the bride of Christ whom he had redeemed from error."

The reference here is to Jesus, who gave his earthly life that we might live. He cleansed us from sin and saved us, and brought us close to God. Hence our bodies are the temple of the Holy Spirit, which dwells in us. They are redeemed by the grace of God and the salvation of Jesus Christ.

SANCTITY OF MARRIAGE

Now concerning the things whereof ye wrote unto me: It is good for a man not to touch a woman. I Cor. 7 : 1.

The Eastern text reads: "Now concerning the things which you wrote to me: It is proper for a husband not to have intimacy with his wife at times." The reference here is to periods of prayer and fasting. On such occasions Easterners fast and abstain from intercourse with their wives. The periods of prayer and fasting are considered holy periods; both men and women purify themselves so that they may become worthy to stand in the presence of God (I Cor. 7 : 5, Eastern text). In biblical times the Hebrews could not touch holy things if they had recently had intimacy with their wives (I Sam. 21 : 4-6). Paul clearly states that such recommendations are not part of the law of the Christian Church, but mere instructions to weak persons (I Cor. 7 : 6).

Paul commends the sanctity of the Christian marriage. He appeals to men and women to love and be loyal to one another in every respect. Marriage is a sacred institution which was ordained by God from the very beginning. No one can change or alter God's command. On the other hand, he denounces immorality and recommends that widows and those who are unmarried, if they cannot endure to remain single, should marry (I Cor. 7 : 9).

FORNICATION

Nevertheless, to avoid fornication, let every man have his own wife, and let every woman have her own husband.
I Cor. 7 : 2.

Prostitution was never legalized among the Jews. The Mosaic law prohibited adultery. Violators of the law were punishable by death. "Thou shalt not commit adultery" (Exod. 20 : 14).

Among the Gentiles, however, fornication was not considered a sin, and men and women often lived together unmarried, as many do today in some parts of the world. Some of the Christians in Greece had been converted to Christianity from paganism. Those who were weak continued to live under the influence of the pagan customs of their countries. Paul, in his epistle, admonishes those who were living unchristian lives to keep away from pagan practices. The Jewish Christians in Corinth could not have any social and religious dealings with such persons. They had accepted Jesus but were still loyal to the Mosaic law. This admonition was also given to the Romans (Rom. 13 : 9).

Jesus upheld the Mosaic law relative to adultery. "Thou knoweth the commandments, Do not commit adultery, Do not kill, . . ." (Mark 10 : 19).

Christians in Corinth, Paul insisted, should live a better life and become an example to the pagan world, both in faith and practice. They were to be a light to shine among the Gentiles. Jesus and his disciples won people to God, healed the sick, and saved the sinners because they themselves lived close to God.

The Council of Jerusalem also had decreed that the Gentile Christians must abstain from fornication (Acts 15 : 29). The Council made no reference to Jewish Christians, simply because converts from Judaism to Christianity were under the Mosaic law.

ABSTINENCE

Defraud ye not one the other, except it be with consent for a time, that ye may give yourselves to fasting and prayer; and come together again, that Satan tempt you not for your incontinency. I Cor. 7 : 5.

Defraud" is a mistranslation. *Glaz,* in Aramaic, means "to deprive." The confusion is due to the similarity of the Aramaic word *glaz,* and another word *gnaz,* to hide. The Eastern text correctly reads: "Therefore do not deprive one another except when both of you consent to do so, especially at the time where you devote yourselves to fasting and prayer; and then come together again, so that Satan may not tempt you because of your physical passion."

To abstain from certain foods and practices during the fasting season is an ancient custom in the East. Ministers and pious men and women always deprive themselves of certain things during periods of fasting and prayer, especially during holy days. This is done to conquer the physical forces and let the spirit dominate the body. The pious try to subdue all wrong thoughts and worldly desires. Consequently, quarrels and troubles cease for a time, the rich distribute food to the poor; merchants stop cheating, stealing, and taking false oaths about prices of goods. Some earnest merchants are therefore reluctant to transact important business during the fast days, because they are convinced that if they cheat, their punishment in heaven will be severe. Then again, marriages, banquets, dances and other social activities are also prohibited during this period.

Before the Ten Commandments were given at Sinai, Moses instructed the Israelites to purify themselves and keep away from their wives for a certain period (Exod. 19 : 15).

THE CONDUCT OF A CONVERT

Is any man called being circumcised? Let him not become uncircumcised. Is any called in uncircumcision? let him not be circumcised.   I Cor. 7 : 18.

The Eastern text reads: "If any man is called, being circumcised, let him not return to uncircumcision." That is to say, if any circumcised man becomes a Christian convert, let him not join the party of uncircumcision. "Let him not become uncircumcised," being impossible, is a mistranslation.

The question of circumcision and uncircumcision was debated by the disciples in Jerusalem. Paul was accused, by the Jewish Christians in Asia Minor, of discouraging circumcision, receiving Gentiles into the church without it, teaching the Jews who were living among Gentiles to disregard the Mosaic law and traditions, and especially of bringing Arameans into the Temple, as in the case of Titus (Acts 21 : 28; Gal. 2 : 3).

Circumcision was an ancient Jewish racial custom. Like many other customs and traditions, it had become an actual doctrine. In the East, customs and manners are highly revered and in due time come to play a dominant part in religion. Even today Christians, Jews and Moslems in the East uphold their ancient customs. For instance, the meat of animals killed by a Jew or Christian is unclean for a Mohammedan. The Jews never eat meat from an animal slaughtered by a Christian or a Moslem. Even certain features and colors of racial apparel must be different, to distinguish the members of one faith from those of another. Thus, converts from one faith to another find themselves changing their customs and adopting those of the new faith. Such changes cannot be made over night. A person may change his faith, but he cannot easily change his customs and manners.

The first Christians were Galileans, members of the Jewish faith. They had been circumcised, as all Jewish proselytes were required to be. When Arameans were converted, the question of circumcision was raised, and the Jewish Christians demanded that they also should submit to this rite. Paul's work at first was chiefly among the Jews and Arameans in Asia Minor. The two outstanding young pastors whom he was training, Titus and Timotheus, had Aramean fathers and Jewish mothers. The Arameans knew that circumcision and the traditions of the elders were a vital part of the Jewish practice but, not being Jews by race, they felt no need to adopt them. This was also the case with the Galileans who accepted the Jewish customs only in part. They did not practice ceremonial ablutions in connection with eating, nor did they fast like the Jews. They did healing and other works of mercy on the Sabbath. Moreover, even though Jesus himself had been duly circumcised in his infancy, he had not recommended that circumcision or any other external features of the Jewish religion be perpetuated. He had not only disregarded many of the practices that were considered sacred and most essential by the Jews, but had bitterly attacked them. The very heart of his teaching was the fact that religion is a purely spiritual matter, and he denounced legalism, racialism or any other doctrine that served to create barriers between the children of God.

UNCIRCUMCISION

Uncircumcision" in this case means the believers who were not circumcised. During the time of Paul there were two Christian groups: The Jews, who were circumcised before their conversion to Christianity, and the Gentile Christians, who were exempt from this Jewish custom (Acts. 15 : 24).

Paul advised the Corinthians to abide in the same way wherein they were called. That is, if they were Jewish Christians to remain so and not attack circumcision and join the Gentile party, or if they were Gentile Christians, not to practice circumcision nor despise their brethren who were circumcised. According to Paul, the matter of circumcision or uncircumcision is not important. The most important thing is the keeping of the commandments of God. Circumcision was a Hebrew racial custom which was practiced four hundred years before the commandments were given.

UNMARRIED OR EUNUCHS

Now concerning virgins I have no commandment of the Lord: yet I give my judgment, as one that hath obtained mercy of the Lord to be faithful.
I suppose therefore that this is good for the present distress, I say, that it is good for a man so to be.
I Cor. 7 : 25–26.

The Aramaic word *mehemna* means both "faithful" and "a eunuch." This is because a eunuch is a faithful servant entrusted with important duties. *Mehemna*, "eunuch," occurs several times in the New Testament. Jesus spoke of men who were born eunuchs, those who were made eunuchs by men, and those who made themselves eunuchs for the kingdom of heaven's sake (Matt. 19 : 12).

The Minister of Finance of the Queen of Ethiopia was

a eunuch (*mehemna*). *Oaraey mehemna khad datey hwa min Coosh.* "And he was met by a eunuch who had come from Ethiopia" (Acts 8 : 27).

Some authorities are inclined to believe that Paul was a eunuch, and that that was the reason he was not married. Be that as it may, Paul, for certain reasons, was not married. It is certain that he was not a Nazarite, for in his early life he was a Pharisee and a persecutor of the Church of Christ.

It is true that some sects taught against marriage. Many men made themselves eunuchs as a means of salvation. This ancient custom prevailed for many centuries. In the second and third centuries it grew to such an extent that it became a menace. It assumed the form of monasticism. Thousands of men left their homes, inflicted injuries upon their bodies, and sought dwellings in deserts and caves. Eunuchs are still to be found in Ethiopia and Arabia. The Turkish Republic abolished the practice some years ago and did away with polygamy.

Paul does not object to marriage: "I have no command from God" means it is not written in the law. If circumstances should require that men should remain unmarried, let them be so. But marriage is holy and ordained by God (verse 28).

VIRGINS' CONDUCT

But if any man think that he behaveth himself uncomely toward his virgin, if she pass the flower of her age, and need so require, let him do what he will, he sinneth not: let them marry. I Cor. 7 : 36.

The Eastern text correctly reads: "If any man thinks that he is ashamed by the behavior of his virgin daughter, because she has passed the marriage age, and he has not given her in marriage, and that he should give her, let him give her in marriage, and he does not sin. Let her be married."

Woman's status in the East is not equal to that of man. When a woman reaches the marriage age (twelve to fourteen) she must marry in order that she may have a home and means of support. There is no way for a woman to secure employment and support herself. Therefore, marriage is preferred. The ancient social and economic conditions make it necessary.

Then again, in the East, parents do not wish to have their daughters remain unmarried. Dowries consisting of sheep, camels and money induce some fathers to give their daughters in marriage as soon as they mature. Nevertheless, there are exceptions to this. A father who has no sons may allow one of his daughters to remain unmarried, if it is her wish. The girls who decide to remain virgins must live a pure life, so that they may not bring reproach upon their parents. Some virgins vow to devote their time to prayer. They remain in the home of their parents, but they are engaged in church work.

Sometimes it happens that some of these virgins under vows change their minds, break their vows, and marry. Others are subjected to undue gossip concerning their behavior and are accused of bad conduct. This kind of gossip disturbs their parents. Some Eastern fathers will seek vengeance if the names of their virgin daughters are reproached. On the other hand, the breaking of a vow is not an easy thing in the East. Most people believe that it brings with it a curse. Nevertheless, when a father discovers that his virgin daughter has changed her mind and desires to be married, he usually gives her his consent and lets her be married.

Paul here admonishes fathers to do justice to their virgin daughters under these circumstances, especially if their conduct is questionable. The Eastern text conveys no hint that the father has the slightest wrong thought toward his daughter. No such case has ever been heard of in the East. But breaking of the vows is not unusual. Virgins are given in marriage even today. All matrimonial arrangements, the choice of a husband and the terms of the dowry, are of course not in her hands, but her father's.

The term "virgin" also means "maiden." All girls who are unmarried are addressed as virgins. There are many references to virgins in the Bible.

VIRGINS

Nevertheless he that standeth stedfast in his heart, having no necessity, but hath power over his own will, and hath so decreed in his heart that he will keep his virgin, doeth well.
So then he that giveth her in marriage doeth well; but he that giveth her not in marriage doeth better.
I Cor. 7 : 37–38.

Marriage is not an easy thing in the East. Courtship between young men and women is unknown. Marriages are arranged by the parents of the parties concerned.

At times, fathers find it difficult to give their daughters in marriage to men who are socially their equals. Under such circumstances they prefer to keep them unmarried (virgins). On the other hand, as some girls bring good dowries, their parents may give them in marriage, irrespective of their future welfare. Virgins are more admired and bring larger dowries than widows.

There are times when parents make a vow in which they pledge to keep one of their daughters unmarried. And some women disregard marriage in preference to a religious vocation, as in the case of Philip, the evangelist, who had four virgin daughters who prophesied (Acts 21 : 9). In such a case, it is said the father "hath power over his own will," for he forfeits any dowry his daughter might bring, and dedicates her to the service of God.

MARRYING A CHRISTIAN

The wife is bound by the law as long as her husband liveth; but if her husband be dead, she is at liberty to be married to whom she will; only in the Lord. I Cor. 7 : 39.

Eastern Christians never give their daughters or sisters in marriage to unbelievers. When a Christian woman marries a Mohammedan or a Jew, she is immediately excommunicated from the Church. But in Europe and other parts of the world, Christian women are given in marriage to Mohammedans, Jews and Hindus.

Paul would permit a widow to marry, but only to a Christian. This is because in the East when a woman marries a pagan she is compelled to adopt his religion. The phrase "in our Lord" means that the widow should marry one who is a believer in Jesus Christ. A man or a woman being saved through Christ should not part with their religion for the sake of marriage.

FOOD OFFERED TO IDOLS

As concerning therefore the eating of those things that are offered in sacrifice unto idols, we know that an idol is nothing in the world, and that there is *none other God but one.* I Cor. 8 : 4.

In some parts of the East, animals are still offered at ancient sacred places and shrines. Sheep, lambs and oxen are slaughtered at the shrine by the member of the faith to which the shrine belongs. The meat is then broiled and eaten by all at the shrine, and some of it is taken to the people in town. Members of one faith might consider themselves defiled if they were to eat meat killed at the shrines of a rival faith. On other occasions, in towns inhabited by both Christians and Mohammedans, the animals may be killed by a Mohammedan, in order that the meat may be declared lawful and sold to both

Mohammedans and Christians. In the case of Christians and Jews, the animal is slaughtered by a Jew so that members of both faiths may eat its meat. If the town is inhabited by Jews and Mohammedans, complications arise, because neither of them could eat meat slaughtered by a member of the other faith.

The Semitic people for long centuries have been worshipers of one God. Undoubtedly, their monotheism was the result of ages of disputes over man-made idols, images, sacrifices, and shrines. This led to a new quest which resulted in the discovery of the living God, and the fact that idols were not gods at all.

Hebrews had for many centuries contended with idol worship and sacrifices to Baal. It took many centuries to do away with paganism and its immoralities and superstitions.

The Gentiles were just emerging from darkness and finding the living God through the preaching of the apostles. It was difficult for them to abstain completely from eating foods which had been offered to idols. At times, meat was available only when animals were sacrificed at the shrines and the meat distributed among the people.

It often happened that a certain member of a pagan family embraced Christianity, but still continued to visit his parents and other relatives and eat and drink with them. It was difficult for him to condemn the food that his parents ate, or to refuse to sit at the meal with them, even though he suspected that the foods set before him might have been offered to idols.

This custom still prevails in the East. A Christian cannot enter a Mohammedan restaurant, or any public place that is patronized by conservative and fanatical Mohammedans.

Paul discards the tradition. He declares that an idol is not a god at all, and therefore that what is offered before it is not an offering. The Christians are admonished to eat anything set before them, without any scruples. In the East a guest must either eat anything set before him or refuse to enter the house when invited. Guests cannot easily make an inquiry about the food which is set before them by the host. Such an act would lead to disputes and quarrels, especially if the guest and host happen to be members of rival faiths (Acts 14 : 13).

IDOLS ARE NOTHING

Howbeit there is *not in every man that knowledge: for some with conscience of the idol unto this hour eat* it *as a thing offered unto an idol; and their conscience being weak is defiled.* I Cor. 8 : 7.

Pastoral people do not depend on meat for food. They eat cheese, buttermilk and other dairy products. Sheep and other animals are seldom killed for food. In many ancient cities and country places butcher shops are unknown. The people eat meat only when certain animals are sacrificed, or at wedding feasts. On such occasions the meat is shared. Portions of raw meat are distributed among the people to be cooked and eaten at home. The other portion is cooked near the shrine and eaten by people who attend the celebration.

The meat of animals offered to gods or idols was eaten by the priests and the people. Portions of it were distributed among the people to be taken home. Only a small portion of it was burned on the altar, and that was supposed to be the share of the deity or the idol at whose shrine the animal was slain. The offering was blessed and the priests ate first (I Sam. 9 : 13). Some sacrifices, such as sin offerings, were eaten only by priests (Lev. 2 : 3).

The Jews were forbidden to eat meat that had been offered to pagan gods. That was because, in olden days, the Jews recognized the gods of the Gentiles. "Ye shall not go after other gods, of the gods of the people which are around about you" (Deut. 6 : 14). Eating of meat or other food that was sacrified to idols was considered an act of worship. Sacrifices were offered as thank offerings to gods or idols. (See comment on I Cor. 8 : 4.)

Centuries after the law was written, the Hebrew prophets discovered that the pagan gods were not gods, and that idols were nothing but deaf and dumb images. Nevertheless, the Jews continued to observe the ancient tradition and abstained from eating meat sacrificed to idols. When they ate food offered to idols they were conscious of guilt. On the other hand, some people ate meat with the understanding that the idol was nothing, and therefore they had no guilty conscience when they ate food offered to them.

When Christian Jews visited the homes of their Gentile neighbors and were invited to eat, if they found out that the animal had been offered to an idol, they were guilty in conscience. This made it hard for members of the Church to visit and eat food with others.

Jesus told his disciples to eat anything put before them. Paul admonishes the Corinthian Christians to eat of such foods if their conscience did not bother them (I Cor. 8 : 4–10). The Council of Jerusalem prohibited eating of things offered to idols (Acts 15 : 29) because at that time most of the Christian converts were of the Jewish faith. There were only a few Gentiles in the Church.

For the laws concerning the sacrifice, and other offerings, see Lev. 1–7.

AN APOSTLE

Am I not an apostle? am I not free? have I not seen Jesus Christ our Lord? are not ye my work in the Lord? If I be not an apostle unto others, yet doubtless I am to you: for the seal of mine apostleship are ye in the Lord.
I Cor. 9 : 1.

The Aramaic word *shelekhy*, "apostles," is derived from the Aramaic word *shelakh*, which means "sent." Any person who is sent on a mission is called *shelekha*, "an apostle" or "a missionary." Nevertheless, the term apostle was somehow used only when speaking about one of the twelve men whom Jesus had appointed and sent to preach.

Paul, Barnabas and Mark were not counted in the ranks of the twelve apostles, but were known also as apostles of Jesus Christ. The Gentiles among whom they were working considered them as such, but in Judea this title was solely reserved for the twelve who had seen Jesus and who were eyewitnesses of his resurrection and ascension.

Paul was convinced that he was entitled to call himself an apostle, on the ground that he had seen Jesus on his way to Damascus and had been commissioned by him to preach the gospel among the Gentiles. In other words, he was an apostle to the Jews and the Gentiles. He opens his epistle by saying: "Paul, called to be an apostle of Jesus Christ." Regardless of his success and sacrifices, however, his claims to the apostleship were disputed by his enemies, especially those of his own race.

A WOMAN CONVERT

Have we not power to lead about a sister, a wife, as well as other apostles, and as the brethren of the Lord, and Cephas? I Cor. 9 : 5.

The Aramaic word *khatha,* "sister," also means "a convert." Thus *khatha atta,* in this instance, means "a convert wife," not "a sister." This term is used to distinguish converts to Christianity from pagans.

In the East, a preacher's wife must be a follower of his religion. No preacher or missionary takes a sister or a strange woman with him. But married priests or preachers are free to take their wives with them if circumstances compel them to do so.

The wives of some of the early Christian converts remained loyal to their pagan religion; the Christians had married pagan women with the hope of converting them to Christianity. But most evangelists whose wives were pagan traveled alone.

This passage indicates that the disciples and missionaries were permitted to travel with converted women only, as in the case of Aquila and his wife Priscilla (Acts 18 : 2). Peter and some of the other disciples were married before they embraced Christianity. Peter's wife was an early convert; and her mother was healed by Jesus. Some of these apostles took their wives with them. Having no means of support, they could not be left behind. Jesus' brothers and their wives were also early converts to the Christian faith. James the brother of Jesus evidently succeeded James the son of Zebedee. He might have taken his wife with him.

Paul here states that he also had the authority to marry a convert and take her with him on his missionary journey and lead the life that other missionaries and apostles were leading. But Paul, being mindful of the churches, realized that such a departure would add to his expenses and thereby burden the small flock of believers and hamper the progress of the gospel.

Those who work for the Church must derive their support from the Church. The worker is worthy of his food. The apostles and missionaries were not paid for their work. They were entitled to support from the Church. When no salary is paid, the worker is worthy of his maintenance. Because Paul chose not to marry, it was necessary for him to do his own cooking, washing and mending, and apparently he took pride in the fact that he was not dependent upon anyone.

Had Paul been married, some features of his life would most certainly have been different, and who shall say that his ministry might not have been more effective? Women have contributed more toward the spread of the gospel than men have. From the very beginning they have been active and loyal supporters of the gospel, and great pillars in every spiritual enterprise.

MUZZLING

For it is written in the law of Moses, Thou shalt not muzzle the mouth of the ox that treadeth out the corn. Doth God take care for oxen?   I Cor. 9 : 9.

The scarcity of wheat in Palestine compels some men to muzzle the mouths of their oxen when threshing wheat. This ancient method is harsh and cruel. The oxen are tied to a pole which is hoisted in the center of the threshing floor, and are driven over the sheaves until the wheat is separated. The process is long and tiresome; it takes about five hours before the oxen are loosened.

The quotation is from Deuteronomy 25 : 4. See also I Timothy 5 : 8. Prior to World War I, soldiers were poorly paid but were fed and clothed. In the East, laborers who are not paid for their services expect to be well fed. The employer makes lavish preparations, and serves bread and other food in great quantities. But when laborers are paid for their work, they eat whatever the employer puts before them. In other words, they do not expect both wages and banquets.

The apostles had the right to receive support from the people to whom they were preaching. They were not paid for their services. All they wanted was their daily bread, so that they might be able to carry on the work which was entrusted to them.

A worker is worthy of his food. Those who preach the gospel must live from it. The apostles, even though entitled to receive support, never let themselves become a burden on their followers. They lived a simple life, and at times worked with their own hands in order to earn money for their expenses.

UNPAID MINISTRY

For though I preach the gospel, I have nothing to glory of: for necessity is laid upon me; yea, woe is unto me, if I preach not the gospel!   I Cor. 9 : 16.

The Aramaic word *ketira* means "obligation." Preachers who are paid for their services are under obligation. This is especially true of Eastern people. They mistrust ministers of the gospel who are paid for their work. Eastern missionaries receive no stipends. They must trust in God and the good will of the converts. Some of the latter give generously as a token of gratitude. Some of the ministers have occupations and others do any type of work necessary. It is said that Thomas was a famous builder. He worked as a mason and preached the gospel to the people in southern India. A large Christian community in Malabar bears his name. His healing power brought him fame and money with which to carry on his work. Paul was a saddle-maker, and he supported himself by means of his trade.

Christians trust those who are not under obligation, and they believe in their preaching. There is no reason to doubt them. They serve and give freely. Jesus told his disciples that, since they had received freely, they should give freely (Matt. 10 : 8). Ministers of the pospel must demonstrate the power of faith in God. They preach a gospel that is full of power and is able to change the lives of people and heal their infirmities. The same gospel provides their daily needs. Men and women who are converted and healed gladly offer all they have to ministers of the gospel.

HUMILITY

To the weak became I as weak, that I might gain the weak: I am made all things to all men, that I might by all means save some. — I Cor. 9 : 22.

The Aramaic word *keriha* means "weak" and "sick." In this instance the word "weak" refers to a lack of discernment or wisdom, and not to physical weakness. Men who lack understanding are often called weak.

Paul, in order to preach the word of God effectively, lived close to the people. He approached them from their own point of view. He dressed modestly, lodged in the homes of the poor, ate with members of the lower classes, and conversed with them in such a manner that no one suspected him of being a learned man. In other words, he humbled himself in order to raise them up. Paul was very strong physically. He had not suffered any illness, as some people wrongly imagine. He speaks "of having a thorn in his flesh." But this is an Aramaic idiom which means, "I am constantly annoyed." Paul's apostleship was questioned by his enemies.

Simple men in the East always suspect the enticing words of wise men; but they understand and trust those who speak their own language. Jesus likewise did not use wise or difficult words. He spoke in the vernacular. He never preached over the heads of the people. He mingled with the rich and the poor, ate with the publicans and those who were called sinners. Jesus humbled himself in order to reach those who were "down and out." Anyone must lower himself when trying to raise those who have fallen.

I CORINTHIANS

SINCERITY

But I keep under my body, and bring it into subjection: lest that by any means, when I have preached to others, I myself should be a castaway.   I Cor. 9 : 27.

The Aramaic text reads: . . . "When I have preached to others, will I despise myself?" In other words, the preacher must live up to his teaching. Easterners judge a preacher by his works and not by his words. A good minister is admired for his faithfulness, hospitality, kindness and healing power.

Jesus condemned the Pharisees and scribes, because they never practiced what they taught. He told his followers to do what they *said* but not what they *did*.

In preaching, it is the doing that counts. It is the life of the preacher that touches the heart of the people, and not his words. Sincere words come from a pure heart.

Jesus, from the day he began to preach until his death, practiced his own teaching. He taught love, and he loved even his enemies. He taught forgiveness, and he forgave those who crucified him. He suffered many hardships and privations to prove the power of his gospel.

THE ROCK

And did all drink the same spiritual drink: for they drank of that spiritual Rock that followed them: and that Rock was Christ.   I Cor. 10 : 4.

The Aramaic word *kepa* (*cepa*), "rock," is often used symbolically, suggesting protection and shelter. One often hears people say: "He has been a rock behind me," which means "he has supported me." "God is my rock" means "God is my shelter or support." Rock also means "truth." "On this rock will I build my church" means "on this truth will I build my church."

During severe sandstorms and heavy rains, pastoral

people take refuge under rocks and in caves. And they often find water from springs coming out of the rocks.

The reference here is to the rock which Moses struck in the desert when the people were thirsty (Exod. 17 : 6; Num. 20 : 7–21).

Striking the Rock

In Arabia, Tripoli, Libya and other places where water is scarce, people depend on wells. The wells are the property of certain men or tribes and they are hidden from their enemies and protected from roaming tribes and from contamination.

During the grazing season the wells are uncovered so that shepherds may draw water for their sheep and cattle and for drinking. When tribes move away they cover the wells with rocks and thus hide them so that rival tribes may not find water. This is done to protect the scanty supply, to discourage other tribes from grazing in their territory, and to prevent their enemies from pursuing them in times of war. When tribes are at peace, wells are rented and water is shared (Num. 20 : 19).

Shepherds of the roaming tribes when passing through arid regions always search for wells. They probe the sand with their staves until they strike a rock and discover a well (Gen. 26 : 32). When Jacob fled from Esau, and went to Haran, he met Rachel at the well. "And a great stone was upon the well's mouth. . . . And they rolled the stone from the well's mouth, and watered the sheep, and put the stone again upon the well's mouth in his place" (Gen. 29 : 2–3).

During severe sandstorms, wells are heavily covered with sand and the marks obliterated. This makes it difficult to find them. Moses had spent forty years in the desert feeding the sheep of his father-in-law. He knew the tribal secrets and the positions of the wells. But when he returned to the desert he found it difficult to locate the wells. It is probable that the native tribe had them hidden in order to prevent the Hebrews from using them and conquering their lands. Moreover, the Hebrews were

I CORINTHIANS 267

dissatisfied with Moses' leadership. They murmured against him and plotted to return to Egypt. This made Moses' task difficult.

When Israel came to Rephidim they found no water for the people to drink. Unrest and dissatisfaction made things harder for Moses. For a while he was unable to find the wells. But when he prayed and sought divine directions the Lord told him where to strike. The place was rocky. No one would have expected to find water there, but God showed him the spot under which there was abundant water for both the men and their sheep.

"Moses smote the rock" means that he bored through it, or found it, just as one says in English, "They have struck oil."

The writer of the book of Numbers clearly explains how water was obtained. When the King of Edom refused to permit passage through his territory, the children of Israel were compelled to return once more to Rephidim and wait to find a new route. "And from thence they returned to Beer." That is, the well whereof the Lord spoke unto Moses. "Gather the people together, and I will give them water." Then Israel sang this song, "Spring up, O well; sing ye unto it: the princes digged the well, the nobles of the people digged it, by the direction of the lawgiver (Moses), with their staves" (Num. 21 : 16, 17, 18). When God had shown the exact spot where the water was, the princes and nobles digged with their staves, under the order of Moses. "He opened the rock, and the waters gushed out; they ran in the dry places like a river" (Psa. 105 : 41). "Which turned the rock into a standing water, the flint into a fountain of waters" (Psa. 114 : 8).

Even today, in Aramaic, Hebrew and Arabic, "well" is called *beer*. In the First World War the Turks destroyed or hid their wells in order to hamper British military operations in the Arabian Desert. The same thing was also done in World War II in Libya, Egypt and Tunisia.

When our spiritual vision is obscured we fail to find the things we need. When we turn to God and seek direction from him our needs are met in a miraculous way. At times the things for which we search are close around us. When Hagar and her son were thirsty in the desert they failed to find the well that was near them; but when Hagar prayed God told her where the well was. "And God opened her eyes, and she saw a well of water; and she went, and filled the bottle (skin) with water, and gave the lad drink" (Gen. 21 : 19).

Christ-Rock

Paul likens Christ to the rock from which the Hebrews drink. Water is symbolical of light and truth. Jesus, while conversing with the woman at the well, spoke of living water (John 4 : 10–14).

It was God who followed the Hebrews, not the stone. Whenever the Hebrews returned to God their needs were abundantly met and their enemies overcome; but when they rebelled and were doubtful they were hungry and thirsty.

Christ is the rock, the truth, from which we drink the living water. He is the fountain which never runs dry. Those who drink from it receive the eternal blessings of this life and the life hereafter.

UNGRATEFUL

Neither be ye idolaters, as were some of them; as it is written, The people sat down to eat and drink, and rose up to play. I Cor. 10 : 7.

The quotation is from Exodus 32 : 6. The Aramaic text reads, "Rose up to quarrel." There is an Eastern saying, "When people have abundant food and water and are at ease, they quarrel among themselves." This is true of many races in the Near East. When they are persecuted and poverty-stricken they are united and humble, but when prosperous they fight among themselves. Then again, during feasts and banquets, when people eat and drink, they often fight with each other.

When the Hebrews were in need they rose up against Moses, and when they were well fed they fought with each other. In other words, they were not grateful. In the Bible the word "play" is used, but it should be "fight." For instance, in II Samuel 2 : 14 "Abner said to Job, Let the young men now arise, and *play* before us." But the young men actually fought with swords!

Paul admonishes the Corinthians to show their Christian qualities and to be content with and grateful for the benefits which they had received through the gospel of Christ. He also reminds them of their forefathers who perished in the desert because they were disobedient and troublesome, and materially and carnally minded.

THE PLAGUE

Neither let us commit fornication, as some of them committed, and fell in one day three and twenty thousand.
I Cor. 10 : 8.

The reference here is to the plague which broke out among the Israelites when they committed adultery with the Moabites at Shittim (Num. 25 : 1–9). Twenty-four thousand died of the disease.

There is some discrepancy between the number of dead as given in Corinthians and that which is given in the book of Numbers. According to Paul, twenty-three thousand persons died in one day; in the book of Numbers the total number of deaths is twenty-four thousand. The difference, I believe, is due to the fact that Paul was quoting from memory. When Paul wrote his epistle to the Corinthians he had no access to the book of Numbers. In those days the Scriptures were written on scrolls and different portions were owned by different people. Few people could afford to possess an entire Bible. Nor could one have carried all the scrolls with him if he had owned them.

In quoting orally from the Bible one is likely to make

mistakes. The difference cannot be blamed on the manuscripts or on Hebrew numerals, as some authorities think. The Hebrew and Aramaic languages use letters for numerals, but numbers like this are written out, so that no confusion should be caused. Dots placed over the letters indicate the higher numerals from the lower ones.

EARLY COMMUNION

For we being many are one bread, and *one body: for we are all partakers of that one bread.* I Cor. 10 : 17.

The Eastern text reads: "For just as the loaf of bread is one, so we are all one body: for we are all partakers of that one bread."

In biblical lands, bread is baked thin and wide. The loaves are broken by hand, and several persons may eat from the same loaf. To eat from the same bread is a token of sincere friendship. Enemies, when at the same table, refuse to eat from the same loaf.

In the early days, communion bread was baked at home and brought to the church. The people traveled long distances to attend the services and to receive instruction. Most of those who came brought bread and other food with them. The loaf, after being blessed, was broken into small pieces, according to the number of communicants. Then other loaves were blessed and distributed among the worshipers. These were called *"bokhra."* Loaves and other food which were brought as offerings were eaten in the church.

This ancient custom is still preserved among the Assyrian Christians. Bread and other food brought to the church are blessed and distributed among the worshipers, choir singers and priests. Small fragments of it are taken home to those who have not been able to attend the service and participate in the holy communion.

CONSIDERATE

Let no man seek his own, but every man another's wealth. I Cor. 10 : 24.

The Aramaic reads: "Let no man seek for himself alone, but let every man seek for his neighbor also." "Seek," in this case, means "be concerned." Some men who ate food sacrificed to the idols knew that idols were nothing; therefore the food which was sacrificed to them could not be defiled. Others, because of their belief in idols, thought that food offered to idols was unclean. Therefore they had a guilty conscience when they ate it. Paul denounced the idols. He said, "We know that an idol is nothing in the world" (I Cor. 8 : 4).

Nevertheless, Paul warns that one should be considerate of his neighbor. "Wherefore, if meat make my brother to offend, I will eat no flesh while the world standeth, lest I make my brother to offend" (I Cor. 8 : 13).

Sheep and cattle are killed at the shrines on certain days, and people invite their friends to eat with them. The whole town eats meat on that day. See verse 18. (I Sam. 9 : 12–13; I Cor. 10 : 27.)

Christians are told to eat anything without question, as far as science is concerned, but they are not to eat certain meats if the eating thereof would offend their weak neighbors.

COVERING THE HEAD

For if the woman be not covered, let her also be shorn: but if it be a shame for a woman to be shorn or shaven, let her be covered. I Cor. 11 : 6.

Covering of women's faces is an old established Eastern custom that is still observed in Palestine, Syria and other parts of the Near East where Moslem civilization predominates. Prior to World War I all Mohammedan women covered their heads. When polygamy was abolished in Turkey, the veil was done away with also.

In these ancient biblical lands, men seldom see women's faces. Women cover their faces when at public meetings, on the streets, and whenever they happen to be in the presence of men. Rebekah covered her head when Isaac came out to meet her (Gen. 24 : 64–65).

The covering of the head in churches grew out of the Jewish social custom. Jewish women veiled themselves when they prayed. Jewish Christians in Asia Minor, Greece and Rome, could not have done away with this established custom without offending the Christians in Palestine and Syria.

On the other hand, in the East it would be difficult for men to worship at places where women were unveiled during preaching or prayers. The men would be looking at the women instead of worshiping. This is because men do not see women's faces on other occasions. Thus to see the face or arms of a woman is unusual.

If Paul were living today he would never have made such recommendations. Circumstances compelled him to discourage women from preaching and reading in churches. There were certain Jewish customs that Paul was unwilling to abolish, though he had fought in behalf of the Gentile Christians and freed them from circumcision and other Jewish ordinances (Titus 3 : 9).

Mohammedans throughout the world, and Christians and Jews in the East, still observe this ancient custom. Women neither speak nor say prayers publicly in churches or other assemblies. During the services they stand or sit by themselves, in a portion of the church which is reserved for them.

CHRISTIAN DISCIPLINE

When ye come together therefore into one place, this is not to eat the Lord's supper.   I Cor. 11 : 20.

The Eastern text reads: "When you gather together therefore, you do not eat and drink as is appropriate on the day of our Lord."

During feasts, banquets and weddings, some men plan to come early so that they may occupy high places and eat from the best dishes. As watches are unknown and time is measured only by the shadows, some men may come an hour or two before the others. On such occasions, no one can tell exactly when the meal will be served.

At a wedding feast food is abundant and all who are invited are fed. It is not so at feasts where food is scarce and attendance large. On such occasions those who come early eat more than they need, while those who come late are left hungry.

Paul rebukes the Corinthian Christians for conducting themselves during the communion as though they were attending a banquet or a feast at a shrine.

Communion is to be taken with reverence, as though one were in the presence of Christ. It cannot be eaten like ordinary bread; one must be worthy of it.

OVER-EATING

For in eating every one taketh before other *his own supper: and one is hungry, and another is drunken.*
What? have ye not houses to eat and to drink in? or despise ye the church of God, and shame them that have not? What shall I say to you? shall I praise you in this? I praise you not.   I Cor. 11 : 21–22.

These gatherings were primarily organized for the purpose of teaching. The early Christian literature was limited to the gospel. The other teachings and traditions were handed down by the word of mouth. People had heard something about Jesus and his teaching, but not enough to meet their needs. Therefore, houses of Christian converts were opened to gatherings which were addressed by an apostle, an elder or a layman who happened to be present.

As most of the members had to come from villages and country places, they had to bring food and wine with them. The meeting lasted for many hours. (In the East some services last from four to five hours.) Some people took advantage of these occasions. They came hungry so that they might eat at the meeting place. Some of them left the meeting and ate the food before the rest were ready. The result was that some went hungry while others ate and drank too much and vomited. Some were sick and others drunk.

EXCESSIVE EATING

For this cause many are weak and sickly among you, and many sleep.   I Cor. 11 : 30.

Invariably Eastern people, during festivals, weddings and on other special occasions, eat and drink to excess. The reason for this is that in these countries food is always scarce and some people are always hungry. But on such occasions there is abundant food, brought by those who attend. One can see women with trays full of bread and dishes containing food entering the wedding house.

On Sunday mornings when communion is celebrated, women bring loaves of bread to be broken and distributed among the people at the church door.

It is true that during the festivals some people come to eat rather than to worship. They all know that on such occasions food is abundant and people share it generously. Jesus on one occasion warned some people who followed him simply because of the bread they received. He knew they were not interested in the truth which he was preaching, but only in the loaves and fishes they ate.

I CORINTHIANS

In verses 21 and 22 Paul warns the Corinthians against Christians eating excessively on such occasions. He admonished them to eat at home before they came to worship. There were many men and women who ate to excess and became sick. This happened quite often when people were hungry and found abundant food to eat (I Cor. 11 : 20–22).

GIFT OF HEALING

For to one is given by the Spirit the word of wisdom; to another the word of knowledge by the same Spirit;
To another faith by the same Spirit; to another the gifts of healing by the same Spirit; I Cor. 12 : 8–9.

Spiritual healing has been practiced in biblical lands since long before the introduction of the Christian religion. When science was in its infancy and medicine unknown, people relied on God for health and comfort. Healers and prophets were found among people of many different races and religions. They all believed in a force, the spirit, which directs the universe and guides the lives of men. They felt the omnipotence and omnipresence of this power and tried to reach it by various means.

Divine healing was predominant among the Hebrews; their concept of God was clearer and truer than that of any other people. Their prophets were sought for healing, guidance and advice by their own people as well as by those of other races. They were known as seers, that is, men with inner understanding. Samuel was looked upon as a seer (I Sam. 9 : 19–20).

Elijah raised the son of the widow (I Kings 17 : 17–24). Elisha healed Naaman of leprosy (II Kings 5 : 9–14). On the other hand, Daniel, Ezra and some of the other prophets were regarded as great seers, wise men and statesmen. They played an important part in the realms of Babylon and Persia.

Healers and men of God rose among the people from time to time. Those who sought their aid and believed in them were healed. Hebrew healers and seers were not college graduates, but men who had infinite understanding of God's power and his omnipresence. They had the gift of healing, simply because their faith in God was strong. The same men who prophesied, also healed the sick and raised the dead. This is because it is the same spirit which does all. The same power which operates a locomotive operates a ship. In other words, some men have many gifts, others but one. For example, Jesus had all the gifts. He healed the sick, raised the dead, fed the hungry, and predicted future events.

Even today in the East the sick and suffering seek the help of men and women who have the gift of healing. The healers lay hands on the sick, and pray and rebuke the diseases. Many people, because of their strong faith, are instantly healed. The faith of the healer strengthens the belief of the sick and connects him with the Spirit of God, which is life and truth.

TRUE AND FALSE PROPHETS

To another the working of miracles; to another prophecy; to another discerning of spirits; to another divers kinds of tongues; to another the interpretation of tongues:
I Cor. 12 : 10.

Discerning of spirits" refers to the ability to distinguish the true prophecy from the false.

There are false prophets, whose prophecies are not true. In the olden days it was assumed that these prophets were inspired by the devil. They were called "prophets of Baal" (I Kings 18 : 22). At times these prophets predominated, persecuted the prophets of God, suppressed the true worship, and exercised a tremendous power over both king and people.

When Ahab, king of Israel, desired to make war against Syria, Jehoshaphat, king of Judea, urged him to inquire of the Lord. Ahab gathered four hundred prophets who prophesied in favor of war. These prophets were deceived by a false spirit (I Kings 22 : 21–23). When the prophet Micaiah was called, he made contact with the true Spirit, prophesied against the war, and warned the two kings of the impending disaster (I Kings 22 : 14–17).

One has to be still and listen to the true Spirit. There are many who prophesy, but few who can interpret a prophecy. Some had the gift of prophesying; others, the gift of interpretation. Some have the gift of languages; others the gift of healing.

All of these gifts are important because they come from the same Spirit. Just as all members of the body are important, all men who have spiritual gifts are important because they are members of the church of Christ. In the spirit is the quality that counts. Therefore, every gift which is derived from the Spirit of God is for instruction, guidance and edification.

CHARITY

Though I speak with the tongues of men and of angels, and have not charity, I am become as sounding brass, or a tinkling cymbal. I Cor. 13 : 1.

Khoba in Aramaic is used in referring to something dear to one's heart, something for which one feels the kind of love that is expressed both in words and in action. In English the word "love" often implies love between a man and woman. The Aramaic word *khoba*, however, has a broader meaning and is seldom connected with sex. It is used when describing human loyalty to God, to our fellow men, and to the higher things of life. The Scriptures speak of God as love.

The word "charity" is derived from the latin word *caru*, which means "dear." It is used not in the sense of giving alms, but rather in speaking of devotion and gratitude to God and men. When men lack this gift, they become as sounding brass, or tinkling cymbals. Love (charity) comes from the depths of the heart and expresses the spiritual qualities of the inner man. When there is charity (love) there is understanding, peace and harmony; the human heart sings spiritual songs with harmonious tunes, which are understood by men and women of all races, creeds and colors.

No one can be close to God and yet be uncharitable. To love humanity is to love God. Our Lord told his followers to love their enemies and pray for those who hated them. "Love thy neighbor as thyself" is the fulfillment of God's commandments.

UNKNOWN TONGUE

For he that speaketh in an unknown tongue speaketh not unto men, but unto God: for no man understandeth him; howbeit in the spirit he speaketh mysteries.
I Cor. 14 : 2.

Speaking in an unknown tongue does not necessarily refer to the use of a foreign language. The phrase sometimes is used in speaking of divining and communing with the Spirit; that is, prophesying.

In the early days of the Christian era, all those who were baptized were supposed to speak in tongues. That was because the apostles on the day of Pentecost were so inspired that all the people heard them in their own languages or dialects (Acts 2 : 4–13). Men with familiar spirits often became ecstatic and spoke in strange tongues, which were not understood by the people. When Saul joined a company of the prophets, the Spirit of God came upon him and he prophesied (I Sam. 10 : 10–11).

Paul admonishes the people to seek spiritual gifts which are helpful, instead of speaking in a strange tongue and uttering mysterious words which no one could understand or interpret. Speaking in mysterious tongues often resulted in confusion and doubt. What was said was debated and questioned and therefore no one received any benefit.

There are various kinds of communications. There are the human and spiritual tongues. When we speak to God we converse with him in a spiritual tongue. In silence we feel his presence, hear his voice and receive guidance from him in a mysterious way. These mysteries can only be explained and understood by those who are inspired by the Spirit of God. Paul discouraged those who tried to speak in strange tongues without the gift of the Spirit of God. In the East, men who speak in several tongues are looked upon as very learned.

The speaker boasted of being able to speak in a mysterious tongue, which he himself could not interpret. (See verses 10–11.)

PROPHECY

But he that prophesieth speaketh unto men to edification, and exhoration, and comfort. I Cor. 14 : 3.

The Aramaic word *mithnabey,* "prophesied," is derived from *neba* (neva), meaning "to spring forth," "foretell," or "to give news." And the Aramaic word *nebia* means "prophet," one who predicts future events or gives advice and instruction.

In biblical days prophets acted as statesmen. They advised and guided kings in political and social matters, and reproved them when they failed to do justice. They sought reforms, instructed and admonished the people in the way of God, warned the people of impending disasters, and foretold future events. They were looked upon as great statesmen and seers who, through the Spirit of God, were able to see a future hope even when everything seemed dark and hopeless. They were feared by kings and revered by the people.

Paul recommends prophecy as a better gift. This is because the prophets acted as instructors in matters of religion. They explained the Scriptures, and advised and guided the people. They were inspired by the Holy Spirit to teach and to lead. (See verse 6.) "For ye may all prophesy one by one, that all may learn, and all may be comforted (verse 31).

SAYING OF GRACE

Else when thou shalt bless with the spirit, how shall he that occupieth the room of the unlearned say Amen at thy giving of thanks, seeing he understandeth not what thou sayest? I Cor. 14 : 16.

Jews and Christians offer thanks before a meal. Christians recite the Lord's prayer or say grace. After they have eaten they offer thanks. The Mohammedans, before they start eating, recite a verse from the Koran, "In the name of God, the Merciful, the Compassionate."

The Hebrews spoke Aramaic, but most of their prayers were said in ancient Hebrew. What they said was not understood by unlearned people. Some of the men preferred to pray in an ancient tongue just to show that they were learned.

Even today some people in the East prefer to pray in ancient languages, which they alone can understand. These prayers create embarrassing situations. Most of those who are present do not know the ancient tongue, and one has to understand a thing before he can say "Amen," expressing his approval.

FOREIGN TONGUES

In the law it is written, With men of other tongues and other lips will I speak unto this people; and yet for all that will they not hear me, saith the Lord.
Wherefore tongues are for a sign, not to them that believe, but to them that believe not: but prophesying serveth not for them that believe not, but for them which believe. I Cor. 14 : 21–22.

The reference here is to the books of Deuteronomy and Isaiah. "The Lord shall bring a nation against thee from far, from the end of the earth, as swift as the eagle flieth; a nation whose tongue thou shalt not understand" (Deut. 28 : 49). "For with stammering lips and another tongue will he speak to this people" (Isaiah 28 : 11). The above prophecies are warnings concerning the invasion of Palestine by foreign nations who would speak with foreign languages and oppress the people. Easterners dread people whose languages they do not know. When one cannot understand the speech of a conquering people, he does not expect mercy or favors. That is one reason why Easterners, especially the Jews, make an effort to learn and speak many foreign languages. It is often said "I will speak in a strange tongue" which means, "I will be harsh with him."

Those who speak many foreign languages are looked upon as wise men. Some of them act as teachers and others as counselors in political and spiritual matters. The people are impressed by their signs and wisdom.

The Jews at various times have been conquered by the Persians, the Romans, the Turks, and finally by the English. Since the first days of captivity, many foreign tongues have been heard in Jerusalem and the Jews have suffered many persecutions and privations.

SPIRIT OF PROPHECY

And the spirits of the prophets are subject to the prophets. I Cor. 14 : 32.

The term "spirits" here means "prophecies." When a man prophesies, he is inspired. The Spirit of God reveals the secrets to him and explains what he is to say.

There were times, however, when certain prophecies were not understood and the prophets prayed God to reveal their correct interpretation. For instance, when Daniel saw the vision of the ram and the goat, he sought the meaning and the angel of the Lord revealed it to him (Dan. 8 : 15). The prophets and men of God were directed what to say and what to do. God guided Moses and Aaron. "And I will be with thy mouth, and with his mouth, and will teach you what ye shall do" (Exod. 4 : 15).

Paul warns against those who prophesied but were unable to interpret their own prophecies. Such revelations were the subject of diverse interpretations and disputes. Some of the things were revealed in symbols, similar to those that Daniel and Ezekiel saw. The prophets, in order to avoid confusion, were admonished to understand the meaning of the symbols before disclosing them to the public. At times, people were divided because of wrong interpretations, which resulted in quarrels among members of the congregation and rivalry among the prophets.

On the other hand, there were many false prophets who had succeeded in creating divisions and confusion among the faithful. Many of these so-called prophets were mad men and fanatics. ". . . The prophet is a fool, the spiritual man is mad, for the multitude of thine iniquity, and the great hatred" (Hosea 9 : 7).

Jesus had warned against false prophets and false Christs. The true prophets were guided by the Holy Spirit. They predicted events before they happened. The sure test of a prophet is his ability to foretell events.

THE SUDDEN RETURN

Behold, I shew you a mystery; We shall not all sleep, but we shall all be changed,   I Cor. 15 : 51.

"Mystery" here refers to the sudden return of Christ. In those days Christ was expected to return at any time and restore the ancient kingdom of Israel. The Hebrew prophets predicted that the Messiah, Christ, would restore the kingdom of David. The early Christians, especially those who were converted from Judaism, were expecting to see these prophecies fulfilled and the scattered people of Israel gathered together.

Those living on that day would not die, but would be transferred from this body into a spiritual body. This transformation was to take place in the twinkling of an eye, at the sounding of the trumpet. And those who had died would rise up and join those who were alive to greet Christ in the clouds (I Thes. 4 : 16–17).

The second coming of Christ will be preceded by the establishment of God's rule on earth. It will take place when all things on earth have been made subject to Christ. "And when all things shall be subdued unto him, then shall the Son also himself be subject unto him that put all things under him, that God may be all in all" (I Cor. 15 : 28).

TWELVE

And that he was seen of Cephas, then of the twelve: After that, he was seen of above five hundred brethren at once; of whom the greater part remain unto this present, but some are fallen asleep.   I Cor. 15 : 5–6.

According to the Synoptic Gospels, the number of the disciples after the resurrection was eleven. "Then the eleven disciples went away into Galilee, into a mountain where Jesus had appointed them. And when they saw him, they worshiped him: but some doubted" (Matt. 28 : 16–17).

According to Mark, Jesus appeared unto the eleven as they sat down to eat (Mark. 16 : 14). When the two followers of Jesus returned from Emmaus to Jerusalem, they found the eleven disciples together (Luke 24 : 33).

Paul here refers to the group of disciples originally known as "the twelve." He was aware that Judas of Iscariot was not among them, but he uses the term "twelve" because twelve is the complete and sacred number. There were twelve tribes of Israel, and twelve months of the year. "The twelve" was the name applied to that inner circle of disciples, irrespective of the number present.

After Christ's resurrection the apostles elected Matthias to fill the vacancy left by Judas of Iscariot (Acts 1 : 23–26) and thus bring their number up to twelve again. He was one of those who had seen Jesus both before his death and after his resurrection. It seems very likely that Paul includes Matthias when he speaks here of "the twelve."

Jesus, after his resurrection, appeared eleven times to his disciples and followers. Those who believed in him saw him. Their eyes were opened. The unbelievers did not see him. They were expecting a political Messiah; therefore, as far as they were concerned, Jesus' mission had been a failure and he had died the death of a malefactor. One needs faith and spiritual eyes to see the risen Christ.

A LATER APOSTLE

And last of all he was seen of me also, as of one born out of due time. I Cor. 15 : 8.

The Eastern text reads: "And last of all he appeared to me also, ignorant and imperfect as I was." Paul refers here to his sudden conversion on his way to Damascus (Acts 9 : 4–6). At that time he was ignorant of the teachings of Christ and was engaged in persecuting the church. In other words, Paul was converted by the grace of God and not because of his faith in Jesus Christ (verse 10). The other apostles, who saw Jesus after his resurrection, believed in him, but Paul was persecuting those who were preaching in Jesus' name and saying that he had risen from the dead.

Paul saw Jesus in a vision. He heard the voice, but those who were with him neither knew what was said nor did they see any man. The whole thing took place like a flash of light. In other words, Paul did not see Jesus in the same manner in which the apostles saw him. This is why Paul's apostleship was questioned.

ADAM

For since by man came death, by man came also the resurrection of the dead. I Cor. 15 : 21.

Adam is derived from the Aramaic word *Ademta,* "red soil." The soil used for pottery is red, like blood. Adam is the symbol of physical or earthly man. He was formed out of the ground and into the ground he returned. ". . . For dust thou art, unto dust shalt thou return." (Gen. 3 : 19). Christ is truth, life and light. He is the symbol of spiritual and eternal man. The first man (Adam) was earthly, but the second (Christ) was spiritual.

The first man (Adam) through his disobedience, lost his spirituality and his original self. For he was created in God's image and likeness. Christ, through his obedience, restored man to his original self, that is, he made him capable of overcoming sin and death.

Just as death reigned because of the disobedience of Adam, life reigns because of the obedience of Jesus Christ. In Adam we all die, but in Christ we rise into a new life.

THROWN BEFORE WILD BEASTS

If after the manner of men I have fought with beasts at Ephesus, what advantageth it me, if the dead rise not? let us eat and drink; for to morrow we die. I Cor. 15 : 32.

The Eastern text reads: "I was thrown to wild beasts at Ephesus."

For many years one of the severest punishments which the Roman authorities inflicted on the early Christians was to throw them before wild beasts in the theaters. Paul, while on his missionary journeys in Asia Minor, was often imprisoned, beaten and stoned. In his second letter to the Corinthians he speaks of being delivered from a great danger (II Cor. 1 : 9–10). He accepted persecution, suffering, hunger and thirst, because of his faith in Jesus and his conviction of the life hereafter.

If there is no resurrection and eternal reward, then why should one suffer for the truth? Jesus went to the cross with secure confidence that he would triumph over death and rise again. Had he not believed in life hereafter, he would never have given his life for us, nor would he have been able to rise from the dead.

Paul apparently is referring here to the Gospel of John: "Verily, verily, I say unto you, Except a corn of wheat fall into the ground and die, it abideth alone: but if it die, it bringeth forth much fruit" (John 12 : 24). Jesus knew that death was not the end of life, but rather the beginning of a larger and richer life. For when a grain of wheat dies, it produces a plant and many other grains. The same power that preserves the seed in the cold, dark earth controls both life and death. Just as a grain remains in the ground a short while before it sprouts, so the dead shall remain for a time in the grave, but will rise again. "It is sown in corruption; it is raised in incorruption" (I Cor. 15 : 42).

DEATH

But God giveth it a body as it hath pleased him, and to every seed his own body.   I Cor. 15 : 38.

The Hebrews, more than any other people, dreaded death. They considered it the end of everything. Those who died were supposed to be cut off from the living God. The Jewish poets drew a dark picture of death. They pictured man as the grass of the field, which grows for a season but soon withers away and is gone. The psalmist says: "The dead praise not thee, O Lord, neither all they that go down into silence." This is why some of the disciples of Jesus were doubtful of his resurrection.

This fear of death is overcome only through the spiritual understanding of life and a new outlook on death. Jesus in his teaching distinguishes between the spiritual body and the mortal body. He told his disciples not to be afraid of those who kill the body, but to fear those who kill the soul. It is the spirit that gives life and causes the body to grow; but the physical man is made of dust and he shall return unto dust.

The spiritual man need not be afraid of death. The spirit (soul) which dwells in man's mortal body is eternal because God is eternal. Through the inner understanding of God and the teaching of Christ, death will gradually lose its hold on men and it will be the last enemy to be conquered. Death still holds its grasp on men because it has allies, sin and fear. When these are destroyed, death will be abolished and man completely restored to his divinity.

Jesus demonstrated his power over death by raising the dead and conquering the grave.

RESURRECTION

So when this corruptible shall have put on incorruption, and this mortal shall have put on immortality, then shall be brought to pass the saying that is written, Death is swallowed up in victory.   I Cor. 15 : 54.

Belief in immortality was quite universal. The resurrection of the dead was believed by the Assyrians, Babylonians and Egyptians. When kings and noblemen died, they were buried with food, clothing, jewelry and all the necessities for the life hereafter.

The Hebrews had lived both in Egypt and Babylon. The Hebrew prophets, because of many national tragedies and injustices inflicted upon their people by their enemies, portrayed a bright future for the oppressed but eternal punishment for the oppressors. The later prophets maintained brighter hopes for a happy future through the Messianic kingdom. As hopes for the restoration of a political state in the line of David diminished, their belief in the ultimate resurrection of Israel was strengthened. They believed that justice would triumph at last, if not in this world, then surely in the other.

The God of the Hebrews was a living God (Job 19 : 25). Pagan gods died. Isaiah cries, "Awake and sing, ye that dwell in dust . . ." (Isa. 26 : 19), and Daniel writes, "And many of them that sleep in the dust of the earth shall awake, some to everlasting life, and some to shame and everlasting contempt" (Dan. 12 : 2). The prophets realized that death was not the end. The earthly injustices and defeats were only temporal. Political Israel was destroyed because of the sins of the people. The defeated Jewish state was to rise up like the dead bones that Ezekiel saw in his vision. This was to come into realization through gradual development, and it was to culminate in the kingdom of God on earth.

Nevertheless, there were diverse opinions and teachings concerning the resurrection. Some of the Jewish sects, like that of the Sadducees, denied any resurrection of the body. Others believed the dead were to be represented by posterity. Some maintained that only the good were to rise up.

Jesus gave his disciples a clearer picture of the resurrection and the life hereafter. According to his teaching, both good and bad are to rise up in the last day and come to the final judgment. The resurrection is to take place at the coming of our Lord, when the righteous and the wicked will be separated (Matt. 25 : 32). On the other hand, the book of Revelation sets a period of a thousand years in which righteousness will reign and evil forces will be destroyed (Rev. 20 : 4). The resurrection will occur at the second coming of Christ.

The earthly man was created of dust and unto dust he shall return. But death has no power over the spiritual man who is the image of God and who existed before the world was created. Jesus, through his death on the cross, destroyed the power of death and Sheol. "But is now made manifest by the appearing of our Saviour Jesus Christ, who hath abolished death, and hath brought life and immortality to light through the gospel" (II Tim. 1 : 10).

Jesus, through his resurrection, proved that death is not the end, but a new beginning. Therefore, those who are born again through faith in Jesus Christ shall rise again. Jesus had power to raise the dead (John 11 : 43–44) and he gave that same power to his apostles (Acts 9 : 36–41).

FIRST DAY

Upon the first day of the week let every one of you lay by him in store, as God hath prospered him, that there be no gatherings when I come.   I Cor. 16 : 2.

According to the Hebrew calendar, Sunday is the first day of the week and Saturday (the seventh or Sabbath Day) the last. God started his work of creating the earth and the heavens on the first day, that is, Sunday; and he rested on the seventh day.

Today many people think of Monday as the first day of the week, and they speak of Saturday and Sunday as the week end. The Jewish week started on Sunday, and some of the most important business activities were begun on that day. The Eastern text reads: "Let each of you put aside and keep in his house whatever he can afford, so that there be no collections when I come."

Corinthian Christians were asked to put something aside every week for the relief of the saints in Judea. This was a simple and easy method. Easterners are frightened when asked to give large sums of money at one time, but seldom refuse to donate small sums. In other words, they can give a dollar a week, but would refuse to give forty dollars at one time.

In the East, when things are pledged to God, they must be offered. Once a gift is promised, no one would dare to refuse to give it. The solemn pledge makes it God's property.

Paul knew that Christians in Corinth had little money and other natural things, and that they could not give large sums at one time. He simplified the matter by asking them to consecrate a small amount each Sunday. Paul's appeal was heeded and the need was met.

AN HOLY KISS

All the brethren greet you. Greet ye one another with an holy kiss.   I Cor. 16 : 20.

Easterners, when greeting one another, kiss each other on the cheek. During the communion those who have not been on good terms become reconciled and kiss each other. Some ministers would not hesitate to kiss women members of their congregation. Such greetings are generally given at the door after the service.

A holy kiss is a token of sincere affection, friendship and harmony, but because of that some persons may use the kiss, as Judas did, for purposes of deception. (Matt. 26 : 48). See also I Thes. 5 : 26.

CHRIST HAD COME

If any man love not the Lord Jesus Christ, let him be Anathema Maran-atha.   I Cor. 16 : 22.

Maran etha is an Aramaic phrase which means, "the Lord has come." *Etha* is past tense and should not be confused with *atheh* (future tense), "will come." This caused considerable uneasiness among the early Christians. They looked for the immediate return of Jesus.

Many Jews in Asia Minor and Macedonia denied that Christ had come. This saying is directed against those who refused to accept Jesus of Nazareth as the promised Messiah and who were looking forward to the coming of another who would fulfill the prophecies, restore the Davidic kingdom, and gather the scattered people of Israel. These men doubted that the prophecies had been fulfilled and that Jesus was the true Messiah. They argued that when the Messiah does come, all prophecies will be literally fulfilled. In other words, they were expecting a political Christ.

Jesus had openly told his disciples that his kingdom was a spiritual one and that he was free from all political implications. He told Pilate that his kingdom was not of this earth. ". . . If my kingdom were of this world, then would my servants fight, that I should not be delivered to the Jews: but now is my kingdom not from hence" (John 18 : 36).

Paul placed all of those who denied Jesus under anathema, that is, a curse. Such men were not to be accepted into the church. The Christian religion is built on the birth, death and resurrection of Jesus Christ. Those who deny him cannot be partakers in his kingdom.

II CORINTHIANS

INTRODUCTION

The author is Paul; he wrote it from Philippi, in Macedonia, and sent it by Titus and Lucas. The probable date is about A.D. 60. Note that Paul never dated his epistles.

Second Corinthians is a supplementary letter to the first epistle to the Christians in Corinth. Some of the Christians, especially those of the circumcision, were hostile to Paul. They attacked his apostleship and made things hard for him. These Christians were still under the influence of Jewish customs and traditions. They did not believe that salvation by grace, through the death of Christ, was sufficient. Paul reminds the Corinthian Christians of his difficulties and trials for the sake of the gospel. He exhorts the Christians to live a pure life. He exonerates himself from attacks and depends upon his apostleship and preaching to prove his sincerity. The Christians in Corinth are asked to share in raising relief funds for the saints in Jerusalem.

A DOOR

Furthermore, when I came to Troas to preach Christ's gospel, and a door was opened unto me of the Lord,
II Cor. 2 : 12.

"And a door was opened unto me by the Lord," is an Eastern idiom. Paul means that God has directed him and removed the obstacles from his way, or that God has given him an opportunity. When times are hard and problems difficult, one often hears people say to one another: "Every door has been closed to me."

On the other hand, in the East, doors are opened to friends and strangers who find favor, but are closed to those who are not welcome. When travelers are not received in one house, they try another, and when a door is opened they rejoice.

Paul was constantly guided by the Holy Spirit and by visions. Thus he was sent to the places where he was most needed and least expected. In many cities he was received by prominent men and women, even city officials. They saw that his needs were met and that the difficulties which lay in his way were overcome. His sincerity and devotion to Christ helped him to find favor in the eyes of the people among whom he preached.

LITERALISM

Who also hath made us able ministers of the new testament; not of the letter, but of the spirit: for the letter killeth, but the spirit giveth life.
II Cor. 3 : 6.

"Not of the letter" means "not according to human interpretation and traditions." The teachings which were taken literally always caused disputes and divisions among the people and proved destructive instead of edifying. Hebrew was a dead tongue. Many of its terms and expressions had become obscure and debatable. The apostle Peter in his second epistle warns against misinterpretation of the Scriptures and in particular the writings of Paul. " . . . Even as our beloved brother Paul also according to the wisdom given unto him hath written unto you; as also in all his epistles, speaking in them of these things; in which are some things hard to be understood, which they that are unlearned and unstable wrest, as they do also the other scriptures, unto their own destruction" (II Pet. 3 : 15–16).

HUMAN LAW

But if the ministration of death, written and engraven in stones, was glorious, so that the children of Israel could not stedfastly behold the face of Moses for the glory of his countenance; which glory was to be done away:
How shall not the ministration of the spirit be rather glorious?   II Cor. 3 : 7–8.

The reference here is to the Ten Commandments which were engraved on the stone tablets (Exod. 20 : 1–18). When Moses came down from Mount Sinai his face shone so the people were unable to look into it. Moses had fasted forty days in order that he might commune with the Lord. Thus the physical forces were subdued to the forces of the spirit, and Moses was glorified with the glory of God which filled Mount Sinai.

Nevertheless, even though Moses was received by God and his face was transfigured, the commandments that he brought down from the mountain contained the sentence of death. The Hebrews for the first time came under the written law. Hitherto they had been a free desert people, guided and directed by the dictates of their own hearts, but now they came under the ordinances of the law. Those who transgressed were put to death. The instrument made no provision for forgiveness.

Paul compares the ministration of the law with the

ministration of the spirit, which is much more glorious because it does not carry with it the sentence of death. The glory of Moses was temporary. The commandments that he brought down from Mount Sinai were hard to keep, and the breaking thereof introduced sin. But the gospel of Jesus Christ was based on the grace of God. Sinners, when they repented, were forgiven. The stone tablets served for a time, and then were lost; but the law of the spirit is eternal.

MOSES' FACE VEILED

And not as Moses, which put a veil over his face, that the children of Israel could not stedfastly look to the end of that which is abolished: II Cor. 3 : 13.

When a person really communes with God, his countenance changes and his face seems to shine. When Moses came down from the mountain into the presence of the people, he covered his face with a veil, but when he went to speak with the Lord he removed the veil (Exod. 34 : 33–35). The Eastern text reads: " . . . that the children of Israel might not look upon the fullness of the glory which was not lasting."

When the law was given, the people were instructed not to come near Mount Sinai lest they die (Exod. 19 : 12). Jehovah was so holy that he could not be approached or seen by sinful men. Then again, the glory was temporary. The law was a good thing, but it could not be kept. Thus the tablets contained the sentence of death.

A veil is symbolical of mystery. The Hebrew faith at that time was based on mysteries. This is because the early Hebrews saw things in part and were unable to understand their inner and spiritual meaning. Even today Mohammedans and Orthodox Jews do not remove their hats during the prayer.

Jesus, in the fullness of time, removed the veil and revealed these mysteries. Today his followers stand before the presence of God unveiled. They converse with him and address him as a loving father. Christ's truth reveals every mystery and dispels the fear of death and sin. His commandments are inscribed on the hearts of men and women, and his glory is everlasting.

VESSELS OF GOLD

But we have this treasure in earthen vessels, that the excellency of the power may be of God, and not of us.
II Cor. 4 : 7.

When rich men entertain, they use silver and gold vessels. The middle class and the poor use earthen cups and utensils. Some wealthy women glory over their silver and gold wares and are less careful about food.

On some occasions, even though silver and gold vessels are used, the food does not taste good, and the banquet is a failure. On the other hand, when earthen vessels are used and the banquet is a success, the credit is given to the women who prepare the food.

Paul likens his body to the simple earthen vessels, suggesting that credit and glory for the work of the gospel may be given to God and not to himself. The teaching of the gospel is a treasure that is contained in earthly bodies. Just as it is the flavor of food that counts, and not the vessels in which it is served, so it is the Spirit of God which does the work, and human bodies are only the instruments through which the Word of God is published.

MARTYRDOM

So then death worketh in us, but life in you.
II Cor. 4 : 12.

In the first and second centuries of the Christian era, many pagans were converted to Christianity through the bravery and martyrdom of the believers. They gladly gave their lives for the sake of the gospel of Jesus

Christ. In some instances even the executioners and judges were converted to Christianity. The believers discarded their earthly lives and went to their death with songs of praise and trust in the life hereafter. Consequently many of the spectators were persuaded to accept Christianity.

Moreover, Christian converts suffered persecutions, hunger and thirst for the sake of those who were brought to Christ. Paul himself had been a persecutor of the followers of Jesus, but later, through the testimony of the martyrs and the grace of God, was led to Jesus Christ.

While Paul and his fellow companions were suffering for the sake of the gospel, the converts derived spiritual benefits and found a new life in the faith of Jesus Christ.

Christian examples of good works and sincere loyalty to Christ are stronger than rituals, preaching and doctrines. Men are like sheep. They must be led by men of God into the true path of life.

SINCERE BELIEF

We having the same spirit of faith, according as it is written, I believed, and therefore have I spoken; we also believe, and therefore speak; II Cor. 4 : 13.

This quotation is from Psalm 116 : 9–10. "I will walk before the Lord in the land of the living. I believed, therefore have I spoken: I was greatly afflicted."

When one sincerely believes in a teaching he is willing to preach it and die for it. There are hundreds of instances where true believers suffered and gave their lives for their teachings. Hebrew prophets were persecuted and imprisoned for the truth which they preached. Many of them died the death of martyrs. Some were stoned, others suffered tortures. It is said that the prophet Isaiah was placed between two wooden planks and then sawed in two.

When one believes in a teaching he cannot help but speak it and teach it. The inner force, the spirit, gives him strength and courage. The thought of life hereafter minimizes the importance of this present, temporary life. The affliction and suffering are soon past, but the eternal reward remains forever.

SPIRITUAL JOYS

While we look not at the things which are seen, but at the things which are not seen: for the things which are seen are *temporal; but the things which are not seen* are *eternal.* II Cor. 4 : 18.

The Eastern text reads: "We do not rejoice in the things which are seen . . ." The Aramaic word *khadenan* means "we rejoice." This refers to joy over the things of the spirit which cannot be seen by the eye of the flesh. This is consistent with Eastern thought. Pious Palestinians, Syrians and Arabs take little interest in material things. They consider this life transitory and temporal. Moreover, pious men are always willing to live or die for their faith.

Paul considers troubles, tribulations and persecutions as temporary and not worthy of consideration when compared with eternal life and everlasting joys. For there is a greater purpose in life than mere living, and physical joys are like shadows. The things for which we crave on this earth are temporal and changing, but the things of the spirit are lasting. This life is like a preparatory school for the life hereafter.

REVERENCE TO CHRIST

Knowing therefore the terror of the Lord, we persuade men; but we are made manifest unto God; and I trust also are made manifest in your consciences. II Cor. 5 : 11.

The Aramaic word *dekhilta* means "fear" or "reverence." The word "terror" is wrongly used here. In the East, bishops, judges, government officials and kings are highly revered by the people. When men and women come into their presence they kiss their hands and stand up until told to be seated. When such important persons speak, the people keep silent. This is done not because of fear, but because of respect for their authority. According to the Eastern text, Paul speaks here of reverence for Jesus Christ. The Aramaic word *Maran* means "our Lord Jesus Christ." The translators confused it with *Maria*, "Lord."

God is often likened to the rulers and kings of this world, who demand reverence and respect from their subjects. Paul wants all reverence and glory to be given to Jesus Christ, whose gospel is the means of salvation to all believers.

REASONING CHRIST'S DEATH

For the love of Christ constraineth us; because we thus judge, that if one died for all, then were all dead:
And that he died for all, that they which live should not henceforth live unto themselves, but unto him which died for them, and rose again.
Wherefore henceforth know we no man after the flesh: yea, though we have known Christ after the flesh, yet now henceforth know we him no more.
Therefore if any man be in Christ, he is a new creature: old things are passed away; behold, all things are become new. II Cor. 5 : 14–17.

The Eastern text reads: "For the love of Christ compels us to reason thus . . ." The Aramaic word *ranenan* means "to reason," and *deninan*, "to judge." The words closely resemble each other. This is why errors in translating would be inevitable.

Paul's logic here is based on faith in Jesus Christ's death and resurrection. Pagans and unbelievers could not see how all could die in one man, and yet live through the one who had died for them. What Paul means is, that Jesus, through his death, destroyed the power of death, and through his triumphant resurrection broke the gates of hell. That is, he tested the bitterest cup of death for all, and won an everlasting victory for those who believe in him. For the old self died in Jesus and the new self rose up in Christ as a new and living creation.

MADE HIM TO BE SIN

For he hath made him to be sin for us, who knew no sin; that we might be made the righteousness of God in him. II Cor. 5 : 21.

This quotation is an Aramaic idiom. It means that God made him to bear our sins, and thus to be looked upon as a sinner.

Jesus was crucified as a sinner. In the East it is often said: "I have become a curse for your sake," or "I have lost my God for you." The people looked upon Jesus as a malefactor and as one who had transgressed the law and blasphemed against God and his holy Temple. Those who were crucified were spoken of as "accursed ones."

Jesus was without sin, but he lowered himself and died the death of a sinner, so that he might reveal God's abundant love for his children. God permitted the death of a righteous man as a means of salvation for his children who had gone astray. In Jesus' death we are reconciled to God.

SPEAKING OPENLY

O ye Corinthians, our mouth is open unto you, our heart is enlarged.
Ye are not straitened in us, but ye are straitened in your own bowels.   II Cor. 6 : 11–12.

"Our mouth is open" is an Eastern saying which means "we have told you everything." When people speak plainly and try to tell everything it is said of them that "they have a large mouth." "Our hearts are enlarged" means "we are relieved." That is to say, we have done our duty and told you the truth.

Paul in his epistle speaks boldly, and warns the Corinthian Christians not to associate themselves with idolaters, but to live a pure life, worthy of those whose bodies are the temples of the living God. The Christians must cleanse themselves of all the evils of the flesh which hinder the truth. He also refers to his suffering and trials for their sakes.

The Eastern text of verse 12 reads: "You are not constrained by us, but are urged by your affections." Paul wants them to know that he has no desire to force his admonitions on them, but that they should listen to him because of their affection for him and his sincere stand for the gospel which he had preached to them. The Corinthian Christians were to come out voluntarily, and not to be enticed by words and threats. They must do their part, just as Paul had done his. He speaks to them as he would speak to his own children.

ALMIGHTY

And will be a Father unto you, and ye shall be my sons and daughters, saith the Lord Almighty.   II Cor. 6 : 18.

The word "Almighty" should not be taken as implying dictatorship. God has the power over all his creation, but he never uses this power as a monarch does over his subjects. His authority over his children is like that of a loving father over his family.

The Aramaic text uses two words *akhid kool,* which means "sustainer of all." God controls the universe in the sense that it all depends upon him. God has power over everything, therefore he is Almighty—capable of doing everything.

Paul admonishes the Corinthians to look to God as a father who is able at all times to direct them and guide them. But they must try to do their part, for God does not use his power to interfere with human will. Man is endowed with free will and with the knowledge of good and evil.

RICH IN POWER

For ye know the grace of our Lord Jesus Christ, that, though he was rich, yet for your sakes he became poor, that ye through his poverty might be rich. II Cor. 8 : 9.

"Rich" in this case does not mean rich in worldly goods, but rich in power and character. In Aramaic, the word *meskena,* "poor," is used when speaking of one's meekness and humility. Jesus was poor. He had no earthly possessions or a place to lay his head, but his needs were divinely met. He could have acquired wealth and become rich, but he denied himself the comforts of this life and died for us.

Paul reminds the Corinthians that their Lord Jesus emptied himself of all worldly glory and honor in order to help his fellow men. Therefore they should respond gladly to the appeal which he was making on behalf of the saints in Jerusalem. In view of the rich gifts which Jesus had given them, they were also to give liberally. It is easier to give money and other goods than to die for others. The Jews gave ten per cent of their earnings to God. The Christians were to give even their lives for the sake of the gospel and for one another.

SHARING

As it is written, He that had gathered *much had nothing over; and he that* had gathered *little had no lack.*
II Cor. 8 : 15.

The reference here is to the manna of Moses' day. The Hebrews were warned by Moses to gather manna according to the number of persons in each family. But because of fear that the supply might become exhausted, some of them gathered more than they were able to consume. The extra supply always spoiled (Exod. 16 : 16–21). But those who gathered what they needed from day to day, had an ample supply.

Paul was raising a fund for the relief of Christians in Judea. He admonished the Corinthians each to give according to his ability, in order that all of them might become partakers in the gift of charity through which Christian love was demonstrated. In other words, Paul was unwilling to lay the whole of the burden on a few rich people who could give large gifts. He did not want to deprive the poor of having a part by sharing in a charitable undertaking through which they would receive eternal benefits and blessings. The giver would be blessed with spiritual understanding and an eternal reward, and the receiver with material things.

SOWING

But this I say, He which soweth sparingly shall reap also sparingly; and he which soweth bountifully shall reap also bountifully.
II Cor. 9 : 6.

In most parts of the Near East, very little wheat is sown in the autumn; most of the wheat and other cereals are sown in the spring.

During the long winters the wheat supplies may be depleted and food become scarce, and yet a portion of the wheat has to be set aside for seed. In such cases the spring sowing is done sparingly. The farmers are reluctant to cast the precious wheat into the ground, when children are hungry at home. This is why the psalmist says: "They that sow in tears shall reap in joy" (Psa. 126 : 5). But when little seed is sown the harvest is poor. On the other hand, those who have abundant seed and sow bountifully, reap also bountifully.

The "seed" in this case represents good works and Christian charity. In the East, doctrines and good works are often called "seed." Paul admonishes the Corinthians to give according to their ability, but those who are blessed with material things he urges to be generous in their gifts. There is a reward for the acts of charity. Those who give generously will receive generously. The Christians must prove their faith by their Christian deeds. Jesus had placed Christian charity above doctrines and creeds. Faith is not sufficient without Christian deeds and charity. Jesus said: "For I was an hungred, and ye gave me no meat: I was thirsty, and ye gave me no drink . . ." (Matt. 25 : 42).

MEEKNESS

Now I Paul myself beseech you by the meekness and gentleness of Christ, who in presence am base among you, but being absent am bold toward you: II Cor. 10 : 1.

This saying is characteristic of the Eastern people who, in writing and conversation, try to humble themselves. The Aramaic word *makikha* means "meek," "gentle" or "humble." "Blessed are the meek: for they shall inherit the earth" (Matt. 5 : 5). (See also Psalm 37 : 11.) In the East, writers and preachers often speak of themselves as being sinners and unworthy to be called Christians. People despise the self-righteous and the proud, but admire the meek. The Scriptures commend the meek and the humble. "The Lord lifteth up the meek; he casteth the wicked down to the ground" (Psa. 147 : 6). Jesus said: "I am meek and lowly in heart" (Matt.

11 : 29). "Blessed are the poor in pride, for theirs is the kingdom of heaven" (Matt. 5 : 3, Eastern text).

Paul does not want to boast of his work or commend himself, like some of the other teachers. Paul's work among the gentiles spoke for itself. In other words, Paul never advertised himself or boasted of his success. He took orders from both James and Peter and went wherever he was sent.

Pride is a heavy burden which tires the bearer as well as those who look at it.

APOSTOLIC RANK

For we dare not make ourselves of the number, or compare ourselves with some that commend themselves; but they measuring themselves by themselves, and comparing themselves among themselves, are not wise.
II Cor. 10 : 12.

"The number" in this case refers to the twelve apostles. The number twelve was maintained for a long time. New men were elected to fill the vacancies which were created by death, desertion and martyrdom. Matthias filled the place of Judas of Iscariot (Acts 1 : 23–26). After the martyrdom of James, the son of Zebedee, it seems that James, the brother of our Lord, took his place. Paul, in his epistle to the Galatians, says: "Then after three years I went to Jerusalem to see Peter, and abode with him fifteen days. But other of the apostles saw I none, save James the Lord's brother" (Gal. 1 : 18–19).

The apostles appointed elders and sent out missionaries. Some of these became bishops or overseers. The apostles were the ones who acted on questions pertaining to the faith and Christian conduct (Acts 15 : 22–30). The rank of the apostles was higher than that of overseers and elders.

Paul was not considered one of "the number." He was sent to Antioch with Barnabas, Judas and Silas (Acts 15 : 25–27).

FALSE TEACHERS

But I fear, lest by any means, as the serpent beguiled Eve through his subtilty, so your minds should be corrupted from the simplicity that is in Christ. II Cor. 11 : 3.

The Aramaic word *peshitotha* in this case means "sincerity." *Peshita* is used to describe one who is sincere, simple-minded and straight. At times the young and the unlearned are called *peshitey,* "simple."

Paul in his epistles warns the Christians to remain sincere and steadfast in the true teachings, which he and the apostles had imparted to them. These teachings were simple and free from complicated theologies. They were based on the true gospel of Jesus Christ.

The Christians in Corinth are likened to a chaste virgin, worthy to be espoused to Christ. Nevertheless, Paul was fearful of false teachers who followed in his footsteps and beguiled the faithful through the introduction of doctrines contrary to the truth which Paul had preached among them. Some of these teachers argued that Paul was not a full apostle, and therefore that his teaching was not authoritative. (See verses 4, 5, 13.) Paul had preached a complete gospel, spoken and taught freely among the Corinthians. The new teachers who appeared among them, instead of strengthening their faith, created divisions among them and made Paul's work harder.

Paul had not seen Jesus in the flesh, but his education and training were of great help to him. He was a scholar and had made a diligent study of the Gospels. After his conversion to Christianity, he went to Arabia and spent several years studying the gospel of Jesus. Being a Hebrew scholar, he soon became an authority. Moreover, Paul consulted the apostles on important matters.

ROBBING CHURCHES

I robbed other churches, taking wages of them, *to do you service.* II Cor. 11 : 8.

The Aramaic word *khalas* means "to deprive" or "to force." But Paul uses it in the sense of "urging" people to give. The term "robbed" is wrongly used. Paul could neither have robbed churches nor forced the people to give him money. He did persecute the church of Christ in Judea and in Syria, but that was prior to his conversion.

In the East, a bishop can ask one of his churches to help another. On some occasions he may make heavy demands on certain congregations in order to help congregations that have suffered persecution. The people respond generously to such appeals, especially when coming from higher authorities and when the money is used to help the poor churches. Bishops are unmarried and have no salaries; they are supported by gifts. When they call on their people for help, no one doubts their sincerity. Some people deprive themselves of many comforts in order to help their brethren.

Paul was an organizer and an overseer of the churches in Asia Minor and Macedonia. The converts never doubted his sincerity. He had denied himself all the comforts of life and suffered many persecutions and privations for the cause of the gospel of Jesus Christ. He did not raise money for his own needs, but for poor and struggling churches.

SATAN AS AN ANGEL

And no marvel; for Satan himself is transformed into an angel of light.   II Cor. 11 : 14.

The word "Satan" is derived from an Aramaic or Chaldean word, *Sata,* which means "to miss the mark," "to mislead," or "to go astray." *Satana* is a verbal noun denoting the action of the verb *sata.* It is used as a noun and an adjective. For example, when an Easterner makes a mistake, he spits on Satan. When he is caught doing something wrong, he says: "It was not my fault. Satan caused me to do it." Such excuses often help men to escape punishment and embarrassment.

It is interesting to know that even today there is a sect of people near Mosul, known as "Devil Worshippers," about 85,000 in number. Their doctrine is that the Satan is a fallen angel who will finally be restored. Therefore, we must not spit on him or curse him, but adore him and be good to him, so that he will be good to us. Spitting and the usage of the name of "Satan" are prohibited among members of this sect, and strangers who visit them must refrain from mentioning Satan's name or cursing him. The doctrine of Satan as a fallen angel is fully accepted in the book of Enoch, in the Apocrypha.

Satan, as a person, is nowhere mentioned among God's creation. In Genesis 3 : 1 it is a *khovey* ("snake" or "serpent") which tempts Eve, and not Satan. There is no mention of angels, Satan, or any other intermediaries. God acts as a father. He reproves Adam and Eve, rebukes Cain, instructs Noah to build the ark, and appears to Abraham, Isaac, Jacob and Moses. In the olden days God seemed to have no advisers, intermediaries, or agents such as angels. According to the Bible, however, in the latter days he seemingly depends on such mediums to carry his messages and execute his orders.

The word "satan" as a noun, is not found in the Pentateuch. It appears once in the book of Numbers, but as a verbal noun, the Hebrew *saten,* which means "to mislead." The angel of God appears to Balaam and tries to mislead him. The early Hebrews had little or no knowledge of Satan and his power.

They attributed everything to God and looked on punishment and suffering simply as a kind of paternal chastising. Their concept of monotheism was so pure that there was no place for Satan as an adversary in a world created and ruled by the God who is the supreme ruler of the universe.

Before and during the captivity, however, Satan appears frequently in Hebrew literature. He is often spoken of as "evil spirit." In the book of Job he appears standing among the sons of God. He freely criticizes God and even rebukes him for being too good and generous to Job (Job 1 : 7–10). In the book of Kings we find him again in the counsel of God, acting as an adviser to mislead Ahab, so that he might fall in the battle against the Syrians. God appears to have accepted his advice as the best that was offered (I Kings 22 : 21–22).

In the New Testament, he is spoken of as a tempter or an accuser. There is much in the Bible about the power of Satan, but it does not blend with the pure Semitic doctrine of one supreme God.

The Jews borrowed the idea of Satan and his doctrine from the Babylonians and Persians during their captivity (605–535 B.C.) A large portion of biblical literature was written during and after this period. Oppression, crookedness, injustice and corruption were so prevalent in Babylon that the Babylonians traced the origin of evil to an independent god *Ahriman,* the god of darkness, who had no relation whatever with *Ormazd,* the god of light. Their system of government had accusers called *Shaytans,* who appeared before the king and accused certain persons such as Daniel, Shadrach, Meshach, and Abednego. Then again, the kings were worshiped as gods and were unapproachable. Their orders were carried out by their ministers and intermediaries. This was not so in the early Hebrew theocratic form of government, where evils were much less, and small tribal affairs were easily settled by the kings, and the people were forgiven without intermediaries.

The Jews found things different in Babylon. They could not associate injustices, corruption and evil with their conception of a pure God, so they borrowed Satan from the Babylonians and reluctantly accepted the doctrine of demonology, as an answer to the prevailing evils which they confronted in Babylon and Persia. On the other hand, Babylonians and Persians were dualistic in their conception of deity. They believed in two gods, the god of good and the god of evil. They acknowledged the existence of evil, therefore they attributed it to *Ahriman*, the god of darkness. They had no idea of man's free will and his power to resist the power of evil.

JEWISH TEACHERS

Are they Hebrews? so am I. Are they Israelites? so am I. Are they the seed of Abraham? so am I.
Are they ministers of Christ? (I speak as a fool) I am more; in labours more abundant, in stripes above measure, in prisons more frequent, in deaths oft.
II Cor. 11 : 22–23.

Teachers and evangelists from Palestine visited the churches in Asia Minor, Macedonia and Greece from time to time. Some of them went to raise money for themselves. They boasted of being the descendants of Abraham, born in Judea. This boasting was aimed against Paul, who was born in Tarsus, in Cilicia.

The simple Christian converts in Corinth looked upon some of these teachers as having come from the Holy Land and being of true Jewish origin. Easterners honor and judge a man by his ancestry and place of birth. For instance, the Turks and Persians honor and revere an Arab teacher of religion to those of other nationalities, regardless of his qualifications and learning. This is because Mohammed, the founder of Islam, was an Arab. The Arabs claim they understand the teachings of Mohammed better than those who cannot speak Arabic and are unfamiliar with Arab customs and manners.

Paul was a Hebrew of the tribe of Benjamin, born in Tarsus; but he had been educated in Jerusalem. The only thing against his apostleship was that he had not been with Jesus. (Paul was born many years after Jesus' death.)

"I speak as a fool" means "I should not say this." Teachers of religion never boast of themselves. Instead they disclaim credit and honor. (Compare II Cor. 12 : 6.) Even Jesus refused to be called "good." Paul boasts of his hard work for the gospel of Christ, his imprisonment, beatings and other hardships. These were the true proofs of his apostleship and his sincerity as a servant of Christ.

Paul does not criticize the true apostle, but he is bitter against the "brethren" who attacked his apostleship.

THIRD HEAVEN

It is not expedient for me doubtless to glory. I will come to visions and revelations of the Lord.
I knew a man in Christ above fourteen years ago, (whether in the body, I cannot tell; or whether out of the body, I cannot tell: God knoweth;) such an one caught up to the third heaven. II Cor. 12 : 1–2.

Paul here is relating a vision which he had seen fourteen years before. The vision is similar to those described in the books of Revelation and Daniel. In a vision one sees men and things as though real. Angels may be seen flying and coming down from heaven. "Hereafter ye shall see heaven open, and the angels of God ascending and descending upon the Son of man" (John 1 : 51).

Paul had seen in a vision a man who was a believer in Christ caught up to the third heaven. He recognized him, but was not sure whether he was in the body or in the spirit.

The Hebrews believed that there were several heavens; one above the skies, the others above the sun and the moon, and still another where God dwells. These heavens were separated by water. "Praise him, ye heavens of heavens, and ye waters that be above the heavens" (Psa. 148 : 4). "The Lord hath prepared his throne in the heavens" (Psa. 103 : 19).

The things which Paul heard were mysterious and could not be repeated. The man Paul saw might have been Stephen. He had seen him stoned, and was greatly impressed by his martyrdom (Acts 7 : 55–56).

Paul had a prophetic gift. He saw visions and was often guided by them. The gift of prophecy was greater than all other gifts (I Cor. 14 : 4–5). "Wherefore, brethren, covet to prophesy, and forbid not to speak with tongues" (I Cor. 14 : 39).

THORN IN THE FLESH

And lest I should be exalted above measure through the abundance of the revelations, there was given to me a thorn in the flesh, the messenger of Satan to buffet me, lest I should be exalted above measure.   II Cor. 12 : 7.

In lands where shoes are lacking and men and women walk barefoot, thorns are a serious problem. During the summer months when wheat is harvested and grass cut, a great many people suffer from thorns. Not having doctors and surgical instruments, men may leave thorns in their feet and hands a long time. Such injuries, even though small, are aggravating. The little thorn may be left in the flesh until it decays. Or it may be pulled out with a small needle. During the summer months people complain more about thorns than any other injuries. They hesitate to walk through fields which have thorns and briers.

"Thorn in the flesh" is an Eastern idiom which means "trouble," "annoyance," or "worry." It is often said "He is a thorn in my flesh," which means, "he bothers me or worries me."

Thorns and thistles are often spoken of allegorically, referring to hardships and enemies. "Thorns also and thistles shall it bring forth to thee" (Gen. 3 : 18). "And there shall be no more a pricking brier unto the house of Israel, nor any grieving thorn of all that are round about them, that despised them; and they shall know that I am the Lord God" (Ezek. 28 : 24).

The thorn in Paul's flesh was the attack which was made against his apostleship. Many people rejected his claim to apostleship on the ground that he had not been with Jesus (I Cor. 9 : 1–3). The title "apostle" was given only to those who had actually seen Jesus and been with him. Paul's enemies tried to belittle his work and attacked his apostleship. These attacks and doubts annoyed him. They were like a thorn in his flesh. Some simple Christians were easily misled and turned against him.

"The messenger of Satan" refers to the false teachers who attacked him.

Paul was not sick, as some commentators think. Indeed, Paul was strong and far from suffering any bodily ailment. He was beaten and stoned. When the ship on which he was sailing as a prisoner went down, Paul not only saved his own life but also helped the others. Indeed, Paul was far from being sick. When he speaks of his infirmities as weakness, he means weakness as a preacher or Christian. Easterners always speak of themselves as being weak and miserable sinners. (See Gal. 4 : 13.) Paul knew that his claim to the apostleship was doubted by some.

PAUL'S APOSTLESHIP

I am become a fool in glorying; ye have compelled me: for I ought to have been commended of you: for in nothing am I behind the very chiefest apostles, though I be nothing.
II Cor. 12 : 11.

Paul's apostleship was questioned by his enemies and rivals. Before his conversion to Christianity, he had been a persecutor of the Church. After his dramatic experience on his way to Damascus, he was healed and baptized by Ananias, a Christian convert at Damascus. But the Christians for some time doubted his sincerity, and feared him. But Paul proved his loyalty to Jesus Christ by his hard work and ceaseless effort to persuade the Jews to accept Jesus as the Messiah. In preaching and healing he was equal to other apostles, but the Christians in Judea disputed his claims to apostleship on the ground that he had not been with Jesus and therefore could not have been a witness to his resurrection. This attack was like a thorn in Paul's flesh.

When a successor to Judas was to be chosen, the eleven apostles selected two men who had seen Jesus and been with him during his ministry. One of them, Matthias, was elected to fill the place left vacant by Judas of Iscariot (Acts 1 : 21–26).

The Gentiles in Macedonia, however, were not concerned about the position and rank which Paul held in Jerusalem. They looked upon him as their apostle. He had given them the gospel of Jesus Christ and endangered his life on their behalf. Nevertheless, Paul always obeyed his superiors, James and Peter. He was sent by them as a missionary to Antioch and on one occasion he was admonished by James. But Paul always fought for the equal rights of the Gentile Christians.

HUMAN WEAKNESS

For though he was crucified through weakness, yet he liveth by the power of God. For we also are weak in him, but we shall live with him by the power of God toward you. II Cor. 13 : 4.

"Crucified through weakness," means crucified in the flesh. What the apostle really means is that Jesus died as a man and not as God. Jesus was tempted, like all of us, but he overcame every temptation. His body was weak, like ours, but he had entrusted it to the Spirit. "And being found in fashion as a man, he humbled himself, and became obedient unto death, even the death on the cross" (Phil. 2 : 8). Then again, Jesus was meek and humble. He did not resist those who crucified him, but he went to the cross like a sheep before the shearer. He had the power to deliver himself, but he did not use it. His spiritual purpose had to be fulfilled.

Jesus suffered and died on the cross as a man and not as God. God cannot be weakened nor can he suffer death. This doctrine is still held by the members of the ancient church of the East. There are, however, some people who believe that God died on the cross. Had God died, no one could have raised him. Jesus lived through the power of God. ". . . Being put to death in the flesh, but quickened by the Spirit" (I Pet. 3 : 18).

The apostles also tried to act and live like their Lord. They were tempted, but they overcame the temptations and trials. They were despised, rejected, and persecuted because of their teaching. But they were powerful in the gospel which they had preached. The Spirit inspired them to teach and preach, protected them from danger, and made their work manifest throughout the world. They had sacrificed their earthly life for something more powerful and enduring.

We are also weak in the flesh, but strong in the spirit. We will suffer death, but we shall live with him through the power of God, who is the origin of life and has power over death.

BE PERFECT

Finally, brethren, farewell. Be perfect, be of good comfort, be of one mind, live in peace; and the God of love and peace shall be with you.   II Cor. 13 : 11.

The Aramaic word *ethigmaro* means "to be complete," or "to attain perfection." An artist who is well versed in his occupation is called *gmera*.

Paul admonishes the Corinthian Christians to attain the highest possible Christian character, both in words and in deeds. He does not want to see them fall short of their Christian ideals when he visits them again.

No one but God is perfect, but through the gospel of Jesus Christ we can strive to attain Christian qualities, which are love, charity, forgiveness and meekness. (See *Gospel Light,* on Matt. 5 : 48, p. 43.)

GALATIANS

INTRODUCTION

This letter was written by Paul from Rome, probably about A.D. 60 to 65. The epistle is one of the pastoral letters, addressed to the churches in Galatia and sent by Tychicus. In this epistle Paul warns the Christians in Galatia to beware of the new teachings and doctrines which were contrary to those which he had given them. Many of the converts had left the churches and returned to their former religions. Paul also speaks of his conversion to Christianity, his former zeal for the religion of his forefathers, and his journey to Arabia and later to Jerusalem. He tries to impress on the Jewish Christians in Galatia that what he had taught them was revealed to him by Jesus Christ, and that anything which differed from it was contrary to it. The epistle as a whole deals with the truth of Jesus Christ. The church is the body of Christ.

The Christians are to be justified by faith; salvation of man is by the grace of God, through the gospel of Jesus Christ and sanctification by the Holy Spirit. The Jewish legalistic codes, traditions of the elders, and the ordinances were a thing of the past. They had served their purpose. The Christians are to live up to the new gospel which was delivered to them by the apostle.

PAUL A STUDENT OF CHRISTIANITY

For I neither received it of man, neither was I taught it, but by the revelation of Jesus Christ. Gal. 1 : 12.

In the East, converts to any faith are taught the doctrines, the laws and the ordinances of the religion which they embrace. Differences in faith are also explained. The new convert, by word of mouth or Scriptures, has to be made acquainted with the religion which he adopts. Young men, after studying their Bibles at home, attend theological schools where they are trained to become ministers and missionaries.

Paul, prior to his conversion, had no knowledge of the teachings of Jesus. For some time he was engaged in persecuting the followers of Jesus. But after his conversion he obtained the teachings of Jesus in writing. Paul needed no teacher; he was a brilliant student and well versed in the Old Testament. Paul was ready for the gospel of Christ; his mind was prepared for it and his inner understanding of the Old Testament helped him to hear Jesus converse with him. That is why he says: "The gospel which was preached of me is not after man." That is to say, Paul was not trained under the guidance of Christian theologians. Therefore he was free from complicated theological arguments. His mind was open to the new gospel, for which he was searching. His teachings were at firsthand, from the original Scriptures which he possessed. (See II Tim. 4 : 13.)

He studied in Arabia (Gal. 1 : 17) and later returned to Damascus and Jerusalem. Paul was called by God to preach among the Gentiles (Gal. 1 : 15).

PAUL'S DESTINY

But when it pleased God, who separated me from my mother's womb, and called me by his grace, Gal. 1 : 15.

In the East, boys are dedicated to God's work before they are born, just as they were in olden times. Their mothers make a vow and pledge the prospective male child to the service of God. Samuel was given to God before his birth. His mother pledged him to be reared in the temple at Shiloh. When Samson was conceived, his mother was told by the angel of the Lord to bring him up as a Nazarite. "For the child shall be a Nazarite to God from the womb to the day of his death" (Judges 13 : 7). Jeremiah likewise was chosen before his birth. "Before I formed thee in the belly I knew thee; and before thou camest forth out of the womb I sanctified thee, and I ordained thee a prophet unto the nations (Jeremiah 1 : 5).

Paul was called and separated by God to serve the church of his forefathers. At the outset, he was trained in Judaism and its mysteries. Later he learned the truth of the gospel of Jesus Christ. Paul was destined to be one of the first apostles to the Gentiles. Before this time, there had been some Gentiles, especially Syrians and Assyrians, in the Christian church. Nevertheless, Paul was responsible for the recognition of the Gentiles, their equality with the Jews, and especially the work in Greece and Italy. Like Jeremiah, he had been called from the time of his birth.

God knows what is in men's hearts before they are formed. He calls and sanctifies men from the time of their birth.

PAUL IN THE DESERT

Neither went I up to Jerusalem to them which were apostles before me; but I went into Arabia, and returned again unto Damascus.　　　　　　　　　　Gal. 1 : 17.

The Arabian Desert has been a place of retreat and inspiration to many prophets and men of God who dedicated themselves to work for the kingdom of God. This region is uninhabited, with the exception of a few tribes always roaming in search of grazing land for their flocks. Arabia is not all desert, for it is inhabited by several million Nomad tribes. In some areas numerous small settlements are to be found, particularly at the edges of the desert and near Mesopotamia.

The Arabian Desert is a wonderful place for meditation and learning, especially for those who are interested in the deeper things of life. The sky is blue at night, decorated with myriads of stars, and the glory of God and the works of his hands are generously manifested. The heaven looks like a crown adorned with costly jewels. When one contrasts this glory and majesty with the barren land he can understand why "the heavens declare the glory of God" to people in the East.

The Arabs live in tents made of the hair of goats. The land, even though destitute of trees and many things with which other lands are blessed, is romantic and inspiring. The Arabs in the past had no schools and institutions of learning. Their knowledge is derived from the study of nature and is handed down from one generation to another. Arabia produced many learned men and philosophers. The Arabs have been responsible for many inventions. It was they who introduced philosophy and science into Spain.

Abraham spent many years wandering in this land and communing with God, who constantly guided and directed him. Moses spent forty years in Arabia as a shepherd. David was born in Hebron, a town at the foot of the mountains of Judea, not far from the desert. He fed sheep at the edge of the desert. Elijah spent several years in this mysterious land. Both John and Jesus went to the desert for prayer and meditation. Nearly all great Semitic religions were conceived in the desert.

Paul went to the Arabian Desert to think things over. He had to examine the Scriptures with a new light. God had called him for a great mission. In the past, Christianity had been contrary to Paul's belief in God. He went into the desert to make a thorough study of the new religion which he had embraced, to divest himself of all Jewish mysteries and teachings, and to learn the things anew. In this silent land Paul studied the gospel of Jesus and became the greatest missionary of all time.

In silence and solitude, when Nature sleeps, one can hear the voice of God and converse with him. The noise of this world often drowns God's voice, and obscures our visions.

BROTHER OF JESUS

But other of the apostles saw I none, save James the Lord's brother. Gal. 1 : 19.

This James should not be confused with James the son of Zebedee, or James the son of Alphaeus (Mark 3 : 18; Luke 6 : 15; Acts 1 : 13). He is a brother of Jesus. The Gospels make mention of Jesus' brothers as James, Joses, Judas and Simon (Matt. 13 : 55; Mark 6 : 3).

Jesus' brothers joined the Christian movement after the resurrection. Prior to Jesus' death, they showed some resentment against the new teaching. But after the resurrection they were found among Jesus' disciples in the upper room in Jerusalem (Acts 1 : 14). James, the brother of our Lord, seems to have succeeded James the apostle, brother of John, who was put to death by Herod Agrippa I. James, Simon Peter (Cephas) and John were considered the pillars of the Church (Gal. 2 : 9).

PAUL DETERMINED

And I went up by revelation, and communicated unto them that gospel which I preach among the Gentiles, but privately to them which were of reputation, lest by any means I should run, or had run, in vain.

But neither Titus, who was with me, being a Greek, was compelled to be circumcised: Gal. 2 : 2–3.

Gilyana, "revelation," comes from the root *gla*, "to reveal" or "uncover." *Gilyana* is a noun. Pentecost is called the Feast of Gilyana. This word seldom is used in other places to denote a vision or warning. *Khizva*, "vision," is the word frequently used in such cases. We often read the "angel of the Lord appeared unto him in a dream (*khizva*)." (Compare Matt. 1 : 20.)

Probably Paul means here that he went up to the Feast of Pentecost. On that occasion many people go up to Jerusalem. Friends and enemies meet there, and feuds and quarrels are settled. Paul was warned not to go to Jerusalem because of the agitation against him. Many of his enemies from Asia Minor were also attending the feast. But Paul had vowed to be in Jerusalem at that particular feast. It was at the feast that Paul was arrested, put in prison, and finally sent to Rome.

Paul, despite the warnings, placed his life in the hands of God and went openly to Jerusalem to the Feast of Pentecost. He was not afraid of his enemies, nor was he afraid to die (Acts 21 : 10–15). While in Jerusalem, he called on the apostles and attended the feast, where he was arrested and imprisoned (Acts 21 : 17–34).

MEMBERS OF CIRCUMCISION

For he that wrought effectually in Peter to the apostleship of the circumcision, the same was mighty in me toward the Gentiles: Gal. 2 : 8.

Members of various sects in the East are known by their peculiar beliefs and practices. Those who believe in the teaching of John the Baptist are called Baptists, because they practice baptism. (A small group of the followers of St. John are found in Mesopotamia. They baptize more than once. They also baptize sheep and cattle before they kill them.)

"They of the circumcision" in this case means the Jewish Christians. This term is used to distinguish between the converts from Judaism and those from heathenism. Peter was the apostle to the people who were brought up according to the Hebrew customs and the Mosaic law. Peter and other apostles were instructed by their Lord to go to no one but "to the lost sheep of the house of Israel" (Matt. 10 : 6). Jesus at first refused to heal the daughter of a Syrian woman who sought his help. He said, "I am not sent but unto the lost sheep of the house of Israel" (Matt. 15 : 24). Paul himself for a long time continued to preach among the Jews, trying to win them to Christ. When he found he was unable to do this and Jewish opposition was becoming strong, he started to preach among the Gentiles (Acts 18 : 6).

Indeed, the work among the Galileans, the Jews of Judea, and the members of the Ten Tribes who were scattered in Mesopotamia, was to come first. Judaism was the depository of God's truth. God's revelation was to be manifested to the Gentiles through members of the Jewish faith. They had the knowledge of God and his commandments. They were the first to be invited to become partakers of the kingdom of God.

Paul himself was a strong upholder of the Jewish faith and a teacher of the law and the traditions of the elders. He gave up Judaism for Christianity, and became an agent through whom the new dispensation was given to the Gentiles in the Roman Empire. Just as Peter was called to preach and minister to the people of the Semitic race and cultural background, so Paul was prepared for the work among the Gentiles in Europe. That is why Paul is known as the apostle to the Gentiles. At times there were clashes between Peter and Paul over the Gentile question. Peter, Barnabas and other Jewish Christians demanded that the Gentiles should keep some of the Jewish ordinances and live like the Jews. But Paul fought for the Gentiles until he freed them from the Jewish customs and traditions of the elders.

LEADERSHIP

And when James, Cephas, and John, who seemed to be pillars, perceived the grace that was given unto me, they gave to me and Barnabas the right hands of fellowship; that we should go unto the heathen, and they unto the circumcision.   Gal. 2 : 9.

After the death of Jesus, James the brother of our Lord, and Peter and John were looked upon as the leaders of the Church. Jesus had warned his disciples against any temptation to seek political leadership. He had told them that the greatest among them must be their servant. He gave them an example by the washing of their feet (John 13 : 5).

These three apostles were far from being political leaders. They gave counsel in spiritual matters and in problems pertaining to faith and Christian conduct. They sent an epistle to the Christians in Antioch, warning them of unnecessary disputes, and told them to abstain from eating blood (Acts 15 : 22–29). They wrote pastoral letters to churches and sent out missionaries to preach the gospel.

James the brother of John was killed by Herod (Acts 12 : 2). It seems that James the brother of our Lord was more highly respected than the apostles. This may have been due to his relation to Jesus, rather than to his rank.

In the East, brothers and relatives of holy men are greatly revered. James the son of Zebedee was one of the closest disciples of Jesus. He might have been taken for the leader of the Christians. Probably that was the reason for his murder.

Paul took orders from James, the brother of our Lord (Acts 21 : 18–26). Then again, from Paul's epistle to the Galatians we see that James was feared and respected more than the other apostles. "But when Peter was come to Antioch, I withstood him to the face, because he was to be blamed. For before that certain came from James, he did eat with the Gentiles; but when they were come, he withdrew and separated himself, fearing them which were of the circumcision" (Gal. 2 : 11–12). Paul also mentions that the brothers of our Lord were married (I Cor. 9 : 5). Nevertheless, the apostles and their followers for many years were in one accord and worked in harmony, with no thought of political leadership or material gains. Both Peter and James were looked upon as the leaders and consulted on matters of faith. Their whole aim in life was the spread of the gospel which Jesus had entrusted to them. And because of this gospel their lives were always in danger. According to Josephus, James the brother of our Lord was murdered during the governorship of Festus.

The church of Christ needs spiritual leadership and overseers. The kingdom of Christ is not the kingdom of this world, but the kingdom of God. The apostles and ministers of the gospel were the princes of the realm of heaven. The church is the depository of God's truth. This truth must be guarded, explained and published by the ministers of Christ.

INFLUENCE OF CUSTOMS

But when I saw that they walked not uprightly according to the truth of the gospel, I said unto Peter before them all, If thou, being a Jew, livest after the manner of Gentiles, and not as do the Jews, why compellest thou the Gentiles to live as do the Jews? Gal. 2 : 14.

The customs and manners of the countries in which prophets and religious leaders were born have always played a dominant part in their teachings, and at times have even obscured their messages. For example, the races which embraced Islam adopt, to some extent, Arab customs. They refrain from eating pork and certain foods which Arabs do not eat, and abstain from wine and strong drinks. This is because Mohammed, the founder of Islam, was an Arab and his religion is based on Arabian customs and manners. Nevertheless, there are some people and races who resent such racial customs and refuse to accept them as an essential part of religion. The Turks, for example, drink wine and eat pork. They are also free from some of the superstitions and traditions which the Arabs and other races hold and observe.

Jesus was born in Palestine. He was reared according to the precepts of the Jewish faith. He obeyed the commandments of Moses and some of the other ordinances which were vital in the Jewish religion, but refused to accept the traditions of the elders, and certain customs which were peculiar to the Jewish people. On the other hand, he had no use for the complicated laws prescribing ceremonial washing of foods and of cups, pots and other household utensils (Mark 7 : 1–9). The Jews had certain dishes and utensils to be used for milk, and others for meat. This ancient custom is still observed by the Orthodox Jews. Jesus never told his disciples and followers not to circumcise, observe the Sabbath Day, pray in the Jewish Temple, and observe the Jewish feasts. Indeed, he was concerned with the vital truths of the Jewish faith.

Peter was a Galilean. He had been with Jesus for three years. He had seen that Jesus observed some of the Jewish customs and respected certain others. At the outset Peter had thought that these customs and practices were a part of the Christian gospel. Indeed, this was the belief of many Jews who had embraced the Christian faith. But later he was told that such practices were not essential (Acts 10 : 9-35).

SALVATION BY GRACE

Knowing that a man is not justified by the works of the law, but by the faith of Jesus Christ, even we have believed in Jesus Christ, that we might be justified by the faith of Christ, and not by the works of the law: for by the works of the law shall no flesh be justified.
But if, while we seek to be justified by Christ, we ourselves also are found sinners, is therefore Christ the minister of sin? God forbid. Gal 2 : 16-17.

According to the old dispensation, justification and salvation were to be attained through the works of the law. Every statute of the law had to be carefully observed; the breaking of one of them was regarded as the breaking of the whole law. This is why the Jews wrote commentary after commentary trying to explain the law and its precepts. Moses, the lawgiver, demanded strict observance of the law. He says, "Cursed be he that confirmeth not all the words of this law to do them" (Deut. 27 : 26).

The Mosaic law, like the law of the Medes and Persians, could not be altered. There was no forgiveness in it. Those who violated it were put to death. Even if a man was found picking grass of the field for fuel on the Sabbath Day, he was stoned. Indeed, the Jews tried hard to live up to the law, they sacrificed and even died for its sake. Yet no one was ever able to fulfill it. This is not all. Every law was saddled with many ordinances and conflicting interpretations on which the authorities were unable to agree. Consequently, the observance of the law was not only difficult but impossible.

On the other hand, the law and the traditions of the

elders took the place of the original law which had been revealed to Moses. This is also true of the Christian law; doctrines and traditions are more emphasized than the commands of Jesus.

Jesus saw this, and therefore ignored the interpretations of the law and the traditions of the elders, not so much that he was against the law, but because these interpretations were too far-fetched and complicated and, in most cases, alien to the spirit of the original law. This is true of all other laws and teachings which, sooner or later, became obscure or conflicting.

Had the Jewish elders and rabbis remained loyal to the teaching of the Hebrew prophet, in their interpretations of the law, there would have been no conflict between them and Jesus.

Paul here rebukes Peter and Barnabas for upholding Jewish customs which he thought were unnecessary. The Galatians were to be saved by the grace of God through faith in Christ, and not through the law. If their salvation was to be obtained by the observance of the Jewish law, then there was no need for the coming of Christ and the new dispensation of grace. Paul puts the Jewish Christians on the spot. They had to choose between the two things: the gospel of Jesus Christ or the old traditions.

When we uphold what Jesus rejected, we then deny that our salvation is by the grace of God, and the death of Jesus. Paul puts it this way: "For if I build again the things which I destroy, I make myself a transgressor." That is to say, if we try to uphold the things which gave way to the law of Christ, we become transgressors of the law of Christ, for by doing so we prove that these laws were valid, and that Jesus was wrong in denouncing them. Therefore, salvation is by the grace of God and the death of Jesus Christ.

FOOLISH GALATIANS

O foolish Galatians, who hath bewitched you, that ye should not obey the truth, before whose eyes Jesus Christ hath been evidently set forth, crucified among you?
Gal. 3 : 1.

The Eastern text reads: "O foolish Galatians, who has envied you?" The Aramaic word *khesam,* "to envy," has been confused with *kesam,* "to bewitch." These two words are very similar and are pronounced almost alike. This saying is characteristic of the Eastern speech, but it cannot be translated into English without loss of meaning. Rival persons use every conceivable method to bewitch or beguile one another. Just like the serpent which beguiled Eve and induced her to break the law of God. The serpent (devil) was jealous of Adam and Eve.

Paul here is referring to the rival teachers who were weakening his work in Galatia. Those false teachers were jealous of Paul's successful work among the Galatians. They came to Galatia to stir up the Jewish converts, preaching obedience to the law and observance of the Jewish customs.

The Galatians, like other Christians in Asia Minor and Macedonia, were continually disturbed by the new teachers who came from Judea. The congregations here were largely made up of Jewish converts and some Gentiles. This made it easier for teachers from Judea to split them. They told the Jews that the observance of the Jewish traditions was essential to their salvation. On the other hand, the Jewish Christians, even though not being strict as their brethren in Judea, were brought under the Jewish laws, and accustomed to the Jewish rituals and other ordinances.

The teachers succeeded in fooling and undermining the Galatians, just as they had done at Colosse and other places. Paul had given them the true teaching of the gospel and told them that Jesus had died for them, and therefore that they were no longer under the law, but under the grace of God. Thus, there was no need to seek protection under the law, but they were to edify themselves by means of the gospel of Christ. Paul upbraids them for going backward instead of forward. He had proved to them the strength of the Christian gospel through miracles and wonders which he had done when working among them. Certainly these works were not the result of Paul's faith in the Jewish traditions, but of his conversion to the gospel of the new dispensation, which is salvation through Jesus Christ.

HEATHENS JUSTIFIED THROUGH FAITH

And the scripture, foreseeing that God would justify the heathen through faith, preached before the gospel unto Abraham, saying, In thee shall all nations be blessed.
Gal. 3 : 8.

The reference here is to God's promise which he made to Abraham when he called him from the land of the Chaldeans and told him to go to the land which he was going to show him. ". . . And in thee shall all families of the earth be blessed" (Gen. 12 : 3). Abraham was blessed through his faith in God.

Moses was born centuries after, and the law was written at a time when the descendants of Abraham had multiplied and become a great people. Therefore, Abraham was not saved or justified by means of the law, but by his trust in the word of God.

At the time of his calling, Abraham was a Gentile and not a Jew. Wherefore, he was not under the law, which came 430 years after. The law was given for several reasons. First, the people did not adhere to the faith of Abraham. Second, the Hebrew people were living under new circumstances and a new order. At the time of Abraham, sin was dormant. It came only as the result of transgression of the law. On the other hand, some laws and ordinances were the result of customs and tribal life; therefore they were temporal and changeable. But the true law, that which is contained in the Ten Commandments, is eternal and in due time was to be revealed and explained fully by Jesus Christ. Jesus came not to destroy the law but to fulfill it.

The Gentiles were called through their faith in Jesus Christ, and therefore there was no need to be under the ordinances of the Jewish law. They were blessed by their faith, just as Abraham was blessed because of his trust in God.

SALVATION

Christ hath redeemed us from the curse of the law, being made a curse for us: for it is written, Cursed is every one that hangeth on a tree: Gal. 3 : 13.

The Aramaic word *porkana* means "salvation" or "deliverance." Thus *porkana* does not literally mean deliverance by means of ransom, but by self-sacrifice and the power of God, the supreme ruler of the universe. Moses delivered his people from the Egyptian yoke, not by the payment of a price, but through much suffering, wisdom and mighty works. On the other hand, the Hebrews took considerable silver, gold and garments from the Egyptians.

Jesus wrought salvation by means of his suffering and death. Jesus, through his death, revealed the truth and thus set men free from the power of evil forces. "And ye shall know the truth, and the truth shall make you free" (John 8 : 32). Jesus died for the truth which he taught.

Thus the term "redemption" does not agree with the Aramaic word *porkana*, "salvation." In Aramaic, an habitual sinner is called a servant or a slave of sin. Men were enslaved to sin, and Jesus, through his teaching and death, freed them. Men saved others from danger by risking their lives.

Sin was the result of transgressions of the law, and offerings were the means by which men sought forgiveness. Jesus gave his life in order to direct us into the true path of life and reveal God's abundant love for us. Jesus gave up all the comforts of this life in order to rescue us from danger and evil.

LAW

In olden days it was conceded by Hebrew theologians that no man can be justified by the law in the sight of God. This is because it was difficult to keep all the laws and ordinances which were founded on the law. Not even prophets and high priests could live up to the law and observe all of its statutes. One may succeed in overcoming the temptation of stealing his neighbor's ox, but he still might covet it. The people overcame the temptation of killing, but they were unable to control their hatred and desire to kill. "Ye have heard that it was said by them of old time, Thou shalt not kill; and whosoever shall kill shall be in danger of the judgment: but I say unto you . . ." (Matt. 5 : 21–22). Jesus himself was looked upon by the Jews as a lawbreaker, simply because he and his disciples when hungry had plucked a few ears of wheat on a Sabbath Day (Mark 2 : 23–24). On other occasions they found fault with them for not fasting and washing their hands before meals.

Thus there was no salvation by means of the law. The commandments were buried under theological interpretations, and therefore the law had become difficult and complicated. Jesus freed us from the curse of the law, so that we might receive the grace of God through faith, and that the promises which God had made to Abraham might be bestowed on the Gentiles also. The law had become a Jewish institution and therefore non-effective. Jesus abolished the sin which came into existence because of the law. Before the law, sin was dead. The law gave it power. But Jesus, through his death on the cross, destroyed the power of sin and gave death a new meaning.

Jesus Christ, the righteous, died the death of a sinner

and was looked upon as accursed of God. Thus his death removed the curse and freed men from the law. Under the law even the righteous were put to death. According to the old law, there was no forgiveness, but the new law, under Jesus Christ, provides forgiveness and salvation from sin and death.

FAITH BEFORE LAW

But before faith came, we were kept under the law, shut up unto the faith which should afterwards be revealed.
Wherefore the law was our schoolmaster to bring us unto Christ, that we might be justified by faith.
Gal. 3 : 23–24.

Philosophers and wise men in the East have always emphasized the power which faith works in man. In countries where people live from day to day, faith in God is essential. Once a Chinese philosopher was asked, "What are the main forces which sustain a government?" His reply was, "An army, food, and faith." Then he was asked which two he considered most necessary, and he said he could do without an army, but that he must have bread and faith. Finally, he was asked which he considered the better of these two? To this the venerable sage replied that he would rather be without bread, for people can live without food for a long time and still exist, but no society or state can exist, once the people have lost faith in it.

Justification by faith existed before Christ, and it is the theme of most religions. Nevertheless, in ancient days, people did not understand the inner meaning of life as we do today, nor did they face the complicated social and economic problems which we confront today. Abraham was justified by faith and declared righteous. He was living at a time when there was no written law and no organized priesthood, but he understood the power of faith and trusted God's word. Melchisedec also was a servant of God. He, like Abraham, was not under the law. That came later. He was known as the priest of the Most High God and a righteous man.

Had the Hebrew people served God faithfully as their forefathers, Abraham and Isaac, did, there would have been no need for the law. Law came because of necessity. The Hebrews, after the patriarchal days, lost most of their spirituality, and became victims of corrupt practices which they learned in Egypt. Hitherto they had been simple people engaged in pastoral life, but now they were learning the ways of a country where the strong devoured the weak and where greed and material things dominated. Abraham was free from all this.

The law was revealed as a medium to guard and preserve some of the sacred things which still survived. These were the Messianic promises which God had made to Abraham. In other words, the law was to be a guardian and pathfinder until the coming of Christ, who was to reveal justification by the grace of God.

If the people had not transgressed the law they would not have been subject to the law and its ordinances. Paul, in his epistle to Timothy, says that the law is not made for the righteous man, but for the lawless and disobedient, for sinners and murderers (I Timothy 1 : 9).

When people respect and obey state laws, they live in a free and larger world and need not fear the authorities who are over them. Only those who disobey the law are in fear of the law and afraid of the authorities. This is also true of the law of God; as long as people live a Christian life and respect the rights of their neighbors, they are free from the law. When laws are not broken, there is no sin and no need for punishment.

SYRIANS

There is neither Jew nor Greek, there is neither bond nor free, there is neither male nor female: for ye are all one in Christ Jesus.   Gal. 3 : 28.

The Eastern text reads: "There is neither Jew nor Aramean, there is neither slave nor free, . . ." The Greek translators, for some unknown reason, changed the word "Arameans" to "Greeks," in many parts of the New Testament. The Aramaic word for Greeks is *"Yonaye."* The word used here is *Aramaye;* that is, Syrians, who lived in Syria, close to Palestine. Many of these people had intermarried with the Jews. When the latter returned from Babylonian captivity, Ezra and Nehemiah denounced these marriages and demanded the people to leave their foreign wives; some of them did, but others were unable to comply with the order. On the other hand, the Syrians were close to the Jews in racial ties, customs and religion. They were of the same stock as the early Hebrews, and their language and culture were the same.

LAW AS A GUARDIAN

Now I say, That the heir, as long as he is a child, differeth nothing from a servant, though he be lord of all;   Gal. 4 : 1.

In the East, the children of overlords and wealthy parents are brought up by servants. Then again, where polygamy is still dominant, children of princes and noblemen are entrusted to the care of officials, servants and rich families, to be brought up. King Ahab had seventy sons who were in the care of noblemen (II Kings 10 : 1). Some people place their children under the guardianship of their faithful servants for training and discipline. At times it is difficult to recognize them from the children of the servants. They dress alike, eat with the servants, and are assigned to manual labor by their guardians. Not until they reach the age of maturity are they recognized as heirs.

Paul argues that we likewise once were under the care of a guardian, that is, the law; but in the fullness of time we were freed by Jesus Christ. Therefore, we are no longer under the guardianship of priests and the law, but under the grace of God and faith in Jesus Christ.

BACKWARD

Ye did run well; who did hinder you that ye should not obey the truth?
This persuasion cometh *not of him that calleth you.*
A little leaven leaveneth the whole lump. Gal. 5 : 7-9.

Paul was always followed by enemies who created disturbances in the churches where he had preached. The Galatian Christians were so misled by the new teachers who had followed in the footsteps of Paul that some of them wavered.

Paul strongly warns them not to go backward but to continue in the new faith which he had given to them. The traditions and Jewish customs were a mere shadow and a thing of the past. Therefore, going backward was the same as stepping from the freedom of Jesus Christ into bondage. This is because, under the old law, all men were in bondage and in fear of sin. The observance of the law was so complicated that no one could comply with it and be declared righteous.

The Galatians were free from these antiquated ordinances and the sins which resulted from the breaking thereof. There was no need to burden themselves with the doctrines which brought no comfort or consolation. They were saved by the grace of God.

The faith of the Galatians was weakened to some extent, but Paul had confidence that the leaven of true Christian teaching remained pure, and that in due time it would strengthen their faith in the gospel of Jesus Christ, and in the pure teaching which he had imparted to them on his previous visits.

NOT UNDER THE LAW

But if ye be led of the Spirit, ye are not under the law.
Gal. 5 : 18.

Laws are generally enacted as the result of crimes and injustices. Where few crimes are committed, laws and ordinances are so few that the people know them by heart. Some of the laws are the result of transgressions against certain established customs and traditions. On the other hand, laws change from time to time; there are things that are unlawful today but which may become lawful tomorrow.

When human conduct rises above material things, the law then will become inoperative. For instance, there are no laws against hospitality, honesty and kindness. Therefore, if we walk in the footsteps of Christ, we are free from the law of man, because we are free from sin.

When the truth was revealed by Jesus Christ, the power of sin over men was destroyed. The law, which came because of human transgression, was repealed and those who live in Jesus Christ are restored to their former selves and made heirs of the kingdom of God. The law, therefore, has power only over those who live under sin and grope in darkness. Those who walk in the light of Jesus Christ need not stumble.

BEARING HIS OWN BURDEN

For every man shall bear his own burden.
Let him that is taught in the word communicate unto him that teacheth in all good things.   Gal. 6 : 5–6.

In the East, articles are often carried on the backs of men and women. Men generally bear burdens of wheat, grass and heavy stones for building; while women take care of the home supplies and carry food, fuel and water. Even little boys and girls do their part and bear their burdens. Everyone has a burden to carry.

During a migration or a caravan journey, when a person is seized with sickness, his burden is carried by others. They thus help him to reach his destination. At times a party of men or a caravan may wait until the sick person is better; otherwise they must carry him with them, bearing his burden.

On the other hand, where people are oppressed and justice is lacking, the stronger men lay their burdens on the weak. One may see in a caravan, certain men of nobility or power walking idly, while their burdens are carried by others. At times a poor man is compelled to carry two or three burdens, one upon another.

Paul admonishes the Galatian Christians to carry their own burdens (that is, not to oppress the poor) and to give a helping hand to the weak.

"Burden" here does not necessarily mean a physical burden; it may be a mental burden—worries and cares.

At times certain people burden others with their problems, not realizing that they also have their burdens to bear. On some occasions a Christian sees another Christian bent under a heavy burden, but, like a Pharisee, he passes by, failing to give a helping hand.

SELECTING OF SEEDS

Be not deceived; God is not mocked: for whatsoever a man soweth, that shall he also reap. Gal. 6 : 7.

"You will reap what you sow" is an old Eastern saying, which means that you will get what is due you. Easterners believe in the law of compensation. That is, a man reaps just what he has sown. The origin of this saying, however, is in the manner of sowing and selecting the seeds.

Before the sowing is done, the farmers determine the kind of seeds which will grow best in certain soil, and the amount of seed which can be spared for the purpose. Thus the seeds are carefully selected. Some farmers, not having a knowledge of the properties which the soil contains, use any kind of seeds, with the result that they reap less. On the other hand, some, because of the lack of seed, sow sparingly, while others sow abundantly. When the harvest comes, the husbandmen are rewarded accordingly. The produce of two fields of the same size and the same soil, may vary to a great degree. Moreover, when seed is bad, the harvest is very poor. Job says, "They that . . . sow wickedness, reap the same" (Job 4 : 8). ". . . But to him that soweth righteousness shall be a sure reward" (Prov. 11 : 18).

Paul wanted the Galatians to be careful about the teachings and spiritual truths which he had entrusted to them; and not to be so concerned over the ordinances and Jewish traditions. He warned them that they must be careful about the seeds which they were sowing, for bad seeds would result in strife and divisions.

The truths of Jesus Christ are the good seed which, when it falls on good ground, produces abundantly; but the seeds of traditions and false doctrines are like tares, which hamper the growth and spread of the Christian gospel. Therefore Christians should be mindful of the true teachings. These are not to be confused with the traditions of men, and the doctrines which are contrary to the gospel of Christ.

EPHESIANS

INTRODUCTION

The author of the epistle is Paul. The epistle was written from Rome during Paul's imprisonment, about A.D. 65, and was sent by Tychicus. Similar epistles were addressed to other churches in Asia Minor and Greece. The purpose of these epistles was to strengthen the bereaved congregations and to inform them about his imprisonment and suffering for the sake of the gospel which he had preached to them.

The Christians in Ephesus are addressed as saints. The first part of the epistle is greeting and thanksgiving for being called into the service of Christ, and exhortations. The Ephesians are well commended for their faith in the Lord Jesus and their love for other Christians. Paul, in this epistle, speaks of the greatness and power of Christ and his dominion over all things. He also reminds the Ephesians of their past, when they lived in darkness, compared with their present life under the gospel of Christ.

As in his other epistles, Paul emphasizes salvation by the grace of God. The Christians are saved through grace and not by works. They are brought close to God through the sacrifice of Jesus Christ. Paul reminds the Gentiles that they have been made fellow heirs and partakers in the promise (covenant), through the gospel of Christ. The Christians in Ephesus were mostly of Jewish origin. There were a great many Gentiles too. Paul spoke at the synagogue and confirmed the faith of the followers of John the Baptist by the laying on of hands (Acts 19 : 1–8). He warns the Ephesians against false teachers and false doctrines.

The epistle contains admonitions relative to Christian conduct. Paul instructs wives to be loyal to their husbands and to love and revere one another as Christ loves the Church. The tone of the epistle shows the closeness of Paul to the Ephesians and their loyalty to him.

EPHESUS

Ephesus was an ancient city in Asia Minor; built about 700 B.C. It was conquered by the Persians in the fourth century B.C. Later the city came under Syrian rule. In the first century B.C. Ephesus was occupied by the Romans.

During the time of St. Paul, Ephesus was the chief city in Asia Minor and the seat of the Roman governor-general. Then again, Ephesus was the center of pagan worship and the See of the Goddess Artemis (Acts 17 : 26–29).

Christianity was introduced in Ephesus by the Jewish Christians. The church for some time was under the leadership of Apollo (I Cor. 1 : 12). He was converted to Christianity by Aquila and Priscilla. Paul visited Ephesus and taught there for some time (Acts 19 : 9).

This epistle was written from Rome in A.D. 63. It was brought to Ephesus by Tychicus. Paul was a prisoner in Rome (Eph. 4 : 1).

The epistle seems to be addressed as a pastoral letter to Christians in the province of Ephesus and not to a particular congregation. This region was evangelized very early. Paul visited the converts on one of his missionary journeys through Asia Minor, and the converts from Ephesus spread the gospel in other adjoining towns. The epistle therefore is addressed to all the converts of this region, of which Ephesus is the chief city.

MARKED

Having predestinated us unto the adoption of children by Jesus Christ to himself, according to the good pleasure of his will,   Eph. 1:5.

The Aramaic word *rashman* means "he had marked us," that is, "set us aside" or "chosen us."

Lambs and calves when given to God are marked on the ears; *Nazarites* likewise are identified by their long hair. This serves as a mark of their consecration to God.

What Paul means here is that God from the very beginning provided salvation for the Gentiles, and marked them to become his children by adoption through Jesus Christ. The Gentiles were destined to be called by God and made heirs of his kingdom.

This salvation is to be earned by faith and Christian works through the gospel which is available to all the people. Paul does not imply that only certain people were chosen, but speaks about the means by which God had made them his sons, through Christ, who was ordained by the foreknowledge of God from the very beginning. Some of the Jews in Ephesus were converted, and a great many Gentiles responded to their calling; others rejected Paul and even tried to kill him.

The determined purpose of God in this case is the salvation which he had provided through the death of Jesus. Therefore, the coming of Christ and his suffering were in accordance with the divine plan.

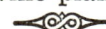

DIVINE MYSTERY

And to make all men see what is the fellowship of the mystery, which from the beginning of the world hath been hid in God, who created all things by Jesus Christ:
To the intent that now unto the principalities and powers in heavenly places might be known by the church the manifold wisdom of God, Eph. 3 : 9–10.

Since the time of the fall of man, God provided means by which evil forces would be destroyed and man restored to his original self. God said to Eve that her seed would bruise the head of the serpent (Satan) (Gen. 3 : 15). Ages later, God's plan of salvation was revealed to the Hebrew prophets who heralded the coming of the Messiah and predicted his rejection, suffering and death.

Paul reminds the Christians in Ephesus of God's promises to the human race, and the salvation and restoration which he wrought through Jesus Christ.

This is why Paul calls it, "The mystery of his will." God's plan remained as a mystery for many ages, to be revealed in the fullness of time through Christ. Salvation was to be offered to the Jews and Gentiles alike, and they were to be united through the baptism of the spirit. God from the very beginning has promised to call the Gentiles into his kingdom and provide for them a means of salvation. "I will call them my people who are not my people" (Hosea 2 : 23; Rom. 9 : 25).

PRISONER OF THE LORD

I therefore, the prisoner of the Lord, beseech you that ye walk worthy of the vocation wherewith ye are called,
Eph. 4 : 1.

"The prisoner of the Lord" means, "I am a prisoner on account of the Lord." In the East numbers are not used; prisoners are known by the charge which has been made against them and the crime which they have committed. In other words, a prisoner is known by his actions.

Paul was imprisoned on account of preaching Jesus Christ. This doctrine was prohibited by the Jewish high priests in Jerusalem. King Herod Agrippa I, took steps to bring to an end this teaching. Christianity was also contrary to Roman law and religion. Nevertheless Paul gloried in the fact that he was a prisoner in the Imperial City and a witness of Christ in the household of Caesar. In many of his epistles he mentions his sufferings and imprisonment for the gospel of Jesus Christ, not as a complaint, but as an opportunity to be a witness of his Lord.

Jesus had warned his disciples and followers of the hardships which they were to suffer for his gospel. He told them that they would be brought before judges, governors and kings for his sake (Matt. 10 : 18).

Paul was a prisoner for the sake of the gospel of Jesus. Being a learned man and a biblical authority, he was greatly feared both by the Jews and the pagans.

CAPTIVITY CAPTIVE

Wherefore he saith, When he ascended up on high, he led captivity captive, and gave gifts unto men.

Eph. 4 : 8.

He led captivity captive" is a mistranslation of an Aramaic idiom, *washwa shvita,* "he has carried away captives and gathered booty." In the East, when a man gives generous gifts to his servants or friends, they say, "He must have plundered a city," just as an American would say, "He must have robbed a bank." When a town or city is captured everything valuable is carried away, and the plunderers give away some of it as gifts to their friends.

Paul is quoting the book of Psalms from memory. The King James Version reads, "Thou hast led captivity captive: Thou hast received gifts for men; yea, for the rebellious also, that the Lord might dwell among them"

(Psa. 68 : 18). But the Eastern text reads, "Thou hast carried away captives: thou hast blessed men with gifts; but the rebellious men shall not dwell before the presence of God."

Jesus' resurrection from death and his ascension into heaven were so triumphant that he became the Lord of heaven and of earth. His great victory over the forces of evil made him the King of kings and the Lord of lords. He distributed rewards to his followers. "Gifts" here refer to gifts of the Holy Spirit which Jesus had promised to his followers. These promises were fulfilled on the day of Pentecost. "And they were filled with the Holy Ghost, and began to speak with other tongues, as the Spirit gave them utterance" (Acts 2 : 1–5).

Then again, the apostles were endowed with gifts of the ministry of healing, prophecy and preaching. (Compare verse 11.)

ANGER

Be ye angry, and sin not: let not the sun go down upon your wrath: Eph. 4 : 26.

Paul quotes from the book of Psalms. "Be angry and yet sin not: . . ." (Psa. 4 : 4, Eastern text).

One cannot avoid being angry when he is provoked, but he can control his anger. "Sin" in this case means "crime." When people are angry at one another, they often lose their tempers and wound or slay one another.

Easterners are easily provoked, but they become reconciled with each other soon. "Let not the sun go down upon your wrath" is an Eastern saying, which means, "forget your trouble as soon as you can." In another part of the scripture we read: "Put not thy servant away in anger" (Psa. 27 : 9). "For his anger endureth but a moment" (Psa. 30 : 5). "Cease from anger and wrath" (Psa. 37 : 8). "Anger rests in the bosom of fools" (Eccl. 7 : 9).

When angry we give room to the devil to operate on us, but when anger is controlled, the devil has no chance to work. Peace and harmony help to create better relations with our neighbors. When anger is overcome, peace and harmony are established again.

STEALING

Neither give place to the devil.
Let him that stole steal no more: but rather let him labour, working with his hands the thing which is good, that he may have to give to him that needeth.
Eph. 4 : 27–28.

Stealing goods from the homes of the people or market places is seldom practiced in the Near East. Pickpocketing and breaking into houses are seldom heard of in the Eastern countries. Such crimes are severely punished by cutting off the hand or nose of the guilty person. Therefore, the people are cautious and hesitate to take the chance. The reference here is to banditry and graft and not to petty crimes.

In the East many people make a living by robbing caravans and travelers on highways. In some regions this practice is not considered a crime, but is looked upon as an occupation. However, if the bandit should happen to be caught by the honest government authorities, he is severely punished. But in most cases, the bandits work together with the government officials or chiefs of the tribes. Some people believe that they have a divine right to raid, rob and oppress others. This is because there are certain regions in the Near East and especially Arabia, where men cannot earn their livelihood by any other means. Therefore, the rights of these people to prey on others have been recognized by certain governments at times. The officials of the government expect a portion of the graft or booty as their share.

Paul here refers to graft, extortion and bribery, which are considered a sin and strongly denounced by the prophets. He warns the Ephesian Christians against making a livelihood by ulterior means, which would expose their Christian conduct and make them a target of the unbelievers.

USELESS

Wherefore he saith, Awake thou that sleepest, and arise from the dead, and Christ shall give thee light. Eph. 5 : 14.

Wicked and corrupt men are often referred to as dead. Likewise men who become useless are looked upon as dead. When people refer to such men, they say, "He is dead," which means, "he does not count for much," or "he is useless." Such statements indeed are very common, and are understood.

The reference here is to those who were sleeping in darkness and drooping in ignorance. They were dead. The Gentiles had been sleeping for many centuries until they were awakened with the sound of the new gospel which heralded the truth and declared freedom and equality to all men throughout the world. God had not forgotten the Gentiles. He visited them in the fullness of time through Jesus Christ, and wakened them through his gospel.

We are in this world for a purpose. We are here to do good and to build on that which we have inherited from our forefathers. When we fail in this sacred duty and trust, we are dead and our lives become useless.

HUSBANDS

For the husband is the head of the wife, even as Christ is the head of the church: and he is the saviour of the body.
Eph. 5 : 23.

Invariably in the East, a husband is the head of his family. Women look to their husbands for advice, support and security. The husband is the bread-earner and the protector of his family. Women look after the children and household affairs, and cook, sew garments and do housework. They are not permitted to engage in business, teach or minister in spiritual work outside of the house.

On the other hand, the husband can buy, sell, and make business agreements without consulting his wife. In other words, in the East a husband is an overlord over his family and his servants. His word is law. Nevertheless there are cases where women have a better business judgment than their husbands. At times some women are discontent with the conduct and inefficiency of their husbands, especially when the latter are careless and extravagant. In such cases, some brave women take things in their own hands and try to admonish their husbands, which results in family quarrels.

This was more true of the women among the Gentiles; they had more freedom than women in Palestine, where ancient Semitic customs and the traditions of men kept them in strict subjugation.

It seems that there was some discontent among men and women in Ephesus. It is likely that when pagans embraced Christianity, their women were told to live according to the Jewish customs. This is true of the Mohammedan religion. Women have little freedom. When a European or an American woman becomes a Mohammedan, she has to give up her freedom and live like Moslem women.

Paul recommends that wives should be obedient to their husbands in matters which concern the family welfare in general. What he means here is that a married couple must be harmonious and co-operative in all matters, with mutual understanding and love. He does not mean that the woman should submit to cruelties or mistreatments or obey their husbands' every command, whether good or bad. Indeed, some Easterners misunderstand these words, and as a result women are considered inferior and at times are mistreated.

In the Moslem and other religions, women have a restricted freedom and have very little to say. They are discriminated against and treated with inequality. In the Christian religion, a husband and wife are one, just as the head and body are one. Paul in many of his epistles teaches on this important question and recommends love and loyalty between husband and wife. He says: "Nevertheless let every one of you in particular so love his wife even as himself; and the wife revere her husband" (Eph. 5 : 33; I Cor. 16 : 16; Col. 3 : 18).

Paul is trying to bring a compromise. Both husbands and wives are to respect and revere one another. Literally, the husband is the head of the woman and her protector, just as Christ is the head of the church and its Saviour. For the gospel of Jesus Christ is salvation to all that believe; to men as well as to women. In Christ, they are not two, but one (Gen. 1 : 27; 2 : 23; Matt. 19 : 5–6).

LOYALTY TO WIVES

So ought men to love their wives as their own bodies. He that loveth his wife loveth himself.

For no man ever yet hated his own flesh; but nourisheth and cherisheth it, even as the Lord the church:

For we are members of his body, of his flesh, and of his bones.

For this cause shall a man leave his father and mother, and shall be joined unto his wife, and they two shall be one flesh.   Eph. 5 : 28–31.

The people of the Holy Land seldom leave their fathers and mothers. They try to preserve the family ties as long as possible. Brothers live together even after their children are married. The Jews are especially noted for their loyalty to their parents. However, there are some exceptions. At times the family house becomes crowded, so that some of the married sons must find new dwelling places. On certain occasions, differences between members of the family cause strained relations. In such cases, some men prefer to put their wives away and choose to remain with their parents and brothers. Easterners, being polygamists (except Christians), could get new wives but could not have another father and mother. Others leave their parents and cleave to their wives.

Paul here is quoting from the gospel according to Matthew (19:5). He supports Jesus' recommendation in this respect. Paul, like his Master, departs from the old established Eastern custom of putting one's wife away, instead of leaving the parents.

See *Gospel Light,* p. 109.

HAVE YOUR FEET SHOD

And your feet shod with the preparation of the gospel of peace;
Above all, taking the shield of faith, wherewith ye shall be able to quench all the fiery darts of the wicked.
Eph. 6:15–16.

"Have your feet shod" is an Eastern saying which means "be alert or in constant vigilance." When men prepared to go on a journey or to feed sheep, they shod their feet. In other words, "have your feet shod" means "be ready." The feet are shod so that in case of emergency a man can start on a journey without losing any time. In the East, where electric lights are unknown, dressing, especially the fastening of shoes, is very difficult.

Until the last war the styles of shoes in many Eastern countries were different from those of Europe and America. Even today, some of the oldest styles are still in use in certain regions where Western civilization has not penetrated. The shoes are very low and are fastened with strings which also are tied around the bottoms of the trousers. When a man is seen dressed in this manner, everyone in town knows that he is ready to start on a journey or on an important mission.

The Christians in Ephesus were warned to be in constant vigilance, ready for any emergency that might occur. The teaching of Jesus was not popular in Ephesus. The church was new and its enemies many. Christians were to arm themselves with the truth and the gospel of Jesus Christ to combat the heresies from within and the enemies from without. Faith in Christ was to be their shield and protection.

PHILIPPIANS

INTRODUCTION

The epistle was written by Paul from Rome during his imprisonment, and was sent to the Philippians by Epaphroditus. As with other epistles, the exact date of writing is not known. It was probably written about A.D. 65. The Church in Philippi seems to have been well organized and orderly, having ministers and deacons. The word "bishop" is not found in the Eastern text. That term is of later origin. There were no bishops at this early time. The term *kashishey*, "elders," might have been changed to "bishops" by the copyists.

In this epistle Paul praises the loyalty of the Christians in Philippi and thanks God for their unity and sincerity in the carrying on of the work. The Philippians remained loyal to the teachings which they had received from the apostles. Paul exhorts them to follow the example of Christ in humility and sincerity. He also warns against false teachers and enemies of the Church. The Philippians are commended for their liberality.

Philippi was an historic and important city in Macedonia. It was noted for the famous battle in which Mark Antony and Cassius were defeated before Octavius about 67 to 70 B.C.

HEART

For God is my record, how greatly I long after you all in the bowels of Jesus Christ.   Phil. 1 : 8.

The Eastern text reads: "For God is my witness of how much I love you through the love of Jesus Christ."

The word "bowels" is used in the King James Version, because the Scriptures refer to the heart, liver and kidneys as the center of love and the other emotions. Even today when Easterners speak of the mind, they use the word heart. "I do not know what is in your heart," means "I do not know what is in your mind." "If riches increase, set not your heart upon them" (Psa. 62 : 10). "Let not your heart be troubled" (John 14 : 1).

Paul here speaks of his sincere love and affection for the Philippian Christians. His nature was sincere and his love pure, like that of Jesus Christ. Paul, like Jesus, was willing to give his life for the sake of the men and women whom he had won to Christ. When one really loves his people he is willing to die for them. When one is ready to die for another, his love is proven. But no love is perfect without the love of Jesus Christ.

SUCCESS IN SUFFERING

But I would ye should understand, brethren, that the things which happened unto me have fallen out rather unto the furtherance of the gospel;   Phil. 1 : 12.

The Eastern text reads: "Now I would have you know this, my brethren, that my work has greatly furthered the gospel." Paul testifies that his imprisonment and all the difficulties which he had gone through had helped the spread of the gospel. The news of Paul's imprisonment was dispatched to all churches in Greece, Macedonia, Asia Minor, Syria and Judea. A great many people who hitherto had doubted his sincerity, now believed that he was a true servant of Jesus Christ.

In the thirteenth verse, according to the Eastern text, Paul says, "And the reasons for my imprisonment have been made manifest by Christ to all Caesar's Court, and to all men."

Paul's trials and testimonies before the governors and before King Agrippa II were a triumph of the gospel of his Master. Many government officials and Jewish leaders heard a true version of Christianity for the first time. Paul, during his trial, made every effort to defend the religion of Jesus and to prove that he was the promised Messiah. His efforts and appeals on his own behalf were secondary. In prison and on board ship, Paul never ceased preaching Jesus Christ.

Persecutions and suffering have always played an important part in religion and science. They have helped to spread the cause of the truth. Personal experiences, examples and deeds are better than words. We understand the system of the past in the present and we will understand that of the present in the future. After all, everything works for the best.

DIVINE IMAGE

Who, being in the form of God, thought it not robbery to be equal with God: Phil. 2 : 6.

The Aramaic word *badmotha* means "image," "form" or "likeness." *Pekhma* means "copy," "duplicate" or "resemblance." Paul implies here that Christ was divine and existed with God from the very beginning. This is in accordance with the teaching of Jesus. When one of his disciples asked him to show them the Father; he said,

"He that hath seen me hath seen the Father" (John 14 : 9). God was manifested in Christ Jesus. Jesus healed the sick and opened the eyes of the blind through the power of God. Jesus said, "The words that I speak unto you I speak not of myself: but the Father that dwelleth in me, he doeth the works" (John 14 : 10). His divine attributes were always evident to those who saw him and talked with him. They recognized Christ in him.

Christ had the power to work miracles and wonders, but he never used them for his own gain. Being the image and likeness of God, he emptied himself of glory and honor and took our form in order to reveal God to us.

At times Jesus spoke of his closeness to God. He spoke of "the glory which I had with thee before the world was" (John 17 : 5). Nevertheless, Jesus never thought that he was robbing God of his glory. And he did not tell people to worship him instead of God. He was simply revealing to man the Christ in him. His whole concern was God's truth.

True, Jesus emptied himself of glory and honor, but not of his divine power. He did this that he might die for us. That is to say, Jesus died as a man, his divine power was always with him. It was with him when he preached and healed the sick, it was with him on the cross, in the grave, and after his resurrection. Death had no power over Christ, who is eternal.

REVERENCE

Wherefore, my beloved, as ye have always obeyed, not as in my presence only, but now much more in my absence, work out your own salvation with fear and trembling.
Phil. 2 : 12.

When Easterners enter the presence of a prince or king, they show reverence. When God's name is mentioned or the Scriptures read, they likewise show reverence. Every one keeps silent, listening as if they were in the presence of God.

The Aramaic word *dekheltha* means "reverence," not "fear" in the sense of being afraid. Paul implies that we should work out our salvation with reverence and not to be hasty and impatient. When a servant stands before a king, he forgets time; his mind is occupied by the presence of the ruler. This is because he pays due honor to him. Moreover, he speaks gently, walks carefully and answers wisely. The apostle demands this kind of Christian conduct from the followers of Christ, in order that they may become an example to the Gentiles who were joining the Christian flock. "Do all things without murmurings and disputings" (Phil. 2 : 14).

VICIOUS GOSSIPERS

Beware of dogs, beware of evil workers, beware of the concision.   Phil. 3 : 2.

Kalbey, "dogs," is used here in an idiomatic sense, meaning "vicious troublemakers and gossipers." There is an Eastern saying: "The dogs bark but the caravan goes on," which is to say, "Let troublemakers and gossipers talk, but you mind your own business." Oftentimes, dogs bark for no reason; and men and women often indulge in unnecessary gossip and variety just to pass their time.

Philippian Christians were criticized by the pagans. Converts to the Christian religion were targets of attacks from their own relatives and neighbors. Then again, there were many false teachers who, through their false doctrines, had succeeded in creating strife and dissension among the converts to Christianity. Christians were especially warned to keep away from the troublemakers who used flattering language. Such people were obviously the enemies of truth.

CIRCUMCISION OF HEART

For we are the circumcision, which worship God in the spirit, and rejoice in Christ Jesus, and have no confidence in the flesh. Phil. 3 : 3.

"Circumcision" here refers to the new covenant. The old covenant demanded that every male must be circumcised. What Paul means here is that the only circumcision the Christians practiced was spiritual. The glory of the Christians was Jesus Christ, and not the covenant of the flesh. The Jews boasted of their circumcision because through it they were made the children of the promise. But Paul argues that circumcision and many other Jewish ordinances were temporal, good only until the time of Christ.

This question of circumcision was raised in this epistle because Jewish Christians in Philippi, like other Jewish converts, had demanded that Gentiles who were embracing Christianity should be circumcised.

Paul, like many of the Hebrew prophets who denounced circumcision, sacrifices and ritualisms, believed in the circumcision of the heart: "Circumcise therefore the foreskin of your heart, and be no more stiffnecked" (Deut. 10 : 16). "And the Lord thy God will circumcise thine heart, and the heart of thy seed, . . ." (Deut. 30 : 6). Jeremiah says, "Circumcise yourselves to the Lord" (Jer. 4 : 4).

Christianity demands a complete change and a new life. The Christians are to demonstrate their faith through good works, charity and Christian love.

CONFIDENCE IN GOD

Though I might also have confidence in the flesh. If any other man thinketh that he hath whereof he might trust in the flesh, I more: Phil. 3 : 4.

Confidence in the flesh" means trust in the Mosaic ordinances and the traditions of the elders, which regulated man's conduct relative to the things of the flesh, but to some extent neglected the spiritual side of life. Indeed, many of these laws governed only the things of the flesh. In other words, they were outward ordinances which were temporal, and were merely symbolical of the things of the spirit which were to be revealed thereafter.

Paul had been a faithful Jew, reared and educated as a strict Pharisee. Nevertheless, he sees no salvation in racial traditions and their various interpretations. He is more concerned with the things of the spirit, which are indestructible and which enrich one's life and soul. Temples and organized worship have come and gone, but spiritual religion is permanent. Confidence in spiritual forces means confidence in the living God.

PAUL WAS A HEBREW

Circumcised the eighth day, of the stock of Israel, of the tribe of Benjamin, an Hebrew of the Hebrews; as touching the law, a Pharisee; Phil. 3 : 5.

Paul was a Hebrew by race, of the tribe of Benjamin, the smallest one among the Twelve Tribes. By religion he was a Jew and a member of the most powerful sect, the Pharisees. Members of this sect believed in the resurrection and were strong exponents of the Mosaic law, ordinances and customs. The sect was also noted for its patriotism and its firm opposition to foreign rulers, taxation and the introduction of alien customs and manners.

Their chief aim was to free their country from the foreign yoke and restore the kingdom of David.

Paul was not of the tribe of Judah, but he was a member of the Jewish faith. Only members of the tribe of Judah were really Jews, but after the Babylonian captivity, the remnants of all the tribes who returned to Palestine were called Jews. This is because political Israel was destroyed, but the center of Jewish worship remained in Judea. The Temple became the only sacred racial relic. Members of other tribes, when they returned to Palestine, were identified by their religion, and even converts from other races were called Jews.

The Jews circumcise in the eighth day and the Mohammedans in the thirteenth year. This is because when Isaac was circumcised he was eight days old, but Ishmael was thirteen years old when he was circumcised (Gen. 17 : 12-25; Gen. 21 : 4).

SHARING IN THE GOSPEL

Notwithstanding ye have well done, that ye did communicate with my affliction.
Now ye Philippians know also, that in the beginning of the gospel, when I departed from Macedonia, no church communicated with me as concerning giving and receiving, but ye only. Phil. 4 : 14-15.

The Eastern text reads: "But ye have done well to share my difficulties . . ."

Paul, throughout all of his missionary preaching, relied on God for his support. In some places he suffered great difficulties; in others he worked as a saddle-maker in order to earn his meager livelihood. In verse 11 he says: "Not that I speak in respect of want: for I have learned, in whatsoever state I am, therewith to be content." Paul knew that at times he must suffer thirst, cold and hunger for the sake of the gospel which he preached. He knew that his teaching would meet with stern opposition from his own people as well as from the pagans.

The Philippians helped him probably more than any other church. He speaks of this kindness not to induce them to send another gift, but to remind them of the good work which he had done to which they had contributed generously and in which they had a part.

For many centuries, Christian missionaries relied on God and the labor of their own hands for support. Some of them left their homes, carrying with them only the Scriptures and a few loaves of bread. They, like Paul, labored with their hands and preached in far-off lands. They trusted in the Lord to help them, protect them and meet their daily needs.

HOLY

Salute every saint in Christ Jesus. The brethren which are with me greet you.
All the saints salute you, chiefly they that are of Caesar's household. Phil. 4 : 21-22.

The Aramaic word for "saint" is *kadeshey*, which means "separated" or "set aside." It was applied to those who devoted their time to prayer, fasting and the work of God. To call a person a *kadisha* does not necessarily mean that he is without sin, but one who has chosen to serve God rather than the world. The term *Kadisha* is generally used in referring to God, Christ and the vessels of the Temple.

The disciples never spoke of themselves as being holy or without sin. Easterners generally are willing to confess their weaknesses. Even when they have done nothing wrong, they say: "I am not worthy, I am a miserable sinner." Such remarks are often seen in the prefaces and at the ends of manuscripts, where the scribes, monks and priests speak of themselves as being wretched sinners and unworthy of undertaking to copy the holy manuscripts.

Jesus did not want the people to address him as good

Master. Not because he was not good or wonderful, but because this title was generally applied only to God. "Holy, holy, holy, Lord God of hosts" (Isa. 6 : 3). "Thy holy child Jesus" (Acts 4 : 27). Any place where God was believed to dwell was also considered holy by the Jewish people (Exod. 3 : 5; 26 : 33).

The members of Caesar's household who had accepted Christ, Paul spoke of as holy, not that they were perfect, but because they were chosen or set aside as partakers in the Christian gospel in the Imperial City.

The time and money which we devote to God's work are holy. When we leave the things of the flesh and work for the things of the spirit, we separate ourselves from worldly things and sanctify our lives to God.

COLOSSIANS

INTRODUCTION

This epistle was dictated by Paul, but written by a scribe. Paul wrote the salutation in his own handwriting. The epistle was written from Rome, where Paul was a prisoner. At the time Paul was writing, Timothy also was in Rome. The letter was delivered by Tychicus, who had carried epistles to other churches. The date of the epistle to the Colossians is not known. Paul, even though a prisoner, was in constant touch with the churches. He always kept informed about the state of the churches and about new teachings that were introduced from time to time.

The epistle is a reminder to the people at Colosse to be wary of philosophers and teachings that might obscure the gospel of Jesus Christ. The apostle warns against quarrels over Jewish holidays, feasts, Sabbath Days and new moons. Paul emphasizes Christian living and faith in Christ. Christ is portrayed as Creator and Redeemer and the image of God, who is invisible. The tone of the epistle is theological. It seems that the Christians in Colosse were disturbed by teachers who interpreted the Scriptures literally and who placed considerable emphasis on the Jewish ordinances as a means of salvation.

The Colossian Christians are addressed as saints and faithful brethren. The church at Colosse seems to have been loyal and firm in the apostolic doctrines. The epistle was sent as a warning against new teachers who had undermined some of the churches in Galatia.

RECONCILIATION

And, having made peace through the blood of his cross, by him to reconcile all things unto himself; by him, I say, whether they be things in earth, or things in heaven.
Col. 1 : 20.

In the East, where courts and judges are unknown, disputes and quarrels are settled through intermediaries. These are selected from among the noblest and kindest men whose reputation as peacemakers is widespread.

In the olden days Hebrew priests tried to reconcile God and man by means of the blood of animals. The pagans offered their firstborn in order to make peace with God. Indeed, the sole purpose of the Jewish priestly system and its elaborate worship was to bring about reconciliation between man and his Creator. God could not be appoached by sinful men. Therefore, the priests acted as intermediaries to effect reconciliation.

The death of Jesus revealed how much God loved the world that he permitted even his beloved Son to die on the cross. Jesus proved that God, the loving Father, was seeking his lost children. Thus, the death of Jesus opened the eyes of men, led them to discontinue sacrifice and yet to draw closer to God. Reconciliation was accomplished through the death of Jesus on the cross.

The animal offerings brought about no reconciliation. Legalistic and theological arguments failed to reveal God's love and his eternal fatherhood. The death of Jesus on the cross was a sacrifice for the sake of all humanity and not for a certain class of people. It was a reminder of God's love for his children and a summons to all people, regardless of race and color, to return to him.

Christianity was the beginning of universal reconciliation. Men were, for the first time, told to love their enemies, and pray for those who hated them. Jesus asked his Father to forgive those who crucified him. He had shown that the way to God was through meekness and gentleness.

Through the death of Jesus, the power of sin and its dominion over men was destroyed. Any enmity between God and man was removed forever. Jesus died because of our sins and disobedience to the law of God. If men had not been dominated by sin, they would not have killed Jesus. It was our sins and ignorance that nailed him to the cross. "For if, when we were enemies, we were reconciled to God by the death of his Son, much more, being reconciled, we shall be saved by his life" (Rom. 5 : 10). It was through the death of Jesus that men gained faith in immortality, and the earthly man once more became a living soul. Death resulted from the enmity between God and man. Jesus by his death on the cross removed sin and death. Death acquired a new meaning, and sin lost its dominion over men. Those who live in Jesus Christ can triumph over both.

SUFFERING FOR THE GOSPEL

Who now rejoice in my sufferings for you, and fill up that which is behind of the afflictions of Christ in my flesh for his body's sake, which is the church: Col. 1 : 24.

Paul suffered persecution, privations and imprisonment for the sake of the gospel of Jesus Christ and the congregations which were under his spiritual care in Asia Minor, Greece and Rome. He often mentions his sufferings and tribulations, but he always boasts of his difficulties and trials because they were inflicted on him for the sake of the gospel of Christ, which had been entrusted to him.

Paul tells the Colossian Christians to rejoice in his sufferings, and not to grieve about his imprisonment and difficulties, because persecution and suffering were bound to come. Jesus had warned his disciples of the trials which awaited them. Believers in the gospel were to be like lambs among wolves. They would be imprisoned and persecuted (Matt. 10 : 17–19). Paul tells the Colossians to make up for the sufferings that he had escaped. That is to say, his sufferings were nothing compared to those of Jesus Christ, who had died the death of a malefactor. The Eastern text reads, "And now rejoice in my sufferings for you, and make up that which is lacking of the sufferings of Jesus Christ in my flesh for his body's sake, which is the Church." Paul is humble in comparing his sufferings with those of his Master. He did not consider beatings, hunger and imprisonment as enough. Paul was ready even to die on the cross or to be beheaded for the sake of the ministry which God had entrusted to him.

WALK IN WAY

As ye have therefore received Christ Jesus the Lord, so walk ye in him: Col. 2 : 6.

"Walk ye in him," means, "be guided by him, or his teachings." In the East it is often asked, "What is your road?" which means, "What is your religion?" In the Scriptures we often find such phrases as "the way of God," which means, "the religion of God." "Noah walked with God," means, "he obeyed God" (Gen. 6 : 9). In the East, when people are on good terms they walk together, but when they are not, they refuse to journey with one another.

Then again, when people walk after their own ways or follow after false teachings, it is said, "They walk in darkness," which means, "They are ignorant." "The people that walked in darkness have seen a great light" (Isa. 9 : 2). "Ye shall walk in all the ways which the Lord your God hath commanded you" (Deut. 5 : 33).

When we walk in the way of God we never stumble. His words, which are truth and life, lighten our path. His commandments serve as a lamp to our feet.

Paul warns the Christians in Colosse against strange

teachings and false teachers who had led some of the people astray from the way of God, and he implores them to remain firm in the truth which he had imparted to them.

BURIED WITH HIM

Buried with him in baptism, wherein also ye are risen with him *through the faith of the operation of God, who hath raised him from the dead.* Col. 2 : 12.

Members of the Eastern churches still practice the ancient rite of baptism. Persons who are baptized are immersed in the water three times. The whole body must be submerged. Baptism by immersion symbolizes the death and burial of Jesus, and the resurrection, or the beginning of a new life for the individual.

Baptism was introduced by John the Baptist. It took the place of circumcision and became the symbol of the new covenant, just as circumcision had been the symbol of the old. The Jews did away with a small portion of the body. The Christians through baptism put away the earthly body and rose with a new spiritually-awakened body. This change is brought about by the Holy Spirit. Water is symbolical of inward cleansing.

Forgiveness is obtained by faith in Jesus Christ and not by mere form, which, like other Jewish ordinances was a mere shadow of the true religion which was to be revealed later. (See *Gospel Light*—article on baptism, p. 158.)

EVIL FORCES

> And *having spoiled principalities and powers, he made a shew of them openly, triumphing over them in it.*
> Col. 2 : 15.

In the olden days evil was recognized as a supreme force independent of the realm of God. Men did not know how to overcome it.

The Eastern text reads: "And by putting off his mortal body, he exposed the powers of evil, and through his person put them openly to shame." That is to say, Jesus, by surrendering his earthly body to his Spirit and to the will of God, overcame the forces of evil and exposed their false claims to authority over men. When he prayed in Gethsemane he said: "The spirit is indeed ready, but the body is weak" (Matt. 26 : 41, Eastern text). Jesus surrendered his body to the will of God and trusted in him with secure confidence that truth would ultimately triumph and that the forces of evil would be put to shame. His resurrection proved the supremacy of God in the universe.

When we sacrifice the lesser for the greater and the material for the spiritual, we then understand Jesus' victory over the forces of evil, and the power which he gave to those who believed in him. His followers were to reveal the truth of the gospel to every people and to every country. They were to expose the false teachings which had enslaved men to the worship of idols. They were given the power and authority to open the gates of heaven to those who would enter.

DATES OF FEASTS

Let no man therefore judge you in meat, or in drink, or in respect of an holyday, or of the new moon, or of the sabbath days: Col. 2 : 16.

Where calendars and clocks are rare the people disagree over the dates of feasts, Sabbaths and other holidays. They have to be informed by the authorities concerning the dates of feasts and fasts.

The Aramaic text reads: "Let no man therefore create a disturbance among you, about the eating and drinking, or about the divisions of the feast days, the beginning of the month and of the day of the Sabbath."

Paul warns the Colossians to beware of teachers who were creating disturbances over the time of observance of certain Jewish feasts, the beginning of months, and the exact hour to observe the Sabbath Day. Agreement on the observance of these institutions was always difficult and resulted in disputes and quarrels. This is because calendars differed and opinions varied. Then again, calendars in those days were not in general circulation. Copies of manuscripts containing calendars were scarce and hard to obtain. The people had to consult priests and elders about the dates of certain feast days. Moreover, there were difficulties in reckoning the time. For instance, the month began with a new moon, but in some countries the moon could not be seen for several days. This resulted in disputes over the exact day and hour. Some of these matters were referred to the high priests, who also, at times, were in disagreement among themselves.

Paul does not imply that the Christian Jews in Colosse should repudiate the Mosaic law. He simply admonishes them to refrain from quarrels over observances, because these were not essentials of the Christian truth. It would not matter if a Sabbath Day or a feast were observed a few hours earlier or later.

On the other hand, a Sabbath cannot fall at the same time in all countries. When you travel in the Pacific Ocean, for instance, you lose or gain a day when you cross the international date line, so that on one island it may be Sunday while on another it may be Monday.

The Jews in Macedonia were not well versed in Jewish traditions, and calendars. They were guided by teachers who came from Judea. The Christian converts of Jewish faith, like Peter, John and James, remained loyal to the Mosaic law and its precepts, but they refrained from controversies over the observances. Jesus was a member of the Jewish faith and kept the Sabbath Day, but he did not observe some of the traditions of the elders. He ate without washing his hands. He healed the sick and permitted his disciples to pluck the wheat on the Sabbath Day (Matt. 12 : 1-2). (For observances, see Lev. 23 : 3-8.)

CHANGES CUSTOMS

Which all are to perish with the using; after the commandments and doctrines of men? Col. 2 : 22.

Eating, drinking and the exact time of observance of feasts and fasts were doctrines of man. That is to say, God would not be angry at the Colossian Christians over the time of the observance of a feast. If they were a few hours early or late in observing the Sabbath, for instance, it would not matter.

The elders of the Jewish faith, however, demanded uniformity and exactness. The people must obey the ruling of authorities in all religious matters. Even today tribal people in the East forget the dates of holidays and feast days. They are reminded of them by the authorities who instruct them as to what to observe and when.

Paul in his epistles calls these ordinances the commandments and doctrine of man. In other words, to Paul the main thing is Jesus Christ and his teaching. The traditions relative to the observances were disputable. The Jewish authorities of the law disagreed in the interpretations thereof. The people were told not to touch this, and not to taste that, and not to handle certain things. These teachers of the law went too far in their interpretations of the Word of God. They even accused Jesus of having broken the Sabbath, simply because he healed a man on the Sabbath Day. There were many other laws, such as washing of hands before eating, of articles of food brought from the market place, and cups and pots (Mark 7 : 2-5).

According to the teaching of Jesus, it is not what goes into a man that defiles him, but that which comes out of man. It is not the exact hour of the observance of feasts and Sabbath Days that counts, but the spirit in which they are observed, and the understanding of God's purpose in ordaining such institutions. Customs are changeable, but truth is eternal. The words of Jesus are eternal truth.

MORTIFYING OF THE BODY

Mortify therefore your members which are upon the earth; fornication, uncleanness, inordinate affection, evil concupiscence, and covetousness, which is idolatry:
Col. 3 : 5.

The doctrine of the subjugation of the body to the spirit is found in the teachings of all major religions. In some countries men inflict severe wounds upon their bodies. In others, they even destroy certain members of the body (Matt. 19 : 12). In the second century some Christians went to extremes in inflicting injuries upon their bodies. A certain movement called Monasticism which flourished in Egypt and part of Europe, was noted for these practices.

The body is controlled and directed by the spirit. "Mortify" in this case means "subdue." Evil desires are subdued or suppressed by means of prayer and fasting. Paul does not mean that men should cause injuries to members of their bodies, as is wrongly interpreted by some teachers of religion. The Aramaic word *amito* means "weaken" or "suppress." When a man is lean, it is said, "his body is dead."

Fasting was recommended both by Jews and Christians for the purpose of weakening the earthly desires of the body. Easterners believe eating and drinking stimulates physical desires, especially when they indulge to excess in eating or in drinking wine.

Prophets and teachers of religion, when they tried to commune with God, sometimes fasted many days and many nights, until their bodies were brought under the control of the spirit. This method enabled them to commune with God. Moses, Elijah and Jesus fasted when they communed with God.

RACIAL EQUALITY

Where there is neither Greek nor Jew, circumcision nor uncircumcision, Barbarian, Scythian, bond nor free: but Christ is all, and in all. Col. 3 : 11.

The Eastern text reads: "Where there is neither Jew nor Syrian (Aramean), circumcision nor uncircumcision, Greek nor Barbarian, slave nor freeman; but Christ is all and in all men."

In the East, when a man changes his religion, he changes his nationality. The convert is identified by the religion which he adopts, or by the race to which the prophet of the new religion belongs. For instance, in Arabia when a Christian becomes a Mohammedan, he is called an Arab. Thousands of Assyrian Christians who, centuries ago, became Moslems, are called Arabs, Turks and Kurds. The Mohammedan religion grants equal rights to all of its members. Likewise, Mohammedans who become Christians, are known by the nationality of the Christians among whom they live.

Paul here admonishes the Colossian Jews not to look down on Syrians, Greeks and Barbarians who had become converts to Christianity. He tells them that they have been united with them in Jesus Christ, who died for all men and freed them from the bondage of sin. On the other hand, some of the Gentiles hated the Jews, and refused to consider the slaves who had become Christians as their equals.

EARLY CHRISTIAN SERVICES

Let the word of Christ dwell in you richly in all wisdom; teaching and admonishing one another in psalms and hymns and spiritual songs, singing with grace in your hearts to the Lord. Col. 3 : 16.

Psalms were sung in the Jewish synagogues and homes. Even though many of the sacred songs are folk songs, they are known as holy songs which are sung during prayers, lamentations and burial services.

It is evident that the church at Colosse was composed largely of Jewish converts. The Syrian and Greek converts knew nothing about Jewish psalms; they had their own psalms (songs) composed by their own poets. The Jews had committed many of their psalms to memory.

In this early period the Christians had no prayer books; during services they used the psalms and other Jewish prayer books and some of the rituals. They also read from the gospels and the books of the prophets and the Pentateuch (the five books of Moses). The Christians continued to use the Jewish prayer book for a long time. It is interesting to note that the order of the Jewish prayer book and its rituals are largely retained by Christian churches.

HUSBAND AND WIFE

Wives, submit yourselves unto your own husbands, as it is fit in the Lord. Col. 3 : 18.

From earliest times, Eastern women have been required to respect and obey their husbands in affairs of the household. The term "subject to their husbands" does not mean enslavement, but loyalty and reverence. The Aramaic word *eshtabdin* is derived from *abad*, meaning "to work," "to serve" or "to worship." The term is used in referring to the child Jesus. "And he went down with them and came to Nazareth and was subject unto them (his parents)" (Luke 2 : 51).

There are times when Eastern women who are mentally strong, despise and utterly disregard the advice of their weak husbands. Some of them take over the management of the household, and let the husband perform the domestic duties, which causes him to become the object of gossip and ridicule among his neighbors. Such women, like Jezebel, who dominated King Ahab, become notorious characters, and are greatly feared by their husbands and denounced by religious authorities.

Oriental priests and preachers of religion always attack such cases and point out such women, just as the prophet Elijah did when he denounced Jezebel. Paul does not mean that women are to be looked down upon, but that women should not usurp the authority of their husbands in domestic affairs. He was aware of the dangers in countries where social customs are different.

Freedom and equality works well in Europe and America where women have progressed to the point where they are the equals of men. But in the East, where women are still ignorant and illiterate, and where the meaning of freedom is not understood, subjection to their husbands is considered proper and expedient. Women, being secluded, have little experience, and they need the guidance of their husbands in matters of business and in the rearing of children. We note that Paul also enjoins husbands to love their wives with due reverence and respect. Christian love overcomes all difficulties and brings harmonious co-operation and reciprocal services.

In Jesus Christ there is no male or female. They are one. Jesus in his teaching never discriminated against women, nor did he say women were inferior to men. From the outset he always spoke of men and women as equals.

Paul was a strict Pharisee and a student of the Mosaic law. In the Jewish religion, women were not equal; they were not allowed to pray together with men or to participate in ceremonies. Nor were they allowed to enter into certain parts of the Temple, or to touch holy things.

It seems that Paul was not, in some respects, completely free from the Jewish customs in which he had been brought up as a child. This is because most of the early Christian converts were of the Jewish faith; the apostles and their co-workers were all Jews. They could not have repudiated all the Jewish social customs, especially those pertaining to the sexes. These were to be observed so that Christians might live a pure and holy life and become examples to converts from pagan religions, whose customs and behavior were different from and inferior to those of the Jews. In other words, time and conditions compelled Paul to make these recommendations.

TREATMENT OF SERVANTS

Masters, give unto your servants that which is just and equal; knowing that ye also have a Master in heaven.
Col. 4 : 1.

The status of a servant in the East is different from that of servants in Europe and America. Most servants are hired without any agreement or understanding relative to the time of work, wages or type of service. However, some employers make verbal agreements with their servants and pay them a small wage. Then again, as servants have nothing to say, their masters determine the wages and type of work. This results in discrimination and injustices. Some servants are assigned to hard work and longer hours, while others sit idle at the gate of their lord or are assigned to easy tasks at home.

On the other hand, servants may be fired without having been paid. The wages of some may be in arrears for two or three years. Not having state laws and unions to protect the interests of the workers, the whole matter is left to the sincerity and integrity of the employers. Some of the latter do fear God and try to do justice to their servants, but others act cruelly and commit injustices to defenseless workers and their families whose labor they exploit. James in his epistle complains against such injustices (James 5 : 4).

LOYALTY TO PAUL

And Jesus, which is called Justus, who are of the circumcision. These only are my fellowworkers unto the kingdom of God, which have been a comfort unto me. Col. 4 : 11.

Ancient and deep-rooted customs are hard to be changed or abolished. The Jewish Christians for a long time continued to circumcise their children. But the Gentiles were free from this duty, for the apostles had agreed not to burden them with this Jewish racial custom.

These Jewish Christians in Colosse were related to Paul by blood and racial ties, and therefore they helped him when he was in need. It seems that at this time there were very few converts of other races who had embraced Christianity. Had not this been the case, Paul would have received some assistance from the Gentile Christians. These Gentile Christians were very generous, as in the case of Titus, Timothy, Luke (all Arameans) and others who stood by Paul even unto death. On the other hand, Paul's arrest and trial was a Jewish affair. Paul was charged with bringing uncircumcised Gentiles into the Jewish Temple. He was also accused by the Jews of being responsible for disturbances in various cities in Asia Minor. Nevertheless, the Jews were divided on some of these questions and charges. Paul always found sympathizers among the minority.

Some of the men who helped him no doubt were Hebrews; that is, they were Jews by religion, but descendants of the Ten Tribes who were scattered through the Roman Empire. Many of these men had no use for the Jews in Palestine. The enmities which centuries before existed between the people of the Northern Kingdom and those of Judea were still remembered. Therefore, many of these Jewish converts rallied on the side of Paul and contributed money for his support and defense in Rome.

MEETING IN HOMES

Salute the brethren which are in Laodicea, and Nymphas, and the church which is in his house.   Col. 4 : 15.

The Aramaic word *etta* means "congregation" or "assembly." The first Christian congregations met at the houses of the converts. The purpose of these meetings was to instruct the people in the gospel of Jesus Christ. The letters from the apostles were also read in these meetings. In those early days scrolls containing the teachings of Jesus were scarce, just as they are today in the East. Therefore, the Christians met together, to discuss the work and to instruct and baptize the new converts. They also went to the synagogue for prayer and other services.

In the course of time, when the small group of Christian converts increased and became powerful, they divorced themselves from the Jewish synagogues and established their own churches for instruction and prayer.

THESSALONIANS

INTRODUCTION

The author of this epistle is Paul. It was written in Athens. Paul had been directed in a vision to go to Macedonia and preach the gospel of Christ (Acts 17 : 9). The exact date of the epistle is not known, because in those days letters were not dated. Nevertheless, this is one of the earliest of Paul's letters addressed to the Christians in Macedonia. These Christian converts were mostly immigrants from Judea. Paul spoke to them in the synagogue and made many converts. "And some of them believed" (Acts 17 : 34). Others opposed him (Acts 17 : 5).

The epistle contains mostly teachings and exhortations, but also mentions the second coming of Christ. The Christians were commended for their strong faith, patience, love, and trust in Jesus Christ. Then again, the converts here were the first fruits of the gospel in Macedonia and Achaia.

The work was accomplished in spite of much suffering and opposition. Paul was shamefully treated at Philippi. He had fled from there and went to Thessalonica, where he began to preach to the Jews in the synagogue.

The apostle admonishes the Thessalonians to remain loyal to the commands of Jesus, to refrain from fornication and other unlawful practices. Paul also speaks of the resurrection of the dead. He tells the people to be watchful and to prepare for the coming of Christ, who will come as a thief in the night.

GOD AS A WITNESS

For neither at any time used we flattering words, as ye know, nor a cloke of covetousness; God is witness:
                                                        I Thes. 2 : 5.

"God is a witness" is an Eastern expression commonly used by Assyrians, Syrians, Turks, Armenians and Arabs. When an oral agreement is made, the parties concerned say, "Let God be a witness between us." Likewise, during arguments and disputes over forgotten debts and deeds, people often say, "I have no witness but God," or "God is my witness."

Easterners make but few written contracts and agreements; most of their business transactions and contracts are oral. Nevertheless, in the buying and selling of important properties such as houses and fields, two witnesses are required to be present when the deal is made. When no witnesses can be found, God is made a witness, as in the case of Laban and Jacob (Gen. 31 : 50). Saying, "God is a witness" is equivalent to taking an oath in the name of God. Then again, in the East, when cases can not be adjudicated in courts, the party suspected of guilt is made to take an oath in the name of God. Many Easterners would much prefer to sustain a loss rather than take a false oath.

Paul's motives toward the Thessalonian Christians were sincere. He had not asked them for any support, nor tried to burden them in any way. God was a witness of his hard labors and trials on their account.

FOSTER MOTHERS

But we were gentle among you, even as a nurse cherisheth her children: I Thes. 2 : 7.

The Eastern text reads, "And like a foster mother who loves her children." In the East, the children of kings, princes and noblemen are entrusted to the care of foster parents. This strange custom grew out of the practice of polygamy. Rulers and rich men who have many wives have more children than they can take care of in their own homes. So they entrust them to the care of servants and faithful citizens, who are granted certain privileges and other remuneration for their faithful services.

This custom was common in biblical days, and it still prevails in some parts of the Near East. "And Ahab had seventy sons in Samaria. And Jehu wrote letters, and sent to Samaria, unto the rulers of Jezreel, to the elders, and to them that brought up Ahab's children (II Kings 10 : 1). Children brought up in this way love their foster parents and do not wish to part from them.

Paul and his co-workers had been like faithful foster mothers to the Thessalonian Christians. They had taken care of them as though they were their own children.

PAUL BITTER AGAINST THE JEWS

For ye, brethren, became followers of the churches of God which in Judœa are in Christ Jesus: for ye also have suffered like things of your own countrymen, even as they have of the Jews:
Who both killed the Lord Jesus, and their own prophets, and have persecuted us; and they please not God, and are contrary to all men: I Thes. 2 : 14–15.

Paul is appealing to the Christians in Thessalonica, reminding them that they are members of the churches of Christ in Judea, and that the Jewish Christians there have suffered much persecution because of their faith.

The Christians to whom the epistle is addressed were largely Jews, inhabitants of Thessalonica. Paul wanted the Thessalonian Jews to know that Christianity was spreading in Judea, and that the converts were meeting stern opposition from their own people. This was an important point. Jerusalem was the seat of the Jewish religion. The Jews who were scattered throughout the Roman Empire were still under the spiritual guidance of the Jewish authorities in Jerusalem, who kept in touch with them by means of letters and emissaries sent from time to time by the high priests. Paul was bitter against the Jews. He charged them with being the murderers of Christ and of their own prophets.

It is true that the Jews persecuted and murdered many of their prophets. Jesus, however, was crucified by the Romans. The Jews of course demanded his death, but the actual killing was done by Roman soldiers. The Jews had no authority to put a Galilean to death. What Paul meant here is that the Jewish leaders incited the people and were the cause of Jesus' death. Paul was bitter toward the Jews of Judea because they had made things hard for him, especially after he had been successful in converting some of their people.

EVIL MEN

Wherefore we would have come unto you, even I Paul, once and again; but Satan hindered us. I Thes. 2 : 18.

Satan in this case refers to hindrances caused by men. Easterners in their conversations and letters blame mishaps on the devil or Satan. When they make a mistake they pretend to spit on Satan. Men whose counsel misleads people or whose actions cause hardship or evil are called Satan. At times the reference is to a person who is well known for his evil acts. Jesus called Simon Peter "Satan." "Get thee behind me, Satan." Of course he knew that Peter was not Satan, but Peter was giving wrong counsel, the kind that Satan would give.

The forces of evil work through human agents. Paul's work was always made hard by false teachers who followed in his footsteps. "And then shall that Wicked be revealed, whom the Lord shall consume with the spirit of his mouth. . . . Even him, whose coming is after the working of Satan" (II Thes. 2 : 8–9). "And the devil that deceiveth them was cast into the lake of fire and brimstone" (Rev. 20 : 10).

Paul met much opposition, but his faith in Christ helped him overcome the power of the forces of evil. Hindrances and difficulties are always bound to come, especially to men engaged in Christian work.

PAUL'S JOY

For now we live, if ye stand fast in the Lord. I Thes. 3 : 8.

"For now we live" is an Eastern expression meaning, "Now we rejoice." When the outlook is discouraging, Easterners say, "We feel like death."

The apostle was happy over the firm faith of the converts in Thessalonica. They had withstood all kinds of opposition and persecution from their own people and had remained loyal to Jesus Christ. This is why Paul was overjoyed at their steadfastness to the teachings of Christ, so strongly evidenced by them in faith and charity.

CHOSEN VESSEL

That every one of you should know how to possess his vessel in sanctification and honour; I Thes. 4 : 4.

"Vessel" in this case refers to the human body. In the Temple the vessels were sanctified before they were used in the worship services. So Paul was called a "chosen vessel." "But the Lord said unto him, Go thy way: for he is a chosen vessel unto me, to bear my name before the Gentiles, and kings, and the children of Israel" (Acts 9 : 15).

The Thessalonians were admonished to observe the commandments of the Lord Jesus. They were told to abstain from adultery and other evil practices common among those who did not know God. Their bodies were the sacred vessels of God and temples of the Holy Spirit. They were consecrated by Jesus Christ and sanctified by the Holy Spirit.

THIEF

For yourselves know perfectly that the day of the Lord so cometh as a thief in the night.
For when they shall say, Peace and safety; then sudden destruction cometh upon them, as travail upon a woman with child; and they shall not escape.
But ye, brethren, are not in darkness, that that day should overtake you as a thief.   I Thes. 5 : 2–4.

In Palestine, the Arabian Desert, and Mesopotamia, where tribal life goes on as of yore, raids often take place during the day while the sheep and cattle are grazing in the plains or on the hills. Arabian tribes raid one another for the purpose of plundering. In this part of the world plundering and the taking of spoil are considered lawful. Even holy men sometimes participate in raids, stealing and breaking into homes. The latter is looked down upon, however, and in most parts of the East is rarely practiced. Nevertheless, the stealing of sheep and goats is common. This is done during the night when the shepherd is sleeping. The thief enters the fold and carries a sheep or a lamb in his arms. Paul is referring to Jesus' words in the gospel of Luke, "And this know, that if the goodman of the house had known what hour the thief would come, he would have watched, and not have suffered his house to be broken through" (Luke 12 : 39).

In many parts of the East, animals occupy the same

room with men and women. In some countries, lambs, sheep and cattle are sheltered for the night in a large room adjoining the family bedrooms. But in some places, sheepfolds may be one or two miles from the towns. In this case, most of the shepherds stay with the sheep.

Jesus' coming will be like that of a thief at night. No man can tell the hour, the month or the year. Therefore, his followers must be constantly alert and ready to greet him.

SIGNS OF HIS COMING

For when they shall say, Peace and safety; then sudden destruction cometh upon them, as travail upon a woman with child; and they shall not escape.   1. Thes. 5 : 3.

Jesus had told his disciples that his second coming would be like that of a thief at night. No one would know the day or the hour. He related several parables to illustrate that his second coming would be sudden and unexpected. He also warned his disciples and followers that false prophets and false Christs would come after him. He told them of the wars, famines and tribulations that would take place before his second coming. He taught that his gospel must first be preached throughout the world before the end would come (Matt. 24 : 5–13).

Jesus related parables in order to impress upon his disciples the suddenness of his coming, namely, the parable of the wise and the foolish virgins, and the parable of the talents (Matt. 25 : 1–14ff).

Paul quoted the sayings of Jesus from the gospels. Word had spread among the Christians that the Lord was coming soon—especially among the Christians in Macedonia, who at the time had no copies of Scriptures and no knowledge of prophecies. The Christians had suffered persecution, and wars and famines were frequent. Therefore, they expected the coming of Christ. These false rumors to some extent were due to the false teachers who, instead of preaching the gospel among the pagans, kept talking about the end of the world. They were the false Christs mentioned in Matthew. "Then if any man shall say unto you, Lo, here is Christ, or there; believe it not" (Matt. 24 : 23–24). Paul did not imply that Jesus was to return soon. He simply admonished the Thessalonians to be ready, for the Lord might come suddenly (Matt. 24 : 43–44). Just as a servant who is watchful for the returning of his master from a journey, Christians must constantly watch and be ready for the coming of the Lord (Mark 13 : 34–37; Luke 12 : 39–40).

DURING THE NIGHT

For they that sleep sleep in the night; and they that be drunken are drunken in the night. I Thes. 5 : 7.

Easterners generally do not indulge in drinking wine and strong drinks, except at wedding feasts and banquets. In some places strong drinks are used only as medicines, while in others, they are not known at all. In Palestine and Syria grapes are abundant, and wine is drunk at meals.

Weddings and feasts are celebrated in the evening. Wine and strong drinks are used to excess and many guests and merrymakers become drunk. Easterners are generally sober, but on such occasions many do get drunk. The wedding celebration continues during the night hours, and drinks are served constantly. One seldom sees a drunken man during the day. Saloons are unknown; all drinking is done in homes. Some people, because of their reputation, refuse to drink during the day, but they would not hestitate to drink at night.

Paul here refers to the gospel according to John: "And this is the condemnation, that light is come into the world, and men loved darkness rather than light, because their deeds were evil. For every one that doeth evil hateth the light, . . . lest his deeds should be reproved" (John 3 : 19–20).

Many crimes and evil acts are committed during the dark hours; thieves break in at night and steal (Luke 12 : 39). Light is symbolic of truth and understanding; but darkness represents superstition, ignorance and unreality.

SPIRIT AND SOUL

And the very God of peace sanctify you wholly; and I pray God your whole spirit and soul and body be preserved blameless unto the coming of our Lord Jesus Christ.
I Thes. 5 : 23.

"Spirit" in this case means "the breath of God," that is, the intelligence which distinguishes between right and wrong. In Aramaic, *rookha* may mean "spirit," "prophecy," "pride," "wind" or "rheumatism."

At times, "spirit" and "soul" are used indiscriminately. In some instances, *naphsha*, "soul," is used in speaking of animate life. It is believed that every person is endowed with a divine spirit which comes directly from God, and with the breath of life, which emanates from matter. Jesus said "It is the spirit that quickeneth; the flesh profiteth nothing" (John 6 : 63). Death destroys only the life which is derived from matter, but the spirit continues and is indestructible. After death, the spirit and the soul combine. There is the spiritual man and the earthly man; one is immortal and the other mortal. "For the word of God is quick, and powerful, and sharper than any two-edged sword, piercing even to the dividing asunder of soul and spirit, . . ." (Heb. 4 : 12).

HOLY KISS

Greet all the brethren with an holy kiss. I Thes. 5 : 26.

Even though kissing is not commonly practiced among Semitic people, it is done at festivals and weddings. On such an occasion, a woman may kiss even a stranger. In the East, people kiss each other on the cheek, and not on the mouth. When men and women greet each other after a long absence, they may kiss. Then again, during church services, when men who have not been on good terms are reconciled, they may kiss each other.

Kissing is a token of sincerity and true affection and a sign that peaceful relations exist between two persons. At times enemies kiss each other in order to conceal their inner motives. "The kisses of an enemy are deceitful" (Prov. 27 : 6). Judas kissed Jesus in order to betray him (Luke 22 : 48).

The Corinthians were instructed by Paul to kiss one another with the holy kiss (I Cor. 16 : 20; II Cor. 13 : 12). The early Christians were always admonished to have holy affection and sincere love toward one another.

II THESSALONIANS

INTRODUCTION

The companions of Paul at the time he wrote this epistle were Silvanus and Timothy.

The epistle was sent as a warning to the Thessalonians to beware of false teachers, troublemakers and especially false prophets who were predicting the imminent return of Christ. Some of these men based their predictions on arguments and on forged letters which they claimed they had received from Paul. Paul admonished the Christians to remain loyal to the truth of Jesus Christ as given to them by himself, both by word of mouth and by epistle.

The epistle no doubt was meant to clear up some misunderstanding created through Paul's mention in his first epistle of the coming of the Lord. The people seemingly took some of his utterances on this matter literally. Paul in his first epistle wrote concerning the coming of our Lord Jesus Christ, "Then we which are alive and remain shall be caught up together with them in the clouds, to meet the Lord in the air: and so shall we ever be with the Lord" (I Thes. 4 : 17). It is likely that the Thessalonians confused this passage with the "day of the Lord" (Isa. 2 : 12).

TRIBULATIONS

Which is a manifest token of the righteous judgment of God, that ye may be counted worthy of the kingdom of God, for which ye also suffer:
Seeing it is a righteous thing with God to recompense tribulation to them that trouble you; II Thes. 1 : 5-6.

Persecutions and sufferings for the sake of the teaching of Jesus Christ were counted as righteousness. The Christians gloried in being persecuted for the sake of the kingdom of God.

Jesus had told his first followers, "Blessed are they which are persecuted for righteousness' sake: for theirs is the kingdom of heaven." At times, Christian converts were brought before judges and governors to be tried. Many officials and court attendants were converted through their testimonies.

The Christians in Thessalonica, like those of other cities, had suffered considerably for the sake of their faith. They were suspected by the authorities and hated by their own people.

FORGERIES

That ye be not soon shaken in mind, or be troubled, neither by spirit, nor by word, nor by letter as from us, as that the day of Christ is at hand. II Thes. 2 : 2.

The forging of letters and documents is an old practice. This is especially true of manuscripts written in the Semitic languages, Aramaic and Hebrew. The change of a small dot may alter the meaning of a word and consequently of the whole sentence. For example, once an Arab caliph sent a letter to a governor-general in Egypt, asking him to welcome the newly appointed governor who was to succeed him. The Arabic words "to welcome" and "to kill" are written alike. The only difference is a single dot which is placed over the one word and under the other. After the letter was written a scribe changed the position of the dot and made the message read "kill him" instead of "welcome him." The orders were obeyed, and the new governor, his family, and the soldiers who accompanied him were killed.

The apostle warned against fake epistles which might be sent to the Thessalonians by false prophets who predicted the sudden return of Jesus and the destruction of the world. There were many such teachers who beguiled the faithful. The converts were led to believe that Jesus was to appear in the flesh soon, and the earth to come to an end. These false rumors were spread by word of mouth and, once circulated, it was difficult to correct them. Most of the alarming news was spread by men and women who claimed that they had the spirit of prophecy. The fact that some of these men had come from Judea made the people believe that they had accurate news about the coming of Jesus.

When we set the time for the end of the world and the coming of Christ, we pretend to know more than Jesus did. He said that no one knows the hour or the day but God himself.

Christians must always be prepared and in constant vigilance. The owner of the house does not know when the thief may come, so he keeps constant watch over his goods. The servant does not know when his master will return, so he stays awake. Jesus will return at a time when no one expects him.

DESTINY

And that we may be delivered from unreasonable and wicked men: for all men have not faith.
But the Lord is faithful, who shall stablish you, and keep you from evil. II Thes. 3 : 2–3.

Easterners believe that every man has a mission in life, and that every mission has an objective. People are called or appointed to these missions, regardless of the difficulties in the way. The more difficult the mission, the more qualified the agent becomes. God does not create the hardships, temptations and persecutions; but he helps us overcome them. These are the result of man's wrong thinking.

Because hardships and trials in this life are inevitable, Easterners believe that God appoints men to suffer in order to carry out their mission.

Jesus warned his disciples of offenses and stumbling blocks, which were inevitable. He blamed those who would be responsible for them. He also predicted that his disciples and followers would be rejected, persecuted and put to death for the sake of his gospel. This suffering was destined to crown them with glory. Paul, in his epistle to the Ephesians, told them not to worry over his tribulations. "Wherefore I desire that ye faint not at my tribulations for you, which is your glory" (Eph. 3 : 13).

Jesus foresaw his own suffering and death. He knew that the high priests and elders would not understand him and that they would reject him. Paul, like Jesus, was aware and ready to give his life for the gospel which was so dear to his heart.

COPYISTS

The salutation of Paul with mine own hand, which is the token in every epistle: so I write. II Thes. 3 : 17.

The epistle was written down by a scribe, but signed by the hand of Paul. It often happens that learned men and high ecclesiastical authorities do not write, but entrust the work to scribes. At times the sender of the epistle gives the scribe an outline of the letter he should compose, of arguments, questions and answers. The rest is done by the writer, who completes the work and reads it to the author before the latter affixes his signature and the salutation to it.

Some writers dictate the whole letter and are responsible for its composition and tone. The scribe merely acts as a copyist.

Paul wrote the eighteenth verse, the salutation, "The Grace of our Lord, Jesus Christ be with you, Amen." The salutation and signature are always written by the sender of the epistle. When the sender is unable to write, he seals the letter with his seal and makes a cross next to it.

Paul was a scholar and a scribe. He knew how to read and write, but on some occasions when he was overwhelmed with work and problems, he sought the aid of other men to do his writing for him.

I TIMOTHY

INTRODUCTION

Paul wrote this epistle from Laodicea of Pisidia prior to his journey to Jerusalem. Timothy, together with several other men, accompanied Paul as far as Asia Minor. Luke, the author of the Acts, states, "These going before tarried for us at Troas" (Acts 20 : 4–7). The epistle might have been sent before Paul's arrival at Jerusalem. In his epistle to the Galatians, Paul mentions Barnabas and Titus, but not Timothy (Gal. 2 : 1–4). It seems that Timothy had been left behind to look after the work in Asia Minor. In his second epistle Paul asks him to bring with him the books which he had left at Troas (II Tim. 4 : 13).

The theme of the epistle is discipline and Christian conduct. The document is a pastoral letter addressed to an elder or overseer of churches in Asia Minor. Timothy is cautioned against hasty judgment and advised concerning the selection of elders and deacons and the general care over the churches. The elders and deacons are to be chosen from among men of good conduct and Christian works.

FABLES

Neither give heed to fables and endless genealogies, which minister questions, rather than godly edifying which is in faith: so do. I Tim. 1 : 4.

"Fables" means "mythologies"; that is, teachings based on traditions which are handed down and circulated among the unlearned. Easterners especially, who are constantly in search of truth and spiritual comfort, are misled at times and may become victims of doctrines and fables that have no foundation.

Such fables often cause disputes and quarrels among the people. Since they are merely traditions based on theories, every teacher has his own interpretation of them, and it is difficult to prove or disprove any of them. Then again, once a fable has been established in the mind of the people, it is difficult to uproot it.

The discussion of these fables resulted in endless arguments. Therefore, instead of concerning themselves with fables, Paul urges the Christians to be mindful of those fundamental truths in the Christian religion which edify and enrich men's souls. Paul gave the same warning to the Christians at Colosse. He admonished them not to dispute among themselves about eating and drinking, the division of the feast days, and the laws governing the keeping of the Sabbath (Colos. 2 : 16–19).

Christians must discriminate between the fundamental truths of their religion and traditions based on theories. Today, for example, Christian denominations agree on most of the teachings of Jesus, but remain divided in respect to rituals, forms and traditions. Every denomination has tried to capitalize on certain of its own traditions and customs. It is the spirit that counts, not the letter.

DELIVERING TO SATAN

Of whom is Hymenæus and Alexander; whom I have delivered unto Satan, that they may learn not to blaspheme.
I Tim. 1 : 20.

The Eastern text reads, "To be disciplined so that they may no longer blaspheme." "Whom I have delivered unto Satan" is an Eastern saying that means, "I have let them suffer in their own evil devices in order to teach them a lesson," or, as Americans say, "I have given them a rope to hang themselves." When people are stubborn and disobedient they must be left alone to suffer the evil consequences.

Paul does not imply that Satan will make good men of them, but that through suffering and disillusionment they will sooner or later find out that they have been wrong. Prior to his conversion, Paul himself was moved by evil forces, persecuting the church of God and imprisoning the followers of Christ. But in due time he came to himself and found that the work he was doing was not of God but of Satan.

Some of these men were renegade converts who had turned against Paul and were causing him trouble. Paul had no power over them. He himself was persecuted for preaching the new gospel; he could not have the men who preached against him punished. All that Paul could do was to let these men suffer through their own evil devices until they were awakened to the truth.

LIFTING OF HANDS

I will therefore that men pray every where, lifting up holy hands, without wrath and doubting. I Tim. 2 : 8.

Semites, when praying, stretch out their arms and lift up their hands as though they were about to receive something. This is a gesture of supplication. When men plead before a high official of church or state, they lift up their hands, making gestures of sincere appeal. When they stand at attention, their hands are folded in front of them. When people beg for mercy they also stretch out or lift up their hands. "Lift up holy hands" means to plead with a sincere heart and motive. Mohammedans, during prayer, often turn around and change the position of their hands.

Christians are admonished to refrain from evil works, so that they may look straight into the eyes of other people and set an example worthy of their faith. Only by good works and Christian conduct will their light shine upon those who live in ignorance and darkness.

MODESTY

In like manner also, that women adorn themselves in modest apparel, with shamefacedness and sobriety; not with broided hair, or gold, or pearls, or costly array;
I Tim. 2 : 9.

The Aramaic text reads, "Let the apparel of women be simple and their adornment modest and refined." Eastern women are fond of necklaces, bracelets, earrings and other ornaments. This is particularly true of Palestinian and Syrian women, who wear lavish apparel, jeweled ornaments, necklaces strung with amber beads, and sometimes necklaces several feet long strung with gold and silver coins. Also their hats may be adorned with many layers of coins hanging one over another.

In the East, banks were unknown until recently. Excess gold and silver coins were used for ornaments. Many husbands took pride in the necklaces of their wives. When the family was in need, the husband took the coins from his wife and used them to buy food, clothing and other necessities. In the East, the wearing of necklaces and costly ornaments may look well on the street and in homes, but it causes disturbances and gossip in the churches. On this occasion women often overdo it, and therefore are criticized. Moreover, the coins and trinkets make a noise and disturb the worshipers. Also, some women wear them just to attract attention and display the wealth of their fathers or husbands.

Paul did not condemn the wearing of jewelry but despised the wearing of it in worship, especially when modesty and simplicity were discarded. He thought it all right for women to wear some jewelry but not to overdo it.

Peter also in his epistle warned against lavish dressing and the adorning of the head (I Pet. 3 : 3). This is because the apostles did not want to see Christian women behaving like pagan women, who dressed lavishly and danced at their temple ceremonies.

WOMAN'S POSITION IN CHURCH

Let the woman learn in silence with all subjection. But I suffer not a woman to teach, nor to usurp authority over the man, but to be in silence. I Tim. 2 : 11–12.

Women take no part in Jewish and Moslem religious services and other ceremonies. They are not allowed to sing, read scriptures, or recite prayers. They generally stand by themselves in a special place where they pray in silence and listen to those who chant and sing. In some Moslem countries women are not allowed to enter the mosque. According to some Moslem authorities, women were created to be servants for men and to make life easy for them. In the East this belief is also held to some extent by Christians. Women are allowed to attend the services with their heads covered, but they take no part in the rituals, nor do they pray aloud or read in the church. Some religious men blame the fall of man on woman. (See verses 13–14.)

Indeed the objection to the participation of women in religious services and in the teaching of the gospel is not based on the teaching of Jesus. It is based on ancient

Semitic customs. Jesus had no women disciples among the Twelve but he never discriminated against women. Jesus was living in the East, and had to respect the established customs and manners. At times, however, he departed from the custom and talked to women openly, so that some of the people, even his disciples, criticized him, as in the case of the woman at the well and Mary of Magdala. Even today such acts would embarrass priests and bishops in the East. They shun the presence of women.

Paul had some reason for not permitting women to preach publicly. Women were veiled, and the veiling of the face was an ancient custom introduced before the time of Abraham. It would have been difficult to abolish such an ancient custom and permit a few Christian women to walk in the streets unveiled. Then again, Christians were few. They attended the Jewish synagogues and the temple services.

In the East the faces of women are seldom seen by strangers. It would be shocking, and even scandalous, to permit a woman to stand before a congregation and read the Scriptures, because she would have to unveil her face in order to read. Such an act would cause great excitement in the congregation. Men would be looking at the woman instead of listening to what was being read.

Such are the Eastern customs and such were the problems that prompted Paul to make this discrimination. Had Paul been living in our day in America or Europe, he would never have thought of making such a recommendation. On some occasions Paul spoke well of women and admonished their husbands to love them and treat them as equals.

Jesus gave his life for both men and women. According to his teachng they stand equal in the presence of God. They are both created in God's image. Moreover, women are entrusted with sacred duties and responsibilities higher than those of men. They are the mothers of the future generations. Religion often means more to them than it does to men.

BISHOP

This is a true saying, If a man desire the office of a bishop, he desireth a good work.   I Tim. 3 : 1.

Episkopos is the Greek ecclesiastical term meaning literally "overseer." But it is usually translated into English as "bishop," "presbyter" or "elder." The Aramaic word is *abona,* meaning "father" or "overseer." The presbyters are elected from among the elderly men. The Aramaic word for priest is *kashisha,* meaning "old man." The term *apeskopa* is also used, especially in the canon law. In the East, a priest who is well known for his piety and devotion to Jesus Christ is called *ava,* "father." *Apeskopa* may have been derived from *ava* or *"abba."* The people look upon such men as fathers and overseers. Deacons and young priests also seek their counsel and blessings.

According to the Eastern text, Paul rarely uses the term "bishop." He uses the term "elder" very frequently (Acts 11 : 30; Titus 1 : 5).

When this epistle was sent to Timothy, the number of Christian congregations (churches) had grown to such an extent that an overseer was needed to appoint new elders to take charge of new congregations and to fill the vacancies which were created by death. The overseers or bishops took orders from the apostles.

MONOGOMY

A bishop then must be blameless, the husband of one wife, vigilant, sober, of good behaviour, given to hospitality, apt to teach;   I Tim. 3 : 2.

During the time of Paul, Christians were very few. The number of converts increased daily, but many of the newcomers into the church of Christ were polygamists. When they embraced Christianity they could not easily put their wives away. Even today, Mohammedans and Jewish priests may have several wives.

"The husband of one wife" refers to an elder who has only one wife. Some commentators believe that what Paul means is an elder who had married only once. The Eastern text uses the term *kashisha,* "elder."

The priests of the church in the East remarry when widowed, but the bishop must be a celibate all his life. This law was adopted later because of the persecution and other difficulties the bishops encountered. Bishops spent most of their lives hiding. Always they were sought by the pagans during persecutions. The priestly celibacy of all ecclesiastical orders in Europe was adopted still later. The priests of the Orthodox or Greek church never marry a second time. This is also true of priests of the Eastern churches that are in union with Rome. They may marry before ordination, but once ordained they may not marry. The Armenian priests may marry before their ordination. They may not marry again if widowed.

It seems, judging from both the language and custom, that Paul here refers to men who have only one wife. The church would not have selected a Christian elder with three or four wives. Family quarrels and troubles would have weakened his reputation.

Jesus made no attack on polygamy, but told his disciples that from the very beginning God had created man male and female. He seemed to take it for granted that a man should have only one wife. He once said, "For this cause shall a man leave father and mother, and shall cleave to his wife: And they twain shall be one flesh" (Matt. 19 : 5).

THE OFFICE OF DEACON

Likewise must the deacons be grave, not doubletongued, not given to much wine, not greedy of filthy lucre;
I Tim. 3 : 8.

Meshamshana, "deacon," in Aramaic means "minister" or "servant"—one who ministers to man's spiritual needs, visits the sick, helps in services, reads the lessons. The Aramaic word for "servant" is *auda*.

In the East, the duties of a deacon are similar to those of a Levite in the Jewish religion. The Levites served in the Temple as assistants to the priests. Their work was confined to temple worship and sacrifices: "And their charge shall be the ark, and the table, and the candlestick, and the altars, and the vessels of the sanctuary wherewith they minister, and the hanging, and all the service thereof" (Num. 3 : 31).

The early Christians adopted the Jewish form of worship, the ceremonials and the priestly order. In many places Christians continued to worship in the synagogues, and went to Jerusalem to worship, make offerings, and pray at the Temple (Acts 21 : 20–24ff).

The deacons took care of the scrolls, read the Scriptures and performed other duties connected with the early simple worship. Years after, when the church became an organized body, the deacons played an important part both in worship and in church administration. In other words, in the East, deacons were and still are assistant ministers. No priest can celebrate communion without the help of two deacons, except in the case of an emergency, when he must have at least one.

SPIRITS

Now the Spirit speaketh expressly, that in the latter times some shall depart from the faith, giving heed to seducing spirits, and doctrines of devils; I Tim. 4 : 1.

"Spirits," in this case, means "prophecies." When men prophesy, they are said to be moved by the Spirit of God. Jesus when he preached in the synagogue at Nazareth said, "The Spirit of the Lord is upon me." On another occasion, when debating with the Jews, he said, "How then doth David in spirit call him Lord" (Matt. 22 : 43).

The "doctrines of devils" in this instance refers to the teachings of devilish men. In the East, doctrines which are not based on the Holy Scriptures are called "doctrines of the devil," and the men who preach them are called "satans."

Paul warned against those who were trying to pervert the truth through lies and hypocrisy. These teachers had departed from the established truths. They were teaching doctrines based on their own theories, thus introducing new practices, such as celibacy, contrary to the law of God. Many of these teachers were carried away by their own deceit, themselves believing the lies and falsehoods which they taught.

CELIBACY

Forbidding to marry, and commanding *to abstain from meats, which God hath created to be received with thanksgiving of them which believe and know the truth.*
I Tim. 4 : 3.

The doctrines of celibacy and abstinence from wine, meat and certain foods were introduced by the Essenes, Sabians and members of other ancient cults who had embraced Christianity.

The members of these cults, which preceded Christianity, refrained from the eating of meat and the drinking of wine and other strong drinks. Some of them went so far in their asceticism that they abstained from eating cultivated plants and vegetables. They preferred to live on wild plants and vegetables that grew in the desert. Their doctrines were supposed to have been based on God's commands concerning food as found in Genesis. "And God said, Behold, I have given you every herb bearing seed, which is upon the face of all the earth, and every tree; in the which is the fruit of a tree yielding seed; to you it shall be for meat" (Gen. 1 : 29). They blamed the fall of man and his short life upon his departure from this command. Many of these people were found in Syria and Asia Minor. Many of them were skilled blacksmiths, silversmiths and iron workers. Some believers in these ancient cults are still to be found in the East.

Marriage was discouraged by them and at times denounced as an evil. Some men inflicted injuries upon their bodies in the hope that they might enter more quickly into the kingdom of God. Jesus, when discussing marriage and divorce, mentioned this custom (Matt. 19 : 11–12).

Paul denounced these doctrines as alien to the Scriptures and not founded on the truth of Jesus Christ. These teachings were similar to the traditions of the Jewish elders, which Jesus had condemned. Celibacy is all right when a man is willing to consecrate his life to God's work. The eating of foods likewise is left to the choice of the individual. "For one believeth that he may eat all things: another, who is weak, eateth herbs" (Rom. 14 : 2).

OLD WOMEN FABLES

But refuse profane and old wives' fables, and exercise thyself rather unto godliness.   I Tim. 4 : 7.

"Fables," in this instance, means "traditions," that is, doctrines that are based on ancient theories and handed down by word of mouth. Paul, in several of his epistles, warned against teachings which sprung up from such theories and from Jewish fables. In his epistle to Titus, he spoke of "Not giving heed to Jewish fables" (Titus 1 : 14). Jesus called them traditions of the elders.

The term "old wives' fables," is derived from colloquial speech. In the East one often says, "I can't believe it; it is a saying of an old woman." This is because in the East, elderly women tell stories. Some of them are like novelists; they spend days telling stories and legends. Where the writing of fiction is unknown, fables are very common. Simple and illiterate men and women believe in some of them.

The teachings found in the fables and legends were contrary to the teachings of Jesus, just as the traditions of the Jewish elders were contrary to the teachings of the prophets.

EARLY EDUCATION

Till I come, give attendance to reading, to exhortation, to doctrine. I Tim. 4 : 13.

Prior to the establishment of the synagogue schools, about 400 B.C., candidates for the priesthood were trained under the care of learned priests and scribes. The priesthood was hereditary. A father taught his son; an uncle, his nephew. For instance, Samuel was trained by Eli, and Elisha by Elijah. At times, the disciples traveled with their masters. Theological schools were unknown; and books were scarce—found only in the possession of priests and kings.

During the Babylonian captivity, synagogue schools were established in Jewish communities, and the learning of the Scriptures was encouraged. Schools of law and higher learning flourished in Mesopotamia. Not only the sons of the learned and the rich went to school, but also those of the poorer classes.

Jesus was born and raised in a poor family. He received his early education at the synagogue school. He was well versed in the Scriptures. Paul debated with the Jews in their synagogues (Acts 17 : 2–3). The synagogue was a place for both prayer and learning. The Jewish learned men were tolerant to some extent. After the service, the people criticized the sermon and debated many of the statements that had been made. The debates helped to spread education and acquaint the people with the Scriptures. Those who could not read nor write, listened to the debates, as they do today in the East.

Timothy's father was an Aramean (Syrian), but his mother was a Jewess (Acts 16 : 1, Eastern text). He had received some religious training from his mother and at the synagogue. Many Syrians who had married Jewish women attended the synagogue. At the synagogue schools the chief studies were the law of Moses, the traditions, and readings from other sacred writings.

Timothy was appointed to take charge of several churches in Asia Minor. He was the chief elder (ava). Paul instructed him to study the Christian gospel and not the Jewish laws and traditions of the elders which Paul had branded as fables, invented by elderly women. The teachings of Jesus had been in circulation prior to Paul's conversion. Paul himself had made a study of them when he went to the Arabian Desert (Gal. 1 : 17). In his epistles he quoted many of the sayings of Jesus. No doubt Timothy had a copy of the gospels which Paul had acquired after his conversion; or perhaps he had confiscated them from the Christians when he was persecuting the churches in Judea. Paul carried his books and scrolls with him. In his second epistle to Timothy, Paul instructed him to bring the books and scrolls which Paul had left at Troas in the house of Carpus (II Tim. 4 : 13). (King James Version mentions an overcoat.) Timothy could not have been made an overseer without having a copy of the gospels. He had to teach and instruct the elders, and this would have been impossible without a copy of the Scriptures containing the teachings of Jesus.

CARE OF WIDOWS

But if any widow have children or nephews, let them learn first to shew piety at home, and to requite their parents: for that is good and acceptable before God.

Now she that is a widow indeed, and desolate, trusteth in God, and continueth in supplications and prayers night and day. I Tim. 5 : 4–5.

In many parts of the Near East, where orphan asylums and homes for old people are unknown, widows and orphans are cared for by relatives, friends and churches. The Mohammedans give a tithe for this purpose. The money is administered by the mosque. The poor receive bread, clothing and shelter.

The Jews also take care of their widows and orphans. Their concern for one another is great; their racial ties are probably stronger than those of any other race. That is why one seldom sees a Jewish beggar. The Scriptures make a strong plea on behalf of orphans, widows and the destitute. "He doth execute the judgment of the fatherless and widow, and loveth the stranger, in giving him food and raiment. Love ye therefore the stranger: for ye were strangers in the land of Egypt" (Deut. 10 : 18–19). "A father of the fatherless, and a judge of the widows, is God in his holy habitation" (Psa. 68 : 5). Indeed, even though at times widows were treated unjustly, they were for the most part generously supported by the rich and the pious.

Nevertheless, Paul warns against such practices, not because he was against Eastern hospitality, but because there were many persons who took advantage of the generosity of pious men and women. Some widows, instead of receiving aid from their relatives, became a burden on the people. This is true today in the East. Many women after the death of their husbands cannot earn a livelihood. They rely for support upon their relatives or the pious. Such cases are so numerous that it is difficult to know which are worthy. Organized charity is unknown, and Easterners hate to turn away anyone who is in need.

WORTHY WIDOWS

Let not a widow be taken into the number under three-score years old, having been the wife of one man,
I Tim. 5 : 9.

The Eastern text reads, "When you select a worthy widow, select therefore one who is not less than threescore years old, and who has been the wife of one man." This command was intended to exclude widows under sixty years of age, and those who had married more than once.

In the East Christian women usually marry only once. Divorces are rare and difficult to obtain. Widows who have married more than once are generally supported by their step-children. Some of them can marry again. On the other hand, widows over sixty, who decide not to marry and who have no male children, may become destitute. They must be supported by pious men and by the churches. Some of them devote considerable time to church work. They light candles, clean sacred vessels, sweep and do other work.

Sixty years of age is the requirement because in the East women usually marry at the age of twelve to fourteen, and when they are sixty they are old women and often addressed as mothers, even though some of them still look young and strong.

This rule generally applies to those widows without a male child who are worthy and unable to support themselves.

YOUNG WIDOWS

And withal they learn to be idle, wandering about from house to house; and not only idle, but tattlers also and busybodies, speaking things which they ought not.
I Tim. 5 : 13.

Among Semitic people, direct courtship of maidens is discouraged and in some countries prohibited. Marriages are arranged by the parents of the parties concerned, and by friends. Virgins shun young men and refuse to converse with them.

Exceptions are made in the case of young widows. This is because widows are not in demand. They must find husbands for themselves. They are permitted to talk to men, and therefore are likely to become the subject of gossip. This is especially true of widows with children. They are forced to transact business, seek the counsel of men, travel with them in caravans, and perform other duties that a maiden is not allowed to perform. Many younger widows thus fall into temptation and are severely criticized.

When Paul wrote this epistle, Christians were living among the pagans. Young Christian widows sometimes left their faith and lived with the pagans. Paul encouraged these young widows to marry Christians, rather than to fall into temptation and lose their faith.

LIVING ON FAITH

Let the elders that rule well be counted worthy of double honour, especially they who labour in the word and doctrine.
For the scripture saith, Thou shalt not muzzle the ox that treadeth out the corn. And, The labourer is worthy of his reward.
I Tim. 5 : 17, 18.

In countries of the East, ministers of the gospel and others who are engaged in church work receive no regular salary for their services; they are supported by gifts and contributions given to the church as offerings. These gifts are either presented to the minister directly or taken to the church to be consecrated. The priests or ministers use a portion for themselves and distribute the rest among the poor. The collection of money during church services is not allowed. Instead, some of the worshipers bring bread and food to church. The ministers, singers and elders share the food after the services.

As a whole, priests and caretakers rely on God for their support. Some of them do work such as farming their fields and attending sheep.

The priests and Levites under the Mosaic law were supported by tithes and offerings which consisted of animals, wheat and fruits. Abraham gave Melchizedek ten per cent of the spoils which he had taken when he defeated the five kings (Gen. 14 : 20). Amos upbraided the people of Israel for not being regular in their tithing (Amos 4 : 4).

During the time of Eli, priests lived lavishly from the sacrifices (I Sam. 2 : 29). Some of the prophets condemned the extravagance of the greedy priests and Levites, and strongly denounced the system of sacrifices and offerings. Hosea said, "I desire mercy, and not sacrifice" (Hosea 6 : 6).

Throughout the Old Testament, one can see that Hebrew priests were well provided for, and that at times they were spoiled by the rich gifts offered in the temple of God. The Mosaic law states that those who work for God must live on the things that are given to God. The quotation, "Thou shalt not muzzle the ox that treadeth out the corn," is from Deuteronomy 25 : 4.

In biblical lands modern scientific agricultural methods were unknown until recent years and in many regions are still unknown. Wheat is cut with ancient implements and threshed under the feet of oxen. The sheaves of grain are laid in a circle, around a pole, similar to a telegraph pole. Oxen are fastened to the pole and a man drives them around and around, treading on the sheaves until the grain is separated from the chaff. The oxen are muzzled because wheat is scarce. Moses objected to this practice. However, there are some people who do not muzzle their

I TIMOTHY

oxen, but let them eat as much as they want of the wheat that they thresh.

Paul implies that the ministers of the gospel must live from the gospel. That is to say, in cases where ministers are not paid, they should be supported by means of gifts and personal contributions. Thus, ministers live on what is given to God, because they serve in his house. If God takes care of an ox, how much more then is he concerned about those who work for him? Paul quotes a saying of Jesus, ". . . For the labourer is worthy of his hire" (Luke 10 : 7). Jesus' disciples received food and other supplies from men who invited them in their homes. They also depended on the generosity of their converts for food, clothing and other needs.

LAYING ON OF HANDS

I charge thee before God, and the Lord Jesus Christ, and the elect angels, that thou observe these things without preferring one before another, doing nothing by partiality.
Lay hands suddenly on no man, neither be partaker of other men's sins: keep thyself pure.
I Tim. 5 : 21–22.

The Aramaic word *tsim,* "lay," is derived from the word *sam,* "to lay down," "to lay a foundation," "to appoint" and "to claim." Thus, *siam eida,* "laying on of hands," also means "to arrest," "to seize," "to ordain," "to accuse" and "to claim." The Aramaic word for "ordination" is *siameda.*

The phrase, "they laid hands on him," is commonly used in the vernacular Aramaic speech. When such phrases, having several meanings, are encountered in speech or in writing, their meaning is determined by the context. In the case of ordination, the word *kashisha,* "elder," is inserted. For example, Ananias laid his hands on Paul and healed his eyes (Acts 9 : 17). Jesus laid his hands on his disciples. The prophets and teachers at Antioch laid hands on Paul and Barnabas when they were sent on their mission. Then again the Jewish rulers laid hands on Peter and John and kept them in prison because it was the Sabbath, but brought them to trial on the next day (Acts 4 : 3). "No one dares to lay hands on him" is a common saying, and it occurs many times in the New Testament.

In olden days in the East men were elected to an office by laying hands on them. The candidates were presented and the people placed their hands on those whom they desired to elect to the office. Balloting was unknown among primitive people. On the other hand, when a man is accused, his accuser generally comes forward and taps him on the shoulder. "He had laid hands on it" means "he claimed it." Assyrians often say, "He has laid hands on my ox," which means, "he seized it by force." "They had laid hands on his daughter," means that the girl had been betrothed to a certain person.

Apparently Paul admonished Timothy not to ordain men hastily; but he might have meant that Timothy should not accuse anyone, elder or layman, unless he was sure of the accusation. Charges against the elders had to be substantiated by two witnesses. In some respects, this whole chapter of the epistle deals with Christian conduct.

Ordination, as we have it today, was hardly known or practiced at that time. The priesthood, composed of bishops, deacons and priests, was also unknown. Jesus had laid his hands on all of his disciples, but not one of them was appointed as a leader. He told them all to be servants. He laid his hands on little children and on the sick. His disciples likewise laid their hands on the converts.

Jesus had some organization among his followers, but it was not like that of Judaism, which he opposed. The leaders were not to be lords of the people, but their ministers. They were to serve spiritually and materially, and not to be served. They were to guard and teach his doctrine and not to create their own system of theology.

WINE OR MEDICINE

Drink no longer water, but use a little wine for thy stomach's sake and thine often infirmities. I Tim. 5 : 23.

In biblical days wine was considered as a medicine and therefore prescribed for both internal and external ailments. This is because in those days, medicines were rare. Wines and liquors were considered to have the power to cure.

Oil and wine were poured on wounds, as in the case of the good Samaritan. "And went to him, and bound up his wounds, pouring in oil and wine" (Luke 10 : 34). Wine contains some alcohol, and in the East it is used as an antiseptic for wounds. Flies are so numerous that bodily injuries are easily infected. The dressing of wounds is rare and difficult. At times the wounded are left helpless, their wounds exposed to flies and other insects. Some native doctors recommend tobacco, instead of wine. Occasionally people who suffer from indigestion drink a little wine with their meals.

Native wines do not contain as much alcohol as foreign wines do. Some people use wine at meals; others drink only during festivals and banquets. Wine is supposed to gladden men's hearts and make them forget their troubles (Psa. 104 : 15). "Give strong drink unto him that is ready to perish, and wine unto those that be of heavy hearts" (Prov. 31 : 6). That is why the soldiers gave vinegar to Jesus when he was on the cross. The Scriptures in many places oppose the use of wine and strong drinks (Habbak. 2 : 5).

Paul does not encourage the drinking of wine, nor does he condemn its moderate use. Many prophets and religious teachers denounced excessive drinking. Paul's advice to Timothy is like that of a doctor to his patient, and it should not be misunderstood.

PUNISHING OF THE GUILTY

Some men's sins are open beforehand, going before to judgment; and some men they follow after. I Tim. 5 : 24.

According to Roman law, or the code of Justinian, a man is innocent until he is proven guilty. This is also true of the Mosaic law and the laws of many other religions. A man's guilt must be proved by two or three witnesses of the crime. Anyone can accuse a man, but the accusation cannot always be sustained by witnesses.

Nevertheless, there are times when the acts of the person accused of a crime are evident before his trial, so that there is no need for witnesses. It is interesting to know that in Persia notorious criminals and bandits when captured are put to death without trial.

On the other hand, some crimes are brought to light only after charges are sustained and the guilty person convicted.

Paul admonished Timothy that the works of some men are well known beforehand and their acts likewise speak for themselves. But there are others whose works are hidden. Therefore Paul warned him to discriminate in these cases, and convict only persons against whom charges are sustained by witnesses, according to the law of the land or the law of Moses. But in the case of persons whose evil acts were evident, he was to use his own judgment.

SPIRITUAL RICHES

But godliness with contentment is great gain.
I Tim. 6 : 6.

The Aramaic word *tegortha* means "trade," "business" and "gain." Both Jews and pagans boasted of their riches and magnificent temples and their elaborate ceremonies. Their ritualistic worship could not be carried on without temples, treasures and other worldly riches. An elaborate priesthood, a huge volume of traditions, a highly spectacular ritual and innumerable costly and impressive liturgical appointments had come to play so large a part in religious worship that the real issues were obscured. Many priests and their associates derived fabulous incomes from treasuries accumulated in the temples and shrines. Very few of them were spiritual leaders of their flocks, or interpreters of God's love for his children.

In contrast to this, the early Christians were paying a high price for their faith, suffering countless privations and persecutions. Their homes and other properties were often confiscated or burned. They carried on their worship in simple dwellings and such secret places as they could find, literally following in the footsteps of their Master, holding a spiritual concept of religion. They were free from temples, shrines, dogmas and traditions, which Jesus had so strongly denounced. To the pagans riches, honors and worldly power were the things that counted most; they had little knowledge of life hereafter.

The Eastern text reads, "But our gain is greater contentment, for it is the worship of God." Paul, like Jesus, warned against the temptations of the material world (Matt. 19 : 24). Christians are to be content with daily bread and simple worship. Their riches consist of spiritual things, the fear of God, true worship and the hope of salvation through Jesus Christ. These are the things that count in a Christian world. God's kingdom and his righteousness are to come first and other things will be added later. The prophets warned against extreme riches and the worship of wealth. "Better is little with the fear of the Lord than great treasure and trouble therewith" (Prov. 15 : 16). "A little that a righteous man hath is better than the riches of many wicked" (Psa. 37 : 16). "Lay not up for yourselves treasures upon earth, where moth and rust doth corrupt, and where thieves break through and steal" (Matt. 6 : 19).

Wealth is a blessing to those who possess it and use it for good, but a curse to those who do not know how to use it. It is not the possession of wealth that is evil, but the worship of wealth and the wrong use of it. Paul warned against materialism, and enjoined upon the Christian converts the earnest pursuit of the treasures that satisfy the soul and endure.

SCIENCE AND RELIGION

O Timothy, keep that which is committed to thy trust, avoiding profane and vain babblings, and oppositions of science falsely so called: I Tim. 6 : 20.

The word "science" in this instance refers to knowledge based on human understanding. Scientific teachings were spread in Asia Minor and Greece by learned men who traced everything to nature, failing to realize that behind nature is a creating and guiding power. The pagan teachers tried to find the meaning of life in the sun and moon and other heavenly bodies that they could see. Their minds could not penetrate the unseen and spiritual, which is the basic reality of life.

Some of these teachers had embraced Christianity, but were polluting the gospel of Christ with pagan teachings based solely on science. This was the beginning of Gnosticism. According to these teachers, salvation was to come through knowledge. Yet what is human knowledge when compared with the wisdom of God? The Christian religion was founded on faith and good works, and its salvation is by the grace of God and faith in Jesus Christ, and not by the definition of physics, astronomy and astrology. Man's limited wisdom of these sciences seems foolish when compared with the infinite wisdom of God.

There is no conflict between true science and religion. Nevertheless, when science and religion are based on theories and not on true facts, they do conflict.

These false teachers rejected the deity of Christ and did not believe in salvation through his death. They also denied the resurrection of the body. In the second century, Gnosticism grew to such an extent that for a time it became a great danger to Christianity. Paul upbraided these teachers and scorned their teachings. He described them as, "ever learning, and never able to come to the knowledge of the truth." That is to say, they were unable to agree.

II TIMOTHY

INTRODUCTION

This epistle was written from Rome, where Paul had been brought before Nero the second time. It is believed that Paul suffered two imprisonments. The document is one of the last epistles written before his death, to a sincere and beloved co-worker whom he often called "my son," and who had been entrusted with important work in Asia Minor.

The epistle deals with the ministers of the gospel (elders), their duties and conduct, and with the congregation which had been entrusted to them. The tone of the epistle is very friendly; indeed, it sounds like a letter written by a father to his son. Paul admonishes Timothy to live a Christian life, to remain firm in the true teaching received from Paul, to study hard and to ordain worthy men to the ministry. He also warns Timothy against philosophers, who taught science above religion, and against fables and doctrines which were causing strife among believers.

The situation of some of the churches in Asia Minor was seemingly grave. The people of this area were of diverse origins. They still held to some of the beliefs they had acquired before they became Christians. Moreover, teachers who were opposed to Paul visited them from time to time, preaching doctrines contradictory to those of Paul and the other apostles. Some of the believers had already deserted Paul, and others were wavering. The epistle also shows beyond doubt Paul's high esteem for Timothy's loyalty, faith and Christian conduct. But even so, Paul, as a Christian father, admonishes Timothy to be steadfast, remain loyal, and fight a hard fight against the forces of evil which were undermining the faith of the converts in that region.

ORDINATION

Wherefore I put thee in remembrance that thou stir up the gift of God, which is in thee by the putting on of my hands. II Tim. 1 : 6.

Basiam edi, "putting of my hands," in this instance refers to ordination. The laying of hands on those who are ordained to minister is an ancient Eastern custom. When sincere friends converse with one another, each places a hand on the other's shoulder, especially when an elderly man is giving advice to a younger one. The hand is symbolic of divine power. Figuratively, outstretched hands indicate a desire to show mercy. "I have spread out my hands all the day unto a rebellious people" (Isa. 65 : 2).

The lifting of the hands indicates a solemn pledge: "And Abram said to the king of Sodom, I have lift up my hand unto the Lord" (Gen. 14 : 22).

The laying of hands on a person is an act of consecration; that is, the act sets aside the person for the service of God, and he is consecrated by the Holy Spirit. "And the Lord said unto Moses, Take thee Joshua the son of Nun, a man in whom is the spirit, and lay thine hand upon him" (Num. 27 : 18).

Jesus laid hands on the apostles, and they in turn laid hands on the men who were chosen to preach the gospel and minister to the people (Acts 6 : 6).

Timothy was ordained by Paul. Paul had taken Timothy with him on many of his journeys and had trained him in the word of God and the ministration to the churches. Paul himself was well educated in all aspects of the Jewish faith and its ministry.

Timothy had the gift of laying hands on those who were selected to minister to the churches that were under his charge. By the laying on of hands he appointed and consecrated them through the Holy Spirit and gave them power to shepherd the flocks of Christ which were entrusted to them.

IMMORTALITY

But is now made manifest by the appearing of our Saviour Jesus Christ, who hath abolished death, and hath brought life and immortality to light through the gospel:
II Tim. 1 : 10.

Before the coming of Jesus, death was dreaded by the Jews, who looked upon it as the inevitable end of life. The people had little idea of immortality; they were not at all sure about a life hereafter. Indeed, the doctrine of the resurrection was in its infancy and much debated. The Pharisees believed in the resurrection of the body, but the Sadducees denied it. On the other hand, pagan gods were thought to die, so their worshipers had no conception of life hereafter. It was believed that when a person died, both his body and his soul perished. In this verse Paul refers to the death of the soul and not the death of the body.

Jesus, through his death and resurrection, destroyed the fear of death and gave humanity a new hope. According to the teaching of Jesus, it is the spirit that gives life; the earthly body is not important. "It is the spirit that quickeneth; the flesh profiteth nothing" (John 6 : 63).

Nevertheless, at the end the body will rise in glory; that is, it will be transformed into a spiritual body. This new hope of immortality was brought to its highest conception through the teaching of Jesus. And since then, it has always been a great comfort to his followers, who look forward to his coming.

Christianity is the religion of the living God. Believers will live hereafter. Life on this earth is only a preparation for the life to come. Christians are exhorted to work for things which are enduring and for life everlasting. Earthly bodies are the temples of the spirit. They must be cared for, kept clean, and dedicated to the Spirit of God which abides in them; but man is a living soul, which is the breath of God. Man is immortal because God is immortal.

SPIRITUAL RELATIONS

Thou therefore, my son, be strong in the grace that is in Christ Jesus. II Tim. 2 : 1.

Here, "son," means literally "my child." Elderly men and teachers when addressing younger men, as a token of sincere affection, call them "my son." Strangers never use this term; one must be well acquainted with a person in order to use it. The Turks use this form of address more frequently than any other people in the Near East. When addressing any young man they know well, they call him *auglim,* "my son."

Timothy was not the son of Paul, as is wrongly supposed by some people. Paul was not married; Timothy was his spiritual son. He was one of the early fruits of his missionary work. Paul uses Eastern mannerisms of speech when writing to some of his closest companions, especially to Timothy, who is so close and dear to his heart that he cannot call him anything else but "my son." Timothy was one of the most loyal co-workers of Paul. He stood by him to the last.

GOLDEN VESSELS

But in a great house there are not only vessels of gold and of silver, but also of wood and of earth; and some to honour, and some to dishonour. II Tim. 2 : 20.

Kings, princes and rich men in some of the Eastern countries use vessels of pure gold and silver, as well as artistic pottery. Gold and silver vessels are generally used at banquets and state dinners; they are for the sole use of the owner. The Eastern text reads, "Some for formal use and occasions of honor, and others for service," that is, general use.

In the East, ordinary pottery and wooden vessels are used for the servants and for unimportant guests. Precious vessels are carefully guarded and used only on important occasions.

Paul admonishes Christians to purge themselves from evil and try to become pure, like golden vessels, fit for the service of their Master. (See Romans 9 : 21.)

HERETICS

Having a form of godliness, but denying the power thereof: from such turn away.   II Tim. 3 : 5.

Apostasy was growing among the Christians in Asia Minor and Macedonia. Paul had been in prison, the churches were left like sheep without a shepherd and in constant danger from men who disguised themselves as Christian teachers. The reference here is to the converts who had departed from the true faith and teaching which had been imparted to them by the apostles. These men were materially minded. Like the Pharisees, they made a display of their faith by wearing long garments, and they taught doctrines based on their own interpretations, which caused divisions in the church. They had already become apostates and departed from the teaching of Christ. They were unwilling to carry the cross and endure suffering for the sake of the truth which had been entrusted to them (II Tim. 4 : 3).

The apostles from the very beginning were aware of these false teachers and of the temptations that would confront the Christian flock. "For such are false apostles, deceitful workers, transforming themselves into the apostles of Christ" (II Cor. 11 : 13). Many of these teachers were posing as apostles. Some were pretending they had letters from the apostles; others succeeded in forging letters from churches in Judea.

When we Christians are confronted with heretics and false teachings, we should always turn to the gospel of Christ as the only true source by which we can be guided. Any teaching that is not based on the gospels is contrary to the teaching of Jesus and his apostles. One must discriminate between theories and traditions and fundamental truths.

JANNES AND JAMBRES

Now as Jannes and Jambres withstood Moses, so do these also resist the truth: men of corrupt minds, reprobate concerning the faith. II Tim. 3 : 8.

Jannes and Jambres were the two famous Egyptian magicians who opposed Moses, and in a few instances duplicated his wonders in the presence of Pharaoh. In Aramaic they are called *Yane* and *Yambres*. These men were highly versed in Egyptian magic and sleight of hand. After enchanting, they cast down their rods, which they turned into serpents (Exod. 7 : 11–12). They also, like Moses, smote the river and turned its water into blood (Exod. 7 : 22). With their highly developed art of magic they succeeded in belittling Moses' miracles and wonders and thus hardened Pharaoh's heart.

These apostates who had left the Christian faith and were opposed to Paul, he likened to the wise men of Egypt who had been successful in opposing Moses. The apostates had caused considerable strife in the churches and led many people astray from the truth of Christ. As a result, others were deserting Paul (II Tim. 1 : 15). Even some of his close disciples and followers had already left the church. Paul complained strongly against these unfaithful men (II Tim. 4 : 10–16).

Many of the religions in Asia Minor were introduced from Egypt and Babylon. The priests of these religions studied magic. Christian converts were still under the influence of the teachings of the pagan religions which surrounded them. Then again, it must be remembered that the Christian flock was very small and insignificant in a world where pagan religions exerted such great social and political influence. In other words, the pagan religions offered more material gains and opportunities than Christianity. The Christians, at the outset, were told to expect persecution and to be ready to die if necessary for the gospel that had been delivered to them. Nevertheless, some converts failed to remain steadfast. The temptations of the world about them made them deny Christ.

BOOKS

The cloke that I left at Troas with Carpus, when thou comest, bring with thee, and the books, but especially the parchments. II Tim. 4 : 13.

Beth ktavey in Aramaic means a "bookcase," and not a "cloak," as wrongly translated in the King James and other versions. It is a small container made of leather in the shape of a saddle-bag. When on a journey, Oriental missionaries and religious men always carry their books with them for devotional and educational purposes. They do not carry extra clothing or shoes, nor do they take their best clothing with them. They generally wear their everyday clothes. This is because styles never change. The same garments are worn all the year round. In some regions, during the winter months, people wear an extra garment. There are a few exceptions to this. Rich travelers, with servants, and government officials sometimes carry an extra robe and embroidered official garments, but the missionaries take only what they are wearing. Travel is hazardous; bandits often rob men of their clothing and money. Those who are carrying much baggage are attacked first, as they are suspected of being rich. That is why Jesus warned his disciples not to carry extra clothes and shoes.

Paul had no extra cloak to be left behind, nor was he

concerned about his clothing, especially on this occasion, when he was in Rome and Timothy at Troas. He would not have asked Timothy to carry a robe such a long distance. Christian converts in Macedonia and Italy who frequently visited him would have provided him with clothes if he had been in need. What Paul asked, was that the bookcase, containing scrolls and books, be brought to him. He carried these books with him for study, for the instruction of his students and for devotional purposes. The scrolls contained the gospel writings, which Paul usually carried with him, and from which he preached and taught, just as the missionaries do today.

We must not forget that Paul had never been with Jesus and that he was a later convert to Christianity. While an enemy of the new faith, he had learned little about Jesus and his teachings; he had heard only prejudiced misrepresentations. After his conversion Paul devoted much of his time to the study of the Scriptures (Four Gospels), which he had copied while in Syria and Jerusalem. The books had been left behind for safety, because books were always in danger of being confiscated and burned. These documents were Paul's most precious possession and he guarded them most jealously.

TITUS

INTRODUCTION

The writer is Paul. The epistle was written from Nicopolis of Macedonia before Paul's imprisonment.

Titus was one of the earliest disciples of Paul. He was an Aramean (Syrian). (Gal. 2 : 3.) Paul took him with him on his various missionary journeys. Titus seemed to be a great organizer. He knew the people in Asia Minor and Macedonia. Paul sent him on important missions and at times left him behind to finish the work which he and his co-workers had started (II Cor. 2 : 13; 7 : 6; 12 : 18; II Tim. 4 : 10). He was with Paul at the Council of Jerusalem (Acts 15 : 4; Gal. 2 : 1–3).

Titus was left in Crete to organize churches and appoint elders over the congregations (Titus 1 : 5). Paul sets forth the qualifications of elders. The candidates were to possess Christian characters, to be hospitable, pure, kind and sober. It seems that conditions in the churches in Crete were bad and apostasy was growing. Paul warned Titus to keep away from fables and genealogies and to reject any heretics.

QUALIFICATIONS OF ELDERS

For this cause left I thee in Crete, that thou shouldest set in order the things that are wanting, and ordain elders in every city, as I had appointed thee: Titus 1 : 5.

Titus was an overseer (bishop) of Crete. Like Timothy, he was empowered to select and train worthy elders and ordain them to take charge of the churches which were growing on the island.

At the outset Titus was sent to Crete by Paul to look after the congregations which the latter had organized on his earlier journey. This appointment resulted in bigger responsibilities.

The term "elders" means "presbyters" or "ministers." They are called elders because Easterners generally do not ordain young men to the ministry. They prefer elderly and experienced men with good conduct. In the East, the people seldom seek counsel of young men; they look up to elderly men for discipline and admonition. Moses was eighty when he began his ministry.

The qualifications of elders, as outlined here, are similar to those which Paul recommended in his epistles to Timothy. The elders must be blameless, sober, faithful and husbands of one wife. That is to say, they must not be selected from among the polygamists. The elders who already were in charge of congregations had been converted from other religions. Both pagans and Jews were polygamists. There were a great many Jewish converts in Crete, as is seen in the tenth verse. Paul calls them, "they of circumcision." Some of these converts had several wives before they became Christians. Paul instructed Titus not to appoint elders and overseers from among these men. There were many converts who had only one wife. These were to be preferred. Paul was careful not to set a bad example. Then again, men who had more than one wife, and large families, would have found it difficult to minister to their congregations, and at the same time take care of their large families. This is true of some of the Moslem and Jewish rabbis who have more than one wife; most of their time is spent settling quarrels among the women and children.

To permit elders or even members of the church to have more than one wife at a time, would have been contrary to the teaching of Jesus and Christian ethics.

Note:—Armenian and Greek churches believe that what Paul meant here is that priests must not marry a second time. When an Armenian priest loses his wife he never marries again. This is also true of the Greeks and other Christians who belong to Monophysitic sects.

BAD ELDERS

One of themselves, even a prophet of their own, said, The Cretians are always liars, evil beasts, slow bellies.
Titus 1 : 12.

The Aramaic reads: "vicious beasts with empty bellies." That is, gluttons, who give themselves to eating and drinking and who, when drunk, act like wild animals. Men of this type were dangerous and greedy. They would pervert church doctrines, accept bribes and do evil things for the sake of money and power.

Paul is strong in his denunciations of some of the elders in Crete who lacked good conduct and spirituality. He instructed Titus to rebuke them sharply and to reject them if they should fail to heed his admonitions.

In the East, it is the conduct and behavior of a priest that counts, and not his sermon. One never hears people talking about good or bad sermons, but one often hears gossip about priests and deacons, especially when they are drunk and acting in a manner unbecoming to their sacred trust.

WOMEN TEACHERS

The aged women likewise, that they be in behaviour as becometh holiness, not false accusers, not given to much wine, teachers of good things;
That they may teach the young women to be sober, to love their husbands, to love their children, Titus 2 : 3–4.

Schools for women were unknown until recent years, when they were introduced by English, French and American missionaries. The Mohammedans for a long time prohibited the education of women. Christians, being a minority, and living among Moslems, were unable to open schools for their women. The problem of educating women was difficult and complicated. Women, with the exception of a few deaconesses, were not permitted to read the Scriptures, and, being of the opposite sex, could not become instructors. Nor could they be instructed by male teachers.

Certain women were instructed by pious elderly women who had acquired their education by constant attendance in church. Many of them are able to recite portions of the Scriptures by heart. They also know the order of the morning and evening prayer, doctrines, rituals and the dates of holidays. Some of them are members of priestly families, and are taught to read. One can see these elderly women giving counsel to girls and young married women, some of whom are looked upon with great respect and reverence. Their religious education is transmitted by word of mouth, and is simpler and purer than some of the teachings which are obtained at some theological schools. There is an Eastern parable, "Learned people always disagree." In other words, pious elderly women can best transmit pure truths, free from complicated teachings of the learned men.

Then again, women in Palestine, Syria, and Mesopotamia seldom drink wine or strong drinks; but women in Asia Minor and Greece use wine. The people of these countries, like the French and Italians, are wine users. Wine is so abundant that it is used instead of water. Paul was not opposed to the moderate use of wine, but he was against excessive drinking, which is costly, dangerous and unnecessary.

SERVANTS AND MASTERS

Exhort *servants to be obedient unto their own masters, and to please* them *well in all* things; *not answering again;* Titus 2 : 9.

Slavery is an ancient institution and is still prevalent in many countries. The status of some servants in Crete and Asia Minor was different from that of servants in Palestine and Syria.

There were two types of servants—those who were hired and were free to leave at will, and those who were purchased and owned as slaves. Many of these slaves were brought from other countries by men who raided villages. Some of these servants hated their masters, not so much because they were subjected to hard labor, but because they remembered the horrors inflicted on their families when they were carried away and sold as slaves.

Paul in other epistles exhorts masters to be kind to their servants or slaves, some of whom were Christians. He likewise admonished slaves and servants to be loyal and faithful to their masters, and to serve them as true Christian servants and not as hypocrites.

Servants in the Eastern countries are paid very little. Some are hired for food and clothes only. Some men treat their servants well and remunerate them for their services; others make them work hard and refuse either to pay them or to let them go.

It seems that many Christian slaves desired freedom from their Christian owners; others wanted equality and higher wages. Paul was facing a problem similar to that which President Lincoln faced in his day. Paul had no power to abolish slavery. It was legalized by the Roman government and no one but the Roman Senate and Caesar could change the law. Nevertheless, Paul as a Christian teacher, urged both servants and their lords to try to understand one another, to be kind and faithful to each other, and to work with mutual understanding so that they might become examples of the Christian gospel. In other words, he appealed to them as Christian brothers.

DEALING WITH A HERETIC

A man that is an heretick after the first and second admonition reject; Titus 3 : 10.

This admonition is taken from the eighteenth chapter of the Gospel of Matthew. "Moreover, if thy brother shall trespass against thee, go and tell him his fault between thee and him alone: . . . But if he will not hear thee, then take with thee one or two more, that in the mouth of two or three witnesses every word may be established. And if he shall neglect to hear them, tell it unto the church: but if he neglect to hear the church, let him be unto thee as an heathen man and a publican" (Matt. 18 : 15–18).

Jesus' advice is still followed by Christian members of the Church of the East. Trifling problems and minor disputes are generally settled between the persons involved. When the disputants find it difficult to agree between themselves, they seek the advice of one or two elderly men who arbitrate the matter. When this fails, the matter is brought before the church as a final tribunal of justice. The guilty person is excommunicated or temporarily ousted from the church. The members of the congregation stop their dealings with him and refuse to eat bread with him or salute him. Many civil and religious cases are tried by bishops and priests. Prior to the First World War the Assyrian patriarch, called "Mar Shimun" (St. Peter), was invested with both spiritual and temporal authority, which he in turn delegated to the bishops and priests.

When one confronts a stubborn person who is unwilling

to see the truth or come to an agreement, why should one continue to deal with him? Most men of this type know the truth of the matter, but they try to pervert it in order to gain their point and further their own interests.

PHILEMON

INTRODUCTION

The epistle was written by Paul while he was in prison in Rome and was sent by Onesimus. The subject of the letter is Onesimus, a servant who had deserted his master. Philemon was a Colossian Christian and a follower of Paul. His servant, who had deserted him, was converted and corrected by Paul. The latter intercedes with Philemon on behalf of Onesimus, begging him to welcome Onesimus and forgive him for his bad conduct. It seems that Onesimus had run away with some money, and after having spent it, was afraid to return to his master. Paul besought Philemon to forgive these matters, on the ground that this servant had become a Christian. Paul's faith in the servant is so strong that he calls him "my son." He promises Philemon that Onesimus will live a Christian life without reproach. Onesimus has proven this through his loyalty to Paul during his imprisonment in Rome.

EASTERN HUMOR

If he hath wronged thee, or oweth thee ought, put that on mine account;
I Paul have written it with mine own hand, I will repay it: albeit I do not say to thee how thou owest unto me even thine own self besides. Philemon 1 : 18–19.

"Put it on my account" is an Eastern idiom which means, "forget it." Just as one says in English, "write it on ice."

In the East, when a man appeals on behalf of a friend, or a poor person, he speaks very frankly and uses peculiar expressions. One often hears a religious man or an elder, while admonishing people and urging them to forgive one another, pointing his finger and saying, "put it on my account," or "I will pay you for it."

Paul had no account with Philemon. He was not a business man, nor was he a borrower. Philemon, being a convert of Paul, owed a great debt to him. Paul makes Philemon feel as though he had a share in his property or that he was a partner. He asks him as a fellow Christian, to forgive his servant and forget the little money that he owed him. Paul knew Philemon well and had confidence in him. The nineteenth verse explains Paul's familiarity with Philemon. He says: "I Paul have written it with mine own hand, I will repay it: albeit I do not say to thee how thou owest unto me even thine own self besides," which means, "If you do not trust the servant, I will make good." Paul, of course, realized that Philemon was not going to ask him to pay this money which the servant had taken from him. In other words, Paul made a strong plea, using some Eastern humor and a friendly appeal.

HEBREWS

INTRODUCTION

The apostle Paul wrote this letter from Italy, probably during or soon after his imprisonment in Rome.

The epistle, like other Pauline writings, is doctrinal, and the author was well versed in Hebrew history, temple worship and especially the priesthood. Eastern Christians have never questioned Paul's authorship of this important document. No one but a well educated Hebrew could have composed such a letter. The early church fathers ascribe fourteen epistles to Paul. The author had been in Italy. The first part of the epistle has been lost. Verse one of chapter one is not the original opening of the epistle. All apostolic letters start with greetings. I believe two or three chapters are missing.

Some of those who doubt Paul's authorship argue that if the epistle had been written by Paul, he would have described the Jewish rituals and temple worship in detail. These men fail to realize that the purpose of the epistle is not to give an account of the Jewish temple rituals and priesthood, but to liken them to Christ. In other words, Paul wrote to the Hebrews, who were well informed about the Jewish religion, in which they had been brought up. He did not need to explain such things to them.

The aim of the epistle is to convince the Jewish Christians that the temple and the priesthood had served their purpose till the time of Christ, but that henceforth they were a thing of the past. Paul wished to warn the Jewish Christians against teachers who were preaching that salvation could be attained by means of the Mosaic law and customs. He declared that these ancient Jewish institutions had served as a shadow pointing to the coming of

Christ. The same warning was made to the Galatians and other churches where converts were falling away and some of them were turning to Judaism.

Paul uses a good analogy in comparing Christ's priesthood to that of Melchisedec. Christ's priesthood is superior to that of Aaron and he himself (Christ) is greater than Moses.

ANGELS

Being made so much better than the angels, as he hath by inheritance obtained a more excellent name than they.
Hebrews 1: 4.

Malakha, angel, also means "messenger" and "minister." The stem of the verb is *malakh*, "to give counsel" or "to advise." Thus, the term is variously used in referring to the angels of the Lord, that is, an order of spiritual agents whose chief functions are giving counsel, advice and guidance, and the performance of various spiritual missions. Angels appeared to men in visions, delivered God's messages, and performed other duties, as in the case of Jacob (Gen. 28 : 12–13) and of Joseph (Matt. 1 : 20) and the Virgin Mary (Luke 1 : 26).

There are many other instances where angels announced news, issued warnings, and helped those who sought God's protection. At times angels acted as spokesmen for the Deity and made promises in the name of God. "And the angel of the Lord said unto her, I will multiply thy seed exceedingly, that it shall not be numbered for multitude" (Gen. 16 : 10).

In the book of Psalms, angels are called spirits. The Aramaic word *rokha*, "spirit," also means "wind." When a man travels fast it is said, "He is like the wind." Spirit knows neither distance nor time. "Who maketh his angels spirits; his ministers a flaming fire" (Psa. 104 : 4). According to the Gospel of Matthew, angels are guardians of men, and stand continually in the presence of God (Matt. 18 : 10). Angels are spoken of throughout the Bible as messengers of God, giving counsel and directing and protecting pious men and women. Those who obeyed God's command were blessed, but the transgressors received just punishment.

The reference here is to the angelic order. Christ's spirit and truth are eternal and therefore higher than the angels. Angels are ministers of men, but Christ is the Saviour of men. Christ existed with God from the beginning, and now has dominion over all things. (See verses 8–14.)

FALLEN ANGELS

For if the word spoken by angels was stedfast, and every transgression and disobedience received a just recompence of reward;   Heb. 2 : 2.

The angels who disobeyed the word of God are called "fallen angels." They were deposed from their rank and place, bound with chains, kept in darkness, and reserved for final judgment.

According to the prophet Isaiah, this group of angels lost first place and fell from grace because of pride and self-exaltation. He apparently considers Lucifer, son of the morning star, as their chief representative (Isa. 14 : 12–13). Jesus referred to this incident when he said, "I beheld Satan as lightning fall from heaven" (Luke 10 : 18). In Genesis, Satan is represented by the serpent who was more subtle than any beast of the field (Gen. 3 : 1).

Fallen angels and the wicked are to face everlasting condemnation. "Depart from me, ye cursed, into everlasting fire, prepared for the devil and his angels" (Matt. 25 : 41). At times, fallen angels are symbolical of sons of God who have fallen from grace.

Paul warns the believer to keep steadfast and loyal in the true teachings, lest they fall from grace and lose the salvation which they had obtained through Jesus Christ. For if God had not spared the angels, how can he spare those who are disobedient? (Compare II Pet. 2 : 4.)

MAN'S POWER

But one in a certain place testified, saying, What is man, that thou art mindful of him? or the son of man, that thou visitest him?
Thou madest him a little lower than the angels; thou crownedst him with glory and honour, and didst set him over the works of thy hands: Heb. 2 : 6–7.

Earthly man was created of dust and unto dust he shall return, but the spiritual man is the image and likeness of his Creator, and his soul is the breath of God, which is life eternal. Therefore, earthly man is lower than the angels, but the spiritual man is the child of God and therefore higher than the angels. The Hebrew text reads: "He made them a little lower than gods. Man has jurisdiction over the works of God, but the angels are ministers and guardians of men."

The reference here is to earthly man, who changes and becomes old, like a garment, and perishes like the grass of the field. What is the mortal body as compared with the stars, the sun, and the glory of God? Nevertheless, mortal man is endowed with tremendous power and knowledge, and thus has become master over the works of God's hand. Through science and truth he has been able to rise and have dominion over the earth. The creative forces within him are limitless, the scope of his knowledge is incomprehensible, and in the course of time man has succeeded in overcoming many of his natural enemies. He has conquered land, sea, and air.

THE DEATH OF JESUS

But we see Jesus, who was made a little lower than the angels for the suffering of death, crowned with glory and honour; that he by the grace of God should taste death for every man. Heb. 2 : 9.

Jesus' death was predicted in the Scriptures and was revealed through the foreknowledge of God to the holy prophets. God knew that men would go astray and fall from grace, and that in the fullness of time his Son would suffer on the cross in order to bring them once more to him. God saw that the death of Jesus was the only means of salvation. This divine plan was a mystery to be revealed in the fullness of time. The death of Jesus was not fatalism, as it may seem, but the means of salvation which was preordained by God. In other words, there was no other means by which men could be saved and directed into the true path of life.

Man was created in the image and likeness of God, with a divine intellect and a will free to choose between good and evil. Had God deprived him of his will, man would never have fallen, but would have been like a machine. He could not have been called a child of God.

God sits on high. He sees what is on the earth and in the sea. He knows the strength and the weaknesses of men, but he does not interfere with man's free will. He guides and directs men into the true paths of life and helps them to rise up when they seek him.

Jesus predicted his own death and resurrection. He looked on the cross as a shame, but also as a glorious victory over the powers of evil and death. Life is the breath of God; death had no power over it. "Behold, we go up to Jerusalem; and the Son of man shall be betrayed unto the chief priests and unto the scribes, and they shall condemn him to death" (Matt. 20 : 18). After his resurrection, when he appeared to two of his followers, he said to them: "Ought not Christ to have suffered these things, and to enter into his glory?" And then "he expounded unto them in all the scriptures the things concerning himself"

(Luke 24 : 26–27). Jesus laid down his life voluntarily, in order to take it again in a larger and glorious way. "No man taketh it from me, but I lay it down of myself. I have power to lay it down, and I have power to take it again" (John 10 : 18).

Jesus, through his death and resurrection, exposed the power of evil forces, crowned man with glory and honor, and restored man's lost divinity. Had he failed in the mission which God had entrusted to him, then our salvation would never have been accomplished.

ETERNAL CHRIST

Wherefore in all things it behoved him to be made like unto his brethren, that he might be a merciful and faithful high priest in things pertaining to God, to make reconciliation for the sins of the people.   Heb. 2 : 17.

The word "made" is not found in the Eastern text. The Aramaic word *nithdamey* means "to resemble." "Therefore it was meet and proper that in everything he should resemble his brethren." He was not made, but took on flesh of his own accord. In the third century Arius taught that Christ was created (made) and therefore was inferior to the Father.

Christ took on human flesh and became like us in every respect except that he did not sin. Jesus hungered, thirsted and was tempted like all of us, but he overcame his temptations. Through his suffering and cross he revealed God's truth and love to those who believed in him, and he reconciled them to God.

He had to become like one of us in order to understand our human weaknesses and be able to lead us to the true path of life. Jesus, through his victory over death and sin, became an example of perfect and original man, created in the image of God. Christ, the eternal truth, life and light, existed with God from the very beginning. John says: "The word was in the beginning, and that very word was with God, and God was that word. The same was in the beginning with God" (John 1 : 1–2, Eastern text).

JESUS LIKENED TO MOSES

Who was faithful to him that appointed him, as also Moses was faithful *in all his house.*
For this man *was counted worthy of more glory than Moses, inasmuch as he who hath builded the house hath more honour than the house.* Heb. 3 : 2–3.

"This man" refers of course to Christ, who existed with God and was appointed by him before the world was made. "The same was in the beginning with God. All things were made by him; and without him was not anything made that was made" (John 1 : 2–3). Jesus, by virtue of his divinity, is greater than Moses and the other prophets who heralded his coming. Moses told the Hebrews that a prophet like himself was to come and that they should listen to him (Deut. 18 : 15–19).

Jesus' faithfulness to God is compared to that of Moses. Even though at times Moses was discouraged and doubtful, his faith in God never wavered. He fought a great fight and overcame many serious obstacles. Jesus, likewise, never doubted God's wisdom; even death on the cross could not weaken his faith in God. Therefore, Moses' loyalty to God is compared to that of Jesus.

SWEARING IN HASTE

So I sware in my wrath, They shall not enter into my rest. Heb. 3 : 11.

"I swore in my wrath (anger)" is an Eastern saying, which means "I did it hastily." When certain things are done hastily, people say "I did it in anger" or "I was impatient." Moreover, Easterners, when making promises in buying or selling, are in the habit of taking oaths, swearing by the Temple and the holy altar. Jesus admonished his followers not to swear by holy things or to take God's name in vain. The quotation is taken from Psalm 95 : 11—"Unto whom I sware in my wrath that they should not enter into my rest."

This refers to the fact that thousands of Hebrews left Egypt, but only two men, Joshua and Caleb, entered the promised land. The others, because of their unbelief, perished in the desert. Joshua led the children of Israel, those who were born and reared in the desert, into the land of promise. There are instances in the Bible where we are told that God repented, that he was sorry after he had decreed severe punishment.

Men swore by things greater than themselves. God does not need to swear by anything, for there is nothing greater than himself. (See verse 18.) The writer likens God to a prophet or a ruler who swears by his head or his position.

The Hebrews, because of their unbelief, were barred from entering into the promised land. Those who believed did enter. Christians likewise must remain loyal in the faith of Christ, lest they be rejected and barred from entering into their heavenly rest. The Hebrews erred because they lacked faith and understanding. The Christians have the gospel of faith and the grace of God. The judgment of those who disobey will be serious indeed.

ETERNAL REST

For if Jesus had given them rest, then would he not afterward have spoken of another day. Heb. 4 : 8.

The reference here is to *Eshoo-Bar-Nun*—that is, Joshua, the son of Nun, and not to Jesus, son of Mary. It was Joshua who led the Hebrews into the promised land about 1400 B.C., defeated many kings, and took over their land. Nevertheless, the Hebrews, even after crossing the river Jordan and conquering more than a score of kingdoms, were unable to find peace and rest. The inhabitants of some parts of Palestine resisted violently, and the struggle for control of the land continued for many centuries after Joshua's death. After the establishment of the monarchy about 1000 B.C. the Hebrews enjoyed brief periods of peace and prosperity, but lasting peace never came.

The confusion in this text occurred because of the similarity between the names of Jesus and Joshua. The Eastern text, when referring to Joshua, always mentions Nun, his father. The correct translation from the Aramaic would be "Jesus, son of Nun." Because of similarity of names the Semites often use the father's or mother's name, or the name of the town. For instance, "Jesus son of Mary," "Judas of Iscariot," "Mary of Magdala," and "John son of Zebedee."

Just as Joshua led the Hebrews into the land of promise after they had spent forty years in the wilderness, so Jesus led them to the truth after they had spent many centuries groping in darkness and superstition, enslaved to the doctrines and traditions of man. A small remnant accepted Jesus as the promised Messiah and entered into the eternal rest.

GOD'S LAW IS ETERNAL

There remaineth therefore a rest to the people of God. For he that is entered into his rest, he also hath ceased from his own works, as God did from his. Heb. 4 : 9–10.

The fourth commandment decrees that the seventh day must be observed as a day of rest. This is because God completed the creation of heaven and earth in six days and on the seventh day rested from his work (Gen. 2 : 2). "Six days shalt thou labour, and do all thy work: but the seventh day is the sabbath of the LORD thy God: . . . For in six days the Lord made heaven and earth, the sea, and all that in them is, and rested the seventh day: wherefore the Lord blessed the sabbath day, and hallowed it" (Exod. 20 : 9–11). The Eastern text reads, "Therefore the people of God must observe the Sabbath."

The Sabbath is to be kept until man enters into eternal rest and dwells forever with his Creator. Palestine is symbolical of heaven, and the Sabbath is a symbol of everlasting rest. The Hebrews, after entering into the promised land, rested from their many desert difficulties and trials. They found food, wine, honey and other comforts and luxuries which are not within the reach of desert dwellers. In other words, they found some physical rest, but were far off from the new Jerusalem and eternal rest. And even after their conquest of Palestine the Hebrews were often harassed and defeated by their enemies.

Joshua brought them into the land of promise, but because it took them many centuries before they were able to subdue some of their enemies, Joshua could not give them eternal rest. David, four hundred years later, spoke of another day.

Therefore, it is necessary for the people to keep the law of God and observe the Sabbath until they enter into the kingdom of God. The law and prophets remain as of yore until all things are fulfilled and the forces of evil destroyed. Jesus did not come to destroy the law and the prophets, but to fulfill them. Christians must labor hard in order to hasten God's reign, so that they may enter into his kingdom and his eternal rest.

TWO-EDGED SWORD

For the word of God is quick, and powerful, and sharper than any twoedged sword, piercing even to the dividing asunder of soul and spirit, and of the joints and marrow, and is a discerner of the thoughts and intents of the heart. Heb. 4 : 12.

In ancient times when guns were unknown, two-edged swords were popular among soldiers, especially the cavalry. The swords were very sharp and could be used backward and forward.

This type of weapon is still made and used among the Arabs who are famous for handling swords. The blade is slightly curved and sharpened on both sides. When the enemy is hit, he is severely cut with the sharp edges. But one has to be an expert in order to use the two-edged sword.

The Word of God is likened to the sharpest type of sword that was known in those days. This is because the Word of God is penetrating and discerns the inner thought and reaches the hidden secrets of the heart. Easterners often say: "His words are very sharp, they cut like a sword," which means that they help to decide matters quickly.

The Aramaic word for "soul" in this verse is *naphsha,* and refers to the breath of earthly life which is extinguished at death. The "spirit" is the divine spark of life which after death passes into eternity. At other times the two words spirit and soul, are used indiscriminately.

TRIED OUT

For we have not an high priest which cannot be touched with the feeling of our infirmities; but was in all points tempted like as we are, *yet without sin.* Heb. 4 : 15.

The Aramaic word *menassi* means tempted, tried, or experienced. The author of Hebrews implies that Jesus was tempted and tried in all points, and that he went through life and its struggles like one of us, but he did not sin.

The office of the Jewish high priest was hereditary. The firstborn son succeeded his father. In some instances the high priest died when his heir was young and therefore inexperienced. Then again, in many cases, the successor was unfit to hold the office. But the Jewish laws which governed the succession of the Jewish hierarchy were similar to those of a monarchy, and the heir, regardless of physical and mental deficiencies, always succeeded to the office. The Jewish hierarchy, after the Babylonian captivity, took the place of the Jewish monarchy. The high priest was ruler over both religious and political affairs, and in due time gained such prominence that he was looked upon almost as a king and could not be approached by the poor and the lower classes. Therefore the high priests were not familiar with their people and did not understand their needs. In fact, they taxed their people heavily while they themselves lived in luxurious palaces.

Jesus, on the other hand, was born and reared in poverty. His folks were simple and innocent peasants. He understood human strength and human weakness. In other words, he rose to the spiritual office of High Priest from the ranks of the common people. He was fully qualified to act as a mediator between God and men because he understood both.

MELCHISEDEC A TYPE OF CHRIST

As he saith also in another place, Thou art a priest for ever after the order of Melchisedec.   Heb. 5 : 6.

When a man is selected to become a high priest or a bishop, he is ordained by another high priest who is greater than himself or by a group of prelates or elders.

Melchisedec was a king-priest. No one knew how he became a high priest or who ordained him, but he was "king of Salem" and "priest of the most high God." He offered bread and wine to Abraham and blessed him (Gen. 14 : 18–19). Abraham gave a tithe of the spoils which he had taken after the defeat of the four kings (Heb. 7 : 2).

Melchisedec's priesthood was hereditary, handed down from father to son. He was the best example of Christ's priesthood, for he was a righteous king of peace.

According to the Mosaic law, none but the descendants of Aaron were to be ordained as priests or high priests. Therefore it was difficult for some of the Jewish Christians to look upon Jesus as a high priest. He was not from the house of Aaron, nor had he been ordained by another high priest or a greater man than himself, as Aaron was ordained by Moses (Exod. 29). Moses was not a high priest but a prophet of God. His office was greater than that of Aaron.

Jesus was ordained by God. His priesthood was from above and therefore abiding forever. "The Spirit of the Lord is upon me, because he hath anointed me to preach the gospel to the poor; he hath sent me to heal the brokenhearted, . . ." (Luke 4 : 18). Jesus' priesthood, like that of Melchisedec, was not of man but of God.

Christ's mission was to bring peace on earth and to judge men in righteousness. "And righteousness shall be the girdle of his loins, and faithfulness the girdle of his reins" (Isa. 11 : 5). And, as a high priest, he was to reconcile men to God. This he did through his suffering and death on the cross. He became a high priest forever (Heb. 6 : 20).

POOR CROPS

But that which beareth thorns and briers is rejected, and is nigh unto cursing; whose end is to be burned.
Heb. 6 : 8.

When fields produce thorns and briers, and crops are poor, they are condemned. Both wheat and thorns are used for fuel. When the wheat is short and briers and thorns are thick it is difficult to separate them. The crop is then abandoned until late in the summer when it is harvested and stored for fuel to be used during the winter months. At times, good wheat fields, because of neglect, are covered with briers and thorns.

In biblical lands coal is unknown and wood is scarce. Thorns, briers, manure and the grass of the field are used for fuel.

The author of Hebrews warns the Jewish Christians to take heed and safeguard the true teaching, so that they may not go backward and receive condemnation, but rather advance in the doctrines and the teaching of Christ (verse 4).

Those who had neglected the true doctrines had become like fields which are covered with thorns and briers and ready to be condemned and used for fuel.

SWEARING BY PATRON SAINT

For men verily swear by the greater: and an oath for confirmation is to them an end of all strife. Heb. 6 : 16.

In many parts of the East where civil courts are unknown, disputes and quarrels that cannot be settled by elders and self-appointed judges are decided by oaths. The disputants are asked to swear by the shrine, the temple or the patron saint. The accused person is given a final chance to either confess his crime or swear. Most people charged with minor crimes choose to confess and make restoration rather than take an oath by the patron saint or the altar. Easterners are fearful of oaths. "And when the people were come unto the wood, behold, the honey dropped; but no man put his hand to his mouth: for the people feared the oath" (I Sam. 14 : 26). "And he that sweareth, as he that feareth an oath" (Eccl. 9 : 12). Those who take oaths are allowed to go free. The judgment is left to God, who knows what is in the heart of men and who punishes the wicked.

Oaths are also used in determining the prices of articles in market places and homes. But on such occasions, oaths are not taken very seriously. This is because in bargaining people often lie. Therefore, oaths in business do not count. The names of God and the prophets are so often taken in vain that no one believes those who invoke them.

Because of all this Jesus admonished his followers not to take oaths. "But I say unto you, Swear not at all; neither by heaven; for it is God's throne: Nor by the earth; for it is his footstool: neither by Jerusalem; for it is the city of the great King. . . . But let your communication be, Yea, yea; Nay, nay: . . ." (Matt. 5 : 34–37). (See *Gospel Light,* page 39.)

MELCHISEDEC

For this Melchisedec, king of Salem, priest of the most high God, who met Abraham returning from the slaughter of the kings, and blessed him;
To whom also Abraham gave a tenth part of all; first being by interpretation King of righteousness, and after that also King of Salem, which is, King of peace;
Without father, without mother, without descent, having neither beginning of days, nor end of life; but made like unto the Son of God; abideth a priest continually.
Heb. 7 : 1–3.

When Abraham returned from defeating the four kings Melchisedec, King of Salem and priest of the most high God, brought him bread and wine, and blessed him.

Abraham, in return for the generous reception and the blessings, gave Melchisedec tithes of all spoils which he had brought with him (Gen. 14 : 18–20).

The Eastern text reads: "Neither his father nor his mother is recorded in the genealogies; and neither the beginning of his days nor the end of his life; but, like the Son of God, his priesthood abides for ever."

In many parts of the Near East, notably in Arabia, Mesopotamia and Kurdistan, both the spiritual and the temporal powers are vested in the person of the tribal chief, who, in Aramaic and Hebrew, is called *maleck,* "king" or "counselor." His advice is always sought in legal, financial, political and religious matters. The high office is hereditary. The king and priest is succeeded by his son or an elder member of his family.

The Aramaic word *komra* means "high priest." In most cases the tribal ruler or high priest presides over all tribal affairs, and appoints elders and civil administrators who in religious and political matters are responsible to him only.

In ancient days, priests and kings often usurped one another's powers. At times, kings became priests and priests became kings. For instance, when King Jeroboam established places of worship in Samaria, he also appointed new priests (I Kings 12 : 28–32). Sometimes Hebrew kings overthrew the priests who sought reforms and demanded justice, and appointed others more favorable to their administration. On the other hand, if a high priest had sufficient prestige and power he might depose the king. Queen Athaliah was thus overthrown by the priest Jehoiada (II Kings 11 : 13–16).

Small tribes, in order to avoid strife and excessive taxation, usually prefer a king-priest as their ruler. Melchisedec was of this ancient order. He was ruler of a small tribe comprising half a district or more. His subjects were chiefly herdsmen and farmers. His authority as a king and a priest was recognized by all of the neighboring tribes who were on friendly terms with his tribe and who worshiped the same Deity. Chiefs of other tribes, whose people were followers of his religion, offered him gifts as a token of friendly alliance, and as a tithe to the Deity who always received a generous share of all spoils and plunders. Then again, when sheep, cattle and commercial traffic passed through his territory, he exacted tithes or duties just as is done today. Some chiefs of powerful tribes demand a small tax from weaker tribes who are under their protection. When a tribe plunders another tribe, the chief of the tribe gives a tithe consisting of money, clothing and livestock to the high priest or to the local priests, as God's share. When the Hebrew army returned from defeating the Midianites, God told Moses to divide the spoils and to give a portion thereof to the priests and the Levites. "And levy a tribute unto the Lord of the men of war which went out to battle: one soul of five hundred, both of the persons, and of the beeves, and of the asses, and of the sheep" (Num. 31 : 28).

Abraham was a new settler in Palestine. He had sought peace alliances with various powerful chiefs. On his return from his defeat of the four "kings" he visited Melchisedec to offer the customary tithes for his victory.

Melchisedec, as the high priest, was entitled to a share of the spoils which Abraham had taken. Melchisedec's father and mother are not mentioned in the Bible because he was a ruler of a tribe which like many other Arab rulers had no written chronicles; perhaps the genealogies had been lost. His name is of Mesopotamian origin, which suggests that he may have been a descendant of an old Aramean family which later had ruled over Salem, which means "peace." Neither the author of Genesis nor Paul attempts to trace Melchisedec's lost genealogy. But his priesthood abided forever.

A PERFECT HIGH PRIEST

And here men that die receive tithes; but there he receiveth them, of whom it is witnessed that he liveth.
Heb. 7 : 8.

The reference here is to the high priests who were mortal and yet received tithes. The human high priests, even though they forgave the sins of their people and made offerings on their behalf, were imperfect and had to make offerings for their own sins also. Moreover, the priesthoods of Melchisedec and Aaron were changeable and temporary. They were symbolical of the perfect and eternal priesthood of Christ, of whom the Scriptures testify that he lives forever.

Today both orders of high priests are extinct. There are no more high priests of the house of Melchisedec, nor of the seed of Aaron, nor are there animal sacrifices and sin offerings. All of these were a foreshadowing of the true high priest and the eternal offering which Jesus made on the cross. Thus Jesus became the true high priest, not through the laying on of hands, sacrificial offerings, or the carnal commandments, but because he was ordained through the spirit and power of God. His priesthood is eternal and unchangeable.

OFFICE OF HIGH PRIEST

For such an high priest became us, who is holy, harmless, undefiled, separate from sinners, and made higher than the heavens; Heb. 7 : 26.

In olden days the high priest was selected from members of an Aaronic family. The candidate was to be without blemish, good looking, of good character, and possessing all good qualities and spiritual power. The high priest was the symbol of holiness. He was to be pure and holy in order to be able to come before the presence of God and ask forgiveness for the people. A high priest was to be free from graft, righteous in judgment, kind and ready to lead the people.

During the period of the judges the office of high priest embodied both spiritual and political power, as in the case of Eli. During the reigns of David and Solomon, high priests were appointed by the kings. At times the high priests rebelled against the kings and deposed them. For instance, Jehoiada, the priest, rebelled against Queen Athaliah. (II Kings 11 : 12–17.)

After the destruction of the first temple the high priesthood lost its purely religious character and tradition and became political. The high priests henceforth were chosen by foreign rulers. The office in most cases went to persons who were in favor of high taxation and were sympathetic toward the alien rule. Piety and good character were no longer required. The once holy office became the center of corruption and intrigues. The people protested in vain against the tyrannical power of the priests and the graft which was associated with their office.

In the East there is still a canon that aspirants to the office of the priest must be both physically and morally without blemish. Men with physical defects cannot be ordained to the priesthood. Morally, of course, no one knows how a priest will turn out after he is ordained.

Jesus Christ is the one high priest without sin or blemish. This is because God had ordained and sanctified him from the very beginning to become a mediator on behalf of sinners. On the other hand, Jesus overcame sin and temptation of the flesh, and thus qualified himself to be a living high priest offering prayer on our behalf. Jesus, as a high priest, is familiar with our human weaknesses and understands the infinite love of God and his mercies.

TRUE PRIESTHOOD

Now of the things which we have spoken this is the sum: We have such an high priest, who is set on the right hand of the throne of the Majesty in the heavens;
A minister of the sanctuary, and of the true tabernacle, which the Lord pitched, and not man.
For every high priest is ordained to offer gifts and sacrifices: wherefore it is of necessity that this man have somewhat also to offer. Heb. 8 : 1–3.

The epistle was addressed to Christian converts of Hebrew origin. Jesus instructed his disciples to go to no one but the lost sheep of the house of Israel (the Ten Tribes). Many of these people were scattered in the region of the river Kabor and in Mesopotamia, where Assyrian kings had settled them when Samaria fell and the kingdom of Israel came to an end in 721 B.C. (II Kings 17 : 5–7).

The author of the epistle is familiar with the Jewish ordinances and temple worship, the priesthood's functions and sacrificial system. The writer, himself a sincere convert to the new religion, points out the limitations and defects of the Mosaic law and the Aaronic priesthood. He pictures them as a symbol of the true priesthood, the living sacrifice, and a new and perfect high priest whose priesthood has no end.

NEW COVENANT

For finding fault with them, he saith, Behold, the days come, saith the Lord, when I will make a new covenant with the house of Israel and with the house of Judah:
Not according to the covenant that I made with their fathers in the day when I took them by the hand to lead them out of the land of Egypt; because they continued not in my covenant, and I regarded them not, saith the Lord. Heb. 8 : 8–9.

The old covenant which God had made with Abraham, Moses and David had become obsolete. The Hebrews failed to live up to its precepts. The promises therein were conditional. The Hebrews were required to obey the voice of God and keep his covenant; but when the terms of an agreement are not respected, the agreement is nullified.

Both Israel and Judah had violated the terms of God's covenant with their forefathers. As a result, the kingdoms of Israel and Judah came to an end, and the people were carried as captives into Assyria and Babylon. Thus the political Israel gave way to a spiritual kingdom through which the Messianic promises made to Abraham were to be fulfilled. . . . "Unto thy seed have I given this land, from the river of Egypt unto the great river, the river Euphrates" (Gen. 15 : 18). The Hebrew prophets foretold the termination of the old covenant and the making of a new covenant to take its place.

God made a new and better covenant established not on conditional terms and ordinances, but on faith in Jesus Christ. "Behold the days come, saith the Lord, that I will make a new covenant with the house of Israel, and with the house of Judah: not according to the covenant that I made with their fathers in that day I took them by the hand to bring them out of the land of Egypt; which my covenant they broke" (Jer. 31 : 31–32).

This new covenant was offered not only to Judah, but to Israel also. It is a universal covenant between God and all believers, irrespective of race and color. Its laws are not engraved on stone tablets which may break, but on human hearts. In the terms of the new agreement life both here and hereafter is secured. In the new covenant God is not an over-Lord, as he was in the old, but a loving Father who forgives his children and seeks them when they go astray.

FIRST COVENANT

Then verily the first covenant had also ordinances of divine service, and a worldly sanctuary. Heb. 9 : 1.

The first covenant was made with Abraham when God promised him the land from the river of Egypt to the river Euphrates (Gen. 15 : 18). God appeared to him, changed his name from Abram to Abraham, and promised him an heir. This was a blood covenant, and Abraham was asked to circumcise all males in his house. (Gen. 17 : 10). This was somewhat like the blood covenant which the Arab tribes make. The men make cuts on their arms and then touch arms so that their blood mingles. By this act a person becomes a full-fledged member of the tribe. One often hears people say: "My blood is of your blood, and my flesh of your flesh," which means "we are brothers."

Years later God appeared to Abraham again and blessed him and promised to multiply his seed and give him an inheritance in the land in which he was living as a stranger (Gen. 22 : 15–18). Later this covenant embodied the Mosaic law—the Sabbath, the tabernacle and the sanctuary, sacrifices and the commandments.

The promise to Noah not to destroy the earth by water was also a covenant (Gen. 9 : 9–17).

Nevertheless, this covenant was a symbol of the true covenant which was sealed through the sacrifice of Jesus Christ. With the new covenant Jesus freed us from the sacrifices, ceremonies and Jewish ordinances. This was done through the grace of God and his love for his children in permitting the death of Jesus on the cross.

THE TABERNACLE

For there was a tabernacle made; the first, wherein was the candlestick, and the table, and the shewbread; which is called the sanctuary. Heb. 9 : 2.

The tabernacle was a large tent erected in the desert, suitable for tribal life and constant migration. It also served as a meeting place for other purposes. The tabernacle contained the mercy seat, the candlestick, the ark of the covenant and other holy relics. (For the construction, materials and style of the tabernacle see Exodus chapters 25–27.)

Four hundred years later, when David had conquered nearly all of Palestine, his son Solomon built a magnificent temple on Mount Zion, to which the people came to worship. For a time the Temple served as a center of worship for all the tribes, but later it was turned into a national museum and treasury. Gifts of gold and silver, as well as animal offerings continued to flow to Jerusalem from all directions. The Temple gradually became the depository for the collection of money and other wealth which the kings could use in case of war or other emergencies. But this fact made the northern tribes jealous.

The break came during the time of Jeroboam. The north revolted against the house of David. Jeroboam erected other shrines in Samaria. This was done to stop the flow of wealth into Judea.

The Temple was Jewish in character. It lacked a universal idea of God. The Gentiles were not permitted beyond the outer court or, as it was called, the Gentile's court. The control of the Temple and its vast treasures was in the hands of the king. The high priest was appointed by him. In due time the teachings and laws were replaced by traditions, mysteries and rituals. In other words, the candle which God had lighted to lighten the word was covered so that it could not give light.

The veil was to be removed by another priest, who had the keys to the holy of holies. Jesus was the new high priest who unveiled the Jewish mysteries, took the cover from over the great candle, and restored the true worship and made it universal.

ARK OF THE COVENANT

Which had the golden censer, and the ark of the covenant overlaid round about with gold, wherein was the golden pot that had manna, and Aaron's rod that budded, and the tables of the covenant; Heb. 9 : 4.

The ark was a box made of shittim wood, two-and-a-half cubits long, one-and-a-half cubits wide, and one-and-a-half cubits high. It was overlaid with pure gold, both inside and out, and had a crown of gold on top of it (Exod. 25 : 10–11).

It was called the ark of the covenant because it contained the tablets of the covenant on which the law was engraved, the pot in which some manna was preserved, and the rod of Aaron which budded. On top of the ark rested the mercy seat with its cherubims.

The ark and other sacred tribal relics were placed in the inner tabernacle, that is, the holy place where the high priest entered once a year to make the offerings for the sins of the people and for himself. This place was separated from the rest of the tabernacle by a veil. The ark, the veil, and other objects in the tabernacle pointed to the true worship which was to be revealed by Jesus Christ.

BLOOD COVENANT

Whereupon neither the first testament was dedicated without blood.

For when Moses had spoken every precept to all the people according to the law, he took the blood of calves and of goats, with water, and scarlet wool, and hyssop, and sprinkled both the book, and all the people,

Saying, This is the blood of the testament which God hath enjoined unto you. Heb. 9 : 18–20.

In Arabia today, as of yore, a covenant is dedicated and sealed with blood. The two chiefs make small wounds on their arms and let their blood mingle. Then too, when a man joins a tribe his blood is mingled with that of one of the members of the tribe. When an important agreement is reached and inaugurated, sheep and oxen are killed and the people celebrate.

The Mosaic covenant was not sealed with human blood, but instead with the blood of animals. "And Moses took the blood, and sprinkled it on the people, and said, Behold the blood of the covenant, which the LORD hath made with you concerning all these words" (Exod. 24 : 8).

The new covenant was sealed with the blood of Christ, which reconciled men and made peace with God. The covenant of the blood was symbolical of the covenant of the spirit. The blood of animals did not eradicate the sin, nor did it bring reconciliation. Jesus through his willingness to die on the cross, destroyed sin, conquered the forces of evil, and wrought everlasting salvation for those who believe in him and look forward to his coming. Thus the sacrifice of Christ was better than those which the Hebrews offered (Heb. 10 : 4). His blood, which was poured out on the cross, sealed the everlasting covenant.

HUMAN ORDINANCES

For the law having a shadow of good things to come, and not the very image of the things, can never with those sacrifices which they offered year by year continually make the comers thereunto perfect. Heb. 10 : 1.

"The law" in this instance means ordinances relative to the sacrifices and rituals which were symbolical of the things to come, and not the Ten Commandments which are eternal. Jesus came to fulfill the law and the prophets, but with his sacrifice on the cross he did away with the animal sacrifices, mysteries and rituals. These served only as a foreshadowing of the holy sacrifice which was to be offered on the cross. A shadow has no essence and therefore is not a reality. The animal sacrifices which were offered every year failed to bring eternal salvation. They reminded the people of their sin, but did not eradicate the sin. But the body of Jesus Christ was offered once as an everlasting sacrifice and a reminder of God's love toward his children.

FIRST PROMISE

Then said I, Lo, I come (in the volume of the book it is written of me,) to do thy will, O God.
Above when he said, Sacrifice and offering and burnt offerings and offering for sin thou wouldest not, neither hadst pleasure therein; which are offered by the law;
Then said he, Lo, I come to do thy will, O God. He taketh away the first, that he may establish the second.
Heb. 10 : 7–9.

The Aramaic text reads: ". . . In the beginning of the books, it is written of me, I delight to do thy will, O God!" "In the beginning of the books" means the five books of Moses. This quotation is from Psalm 40 : 8. The psalmist is speaking of the Messianic promises which were made to Eve. "And I will put enmity between thee and the woman, and between thy seed and her seed; and it shall bruise thy head, and thou shalt bruise his heel." The fall of man was temporary. Evil was to be destroyed by a Saviour who was to come from the seed of Eve. This Saviour was Christ. Moses also told the people that a great prophet was to come after him. The prophets often denounced the animal sacrifices and told the people that God was displeased with their offerings.

The animal sacrifices were a reminder of the people's sins and a means through which to seek temporary forgiveness. To atone through the blood of animals was a custom as old as the Bible itself. Cain and Abel were the first to offer sacrifices (Gen. 4 : 4).

On the other hand, the offering of animal flesh on the altar was a universal custom. Abraham offered sacrifices four hundred years before the law was revealed. Pagans offered animals to their deities.

All these sacrifices pointed to the coming of Jesus and his suffering on the cross, and the proclamation of a universal religion based on love, truth and understanding.

ENOCH

By faith Enoch was translated that he should not see death; and was not found, because God had translated him: for before his translation he had this testimony, that he pleased God. Heb. 11 : 5.

Enoch was believed to have been taken up into heaven or transferred from this life into the life hereafter without experiencing death. Evidence of his transfiguration and ascension is based on the book of Genesis. "And Enoch walked with God: and he was not; for God took him" (Gen. 5 : 24). "God took him" in Aramaic means "he died." When holy men die, it is said that "they are with God." "God had invited them, or they are asleep." Those who live according to the will of God and keep his commandments never suffer the death of the soul. They are transferred into the other world. "We know that we have passed from death unto life, because we love the brethren. He that loveth not his brother abideth in death" (I John 3:14).

It is assumed that no one saw Enoch's body and that the place of his burial, like that of Moses, is unknown. Moses and Enoch walked with God and did his will. They were divinely protected and guided. They were healthy until the time of their departure from this life. Then, without physical suffering, they were transferred into the life hereafter. Death has no power over those who walk with God and do his will. God, who is the author of life, can save from death. "I will ransom them from the power of the grave; I will redeem them from death" (Hosea 13:14).

The Hebrews believed that when men die, their souls are held in Sheol, a place over which God has no jurisdiction. "For in death there is no remembrance of thee: in the grave (Sheol) who shall give thee thanks?" (Psa. 6:5.) Moses and Enoch were exceptions. Their souls did not remain in Sheol, but went to heaven. Jesus remained three days in Sheol, then rose from the dead and ascended into heaven.

ABRAHAM'S FAITH

By faith Abraham, when he was called to go out into a place which he should after receive for an inheritance, obeyed; and he went out, not knowing whither he went.
Heb. 11:8.

In biblical days the world was uncharted and maps were unknown. Travelers depended entirely on the information which they could obtain while traveling from one place to another. Even today, tribesmen in the Arabian Desert and other parts of the Near East have little knowledge of the globe and its vastness. The chiefs of the tribes and their wise men know little about the lands which lie beyond their borders. Therefore, **in migrating** from one place to another they must trust God to guide them. They cannot know the difficulties which lie ahead, or the kind of reception they will receive from other tribes. Some tribes welcome an immigrant and give him a temporary grazing permit. Others are hostile and refuse grazing rights and the use of wells.

Abraham wandered for many years in the Arabian Desert, searching for fertile pastures and wells for his flocks. His family and the many members of his household—servants and relatives—lived in tents made of the hair of goats. In some places Abraham and his tribe were well received; in others the people were hostile. At times he fought against raiding Arab kings (Gen. 14 : 14–17). Abraham trusted in God and was told in a vision to leave his country and his people, and to go to a land which God was going to give to his descendents. (Gen. 12 : 1–5).

It takes strong faith, courage, and trust in God to leave one's home, fields, pastures, friends and relatives in exchange for a mere promise given in a vision. But Abraham believed in this promise, even though it was not to be fulfilled in his own day. He knew God was trustworthy and that the promise would be fulfilled in due time. This is why Abraham was declared righteous and came to be known as the father of believers.

Men must learn to trust in God and let him lead them and guide them through life. Everyone has a call and a mission in this life. We do not know what our mission is in life, nor do we know when it will be fulfilled. Therefore, we must listen to God and trust in his Word.

STARS AND SAND

Therefore sprang there even of one, and him as good as dead, so many as the stars of the sky in multitude, and as the sand which is by the sea shore innumerable.
Heb. 11 : 12.

In the East large mathematical figures were not known by the general public; few people understood the meaning of figures over one thousand. "As the stars of the sky and the sand by the sea" is an Eastern way of suggesting a very large number. Some people also speak of the leaves of the trees and the hairs of the head.

Abraham's seed increased so rapidly that the Egyptian pharaohs were alarmed. They commanded that all male children be killed at birth. ". . . If it be a son, then ye shall kill him: but if it be a daughter, then she shall live" (Exod. 1 : 16).

The increase no doubt was due to God's blessings which were bestowed on Abraham, Isaac and Jacob. God had promised Abraham a land. His descendants were to increase and become strong in order to possess this land. In other words, Abraham and his children were led by God; thus they overcame their difficulties and prospered and increased even in countries where poverty and sickness were prevalent.

GOD IS ABLE

Accounting that God was able to raise him up, even from the dead; from whence also he received him in a figure.
Heb. 11 : 19.

When God told Abraham that Sarah, his wife, would bear a son, Abraham was a hundred years old and Sarah ninety. She had been childless and at this age was too old to have a child. God nevertheless assured Abraham that Sarah was going to have a child and that his name would be called Isaac, meaning "laugh." This is because Abraham laughed in his heart when God told him that he was going to have a child in his old age. "Then Abraham fell upon his face, and laughed, and said in his heart, Shall a child be born unto him that is an hundred years old? and shall Sarah, that is ninety years old, bear?" (Gen. 17 : 17.)

Thus, the birth of Isaac, and Abraham's willingness to offer him to God, served as a parable through which Abraham's faith in God was confirmed. The birth of Isaac was the beginning of the covenant between God and Abraham. It proved beyond doubt that what is impossible for men is possible for God. The Eastern text reads: "And he reasoned in himself, it is possible for God even to raise the dead."

Faith is the substance of things that cannot be seen. One needs spiritual vision to see beyond this world. By spiritual understanding, what is unseen becomes a manifest reality. Faith helps one to find direction and guidance. In faith there is hope and strength. Without faith man is like a ship with a broken rudder drifting in the sea.

FAITH OF HEBREW LEADERS

And what shall I more say? for the time would fail me to tell of Gedeon, and of Barak, and of Samson, and of Jephthae; of David also, and Samuel, and of the prophets:
Heb. 11 : 32.

All of these great Hebrew leaders rose to power during times of crisis and national emergency, when everything looked dark and hopeless and people were in despair. Their victories were accomplished by faith and trust in the infinite power of God, who rules all and knows all. There were no other forces to rely on. The Hebrews had prophets. Except for their faith and trust, they were poorly armed to make war against strong and well-organized kingdoms. In many instances, they suffered severe defeats from their enemies. But when they turned to

God, a great leader and deliverer rose up from among them.

Gideon was a great leader and military genius. His exploits as a leader and general made him a national hero. His faith in God was so strong that he dismissed thousands of his soldiers and chose to fight against the army of Midian with only three hundred men (Judg. 7 : 4–9). The other Hebrew leaders mentioned here were also courageous and daring. Their faith in God was so strong that they were able to meet every emergency and save their people from their enemies.

When we rely on God, our vision is cleared and our way prepared. By faith things which are unseen are revealed and unreality is made real. Gideon was told by God in a vision how to prepare to meet his enemies.

The exploits of the leaders mentioned here are recorded in the book of Judges: Gideon, chapter 6; Barak, chapter 4; Samson, chapter 13; and Jephtha, chapter 11.

PROPHETS RAISED THE DEAD

Women received their dead raised to life again: and others were tortured, not accepting deliverance; that they might obtain a better resurrection: Heb. 11 : 35.

Some of the Hebrew prophets, like Jesus and his disciples, healed the sick and raised the dead. Elijah raised the son of the widow of Zarephath in Syria. The miracle was performed through the power of prayer. Elijah prayed to God and asked him to restore the child's soul. His request was granted and the child was restored to life (I Kings 17 : 17–23).

Elisha, like his master Elijah, performed miracles and wonders. He raised the son of the Shunnamite woman. He cured Naaman, captain of the host of Syria, of his leprosy (II Kings 5 : 14–17).

The miracles and wonders in the New Testament were a continuation of those which were wrought by the prophets. Nevertheless, there was a period in which no prophets rose among the Israelites, and as a result, divine healing was lost until it was once more restored through Jesus Christ. Jesus' miracles and wonders were greater than those of the Hebrew prophets. This is because his understanding of God was infinite, while the Hebrew prophets, when they were in difficulties and despair, doubted God's wisdom and complained.

BASTARDS

But if ye be without chastisement, whereof all are partakers, then are ye bastards, and not sons.
Furthermore we have had fathers of our flesh which corrected us, and we gave them reverence: shall we not much rather be in subjection unto the Father of spirits, and live? Heb. 12 : 8–9.

Where moral laws are strictly observed and violators punished by death, illegitimacy is hardly known. Children thus born are generally destroyed. There are, however, cases where women marry after they are suspected of having conceived. Children thus born are kept, but are considered bastards and are treated differently and brought up undisciplined. Then again, education and discipline, being religious, are conducted in the synagogue and the Temple. According to the Mosaic law, bastards were excluded from certain privileges and rites.

"A bastard shall not enter into the congregation of the Lord; even to his tenth generation shall he not enter into the congregation of the Lord" (Deut. 23 : 2).

The Hebrew Christians were brought up and disciplined like legitimate children. They were converted to Christianity by the apostles of Christ. Paul demands of them to live up to their faith, discipline and calling. They had no excuse for their falling back and deserting the faith of Christ.

ENTERTAINING ANGELS

Be not forgetful to entertain strangers: for thereby some have entertained angels unawares.   Heb. 13 : 2.

Easterners are noted for their hospitality toward strangers and wayfarers. As hotels and inns are scarce, strangers and travelers depend on the generosity of the people for lodging and food. And when they leave the house or tent that has sheltered them they are usually given sufficient food to carry them to the next camp or town. The family, even the little children, may go to sleep hungry, but the stranger must be fed first and fed well.

Upon arrival in a town, strangers are invited into the homes of the people of the town. Food is provided, and water for their feet. When the caravan is large and travelers are too many, some of them find it difficult to obtain lodging places. For instance, Joseph and Mary had to stay in a stable when they went to Bethlehem (Luke 2 : 7). Some travelers may even have to spend the night in the street or in a near-by field. ". . . He sat him down in a street of the city; for there was no man that took them into his house to lodging" (Judg. 19 : 15).

Generally speaking, Easterners believe in hospitality. They are aware that they themselves some day may be strangers and in need of food and lodging. They entertain people because they expect to be entertained. Then again, as in the East, one may be surprised by the unexpected entrance of a nobleman into his house. At times the host knows nothing about his guest until the time of his departure. This is because strangers do not disclose their identity until they are received. This is why Easterners, especially Arabians, welcome every guest who happens to seek shelter under their roof. Men of God are often called angels.

Abraham entertained angels, set food before them, and gave them water to wash their feet (Gen. 18 : 1–8). He also was generous toward the travelers and strangers who stopped at his tent or passed by his camp. He fed them and gave them water to refresh themselves. This is in accordance with the teaching of Jesus. "For I was an hungred, and ye gave me meat: I was thirsty, and ye gave me drink: I was a stranger, and ye took me in" (Matt. 25 : 35).

BURIED OUTSIDE

Wherefore Jesus also, that he might sanctify the people with his own blood, suffered without the gate. Heb. 13 : 12.

Jerusalem is a walled city having four gates. The city proper, the Temple, and other historic sites are all within the wall. The cemeteries and tombs of the kings of Judah are in the valley of Kedron, outside of the city. Easterners generally bury their dead outside the city wall.

Jesus was crucified in a place called *Golgotha,* about a mile from the city and a short distance from Gethsemane (Matt. 27 : 33). He was buried in a grave near by. This is because in the East, strangers and criminals cannot be buried in sacred ground.

The place now supposed to be the site of the holy sepulcher, where Jesus was buried, was designated by Queen Helene when she visited Jerusalem after the conversion of her husband in 318. Golgotha resembles a human skull. It proves beyond doubt that Jesus died outside the gate, according to the Scriptures. This is because Jesus died the death of a sinner in order to save those who had gone astray. He offered himself not only for the Jews but for the Gentiles also.

JAMES

INTRODUCTION

The author of the epistle is either James the son of Zebedee, or James the brother of our Lord.

James the son of Zebedee, and a brother of John, was one of the first disciples of Jesus (Matt. 4 : 21; 10 : 2; Mark 3 : 14ff; Luke 6 : 13ff; Acts 1 : 13). James and his brother John were intimate with Jesus. They were with him on many special occasions (Matt. 17 : 1; Mark 5 : 37). James the apostle was probably the leader of the church in Jerusalem. He was murdered by King Herod Agrippa I (Acts. 12 : 2).

James, the brother of our Lord, should not be confused with James, the son of Alphaeus. He is called James *Zaora,* the young, to distinguish him from James the son of Zebedee (Mark 15 : 40).

After the murder of James, the son of Zebedee, James, the brother of our Lord, acted as leader of the Christians. At times he and Peter presided over the councils and other important meetings. As the son of Joseph, the husband of Mary, he was given due honors and respected by the converts. He was not one of the twelve apostles. That is why he addressed himself as a servant of Jesus Christ. James joined in the Christian movement after the resurrection.

It is possible that Joseph had other wives besides Mary. The Jews, like the Mohammedans, are polygamists. Even today many Jews in the East marry more than one woman. When Jesus proclaimed himself as the Messiah, the Galileans said, "We know his brother and sisters."

Paul met James in Jerusalem. He says in his epistle to the Galatians, that he went to Jerusalem to see Peter and stayed there for some time and saw James, the brother of our Lord (Gal. 1 : 19). Paul met James again in Jerusalem before his arrest (Acts 21 : 18). Paul mentions that the brothers of our Lord were married and brought their wives with them.

This epistle or pastoral letter is addressed to Christians of Hebrew and Galilean origin who were scattered in northern Palestine, Mesopotamia and Asia Minor.

The epistle emphasizes Christian works. This is in conformity with Jesus' teaching. He told his disciples that doing is what counts. "If you love me keep my commandments." The epistle is brief, but plain and well written. It shows that the author is a sincere and simple Christian who knows little of Jewish theology and rituals, but one who had heard Jesus preaching a practical religion and denouncing the literal interpretations and traditions of the elders. "For if any be a hearer of the word, and not a doer, he is like a man who sees his face in a mirror" (James 1 : 23, Eastern text).

The teaching of James in many respects sounds like that of Jesus. "Swear not, neither by heaven, neither by the earth, neither by any other oath: but let your yea be yea; and your nay, nay; lest ye fall into condemnation" (James 5 : 12). James preaches a gospel of practical Christianity free from theological complications. The epistle was written earlier than those of Paul.

THE FADING FLOWER

But the rich, in that he is made low: because as the flower of the grass he shall pass away.
For the sun is no sooner risen with a burning heat, but it withereth the grass, and the flower thereof falleth, and the grace of the fashion of it perisheth: so also shall the rich man fade away in his ways. Jas. 1 : 10–11.

In arid lands and deserts, where the rainy season is short, the life of flowers is brief, and grass withers under the intense rays of the sun. When the rain falls, and the scorched ground is soft, the grass starts to grow and flowers bloom. When the rain is over and the sun is hot, then the tender grass withers and the flowers fade. That is why the Scriptures so often liken men to the grass and flowers of the field. "He cometh forth like a flower, and is cut down: he fleeth also as a shadow, and continueth not" (Job 14 : 2). "All flesh is grass and all the goodliness thereof is as the flower of the field" (Isa. 40 : 6). Jesus also compared men with the grass of the field, which God clothes with such beauty even though it lives only for a day (Matt. 6 : 30).

James admonishes the believers to be humble and meek. He tells the rich to rejoice in their meekness, because their lives are short like that of the flower of the field, which blooms and fades in a day.

In a changing world like ours, pride, glory, and material things vanish like a flower, but meekness and gentleness endure forever.

GOD TEMPTS NO ONE

Let no man say when he is tempted, I am tempted of God: for God cannot be tempted with evil, neither tempteth he any man: Jas. 1 : 13.

The followers of some of the Eastern religions attribute to God everything that happens. The people of Semitic origin believe that God tries men to test their strength. When they are prosperous and happy they say, "God has blessed us." When they lose their wealth they say, "God gave and God has taken it away." When Job received the sad news of the death of his sons and the loss of his wealth, he fell down upon the ground, worshiped the Lord, and said, "Naked came I out of my mother's womb, and naked shall I return thither: the Lord gave, and the Lord hath taken away; blessed be the name of the Lord" (Job 1 : 21). Likewise, temptations and mishaps in life are blamed on God. For instance, when the Hebrews won victories over their enemies, they credited them to their God; they felt that God had been on their side. When they were defeated, they said that God had deserted them. This made it easier for the people to bear defeats.

The Mohammedans believe that everything is preordained by God. When a man is killed or dies of illness, they believe that God has decreed the man should meet with such a death.

Of course, God knows the hearts and thoughts of men, but he does not tempt men with evil. God tries men, just as he tested Abraham and asked him to offer his son. "And it came to pass after those things, that God did tempt Abraham" (Gen. 22 : 1–3).

It is the devil that tempts men, and not God. Jesus was tempted by Satan, and not by God (Matt. 4 : 1). He taught his disciples to pray that they would not be permitted to be tempted or tried out beyond their strength. "Awake and pray, that you may not enter into temptation; the Spirit indeed is willing and ready, but the body is weak" (Mark 14 : 38, Eastern text).

God stands by us and is always ready to help when we fall into temptation or are tried beyond our strength. As a loving father he is always ready to rescue and to succor us.

FACE IN A MIRROR

For if any be a hearer of the word, and not a doer, he is like unto a man beholding his natural face in a glass:
Jas. 1 : 23.

"Face in a mirror" is an Eastern saying which suggests unreality. In a mirror we see only an image, which cannot be touched. Another similar idiom, "It is like a shadow," is used to describe wishful thinking or false sympathy.

Glass was discovered several centuries before the Christian era. Mirrors were made of glass and shiny metals. Paul used this illustration in his epistles to the Corinthians: "For now we see through a glass, darkly; but then face to face" (I Cor. 13 : 12).

Faith without good works, or an idea that is not put into practice, is like the image of an object in a mirror. Some of the finest inventions in our days, once were merely ideas mirrored in the minds of the inventors. These mental images became realities through faith and action.

Thus theologies are ideas and theories that need to be made into realities.

TRUE RELIGION

Pure religion and undefiled before God and the Father is this, To visit the fatherless and widows in their affliction, and to keep himself unspotted from the world. Jas. 1 : 27.

All three of the great Monotheistic religions—Christianity, Judaism and Mohammedanism—stress charity and hospitality. In the East, Christians, Jews and Mohammedans try to demonstrate their sincerity and loyalty to their religion by acts of charity. Their tables are always ready for strangers and the needy. They seldom talk or boast of the superiority of the doctrines of their faiths. They believe in deeds. Words and sermons do not count. A man's faith and religious devotion is proven by his actions.

When the rich do something for the poor, they believe they are doing it for God, who is the father and protector of the poor and the fatherless. The psalmist says: "The poor committeth himself unto thee; thou art the helper of the fatherless" (Psa. 10 : 14).

James' admonishment is in accordance with the teaching of his Master. Jesus in his discourses stressed the importance of charity as a means of salvation. He warned against faith without works. Men are not saved just by calling him, "My Lord, my Lord," or by doing wonders in his name, but by the good works they do. "Verily I say unto you, inasmuch as ye did it not to one of the least of these, ye did it not to me" (Matt. 25 : 45).

Pious works are the true demonstration of a man's faith in God and devotion to his religion. Faith (religion) without good works is dead (Jas. 2 : 14–17).

JUDGING BY APPAREL

And ye have respect to him that weareth the gay clothing, and say unto him, Sit thou here in a good place; and say to the poor, Stand thou there, or sit here under my footstool: — Jas. 2 : 3.

In biblical lands, men who are dressed in expensive clothes and wear costly jewels, are highly respected and honored. They are welcomed into the homes of the people. During feasts and banquets they are given places of honor. This is largely due to the scarcity of clothes in the East. Only the rich can have expensive garments and precious jewelry. Customarily, during weddings and banquets, people wear many garments in order to receive respect and admiration. When a man is short of clothes and jewelry he may borrow from his friends and neighbors (Exod. 12 : 35).

Those who are poorly dressed are given less important places and less attention. At times poorly dressed men are refused a seat. Jesus was familiar with this peculiar Eastern custom. "And when the king came in to see the guests, he saw there a man which had not a wedding garment: And he saith unto him, Friend, how camest thou in hither not having a wedding garment? And he was speechless" (Matt. 22 : 11-12).

James condemns this ancient practice which caused men to be judged by their clothes instead of their hearts and Christian conduct. The poor were discriminated against. The discrimination was contrary to the gospel of Christ. It was all right for the pagans and the unbelievers to adhere to this ancient practice, but not for Christians, who had been made equal through the gospel of Jesus Christ, and his blood, which was shed for all of them. (See *Gospel Light,* page 124.)

POOR OPPRESSED

But ye have despised the poor. Do not rich men oppress you, and draw you before the judgment seats? Jas. 2 : 6.

In many cities and provinces the government is controlled by the rich, who act as representatives of the central government in legislative and judicial affairs. They collect taxes, maintain law and order, and perform other official duties. Most of the civil positions are acquired by bribes and promises of good revenues. In return, the federal government bestows upon the rich unlimited authority.

To make their promises and pledges good, the rich oppress the poor and levy heavy taxes on them. In the East, a rich man seldom taxes another rich man, fearing revenge. The rich escape with a small gift, but the poor work hard in order to support the rich who act as local officials. Those who fail to pay the full amount levied on them are brought before the judge, imprisoned and made destitute. This is why Jesus said: "And again I say unto you, It is easier for a rope to go through the eye of a needle, than for a rich man to enter into the kingdom of God" (Matt. 19 : 24, Eastern text). This type of rich man should not be confused with those who are blessed and made rich by the hand of God. When wealth is acquired by means of labor and justice, it is a blessing of God, but when it is acquired by confiscation and unjust methods, it is a curse. Men should be content with the labor of their own hands and satisfied with what God has given them. "Give me neither poverty nor riches; feed me with food convenient for me" (Prov. 30 : 8).

Christians are warned to be impartial to the poor. Discrimination and impartiality are a violation of Christian conduct and of the law. Rich men among the Christians are to set a good example to the unbelievers. (See *Gospel Light,* page 115.)

FAITH AND WORKS

Ye see then how that by works a man is justified, and not by faith only. Jas. 2 : 24.

Faith is the substance of things that are unseen, but works are the fruits of faith. Both faith and works are connected like the body and the soul which cannot be separated. Or faith is like roots of a tree, and works are like the leaves and fruit. One is unseen and the other seen.

Faith without works is dead. That is to say, faith must be demonstrated by action. An idea must be put into practice. What seems to be unreal must be made real. Many men have sufficient faith to do wonders, but they do not use it. Mere confession of belief in God is not enough. One must prove one's faith by works. Any person can believe in God. Even sinners believe in God and are afraid of him when they commit a crime, but good works speak for themselves, and bear testimony of good faith. When we see a man living a Christian life, we know that he believes in God. Abraham believed in God; his belief was proven by his works. Had he not walked in God's way and done his will, no one would have recognized him as a servant of God. Other men in his day believed in God, but they lacked good works.

James stresses the importance of works. True followers of Jesus are to demonstrate their faith with works of charity, hospitality and brotherly love, and not by mere words and confessions. Jesus, through his teaching, stressed the importance of good works and charity. He told his followers that they must do the will of his father. When they fed a hungry person or clothed one who was naked, they did it for him. "For I was an hungred, and ye gave me meat: I was thirsty, and ye gave me drink: I was a stranger, and ye took me in" (Matt. 25 : 35–46).

RAHAB'S FAITH

Likewise also was not Rahab the harlot justified by works, when she had received the messengers, and had sent them out another way? Jas. 2 : 25.

In Eastern countries, even though moral laws are strongly enforced and the guilty severely punished, harlots are to be found in many large cities. Houses of prostitution are prohibited, so harlots operate secretly. They are generally known to strangers and outcasts who are unwelcome in the homes of the people.

The spies whom Joshua sent from Shittim no doubt disguised themselves so that they would not be suspected. They probably entered the city gate wearing old and tattered garments and sought lodging among the lower classes and women of questionable character. Moreover, Rahab's house was near the wall, an easy place from which to escape if they should be apprehended.

Rahab took them in, hid them and helped them to escape over the wall. Rahab was confident that the Hebrews would triumph over her people and destroy the city. This is why she made the spies swear that when the city was taken, she and her family would be spared. The spies promised her and her family safety in return for her kindness (Josh. 2 : 1–16).

Rahab accepted these promises on faith. The Hebrews were instructed by Moses to destroy all people who resisted them. Rahab proved her faith by letting the Hebrew spies down by a cord through the window. In hiding the enemies and leading them to safety, she risked her own life and the lives of her relatives. When Jericho was taken and its inhabitants slain by the sword, Rahab and her people were spared (Josh. 6 : 21–23).

Note: The author of the epistle to the Hebrews states that Rahab was saved by her faith (Heb. 11 : 31). James says that she was justified by her works. That is, her works confirmed her faith. She believed that God was on the side of the Hebrews, and therefore she acted accordingly (Josh. 2 : 9–12).

THE POWER OF TONGUE

Even so the tongue is a little member, and boasteth great things. Behold, how great a matter a little fire kindleth! And the tongue is a fire, a world of iniquity: so is the tongue among our members, that it defileth the whole body, and setteth on fire the course of nature; and it is set on fire of hell. Jas. 3 : 5–6.

Fluent speakers and orators are often described as having tongues of fire. "His tongue is like fire" is an Eastern idiom meaning, "he is a convincing speaker," one who removes all doubt. Fire burns up everything inflammable. "And there appeared unto them eleven tongues like as of fire, and it sat upon each of them" (Acts 2 : 3). In the East when one converses well in a foreign language, it is said, "He knows it like water." "Write the vision, and make it plain upon tables, that he may run that readeth it" (Hab. 2 : 2). Another idiom is, "His tongue is like a sharp sword."

In the East, word of mouth, especially gossip, spreads like fire. Once a false report is published, it is hard to suppress it. Isaiah likens the tongue to a devouring fire (Isa. 30 : 27). Job says: "Thou shalt be hid from the scourge of the tongue" (Job 5 : 21). "Death and life are in the power of the tongue: and they that love it shall eat the fruit thereof" (Prov. 18 : 21).

Just as the tongue may be used to cause harm, it may also be used for good. The tongue spreads the Word of God, bestows blessings, utters praise, words of comfort, exhortation and prayer. "A wholesome tongue is a tree of life: but perverseness therein is a breach in the spirit" (Prov. 15 : 4).

Both the tongue and fire may be used for good and for evil. With the tongue we may bless or curse, and with fire we may forge implements of peace or weapons of war and destruction. The simile used by the apostle is perfect, for it takes only a spark or a word to destroy a country.

GOD'S PRESENCE

Go to now, ye that say, To day or to morrow we will go into such a city, and continue there a year, and buy and sell, and get gain: Jas. 4 : 13.

The Aramaic words *"abdinan,"* "we will work," and *"abrinan,"* "we will pass time," or "cross over," are written alike. A small dot placed over the third letter causes the change in meaning. This similarity of words makes it difficult for foreigners to understand the meaning, especially in the case of bad manuscripts with carelessly placed dots.

In this case, the translator confused the two Aramaic words. The Aramaic reads, "And will work there a year, and will trade and prosper." Easterners, when going to foreign countries, often say to their families and friends, "I am going to America for a year to work and make money and return home." Then again, men from small towns where there is no work, often spend the winter or a whole year in larger cities, where they find work to ply their trades. Easterners generally go away for a year, but when they fail to earn enough money, they stay more than a year. Until recent years, Assyrians, Arabs, Syrians and Armenians came to America for a short stay. When they had earned a few hundred dollars they returned to their native lands and became rich. This was largely because of the value of the American dollar and the scarcity of money in the East.

When Easterners leave their homes, or start some undertaking, they always say, "With God's power, if God permits, I am going away to work" or, "I am going on a journey." God's presence is needed in everything we start to do. We need his help and his divine guidance at home, in the field, and in the lands to which we go. For our life is the breath of his mouth and our bodies, the work of his hand.

WAGES OF REAPERS

Behold, the hire of the labourers who have reaped down your fields, which is of you kept back by fraud, crieth: and the cries of them which have reaped are entered into the ears of the Lord of sabaoth. Jas. 5 : 4.

Where money is scarce, commodities are used as a medium of exchange. Reapers and laborers are paid in wheat, butter and cheese. Wheat cutters are generally paid in wheat, and the wages of a shepherd are bargained in terms of butter, sheep or lambs. Laban paid Jacob with sheep and cattle (Gen. 30 : 28–43).

Wheat reapers are hired during the harvest only. Each reaper is paid according to his ability. Some are paid a bushel a day; others receive more. In some cases, the reapers cut the wheat by piecework. The owner of the field supplies them with food (two meals a day). The wages are paid in October when the wheat is threshed. The reapers and creditors meet the owner of the harvest at the threshing ground to be paid in wheat. The creditors must be paid first. The reapers' wages depend entirely upon the honesty and integrity of the owner of the harvest. If he does not want to pay, no one can force him to do so. Some of these men make excuses, such as the excuse that the harvest has fallen short or that they have had too many creditors to pay. In the East, there are no laws to compel employers to pay employees; the entire matter depends upon the oral agreement between employer and employee.

Powerful politicians, government officials and rich men generally refuse to pay their workers. They defer the payment from one month to another. Some of them draft laborers by force during the harvest season, and others promise to pay but fail to keep their promises. The families of the unpaid laborers suffer hunger and privations and become destitute in winter.

Religious men always act as intermediaries to secure payments in cases where injustice is done to laborers. James here bitterly condemns the rich of his day who defrauded wheat cutters, whose livelihood depended upon their work during the summer months.

CONFESS

Confess your faults one to another, and pray one for another, that ye may be healed. The effectual fervent prayer of a righteous man availeth much. Jas. 5 : 16.

"Faults," in this instance, means "offenses." That is to say, faults committed against one another. These are not considered as sins and therefore are forgiven. Easterners generally confess their faults to one another. Confessions are followed by restitution. Stolen articles are returned, damage is repaired and apologies made.

Such faults are detrimental to those who keep them secret. On the other hand, confession relieves the heart and establishes confidence and neighborly relations. Evil acts cause worries that may result in sickness. When the mind is obscured, the whole body is in darkness. Once the worries are destroyed, the mind is freed, the vision becomes clear, and the body is whole.

One needs no intermediary in order to confess his faults and make reparation. God knows the secrets of our hearts. We must confess our faults to those to whom we have done wrong. We cannot become reconciled with God until we are reconciled with those to whom our words and actions have been injurious.

I PETER

INTRODUCTION

The author of the epistle is Peter, the apostle. He was writing from the province of Babylon, and not the city of Babylon, the capital of the Chaldean Empire. The names of cities and those of provinces have often caused confusion. Some authorities maintain that Babylon was in ruins during the time of the apostle, and therefore they think Peter might have meant Rome. This is a misleading conclusion. Babylon had been conquered by Alexander the Great about the year 301 B.C. We do not know when the city was destroyed. It had remained intact during the Persian and Greek periods. And even though the metropolis of Babylon was destroyed, the surrounding towns and villages were still standing.

Peter preached in the province of Babylon. Both the members of the Ten Tribes and many of the Jews were settled in this region. Peter was a Galilean. He spoke a dialect of Aramaic which was spoken in Mesopotamia.

Peter sends the greetings of the church in Babylon (I Pet. 5 : 13). The epistle is addressed to Hebrew and Jewish Christians, and it emphasizes the death and suffering of Jesus, and the reconciliation through his death. Christ is spoken of as "a Lamb without blemish" who was "fore-ordained before the foundation of the world." Jesus is likened to the cornerstone which was rejected by the builders. The rest of the epistle covers admonitions, exhortations and salutations.

THE ELECT

Peter, an apostle of Jesus Christ, to the strangers scattered throughout Pontus, Galatia, Cappadocia, Asia, and Bithynia,
Elect according to the foreknowledge of God the Father, through sanctification of the Spirit, unto obedience and sprinkling of the blood of Jesus Christ: Grace unto you, and peace, be multiplied.
Blessed be the God and Father of our Lord Jesus Christ, which according to his abundant mercy hath begotten us again unto a lively hope by the resurrection of Jesus Christ from the dead, I Pet. 1 : 1–3.

To the strangers" here means the Hebrews who were scattered among the Gentiles throughout Asia Minor. Many Jews, because of persecution, had fled from Palestine and were sojourning in Asia Minor. The Eastern text reads, "to the chosen ones and pilgrims."

Many of these people had been converted to Christianity by the seventy evangelists who were sent out by Jesus. Some may have been converted later by Paul and Barnabas on their several missionary journeys in that region. Be that as it may, Christianity had spread widely among the Hebrews prior to the death of Jesus.

Peter reminds them that they were the elect ones, members of the chosen people and the elect of Jesus Christ. They were first elected through the foreknowledge of God, and later by grace and faith in Jesus (Rom. 9 : 11; I Pet. 1 : 23). "Elect" is another term used for "the chosen"—"them that are sanctified in Christ Jesus, called to be saints . . ." (I Cor. 1 : 10). Thus, all who believed in Jesus Christ were the elect of God.

Election in the flesh failed to bring salvation. It is the election to the gospel of Jesus Christ which Peter is trying to emphasize. The gospel to which they were elected was the fulfillment of the promises that had been made to

Israel, God's chosen people. The Jews who had accepted the gospel had become the heirs of the promises which God had made to Abraham and David. These promises were fulfilled only in Jesus Christ. For in him were all the people of the world blessed.

LIVING STONES

To whom coming, as unto a living stone, disallowed indeed of men, but chosen of God, and precious, I Pet. 2 : 4.

Living stone" in this case means a "strong stone." Strong stones are hard to be hewn. Therefore, they are rejected by builders for foundation stones. Softer stones are preferred. Then again, Easterners often say, "He is a stone behind me," which means, "He is my protector." In the East, when people fight, they often seek protection behind stones. The psalmist asks, "That our daughters may be as corner stones, polished after the similitude of a palace" (Psa. 144 : 12). Even the writer of Genesis speaks of "the stone of Israel" (Gen. 49 : 24). And the psalmist spoke of "The stone which the builders refused" (Psa. 118 : 22).

Good stones are selected and placed in the best parts of temples and palaces. Christian converts are admonished to be pure, so that they may be used as stones in the temple of God, which is the church of Christ. Christians throughout the world were rejected and despised, but were to become cornerstones in the spiritual temple which was rising on the ruins of the old.

I PETER

PREACHING IN SHEOL

By which also he went and preached unto the spirits in prison;   I Pet. 3 : 19.

The Aramaic text reads, "And he preached to the souls imprisoned in Sheol." Sheol is the place where the departed souls await resurrection. It is a place of silence and inactivity. It was supposed to be somewhere under the ground, beyond the reach of the forces of the universe and of the living God. "For in death there is no remembrance of thee: in the grave who shall give thee thanks?" (Psa. 6 : 5). Those who were in Sheol were cut off from the rest of humanity and from the living God. The gates of Sheol were so securely locked that there was no way of escape, nor was there any deliverer. Jesus not only defied the mysterious Sheol and conquered death, but he also gave his disciples and the church the assurance that they will not be held in it. "And the gates of hell shall not prevail against it" (Matt. 16 : 18).

CHURCH ADMINISTRATORS

The elders which are among you I exhort, who am also an elder, and a witness of the sufferings of Christ, and also a partaker of the glory that shall be revealed: I Pet. 5 : 1.

The term "elders" means "ministers" or "presbyters." Elders were selected by the apostles to take care of Christian converts, lead them in prayer, admonish them, and teach the doctrine of Christianity. The term "elders" is used simply because in the East such offices are held by elderly men, whom the younger people honor and respect. They are also called "white-bearded men."

The Jews likewise appointed elderly men to high offices in their church. Moses appointed seventy elders to judge the people and look after their spiritual welfare. The elders always laid their hands upon the animals which were offered for sin offerings. "And the elders of the congregation shall lay their hands upon the head of the bullock before the Lord . . ." (Lev. 4 : 15). In the Jewish religion the elders were not priests, nor were they permitted to perform priestly functions. They were appointed and consecrated for other work, mostly judicial and administrative. In those days religion and government were one. Priests and elders functioned under the leadership of Moses, who was supreme in both political and spiritual matters. The Lord gave of the Spirit to the seventy elders (Num. 11 : 25).

The elders which the apostles had selected were not priests in the sense of the Aaronic priesthood, but ministers of the people. The apostles had nothing to do with the Jewish rituals, sacrifices and other ordinances of the Jewish law, which governed worship and which could be administered by no one but *kaney,* priests who were appointed and consecrated for this duty. On the other hand, there is nothing in the gospel to indicate that Jesus wanted his disciples to adhere to the Jewish temple rituals and sacrifices. He had often denounced them.

Christian elders were appointed to serve and not to be served. Jesus, after he ate the Last Supper, told his disciples to minister to one another, and that he who would be the greatest among them must serve the others. He washed their feet as an example. His disciples were not to be lords over their people, as the leaders and the priests of other religions were.

Elders were elected from among men who were noted for their piety, humility and kindness, and who could serve freely. They were to be like shepherds who loved and cared for their flocks. Peter is supporting the command of Jesus relative to the ministry of the gospel. Peter had been with him during the Last Supper when Jesus explained to them the duties and functions of those who were to become leaders among them.

CHRIST SHEPHERD

And when the chief Shepherd shall appear, ye shall receive a crown of glory that fadeth not away. I Pet. 5 : 4.

In many instances, a "chief shepherd" is the head of the tribe. A number of hired shepherds, who work under him, go to the mountains with the sheep and look after the welfare of the flocks during the summer months. The chief shepherd stays at home or at camp. He seldom attends the sheep.

The sheep are often visited by the chief shepherd, who advises on important matters, such as grazing, water and the general welfare of the sheep. He also bestows honors on faithful and hard working shepherds.

The chief shepherd is Jesus Christ who, at his coming, will reward all those who minister faithfully to his flocks.

PETER WROTE FROM BABYLON

The church that is at Babylon, elected together with you, saluteth you; and so doth Marcus my son. I Pet. 5 : 13.

Many years after the resurrection, Peter went to Mesopotamia preaching the gospel to the descendants of the Hebrews who had been carried captive by Assyrians and Babylonians. After the fall of the Chaldean Empire 539 B.C., a small number of Jews returned from Babylon under Ezra and Nehemiah, but the bulk of the people, especially the wealthy and those who had found favor in the eyes of the Persian kings, preferred to stay in the rich Persian provinces rather than to return to the barren hills of Judea.

Babylon was conquered by Cyrus but was not destroyed. The city remained intact during the Persian reign. It was conquered by Alexander the Great, after his defeat of the Persian armies at the Battle of Arbela.

The city at last was destroyed, according to the prophecy, probably by floods. A new city was built near the ruins of the old, by Seleucus, one of the generals of Alexander.

Peter in his epistle refers to the Christians in the province of Babylon. Even today there are many Christians in the province of Babylon. They are called Chaldean Christians. And the title of the head of the church of the East is Mar-Shimun, that is, "Lord Peter."

It was natural for Peter to preach among the people of his own race and language. At this time he was an old man.

When Paul returned to Jerusalem, he was received by James, the brother of our Lord. Peter had left Jerusalem and Antioch on a preaching mission, visiting churches in Mesopotamia. A late tradition states that Peter was martyred in Rome, but there is no actual evidence of it.

II PETER

INTRODUCTION

The author of this epistle is the apostle Peter, and he was writing from Mesopotamia. This epistle is a supplementary pastoral letter, written a short time after the first.

The apostle, like Paul, warns against the apostasy which was to result from the teachings of the false teachers who were denying most of the fundamental doctrines of Christianity and, in particular, the doctrine of salvation through the death and resurrection of Christ. The new teachers are called false prophets, whom he condemns in strong words.

The apostle also assures the churches of the certainty of Christ's coming in judgment at the last day. The converts in Asia Minor had become weary of the doctrine of the second coming—many of them had been expecting the immediate return of Christ and a change in the worldly order. Peter warns against that belief. He tells them that one day is with the Lord as a thousand years, and a thousand years as one day. The Christian must be patient.

OLD PROPHECIES FULFILLED

We have also a more sure word of prophecy; whereunto ye do well that ye take heed, as unto a light that shineth in a dark place, until the day dawn, and the day star arise in your hearts: II Pet. 1 : 19.

Jesus, on many occasions, had predicted his suffering, his death on the cross, and his resurrection. These prophecies, together with those of the Old Testament, were fulfilled. The predictions made by Jesus were a greater proof of the divine inspiration of the Hebrew prophets. Jesus' utterances concerning his suffering and death were recent. Most of the people who had seen him and been with him had heard him predict his death on the cross.

The Old Testament prophecies were made many centuries before. They had become the subject of diverse interpretations. Some of the people could not associate them with Jesus' sufferings and his death on the cross.

Peter declares that these prophecies were the inspired word of God. They shone like the sun throughout the ages, pointing to the coming of a great Deliverer and Saviour.

ONE PROPHECY CONFIRMS ANOTHER

Knowing this first, that no prophecy of the scripture is of any private interpretation. II Pet. 1 : 20.

Prophecy deals with things which are to happen in the future. The prophet surveys the past and present and through divine wisdom foretells things which are to come years or centuries thereafter. Thus, a prophecy foretelling things which are to take place a hundred years hence, cannot of itself confirm those events, because they have not yet taken place. What a prophet sees in advance, other men do not see. If all men saw what a prophet sees, then there would be no need of prophecy.

Many prophets were slain or imprisoned because their prophecies were unacceptable to the politicians, kings and princes of their day. The prophets themselves were powerless. They could not make the foretold things happen, so that they might vindicate themselves and prove their prophecies. They had to wait until the time of fulfillment. When the things which were predicted became a reality, strange as it may seem, the prophets who had been slain for the predictions, which at the time had seemed preposterous, were honored and worshiped by the descendants of those who had murdered them.

One prophecy helps to explain and sustain another. That is to say, the prophet Jeremiah, who lived many years after Isaiah, was in a position to confirm and explain Isaiah's prophecy because some of the events predicted were taking place in his day. And what Jeremiah predicted was confirmed by prophets who followed him. Thus, all prophecies are bound together. One helps to explain another, because all are derived from a divince source.

ANGELS AS MINISTERS

For if God spared not the angels that sinned, but cast them *down to hell, and delivered* them *into chains of darkness, to be reserved unto judgment;* II Pet. 2 : 4.

Malakhey, "angels," means literally "messengers" or "ministers" of God. Angels are not mentioned in the list of God's creatures in Genesis. The first references made to them are in the account of the angel of the Lord who appeared to Hagar, and in the story of the two angels visiting Abraham before the destruction of Sodom and Gommorah (Gen. 16 : 7; 19 : 1). When Jacob was on his way to Padan-aram, he saw in a dream a ladder with angels ascending and descending upon it. Moreover Jacob, on his return, wrestled with an angel, and in a vision he saw a host of angels (Gen. 32 : 1–2; 24 : 32). The psalmist marvels that God has made man only "a little lower than the angels" (Psa. 8 : 5).

Angels are known as ministers of the Lord, carrying out his orders. In the case of Balaam we read, "The ass saw the angel of the Lord standing in the way, and his sword drawn in his hand" (Num. 22 : 23). Jesus spoke of angels, and they ministered to him on several occasions. The angel of the Lord appeared in dreams to Joseph (Matt. 1 : 20; 2 : 13–19).

Angels are mentioned in many books of the Bible, especially in the New Testament. The book of Revelation speaks of them frequently. The ministers who were in charge of churches in Asia Minor are addressed as angels, since they too were ministers or messengers of God.

SATAN, A FALLEN ANGEL

The early Hebrews had no such word as Satan. All power in earth and in heaven belonged to God only. Satan is a later term. In the early days Satan is represented by a serpent (Gen. 3 : 2–13). This is because serpents are greatly feared by people who dwell in the desert. Many Hebrews died of snake bites when they encamped in Edom (Num. 21 : 6–9).

The early Hebrews believed that everything which God had created was good, and that evils such as snakes and hardships were employed as God's agents to reprove and correct the people and make them return to God. For instance, according to the writer of Numbers, snakes were sent by God. "And the Lord sent fiery serpents among the people, and they bit the people; and much people of Israel died" (Num. 21 : 6). When Israel repented, the snake bites proved harmless (Num. 21 : 9). On the other hand, the Hebrews attributed some of the evil to pagan gods in whose lands they traveled and among whose people they lived.

Centuries later the Hebrew prophets discovered that the God of Israel was the God of the whole world and that Gentile gods were not really gods, but only dumb idols, and that even Satan was originally a creation of God and was good, but because of disobedience and false pride had fallen from the presence of God. "How art thou fallen from heaven, O Lucifer, son of the morning! how are thou cut down to the ground, which didst weaken the nations!" (Isa. 14 : 12–15.) Then again, in Genesis we read that the serpent was cursed by God (Gen. 3 : 14). The Hebrew prophet could not subscribe to Babylonian and Persian doctrines of two gods—the god of good and the god of evil. They believed in one God who was the Creator of all things in heaven and on the earth.

According to the Bible, even though Satan had fallen and was cursed, he retained his power and used it to punish the people when they went astray, to tempt them and to accuse them. The Hebrews believed that Satan had a place in this world, and certain work to do. Satan tried to tempt Jesus, but he failed (Matt. 4 : 1–10). He tempted Judas of Iscariot and caused him to betray his Master and later to kill himself.

Paul calls him "the prince of the power of the air" (Eph. 2 : 2). Jesus calls him a liar and a murderer (John 8 : 44). when the truth is known, the power of Satan will come to an end, and Satan himself will be destroyed.

BALAAM

Which have forsaken the right way, and are gone astray, following the way of Balaam the son of Bosor, who loved the wages of unrighteousness; II Pet. 2 : 15.

Balaam, the son of Beor, was an Aramean prophet, probably related to the Hebrews (Num. 22 : 5; 23 : 7). He was invited by Balak, the son of Zippor, king of Moab, to curse the Israelites who had destroyed the

Amorites and were ready to make war against Moab and Midian. The elders of Moab and Midian offered Balaam rich gifts if he would curse Israel. Balaam, aware of the sins which the children of Israel had committed in the desert, thought he could curse them and thus receive rich gifts and favors from the kings of Moab. The temptation for money and glory was so great that, had the Lord not warned him, he would have cursed the Hebrews.

He started out to go to the court of Balak, but the angel of the Lord stood in his way and stopped the ass on which he rode. Then the dumb ass spoke and the prophet realized his mistake (Num. 22 : 20–36).

The inner truth spoke to him and warned him of his greed. There is always an inner voice which guides and directs us to the way of truth. Balaam knew the truth, but his desire for kingly rewards tempted him.

Peter warns against greedy teachers who were perverting the truth for the sake of filthy lucre and worldly honors. These men are likened to Balaam who is known as a hireling prophet, ready to sell his gift of prophecy for worldly gains which perish. (Compare Jude, verse 11.)

DRY WELLS

These are wells without water, clouds that are carried with a tempest; to whom the mist of darkness is reserved for ever. II Pet. 2 : 17.

In Palestine and other regions when the rain is scanty, some wells and brooks dry up suddenly and are abandoned until the rainy season. Moreover, earthquakes change the course of underground water and cause wells and brooks to dry up. Such changes may be so sudden that travelers and shepherds may come to the wells day after day, and then the next time they come are surprised to find the once deep and prolific wells dry and polluted.

The false teachers are likened to these dry and abandoned wells which have every appearance of a water source, but no water. These teachers have every resemblance of teachers of the truth, but they are like dry wells full of filth and corruption. The thirsty and hungry truth-seekers are disappointed. Just as the thirsty travelers are deceived by the appearance of a dry well, Christians are often misled by false philosophers and their strange doctrines which at first sound good, but are far from the truth of Jesus Christ.

A THOUSAND YEARS

But, beloved, be not ignorant of this one thing, that one day is with the Lord as a thousand years, and a thousand years as one day. II Pet. 3 : 8.

Peter is quoting here from Psalm 90 : 4. "For a thousand years in thy sight are but as yesterday when it is past, and as a watch in the night."

Prophets and apostles knew that for God there is no time or distance. The nights and days, caused by the turning of the earth, have no effect on God, who dwells in the heavens and who is the Creator of all the planets and heavenly bodies. Therefore, in the realm of the spirit there is no time. On the other hand, time can be reckoned only by physical senses which are subject to the earth and planets around it. The human senses are temporal, and time is relative. On the other hand, God is eternal, from everlasting to everlasting. Not only are a thousand years like yesterday to him, but a million years are like a minute.

Peter, like Paul, warns against impatient expectation of the coming of the day of the Lord, the immediate return of Christ, and the end of this world. Christians in his day were expecting the immediate return of Jesus and the destruction of the earth and the heavens. Many speculative doctrines were spread by these false and destructive teachers, who were like wolves clothed in sheepskin.

THIEF AT NIGHT

But the day of the Lord will come as a thief in the night; in the which the heavens shall pass away with a great noise, and the elements shall melt with fervent heat, the earth also and the works that are therein shall be burned up.   II Pet. 3 : 10.

In biblical lands, shepherds and sheep owners are in constant fear of thieves who come at night to steal their sheep and cattle. During the summer months the sheep are kept in an open sheepfold or field, and are guarded by one or two shepherds who walk around the fold in turns. In the winter they are kept in large covered buildings.

The thieves come at night, hide themselves near the fold, and when the shepherds are asleep they draw near the edge of the fold and steal some of the sheep. When the presence of thieves is disclosed, the shepherds keep constant vigilance over their flocks. It is said that good shepherds on such occasions sometimes injure one of their fingers and put salt in the wound so that they might keep awake all night. Then again, thieves may even break into buildings where the sheep are kept at night.

The reference here is to the words of Jesus in the Gospel of Matthew. Jesus warned his disciples and followers of his second coming and the end of the world. He told them to watch and keep alert, for no one knows the hour and the day, except his Father only. His coming will be like that of a thief at night when the shepherds are asleep or careless (Matt. 24 : 43).

PAUL'S WRITINGS DIFFICULT

As also in all his epistles, speaking in them of these things; in which are some things hard to be understood, which they that are unlearned and unstable wrest, as they do also the other scriptures, unto their own destruction.
II Pet. 3 : 16.

The apostle Peter admits that some of the writings of Paul were hard to understand, especially by those who were unlearned. These and some other portions of the Scriptures were misinterpreted and debated by the elders and teachers.

Paul was a Jewish scholar. He spoke and wrote like a learned man. Learned men often cannot express in simple language what they want to say or write. Their manner of writing may be complex and difficult to interpret. The other apostles were fishermen. Not one of them was educated; they spoke plainly and directly, using simple terms. Consequently, their writings are easier to understand. This is also true of the Gospels. They are simple and direct. This is because our Lord in his preaching used the common or vernacular Aramaic. His audiences were composed of simple and unlearned folk.

Most of the controversies which arose over the interpretation of the Scriptures were due to mistranslations of Aramaic and Hebrew words and terms of speech. It was difficult then, just as it is today, to transmit the thought, idioms and manners of speech from one tongue into another without the loss of meaning.

Paul no doubt wrote many epistles or pastoral letters. Some of them were lost, some may have been rejected, and others were destroyed during the persecutions. Fourteen of his epistles have survived. Some of the difficulties and obscurities are due to mistranslation and misunderstanding of Semitic customs and manners.

FIRST EPISTLE OF JOHN

INTRODUCTION

The author of the epistle, according to tradition, is the apostle John, the son of Zebedee, who is also the author of the Fourth Gospel and the book of Revelation. The style of writing and the subject matter resembles that of the Fourth Gospel.

The epistle is a pastoral letter addressed to Christian converts whom the apostle calls "little children." The apostle reminds them of their fellowship with the Father and with his Son Jesus Christ. He admonishes them to live up to their faith, walk in the light, and demonstrate their faith through good works and love. Christians must show that they are the true followers of Jesus by living up to his words and not by mere acknowledgment of his name. They must walk in the light of Christ. Sins are forgiven through Jesus Christ, who is an advocate with the Father.

The apostle, like Peter and Paul, warns against false teachers and the spirit of anti-Christ which is to come. The believers are admonished to love one another, just as God loved them, to the extent that he sent his Son to die on the cross for them. They must live a perfect life and keep away from idols.

The date of the epistle is generally placed about 90. I believe it was written much earlier.

LIGHT—TRUTH

This then is the message which we have heard of him, and declare unto you, that God is light, and in him is no darkness at all. I John 1 : 5.

In the Scriptures God is often likened to light, which symbolizes truth and understanding. Darkness is symbolical of evil forces and ignorance. The Babylonians and Persians had a dualistic conception of God. They believed that there were two gods: Mazda, the god of light, and Ahriman, the god of darkness.

The presence of God dispels the darkness and enlightens man's consciousness with understanding, just as the light of the sun dispels the darkness. With the light of the sun and other heavenly bodies, we see things partially. When our hearts are lighted with truth, we see things as they really are. ". . . In thy light shall we see light" (Psa. 36 : 9). "O send out thy light and thy truth" (Psa. 43 : 3).

Then again, it is the inner light which reveals the secrets of nature and discloses the things which cannot be seen by the eye. For the inner light (truth) existed before the sun and moon were created. Jesus said, "I am the light of the world: he that followeth me shall not walk in darkness, but shall have the light of life" (John 8 : 12). Those who walk under his light and live like him will never stumble. They become the children of light and sons of God.

FALSE SPIRITS

Beloved, believe not every spirit, but try the spirits whether they are of God: because many false prophets are gone out into the world.   I John 4 : 1.

"Spirit" here means "prophecy." This is because the person or prophet is moved and inspired by the spirit to see that which is hidden from the eye of the flesh, and thus predicts things to come. "The spirit of the Lord came upon me" means, "I prophesied."

The apostle warns against false prophecies derived from the inspiration of evil forces, astrologers and magicians. It often happened that Christians were misled by false prophets and soothsayers, who predicted things which were not true, and taught doctrines which were contrary to those imparted by the apostles. In general, the apostles warned against the false prophets who constantly predicted the immediate return of Christ and the destruction of this world.

Just as one is inspired and led to do good work, he may be moved by wrong ideas and false motives to mislead and deceive. Wherever the truth has been preached, the forces of evil have stood in opposition.

Some of the false teachers, who were moved by evil forces, were denying that the Messiah (Christ) had come in the flesh. They were falsely prophesying that the true Messiah had not come and that he was to appear later. These men are distinguished from the true prophets by their teachings and evil works.

I JOHN

TRUE SPIRIT

Hereby know ye the Spirit of God: Every spirit that confesseth that Jesus Christ is come in the flesh is of God:
And every spirit that confesseth not that Jesus Christ is come in the flesh is not of God: and this is that spirit of antichrist, whereof ye have heard that it should come; and even now already is it in the world. I John 4 : 2–3.

The word "spirit" (soul) in some instances is used for "persons." People often say "How many souls are in this house?" "All the souls that came with Jacob into Egypt, which came out of his loins, besides Jacob's sons' wives, all the souls were three score and six" (Gen. 46 : 26).

The Eastern text reads: "The spirit of God is known by this: Every prophecy which declares that Jesus Christ is come in the flesh is from God." There were many false prophets and teachers who were hostile to Christianity and were not from God. They denied that Jesus of Nazareth was the promised Messiah. Both Paul and Peter strongly denounced these teachers and false prophets who were undermining the churches. The belief that Christ had come and had been crucified and risen from the dead was the only means of salvation (Rom. 10 : 6–9).

WATER AND BLOOD

This is he that came by water and blood, even Jesus Christ; not by water only, but by water and blood. And it is the Spirit that beareth witness, because the Spirit is truth.
I John 5 : 6.

"Water" in this instance means "baptism by water." This kind of baptism was first introduced by John the Baptist as a means of initiation and as a symbol of cleansing from sin. Jesus was baptized by John in the river Jordan. Later he was to baptize others with the Holy Spirit and with fire (Matt. 3 : 11).

Arabs made covenants and sealed them with blood. When a man became a member of a tribe his blood was mixed with the blood of one of the members of the tribe. The ceremonial entitled the new member to all tribal privileges. The mixing of blood made him one with the members of the tribe which he had joined. In some cases, an animal was sacrificed and its meat shared. The blood was sprinkled on the people or put on their foreheads. When Jacob and his father-in-law, Laban, made a covenant between them they offered sacrifices and ate together (Gen. 31 : 54).

Jesus, in making a new covenant, offered his own blood as an everlasting sacrifice, an offering which did away with the blood of dumb animals.

SIN NOT WORTHY OF DEATH

If any man see his brother sin a sin which is not unto death, he shall ask, and he shall give him life for them that sin not unto death. There is a sin unto death: I do not say that he shall pray for it.   I John 5 :16.

According to the Scriptures, there are various degrees of sin, since some sins are forgivable and others are unforgivable. Jesus said that whosoever blasphemes against God and against the Son will be forgiven, but those who blaspheme against the Holy Spirit cannot be forgiven. Certain sins committed unknowingly are known as faults which are forgivable, but sins such as murder, blasphemy and denial of Christ are unforgivable.

The Eastern text reads: "If any man see his brother sin a sin which is not worthy of death, let him ask, and life will be granted him, who has not committed a sin worthy of death. There is a sin worthy of death. I do not say that he shall pray for it." Even in the Mosaic law, some sins were worthy of death and others were not. When certain laws were broken, the guilty persons were punished by death. Minor offenses or sins, however, were forgiven, the guilty persons merely being chastised, fined and set free.

Sins are forgivable through repentance and the acceptance of Christ. "For the wages of sin is death; but the gift of God is eternal life through Jesus Christ our Lord" (Rom. 6 : 23).

Probably what John refers to here as "sin unto death" is the denial of Christ. Some of the Christians were deceived by false teachers who denied that Christ had come (I John 4 : 1–3ff). Others denied his resurrection from the dead. These were grave sins. If Christ has not come, how can one receive forgiveness in his name? Those who thus denied Christ were both physically and spiritually dead.

II JOHN

INTRODUCTION

The writer is commonly supposed to be the apostle John. One argument against this view is that he does not identify himself as an apostle of Jesus Christ. John was one of the closest friends of Jesus and a pillar of the Church. The author of this letter may have been another John who was an elder in charge of a small congregation, as it is seen from verse 1. An elder is not an apostle, but rather a presbyter or minister. The apostles appointed elders by the laying on of hands. They themselves had been ordained by Jesus Christ.

The purpose of the epistle is commendation, exhortation and warning. John commends the church and its members for remaining in the truth of Christ. He exhorts the Christians to love one another. He also warns them of deceivers who had gone out misleading converts.

A LETTER TO A CHURCH

The elder unto the elect lady and her children, whom I love in the truth; and not I only, but also all they that have known the truth; II John 1 : 1.

The brief epistle is from an elder to the chosen assembly (church) and its members. That is, from a minister to the church assembly or mother church.

In the East, church members are called "sons and daughters" of the church. The bishop is called *"Abona,"* derived from the Aramaic word *"Abba"* or *"Ava"* (father). The patriarchs, in their pastoral letters, address their people as "sons." The minister of one congregation, when writing to another, addresses the minister as "brother," and the congregation is called "mother church" or "sister church," according to its rank. These terms were used by the early converts to Christianity to distinguish the believers in Jesus from the Jews and pagans. They are still used by bishops and ministers of the churches in the East.

The word *Koria,* translated "lady" in our English versions, means "village." Small churches and missions in the little villages are generally under the leadership of an archdeacon.

In this passage, the apostle is not addressing a lady and her children, but a Christian assembly, consisting of several small congregations. John exhorts its members, of whom he had heard many good reports, and admonishes them to treasure and hold fast to that which was given to them when they accepted Christianity. To live a life of love, one toward another. John, the elder, further warns them against any corruption of their teachings, and against anti-Christs, that is, the teachers who had gone forth teaching that Jesus had not actually come in the flesh. In the verse 13 the members of the sister church send their greetings to the assembly or mother church.

GREETINGS FROM MEMBERS

The children of thy elect sister greet thee. Amen.
II John 1 : 13.

The Aramaic word *etta,* "church" or "congregation," is feminine; therefore a church is called "sister." The Church of the East, when speaking of Orthodox and Roman Catholic churches, uses the term "sister churches."

The apostle sends greetings from the members of the mother church to those of a small congregation in a country town.

The elect church is one of the mother churches in Judea or Antioch. Bishops, when writing to members of their churches, often use the term "My son." (Compare I John 2 : 1; II John 1 : 4.)

III JOHN

INTRODUCTION

This epistle, like First and Second John, is supposed to have been written by the apostle John, the author of the Fourth Gospel. But in this epistle, as in the second, the author addresses himself as an elder.

The epistle is addressed to Gaius, a faithful Christian worker. The author rejoices in the good news concerning the faith of Gaius and his people and their loyalty to Christ. The church had stood steadfast to the true apostolic doctrines. The author writes briefly, hoping to meet his beloved friend soon.

The second and the third epistles of John are not included in the authorized Eastern text of the Peshitta, but are included in other texts.

INK

I had many things to write, but I will not with ink and pen write unto thee: III John: 13.

Black ink was invented several centuries before Christ. Since the introduction of the present alphabet, about the ninth century B.C., ink made of oak galls has been used by scribes in the Near East. The galls are boiled and the essence extracted. A little sulphur is mixed with the substance, which causes it to turn black.

All ancient biblical manuscripts, liturgies and other literature were written with oak ink. This kind of ink is still used in many parts of the East. *Aleppo* in Syria is noted for good oak galls, which are exported to other places. Not all kinds of oak trees bear this kind of galls, and those that do, may bear them only once in every two or three years.

The pens commonly used are made of red reed, called in Aramaic "cania." This is where we get our word "cane."

JUDE

INTRODUCTION

Jude is an abbreviated name for Judas. The Aramaic is *Ehoda*. Two Judases are mentioned among the apostles —Judas of Iscariot and Judas, brother of James (Luke 6 : 16). There are also two apostles who are called James —James, son of Zebedee, and James, son of Alphaeus.

The author of the epistle is Jude, brother of James (verse 1). But we do not know which James it is. Even though Judas, the brother of James, is listed among the Twelve, little is known about him.

Jude instructs the Christians to remain loyal to the true faith which was delivered to the saints, that is, the chosen ones. Like Paul and Peter, he warns against false teachers, mockers and deceivers who were to appear among them. Heresies were spreading fast and many of the believers were enticed by destructive pagan doctrines which were contrary to the truth of Jesus Christ.

The date of the epistle is not known, but is placed between 60–65.

JUDE

Yet Michael the archangel, when contending with the devil he disputed about the body of Moses, durst not bring against him a railing accusation, but said, The Lord rebuke thee. 9th verse.

The quotation here is taken from the book of Zechariah. "And the Lord said unto Satan, The Lord rebuke thee." (Zech. 3 : 2). Zechariah, in his vision, saw Joshua, the high priest, standing before the angel of the Lord, and Satan standing at his right hand to resist him.

It is said that angels and the devil fought over the possession of the body of Moses when he died on Mount Nebo in the land of Moab and was buried in a valley over against Bethpeor. But no man knows where his sepulcher is (Deut. 34 : 1–7).

"Angel" is symbolical of God's truth. "Devil" means opposition to the way of God. God's truth rebukes evil and exposes its falsehood. When temptations are too strong to be overcome, we must pray and seek God's help to overcome them.

THE REVELATION

INTRODUCTION

The book of Revelation is considered the hardest book in the Bible to understand. For centuries, it has been the subject of diverse interpretation and a basis for new doctrines. Many people confess that they cannot get much out of its reading. Some refuse to read it, while others belittle its message. This is why the book of Revelation is seldom read in church services.

Indeed, the title of the book speaks for itself and its message. The Aramaic word *giliana*, "revelation," means also "vision" (dream). The author does not claim that his work is based on actual facts. The book must be treated as a work based largely on one or several successive visions, as in the case of certain portions of the books of Daniel, Isaiah and Ezekiel. Therefore, before one undertakes to study this portion of the Scriptures and gain by it, he must realize that he is reading a book based on a vision or visions. The reader must believe in divine revelations and in the inspiration of the Holy Spirit to explain the mysteries. A large portion of the Bible is based on visions that men of God saw.

In a vision one often sees things in symbols, which may or may not be interpreted in the same vision. For instance, Daniel, famous as an interpreter of visions, dreams and mysteries, at times was unable to understand the meaning of certain symbols. He prayed to God to decipher the symbols and reveal to him the mysteries (Dan. 2 : 19; 8 : 15–16).

The book of Revelation differs from other apocalyptic books in the Bible, in that it deals with world-wide problems and covers past, present and future. It starts with seven pastoral letters addressed to seven angels (elders) in charge of seven churches, and ends with the battle of Armageddon, the destruction of the evil forces and the establishment of the kingdom of God.

The reader must study Oriental symbolism. This is because parts of the book of Revelation are revealed and written in symbols referring to problems and events yet in the remote future.

Then again, dreams and visions take place in two ways: First, direct verbal communication, or conversations. Second, in symbolic language. Sometimes the person is instructed directly what to do and what not to do. On other occasions, the warning is given in symbols. This order is clearly seen throughout both the New and the Old Testament books. Therefore, the reader of the book of Revelation must acquaint himself with the Old Testament prophecies, their symbolism and the interpretations thereof.

The book of Revelation differs from the Old Testament prophecies in that it deals with events yet to come. The Old Testament prophecies have been fulfilled. But both were written for the people of the Semitic race, who understand the language, signs, symbols and customs. Many signs in Revelation are similar to those in the books of Genesis, Isaiah, Ezekiel and Daniel. Cows, rams, wild beasts, horses, calves, birds and other living creatures are variously employed.

The book is the revelation of Jesus Christ which he gave to the apostle John while he was on the Island of Patmos about A.D. 90. John then related his vision to a scribe who wrote it down. The apostle received the vision in his own language, Aramaic. The work was later translated by Jewish Christians into Greek for the use of Greek converts. The vision might have taken place many years before it was recorded. For instance, Jacob's and Joseph's dreams were not written down until many centuries after they occurred.

The book of Revelation appeared late and consequently was rejected by Christians in the East until the fifth century. It was not included in Peshitta or the authorized

New Testament text which is still used by the ancient churches of the East. However, it is included in later Aramaic texts.

The book must have been written during or prior to the reign of Nero, about A.D. 64, when the persecution against the Christians began, and before the outbreak of the Jewish war under Vespasian in A.D. 67.

One should note that the number 666 refering to John's writings must have been prior to the year 64 when Nero loosed his wrath on the Christian church.

The book, besides its prophecies, contains admonitions to the seven churches in Asia Minor, the elders of some of which had become corrupt. The central theme is Christ, his church, his kingdom, and the Day of Judgment. It portrays Christ as a lamb, and the church as the bride of the Lamb, and declares the ultimate victory of the Lamb over the beast and the establishment of the heavenly Jerusalem.

REVELATION

The Revelation of Jesus Christ, which God gave unto him, to shew unto his servants things which must shortly come to pass; and he sent and signified it by his angel unto his servant John: Rev. 1 : 1.

The Aramaic word for "revelation" is *giliana,* derived from *gala,* which means "to reveal," "uncover" and "predict." Thus, the book of Revelation deals with things which are to come. Then again, "revelation" is another term for "vision," but the book of Revelation covers a larger scope of things and time than a vision. It is a series of visions covering several important events which are to come.

Eastern people, especially the Semites, believe in visions, and are to some extent guided by revelations and dreams. They are advised and warned in visions. Some men would cancel business engagements, stop buying or selling, or even refuse to go on a journey because of a vision they had seen. Joseph was told in a dream to flee to Egypt. Paul was instructed in a vision to go to Macedonia, and Peter to Caesarea.

Revelations and visions generally take place at night when the mind is free and at rest. Moreover, sleep, to some extent, eliminates the sense of time which is created by events. For example, if a person sleeps ten hours or ten days, he would not know the difference. Some visions and dreams, however, take place in the day time.

The prophets and men of God rose above the material world and were able to see the whole course of life and the destinies of the nations. They were moved by the Holy Spirit to see many things in symbols and to interpret the meaning of the symbols. One has to understand the symbols in order to know the meaning of the visions. For instance, Jacob's dream of the ladder to heaven indicated that he would overcome the difficulties with his brother Esau. Ascending and descending a ladder means peace and harmony (Gen. 28 : 12). Joseph's dream of sheaves (Gen. 37 : 6–8), his interpretation of Pharaoh's servants' dreams (Gen. 40 : 5–13), the dream of Pharaoh about the seven cows (Gen. 41 : 1–8), the dream of Nebuchadnezzar (Daniel 2)—all of these were revealed in Oriental symbology.

God appeared to Abraham, Isaac, Jacob and the prophets in visions and dreams.

Some of the writings of the prophets are based entirely on the visions they saw. "The vision of Isaiah the son of Amoz, which he saw concerning Judah and Jerusalem . . ." (Isa. 1 : 1). "Now it came to pass in the thirtieth year, in the fourth month, in the fifth day of the month, as I was among the captives by the river of Chebar, that the heavens were opened, and I saw visions of God" (Ezek. 1 : 1). "In the third year of the reign of king Belshazzar a vision appeared unto me, . . ." (Dan. 8 : 1). "The vision of Obadiah" (Obad. 1 : 1). "And the Lord answered me, and said, Write the vision, and make it plain upon tables, that he may run that readeth it" (Hab. 2 : 2). Many other prophets use such phrases as "And the word of the Lord came unto me," "And I saw," or "And the Lord appeared unto me."

In many instances a vision takes place in a familiar setting.

The apostles were inspired by the Holy Spirit. They were able not only to predict the future, but also to interpret past prophecies. The prophets in olden days saw only future events, but the apostles could see both past and future. This is because all prophecies were fulfilled in Jesus Christ. The Jewish mysteries were unveiled. The apostles had a larger vision of the world than the prophets. They were preaching a universal religion which in due time was to be embraced by all people. (See the introduction to the book of Revelation.)

NUMBER SEVEN

John to the seven churches which are in Asia: Grace be unto you, and peace, from him which is, and which was, and which is to come; and from the seven Spirits which are before his throne; Rev. 1 : 4.

Seven is an Oriental sacred number symbolizing completeness, and is often used in figurative speech. Seven is an odd number and works well in art. Then again, when a king sits in council he generally has three ministers on each side of him, so that the group consists of seven men, making a quorum. The Jewish and Mohammedan calendars are based upon the phases of the moon, and thus their months had twenty-eight days. Seven was a quarterly division of this unit.

Seven, moreover, was the number of planets known to the ancients. There were seven candles on the golden candlestick in the Temple, and Abraham had seven sacred wells. Beer-sheba literally means "seventh well."

Rokha may mean "spirit," but here it means "wind." It is symbolic of omnipresence. The word of God spread as though carried by the wind. In the East, when a man runs fast, it it said that he "runs like the wind." Standing before God's throne suggests readiness to receive God's commands and to carry them to the utmost parts of the earth. Where the telephone is not known, messengers stand constantly before kings and governors, ready to carry written or verbal messages at any time. Easterners picture God as an Oriental, a king sitting on the throne, surrounded by angels and messengers who act as servants.

ALEPH AND TAU

I am Alpha and Omega, the beginning and the ending, saith the Lord, which is, and which was, and which is to come, the Almighty. Rev. 1 : 8.

The Eastern text reads: "I am Aleph and Tau," the first and the last letters in the Semitic alphabet. Alpha and Omega are the first and last letters in the Greek alphabet. In Aramaic the letters are also used to indicate numbers; alpha means one and tau four hundred. Every word or number must be written with the alphabet, which begins with aleph and ends with tau. Aleph is the first letter in the name of God, "Alaha," and the Hebrew "Alohem." Tau is the last, which means "the end." That is, he who was, and who is to come, the Almighty. The one who has power over both life and death.

Aleph and tau are symbolical of Christ's eternal existence with God. Jesus of Nazareth was like one of us, with the exception that he was without sin. But Christ, who was manifested in him, existed with God from the very beginning. That which has been with God from the beginning will be with God forever, world without end. As God is eternal, so is the Son.

SEVEN CANDLESTICKS

And I turned to see the voice that spake with me. And being turned, I saw seven golden candlesticks: Rev. 1 : 12.

Candlestick" (lamp stand) here is symbolic of truth. Seven candlesticks are symbolical of the seven luminaries and seven centers of truth established in Asia. Gold is symbolical of purity. The Christian doctrine preached by the apostles was pure as fine gold, but to some extent had been corrupted through the teachings of false teachers who followed in the footsteps of Paul. Nevertheless, the seven churches shone in the dark pagan world just as the lamp with seven candles had shone in the Jewish Temple.

Churches which still adhere to the teaching of the apostles stand as great candles shining into the world. As long as men adhere to the teaching of Christ, they walk in the light. Their good deeds make their light shine before men.

PRIESTLY ROBE

And in the midst of the seven candlesticks one like unto the Son of man, clothed with a garment down to the foot, and girt about the paps with a golden girdle. Rev. 1 : 13.

The Son of man" of course is Jesus Christ. The term is a literal translation of Aramaic *Barnasha,* son of man, a human being. Jesus used this term more than the term "son of God." Jesus was man, and the Christ in him was God. The long garment is significant of Jesus' priesthood. Priestly robes covered all parts of the body, even the feet. Jesus was a priest after the order of Melchisedec. "As he saith also in another place, Thou art a priest forever after the order of Melchisedec" (Heb. 5 : 6). Jesus, like a high priest, offered prayers on behalf of the people and at last he sacrificed his own earthly life for their sake.

The golden girdle implies kingly power. The son of man was to have dominion over all things in heaven and earth.

WHITE

His head and his hairs were white like wool, as white as snow; and his eyes were as a flame of fire; Rev. 1 : 14.

White is symbolical of light and purity. Clothing of other colors is made through a dyeing process from white material. Thus white is original and pure, and its color does not change or fade. Black is symbolical of dark-

548 NEW TESTAMENT COMMENTARY

ness, disaster and grief, and is worn for mourning. Easterners often say, "My days have been white," which means, "I have been happy and prosperous." "My days have been black" means "I have gone through difficulties, suffering and misfortunes."

Green is the Mohammedan symbol for wisdom, and is used for turbans which are worn by the learned. Wisdom must be acquired by long experience and trials. In the East, when green-colored material is desired, it must first be dyed yellow. White material is always admired because it can be made into other colors, but dark material cannot. There is an Eastern proverb, "No color can be dyed over the black," which means "a man of bad reputation does not suffer from shame."

Easterners picture angels as having white garments and white beards. The long beard and the white hair are symbolical of knowledge. This is because in the East, only elders are chosen to act as judges and statesmen. They are known as "wise men." The priests also wear white robes during services. The white, clean garment signifies purity.

Jesus appeared to John in the form of a high priest ready to enter into the holy of holies.

FIERY EYES

In countries where letters of recommendation are seldom used, strangers are judged by their eyes and the expression of their faces.

Eyes "as a flame of fire" suggests sincerity and conviction. Some men in the East have strong and beautiful eyes, which express their wisdom, sincerity and deep convictions. In describing one's eyes, people often say, "they burn like fire," which means that they express truth, sincerity and frankness. When men are cold and insincere, it is said, "their eyes are cold as ice." Eyes reveal the inner secrets of the soul, and have been called the windows of the soul.

FINE BRASS

And his feet like unto fine brass, as if they burned in a furnace; and his voice as the sound of many waters.
Rev. 1 : 15.

The Eastern text reads: "And his feet were like the fine brass of Lebanon, and as though they burned in a furnace; . . ."

Lebanon brass is famed for its fine quality and strength. When it is burnished it shines like gold. Brass is symbolical of strength and endurance. (Compare Daniel's vision of the beast "whose teeth were of iron, and his nails of brass; which devoured, brake in pieces, and stamped the residue with his feet,"—Dan. 7 : 19.)

Before steel was known, brass was considered one of the strongest metals and was as valuable as copper. This is because other metals could be broken by it. Manganese and other ores now used to make steel were unknown in those days, but copper and brass were processed to make them very hard and strong.

The gospel of Christ was destined to break down pagan religions, traditions and fables. Fine brass is symbolical of the clarity and strength of the message of the Christian gospel. Just as burnished brass attracts the eye, the true Christian gospel appeals to the minds of people whose religions are inferior.

Water is symbolical of light, and "the sound of many waters" is the announcement the gospel of Christ was to make throughout the world. The Christian gospel was to spread and, like a mighty river, water the dry fields.

SEVEN STARS

And he had in his right hand seven stars: and out of his mouth went a sharp twoedged sword: and his countenance was as the sun shineth in his strength. Rev. 1 : 16.

Seven, twelve and forty are numbers frequently used in the Bible. There were seven candlesticks (verse 12) and seven churches (verse 4). Seven suggests completeness. In this instance it denotes the seven churches to whom the book is addressed. The adoption of the number may have been due to the common belief in ancient times that there were seven planets—sun, moon, Mercury, Venus, Mars, Jupiter and Saturn. The tabernacle was symbolic of the temple in heaven. The seven stars (planets) lighted the heavens, just as the candlestick with its seven candles lighted the Temple.

The "sharp twoedged sword" coming out of his mouth suggests an eloquent speaker who can answer any question and solve any problem.

The sun is symbolical of power and light. It is the source of life on this planet and its heat is self-generated. Prior to the introduction of Judaism, and even after the rise of Christianity, the sun was worshiped by many races throughout the world.

Christ's teaching, likewise, was of himself. He was fully in accord with God and understood God's infinite wisdom. Like the sun's rays, his teaching was to reach the outermost parts of the universe.

THE FIRST AND THE LAST

And when I saw him, I fell at his feet as dead. And he laid his right hand upon me, saying unto me, Fear not; I am the first and the last: Rev. 1 : 17.

"I am the first and the last" is an Eastern saying which means, "I am the only messenger." When people are warned of impending action by a powerful ruler, the de-

THE REVELATION

cree may say, "This is the first and the last messenger," so that the subjects may think things over quickly and give a prompt answer. In other cases, messenger after messenger is sent, and the tone of the message is changed in order to bring about a reconciliation.

The Jews who had repudiated Jesus were still expecting a Messiah, in accordance with their literal understanding of the Messianic mission. They believed the Messiah would lead the people to victory and material prosperity. Jesus had not done away with war, nor had he made nations break their implements of war and make them into plows, nor had he freed the Jewish state from the Roman yoke. Jews throughout the world still expect the sudden appearance of a Messiah like David, who will establish the Jewish state. Through the years many credulous persons were deceived by bandits and other pretenders to Messiahship.

Jesus, by his resurrection and victory over death, proved to his disciples that he was the first and the last—the only true Messiah.

False Messiahs have appeared from time to time to deceive and mislead the people, but the truth has always triumphed. The Messiah has come and the world will see no one else like him.

"I WAS DEAD"

I am he that liveth, and was dead; and, behold, I am alive for evermore, Amen; and have the keys of hell and of death.
Rev. 1 : 18.

"I was dead and behold I am alive" is an Aramaic idiom, meaning, "I was unrecognized (unknown) but now I am well-known." In the East, when a religious or political leader loses his power and influence, men say, "He is dead." Likewise, when he comes back to power, they say, "He has come back to life," meaning that he is powerful and influential again. Then again, when a man is considered as lost or dead, and then is found alive, it is said, "He was dead and now is alive." Note the case of the prodigal son: "For this my son was dead, and is alive again;" (Luke 15 : 24).

Jesus died on the cross as a man, not as God. Christ the Messiah, who is the divine promise of God, did not die. (This teaching is still held by the Assyrians or the remnant of the older church in the East.) Christ is the word of God, the fulfillment of God's promise to mankind. He was recognized by the prophets who heralded his coming, but in the latter days the prophecies were obscured by traditions, rituals and literalism, and confused with a materialistic Messiah. So he was "dead"—that is, he was unrecognized, or forgotten. The Jews, after the fall of the Davidic kingdom, lost their concept of a spiritual Messiah, and forgot their divine mission to the world. So they were looking for a political leader to restore the kingdom, with the freedom and material prosperity which they had lost to foreign rulers.

Jesus, after his death, became known and recognized by Galileans, Jews and Gentiles. The truth became manifest, and spiritual things triumphed over traditions and materialism. The power of the gospel was felt all over the world. Jesus was proclaimed the King of Kings.

SEVEN STARS

Unto the angel of the church of Ephesus write; These things saith he that holdeth the seven stars in his right hand, who walketh in the midst of the seven golden candlesticks; Rev. 2 : 1.

The one who holds seven stars in his right hand is Jesus Christ (Rev. 1 : 13). The seven stars represent the seven ministers who were in charge of the seven churches. The right hand is symbolical of power and authority. The seven golden candlesticks are the seven churches, founded on the true apostolic teaching.

Gold is a symbol of purity. The truth on which the

seven churches stood is like a flickering lamp. The congregations were threatened by false teachers, love of money and other worldly things, but like lighted golden lamps, they shone in the midst of darkness. Christ's truth was manifested from all directions, so that the defects of these churches were evident and the works of false apostles were brought to light. The minister of the church at Ephesus is commended for his patience and long-suffering.

NICOLAITANES

But this thou hast, that thou hatest the deeds of the Nicolaitanes, which I also hate.

He that hath an ear, let him hear what the Spirit saith unto the churches; To him that overcometh will I give to eat of the tree of life, which is in the midst of the paradise of God. Rev. 2 : 6, 7.

"Nicolaitanes" are members of a sect, probably founded by Nicolaus, one of the false teachers whom the author of Revelation calls "liars" (Rev. 2 : 2). There were many such teachers who posed as apostles and preyed on the faithful. Many of these men taught doctrines contrary to those given by the apostles. Through their cunning and false philosophies they succeeded in creating divisions and strife in the churches. This was especially common among the churches in Asia Minor, far from the mother church in Antioch. The converts knew little about theological doctrines. They depended on teachers from Judea and Syria who visited them from time to time. Paul, Peter and other apostles warned the faithful against these dangerous men.

Heresies were thriving in many of these newly established churches. Some Jewish converts had already left the church and gone back to Judaism. Many Gentile converts were still under the influence of pagan cults. The seeds of controversies and strife were so deeply rooted that the security of the church was threatened.

SECOND DEATH

He that hath an ear, let him hear what the Spirit saith unto the churches; He that overcometh shall not be hurt of the second death.   Rev. 2 : 11.

The "second death" is the death of the soul. This death is caused by sin. Jesus told his followers not to be afraid of those who destroy the body, but to fear only those who kill the soul.

"It is the spirit (soul) that quickeneth; the flesh profiteth nothing: The words that I speak unto you, they are spirit, and they are life" (John 6 : 63).

Those who walk in the way of God and overcome sin need not be afraid of the death of the soul. These men shall never taste of real death—the second death. (See Rev. 21 : 8.) The prophets, apostles and men of God who fought for justice and preached the gospel of truth are not dead. They still live in spirit. The teachings for which they sacrificed their earthly lives remain as a guiding influence, comfort and consolation for millions of their followers.

SIN OF BALAAM

But I have a few things against thee, because thou hast there them that hold the doctrine of Balaam, who taught Balac to cast a stumblingblock before the children of Israel, to eat things sacrificed unto idols, and to commit fornication.   Rev. 2 : 14.

In the book of Numbers we are told that Balaam, through his counsel, caused the children of Israel to trespass against the Lord. The Hebrews were enticed to commit adultery with the Midianite women. The name of the act was called *peor*. The children of Israel, as a result, suffered from a plague. Thousands of them perished (Num. 31 : 15).

Balaam was tempted by rich rewards which Balak, the

king of Moab, offered him. When he saw that he could not curse a people which God had blessed, he used other means to weaken their morale. (See II Pet. 2 : 15.)

The Christians in Pergamos were corrupt. They were living where Satan's throne is. The minister of this church had remained loyal to the faith of Jesus, but had been negligent in his duty toward his flock. Immorality was prevalent among the people. Many of them were suffering from venereal diseases. This condition was the result of the teachings of men who, like Balaam, sought to weaken the Christian congregation. (Compare verse 2.)

HIDDEN MANNA

He that hath an ear, let him hear what the Spirit saith unto the churches; To him that overcometh will I give to eat of the hidden manna, and will give him a white stone, and in the stone a new name written, which no man knoweth saving he that receiveth it. Rev. 2 : 17.

"Hidden manna" means spiritual food, that is, truth and life eternal. Bread and water are often used symbolically, meaning truth. Jesus told his disciples that he was the bread of life that had come down from heaven, and that whosoever drinks from the water which he gives shall never thirst (John 4 : 14).

Manna was the mysterious food which the Hebrews ate when traveling in the desert. No one knows where it came from. The word manna means, "What is it?" (Exod. 16 : 13-15.) (See also *Gospel Light*, page 341.)

White stone

White stones are often used for writing and especially for seals. White stones with inscriptions are placed over the graves of the rich, noble and holy men. White is symbolical of purity and holiness. The new name suggests a changed nature or a new creature. When a person changes his life, no one understands the forces that cause the change, except the person who changes. When a sinner repents he is called a new man. The minister in charge of the church at Pergamos had failed to live up to the gospel that had been entrusted to him. Nevertheless, some of the members of the congregation were trying hard to overcome the temptations.

SPIRITUAL DEATH

And unto the angel of the church in Sardis write; These things saith he that hath the seven Spirits of God, and the seven stars; I know thy works, that thou hast a name that thou livest, and art dead. Rev. 3 : 1.

"Thou livest, and art dead" is an Eastern saying which means "You are done." When a man's influence and power are lost, men say, "He is dead."

John is writing to the angel, that is, to the messenger of the church at Sardis in Asia Minor. Paul, on his missionary journeys, and the apostles had appointed elders and overseers to look after the churches of God, to teach and to preach. Because of the high position they occupy in the church, they are here called angels—that is, God's men. For these men spoke for God and stood in his presence.

Many ministers, however, had failed to carry on the work which was assigned to them, and therefore their influence and power as teachers of the true religion was dead. Jesus told his followers not to be afraid of those who kill the body, but only of those who kill the soul. The elder in charge of the church in Sardis was physically alive but spiritually dead.

He was successful and probably prosperous. He had a good name. The people in Sardis honored him and sought his advice. Nevertheless, he was spiritually bankrupt. He had sold out his faith for temporal power and worldly gain.

BLOTTED OUT

He that overcometh, the same shall be clothed in white raiment; and I will not blot out his name out of the book of life, but I will confess his name before my Father, and before his angels. Rev. 3 : 5.

In olden days the names of valiant men who had done worthy deeds were recorded in the chronicle of kings, that is, the royal book of records (Esther 6 : 1–2). If men who had been honored were later disgraced, their names were blotted out. The records were engraved on tablets or written on sheepskin, and in such a case the writing was removed and the tablets and parchment reused.

This reference to a book and blotting out of names is figurative, of course. Easterners often speak of God in human terms, as though he were an earthly king ruling his subjects. "And the Lord said to Moses, Whosoever hath sinned against me, him will I blot out of my book" (Exod. 32 : 33).

Those who have fought a good fight and overcome the temptations of this life will be recorded in the book of life and cited for great honors in the world to come. The names of those who fail will be blotted out and their memories forgotten.

OPEN DOOR

I know thy works: behold, I have set before thee an open door, and no man can shut it: for thou hast a little strength, and hast kept my word, and hast not denied my name.
Rev. 3 : 8.

"An open door" is an Aramaic idiom meaning "an opportunity." It is often said "If God will open the door, I will go on a journey or start a certain project." "No one can shut the door," is a way of saying that no one can take away your opportunity. In the East, when a man faces a difficulty or dilemma, he says, "Every door is shut to me."

The minister of the church in Philadelphia was physically weak, but spiritually strong. He had remained steadfast in the true teaching and had lived up to the responsibility that was placed upon him.

AMEN

And unto the angel of the church of the Laodiceans write; These things saith the Amen, the faithful and true witness, the beginning of the creation of God;   Rev. 3 : 14.

"Amen" refers here to Christ. The word is rarely used this way. It is often used as the last word of an oral treaty or a promise, as the equivalent of an oath.

"Amen" is derived from the Aramaic adjective, *amina,* meaning "faithful," "truthful" and "trustworthy." Jesus is portrayed as the faithful witness who preached the gospel of truth and acted according to the will of God. "For all the promises of God in him are yea, and in him Amen, unto the glory of God by us" (II Cor. 1 : 20).

Jesus was the first and the last. He is the seal of the prophets.

LUKEWARM

So then because thou art lukewarm, and neither cold nor hot, I will spue thee out of my mouth.   Rev. 3 : 16.

"Lukewarm" comes from an Eastern idiom meaning, "neither good nor bad." That is, something unpleasant or of no use. For instance, Easterners drink water either cold or hot (boiled). Lukewarm water is so unpleasant to drink that it makes one want to spit it out. If one drinks very much lukewarm water it may even cause him to vomit.

The reference here is to Christians who were religiously-minded, but not living according to the teachings of their faith. They were not as bad as others, but they were lacking in character and Christian ethics. In other words, they were "lukewarm."

Said Jesus, "Either produce like a good tree with good fruits; or produce like a bad tree with bad fruits; for a tree is known by its fruit" (Matt. 12 : 33, Eastern text).

Men cannot be both good and bad. They must be one or the other. There is no such thing as a person half saint and half sinner. Jesus said, "No man can serve two masters"; that is, no man can serve both God and the devil (Matt. 6 : 24).

ANOINTING THE EYES

I counsel thee to buy of me gold tried in the fire, that thou mayest be rich; and white raiment, that thou mayest be clothed, and that the shame of thy nakedness do not appear; and anoint thine eyes with eyesalve, that thou mayest see. Rev. 3 : 18.

Anointing of eyes is an ancient Eastern custom. The lack of water and sanitary conditions causes considerable eye trouble. Babies are often exposed to dirt, flies and other insects, which cause irritation of the eyes. Then again, during the threshing season, one often sees men and women with red, swollen eyes. Various oils and home-made medicines are often used as eye remedies.

On the other hand, women often anoint their eyes when they go to weddings or other social affairs.

Jezebel anointed her head, painted her face, and darkened her eyes when Jehu entered Jezreel (II Kings 9 : 30).

The writer of the book of Revelation speaks of spiritual blindness. "Anoint your eyes" is used here in a figurative sense, meaning "search for spiritual understanding." That is, to regain the spiritual sight which was lost.

STANDING AT THE DOOR

Behold, I stand at the door, and knock: if any man hear my voice, and open the door, I will come in to him, and will sup with him, and he with me. Rev. 3 : 20.

Doorbells are unknown in most parts of the Near East. Strangers, guests and neighbors knock at the door and wait until it is opened. At times, because of noise in the house, no one hears the knock, but the person keeps knocking until someone opens the door. Some houses have long alleys connecting the house with the main entrance; others have a courtyard, with a high wall and a door. In such cases the stranger knocks at this outer door and it is very difficult for those inside the house to hear the sound of the knocking. (See Acts 12 : 13.)

When guests or strangers enter a house the host or his wife usually sets the table before him. No matter what house a stranger may enter, he is given bread and water, and the host generally eats with the guest. To feed a stranger and give him water and lodging is considered absolutely essential as a sign of hospitality. And even if the guest is not hungry he must eat, as a token of friendship.

The reference here is to Jesus, who knocks at the door of our hearts. When we hear his voice and let him in, he dwells in our hearts and guides us into the true paths of life. (See *Gospel Light,* page 259.)

THE THRONE

And immediately I was in the spirit: and, behold, a throne was set in heaven, and one sat on the throne.
And he that sat was to look upon like a jasper and a sardine stone: and there was a rainbow round about the throne, in sight like unto an emerald. Rev. 4 : 2–3.

The throne is symbolical of power and dominion. In the East, emperors and kings sat on their thrones when judging the people, and on feast days. This was due to the fact that ordinary seating facilities were unknown. Small

THE REVELATION

thrones also were provided for the princes of the realm. The thrones served as platforms so that the rulers and princes could be seen by everybody.

The one sitting on the throne is God. The reference here is to the Judgment Day. The precious stones are symbolical of purity and holiness. Thrones usually are ornamented with costly stones of many colors and gold. The ephod which the Jewish high priest wore, had twelve precious stones representing the Twelve Tribes of Israel (Exod. 39 : 8-14). The rainbow suggests the omnipresence of God and everlasting peace (Gen. 9 : 13-16). The color of the stones is symbolical of the glory of God. At the time of the Judgment Day, all darkness will be dispelled and the brilliance of the glory of God will shine throughout the universe (Ezek. 1 : 26-28).

Green indicates wisdom. Emerald and jasper stones are green. Gold represents prosperity, power and happiness that is waiting for those who are saved. The crown is symbolical of honor and glory, which belongs to God alone. This simile is taken from Oriental symbolism.

PAST AND PRESENT UNIFIED

And round about the throne were four and twenty seats: and upon the seats I saw four and twenty elders sitting, clothed in white raiment; and they had on their heads crowns of gold. Rev. 4 : 4.

The twenty-four seats represent the old and the new covenants. They are set for the princes of the realm —the twelve apostles and the heads of the Twelve Tribes of Israel.

White is symbolical of purity, judgment, and sanctification. The priests, before they entered into the holy of holies, sanctified themselves and put on white linen garments. "And they made coats of fine linen of woven work for Aaron, and for his sons" (Exod. 39 : 27). After the final resurrection the old and the new orders will be united.

FOUR CREATURES

And before the throne there was a sea of glass like unto crystal: and in the midst of the throne, and round about the throne, were four beasts full of eyes before and behind.
And the first beast was like a lion, and the second beast like a calf, and the third beast had a face as a man, and the fourth beast was like a flying eagle. Rev. 4 : 6–7.

These four beasts (living creatures) should be distinguished from the beasts mentioned in the thirteenth chapter of Revelation. The latter, in the Eastern text are called *khaywat shina*, "the savage beasts." They are symbolical of tyranny, violence and deception.

The beasts referred to here are the four living creatures which stand with the angels around the throne of God (Rev. 7 : 11). They are similar to those mentioned in the book of the prophet Ezekiel (Ezek. 1 : 5–12). They are identical with the seraphims that Isaiah saw in his vision. "Above it stood the seraphims: each one had six wings; with twain he covered his face, and with twain he covered his feet, and with twain he did fly" (Isa. 6 : 1–6).

The eyes before and behind are symbolical of past and future. The living creature could see the things that are past and the things yet to come, and judge them accordingly. The beasts were full of eyes, this meant they could see in all directions and were omniscient. In the spiritual realm there is no past or future. (See verse 8.)

The lion represents dominion, the calf symbolizes strength, the man suggests intellect, and the flying eagle means omnipresence. Thus the summary of the four living creatures is authority, strength, omniscience and omnipresence. These are all characteristics of Christ as King of kings and Lord of lords.

THE SCROLL

And I saw in the right hand of him that sat on the throne a book written within and on the backside, sealed with seven seals. Rev. 5 : 1.

Ketava in Aramaic means "letter" or "book." "Book" in this case refers to a scroll. Bound books were unknown until the second and third centuries.

Most scrolls were written on one side only, because they contained Scriptures which were in constant use. Nevertheless, epistles and decrees were written on both sides, in order that all of the letter could be inscribed on one scroll. After being read, the scrolls were kept in the archives.

This scroll was a decree, written on both sides and sealed. The seal indicates the importance of the message that the document contains. Ordinary scrolls were not sealed, but a king's decrees were all sealed. The scroll was rolled, fastened and the seal placed upon it.

When scrolls or letters containing imperial decrees are opened, there generally is fear and anxiety as to their contents. They may contain notices of rewards, removals, executions or other unexpected decrees. Such documents are opened on solemn occasions by important government officials in the presence of notables and dignitaries.

The number seven here symbolizes the completeness of the message. The sealed scroll is symbolical of sealed mysteries, which are to be revealed. Scrolls containing sacred writings are not supposed to be opened or handled by everybody. They must be opened and read only by the high priests. As an example, the ark of the covenant, in which the sacred tablets of the law were kept, was untouchable. Even those who touched it by mistake died (II Sam. 6 : 6–7).

The unusual and mysterious scroll was opened by Jesus Christ who is the high priest of the Christian religion. Jesus had conquered Satan and his forces, and therefore God had given him power and dominion over all things in heaven and on earth. Through his death he has unveiled the mysteries of the Jewish religion and made the sacred writings an open book.

WHITE HORSE

And I saw, and behold a white horse: and he that sat on him had a bow; and a crown was given unto him: and he went forth conquering, and to conquer. Rev. 6 : 2.

An Oriental potentate always rides on a white horse. Princes and high government officials prefer white horses on important occasions. When a king or a conquering general enters a city, he is met by a delegation of notables with a saddled white horse, which is presented as a token of welcome. Pure white horses being scarce are found only in the possession of kings and wealthy men.

White is symbolical of purity and power. In the East, material of all colors, with the exception of black, is white before it is dyed. The bow indicated strength, conquest and expansion of the realm.

This vision of horses is similar to the vision of chariots with horses of different colors, which was seen by the prophet Zechariah (Zech. 6 : 1–7).

RED HORSE

And there went out another horse that was red: and power was given to him that sat thereon to take peace from the earth, and that they should kill one another: and there was given unto him a great sword. Rev. 6 : 4.

Red horses (reddish brown) are numerous in the Near East. They are used by soldiers. Most of the famous Arabian horses are red. They are noted for their speed and endurance.

Red is the symbol of blood, and the red horse symbolizes great destruction of life. The king's bodyguards wore scarlet clothes, indicating that they were ready to shed blood and to die, if necessary, for their ruler. "The shield of his mighty men is made red, the valiant men are in scarlet: the chariots shall be with flaming torches in the day of his preparation, and the fir trees shall be terribly shaken" (Nahum 2:3).

BLACK HORSE

And when he had opened the third seal, I heard the third beast say, Come and see. And I beheld, and lo a black horse; and he that sat on him had a pair of balances in his hand.
Rev. 6:5.

A black horse is symbolical of death, famine and destruction. When a warrior is killed in battle, his horse is saddled in black, and led in the burial procession, following the bier. Most men in the Near East prefer red horses, which are most numerous. Princes and kings generally ride on white horses. Black horses are generally used for draft purposes. Superstitious people consider black a bad omen and are reluctant to own a black horse. When a man dies, his relatives wear black. Black, like darkness, is the symbol of mourning and despair.

The balances (scales) are symbolical of justice. Death, famine and destruction were at hand, the people had gone astray, corruption and injustice prevailed. The old order was ready to be destroyed and a new order, based on justice, was to be substituted. This new order could not come without suffering. Whenever evil is removed, the good usually suffer with the bad.

MEASURE OF WHEAT

And I heard a voice in the midst of the four beasts say, A measure of wheat for a penny, and three measures of barley for a penny; and see thou hurt not the oil and the wine.
Rev. 6 : 6.

During wars the prices of wheat and other foods change. The invading armies take spoils from the lands which they conquer. Food and other necessities become scarce, and the people are ravaged by famine, especially the residents of the cities besieged by the invading armies. (Compare II Kings 7 : 4.) When the siege is broken, and the invading armies defeated, prices of wheat drop. "Then Elisha said, Hear ye the word of the Lord; Thus saith the Lord, To morrow about this time shall a measure of fine flour be sold for a shekel, and two measures of barley for a shekel, in the gate of Samaria" (II Kings 7 : 1).

Trees and vines are generally spared during wars. The Hebrews in their conquest of Palestine were admonished by Moses not to harm trees. The conqueror depends on the fruit of the trees for sustenance.

Famine, death and destruction are followed by a period of prosperity or vise versa. This is generally the case. Compare Pharaoh's vision of seven fat and seven lean cows, and of seven full ears of wheat and seven withered ears (Gen. 41 : 18–28).

"A measure of wheat for a penny" indicates that food must be abundant because of a period of prosperity.

PALE HORSE

And I looked, and behold a pale horse: and his name that sat on him was Death, and Hell followed with him. And power was given unto them over the fourth part of the earth, to kill with sword, and with hunger, and with death, and with the beasts of the earth. Rev. 6 : 8.

When a land is invaded and ravaged, the beasts of the field suffer just like their owners. Grass is scarce, and whatever fodder is found in villages and cities is confiscated. The only horses left in the land are those which the soldiers of the conquering forces have rejected. These are famished, pale, and ugly to look at.

The pale horse represents death, famine and destruction. Death is the wages of sin and disobedience, which often accompany a period of luxury and prosperity. Injustice, greed and lawlessness cause men and animals to suffer alike. According to this picture, the population of cities declines rapidly, and the remnant of the people and domestic animals become the prey of wild beasts.

After the conquest of the Northern Kingdom by the Assyrians, the inhabitants of the province of Samaria were attacked by lions. "And so it was at the beginning of their dwelling there, that they feared not the Lord: therefore the Lord sent lions among them, which slew some of them" (II Kings 17 : 25).

IMMORTALITY

And when he had opened the fifth seal, I saw under the altar the souls of them that were slain for the word of God, and for the testimony which they held: Rev. 6 : 9.

The Hebrew people believed that life continued after death. When a man died, his soul went to Sheol, the place of departed souls. Life continued, but the departed souls remained inactive. Death temporarily suspended the physical life, they thought, but it did not destroy its existence. The body was considered a temporary place in which the soul dwelled. Peter, in his epistle, calls it a "tabernacle" (II Pet. 1 : 14).

Death was the result of man's disobedience to the Creator. But now we know that the body is to rise again in glory. Jesus went to Sheol, where he preached to the souls of the departed ones. But he was the only one to come out of Sheol. That is, he was the only one who conquered the grave.

This verse describes the souls of those who had been slain for the Word of God and the gospel of Jesus Christ as waiting not in Sheol, but under the heavenly altar. The bodies of these men had turned into dust, but their souls were alive and waiting for their resurrection, when they would be clothed in a glorious and indestructible body.

EARTHQUAKES

And I beheld when he had opened the sixth seal, and, lo, there was a great earthquake; and the sun became black as sackcloth of hair, and the moon became as blood;
Rev. 6 : 12.

An earthquake is symbolical of war, disturbances and uprisings. An eclipse of the sun suggests impending disasters and calamities. In the East, when the sun or moon is eclipsed, the soldiers fire their guns into the air. The noise of the gun is supposed to dispel the bad omen. The red moon means bloodshed. Wars and revolutions are caused through ignorance and misunderstanding. And the ignorance is due to lack of truth. In the East, robberies and murders are generally committed at night. National calamities are always preceeded by dark days, when the eyes of the rulers and their advisers are blinded with greed, hatred and love of material things (Matt. 24 : 38).

When the Day of the Lord is at hand, nature will share in the grief of the inhabitants of the earth. The sun and moon will be dark and the stars will not shine. There will be no place of refuge, either in houses or in the mountains. The people will run around bewildered and hopeless (Joel 2 : 9–11). "Immediately after the tribulation of those days shall the sun be darkened, and the moon shall not give her light, and the stars shall fall from heaven, and the powers of the heavens shall be shaken" (Matt. 24 : 29).

But the dark days will be followed immediately by the coming of Christ and the shining of his glory. The earthly temples will be replaced by the heavenly temple and the new Jerusalem. The light of the sun and moon will no longer be needed. New heavens will take the place of the old, and the glory of God will lighten the whole universe.

WINDS AND ANGELS

And after these things I saw four angels standing on the four corners of the earth, holding the four winds of the earth, that the wind should not blow on the earth, nor on the sea, nor on any tree. Rev. 7 : 1.

Centuries ago it was supposed that the earth was flat, resting on four pillars and having four corners. Sun, moon and winds were guarded by angels who had charge of all the forces of nature. This ancient belief was almost universally held until the sixteenth century, when science at last removed the veil of mystery from the physical universe.

Arabs and other primitive people still believe, however, in guardian angels of natural forces and man. This is because Easterners believe that God is behind all changes in the universe, that stars and other heavenly bodies are held by his mighty power, and that the angels are God's messengers appointed to minister to men, carry out God's orders and deliver his messages.

The four winds thus represent the four corners of the earth. And the number four has special significance. Revelation speaks of four beasts, four corners of the earth, four winds and four angels. "Daniel spake and said,

I saw in my vision by night, and, behold, the four winds of the heaven strove upon the great sea. And four great beasts came up from the sea, diverse one from another" (Dan. 7 : 2–3). Moreover, four is one third of the number twelve, which is the sacred number, the number of months in a year, the number of tribes of Israel, and the number of Christ's disciples.

The winds are symbolical of great changes in heaven and earth.

MARKED

And I saw another angel ascending from the east, having the seal of the living God: and he cried with a loud voice to the four angels, to whom it was given to hurt the earth and the sea,

Saying, Hurt not the earth, neither the sea, nor the trees, till we have sealed the servants of our God in their foreheads. Rev. 7 : 2–3.

"Sealed," in this case, means "marked," "ordained" and "set aside." That is, their fate was determined. In the East, both cattle and sheep are "earmarked" with the mark or seal of their owner. Moreover, servants and slaves were marked so that in case of desertion, their ownership could not be disputed. The sealing was done by heating an iron seal and touching it to the foreheads of men.

The angels were instructed not to carry out their orders of destruction until the remnant was marked with the seal of God, so that they might spare all those who were chosen and anointed by the Holy Spirit. When the angel was ordered to smite the firstborn of the Egyptians, the Hebrews marked the entrances of their houses with the blood of the lamb so that the angel of destruction would spare their own firstborn (Exod. 12 : 12–13).

THE NUMBER OF THOSE SAVED

And I heard the number of them which were sealed: and there were *sealed an hundred* and *forty* and *four thousand of all the tribes of the children of Israel.* Rev. 7 : 4.

The number in this instance is used figuratively. The number one hundred and forty-four thousand represents the remnant of Israel. Twelve thousand from each tribe are to be sealed. According to the prophecies, the Messiah will gather the scattered remnant of Israel. A portion of Israel will be saved, because of God's promises to Abraham and Jacob. The Hebrew race will be represented in the above number.

During the time of Elijah the remnant of Israel was seven thousand. Seven is another sacred number (I Kings 19 : 18; Romans 11 : 4). However, it is not the number that counts here, but the truths and Messianic hopes which the remnant represents. The one hundred and forty-four thousand is symbolical of heaven, and of the spiritual truth which the Jewish race represented. Always a remnant of Israel was preserved so that the world might be blessed by the divine promises which were fulfilled in Jesus Christ.

The number of those who will be saved after the judgment will be many times larger.

PAGANS CONVERTED

After this I beheld, and, lo, a great multitude, which no man could number, of all nations, and kindreds, and people, and tongues, stood before the throne, and before the Lamb, clothed with white robes, and palms in their hands;
Rev. 7 : 9.

The great multitude here represents the remnant of those who are to be saved of the Gentile nations. The people of all races from the four corners of the earth are to sit with Abraham, Isaac and Jacob in the kingdom of

God. "Clothed with white robes" suggests that this multitude has been purified. Palms are symbols of praise. The "Lamb" of course is Jesus, called the Lamb of God. "Behold the Lamb of God, which taketh away the sin of the world" (John 1 : 29). In the ancient Jewish sacrificial system lambs were slain for the sins of the people. Jesus died for the sins of the whole world.

Both Jews and Gentiles who believe in him are to participate in his second coming. There will be a remnant from all races and tongues which will greet him at his coming, in much the same manner in which his followers greeted him with palms when he entered Jerusalem (Matt. 21 : 8).

SUNLIGHT

They shall hunger no more, neither thirst any more; neither shall the sun light on them, nor any heat.
Rev. 7 : 16.

The Eastern text reads, "neither shall they be stricken by the sun, nor by the heat." Palestinians and Arab dwellers in the desert are always fearful of the sun's rays. During the summer months travelers and farmers are often stricken by the sun. Some of those who are stricken lose their sight temporarily, and a few permanently. Therefore, people in many parts of Palestine, Syria and Arabia stop working during the hottest hours of the day. At times in July and August the heat is as high as 125 degrees or more. Shepherds bring their sheep in under the sheds. Workers return home or sit under the shadows of trees.

The believers who have been purified through their sufferings and wear white robes cleansed with the blood of Jesus Christ will no longer suffer. They will dwell in heaven where, instead of the sun's rays, the light from the presence of God will shine on them.

TEARS

For the Lamb which is in the midst of the throne shall feed them, and shall lead them unto living fountains of waters: and God shall wipe away all tears from their eyes.
Rev. 7 : 17.

Water is always scarce in Palestine and Arabia. In Jerusalem and some other ancient cities, the people depend on rain water which is caught and stored under the house during the rainy season. One of the people's fondest desires is to find brooks and deep wells with abundant water. "Living fountains of water" means running streams. The shepherds depend on brooks and rivers to water their flocks. This is why water is so much mentioned in the Bible.

Living water is symbolic of eternal life. In the East, when people want to speak of something as being especially abundant and easily acquired, they say, "It is like running water." The apostle here is using the same simile that Jesus used when he spoke to the Samaritan woman at the well and promised to give her living water (John 4 : 10–11).

When children cry, their parents wipe away their tears and comfort them. During funerals, in the East, one may see strangers wiping away one another's tears, especially the tears of the closest relatives of the dead person. The wiping is done by the hand.

God was considered by the Jews as the Father of their race, who chastised them when they went astray, and comforted them and wiped away their tears when they returned to him. "And the Lord God will wipe away tears from off all faces" (Isa. 25 : 8).

SEVEN

And when he had opened the seventh seal, there was silence in heaven about the space of half an hour.
And I saw the seven angels which stood before God; and to them were given seven trumpets. Rev. 8 : 1–2.

Seven, like four, twelve and forty, is a sacred number, and is frequently used in the Bible. Note the references to "the seven Spirits of God, and the seven stars" (Rev. 3 : 1), "the seven churches" (Rev. 1 : 4), "the seven golden candlesticks" (Rev. 2 : 1), and "the seven thunders" (Rev. 10 : 4). The seven days of the week, and the seven planets. Number seven is often used in Aramaic conversation. Jesus told his disciples to forgive those who offended them, not merely seven times, but seventy times seven.

The seven seals suggest the seven secrets which are to be revealed. The seven trumpets signify that the secrets will be disclosed and published. In warning his hearers not to publish their deeds of charity, Jesus said, "When thou doest thine alms, do not sound a trumpet before thee" (Matt. 6 : 2).

In this case, each trumpet is to announce a woe. The great tribulation will be sevenfold. Each woe will be announced by an angel. The great catastrophe will be followed by a period of restoration and salvation. Many men will survive and triumph over these tribulations (Rev. 7 : 14). These and a remnant of Israel will be saved and receive the great reward of eternal life for the suffering which they endured for the sake of their faith. (See number seven and twelve.)

EAGLE

And I beheld, and heard an angel flying through the midst of heaven, saying with a loud voice, Woe, woe, woe, to the inhabiters of the earth by reason of the other voices of the trumpet of the three angels, which are yet to sound!
Rev. 8 : 13.

The Eastern text reads, "And I beheld, and heard an eagle having a tail red as it were blood, flying through the midst of heaven, saying with a loud voice, Woe, woe, woe to those who dwell on the earth, by reason of the other sounds of trumpets of the three angels, which are yet to sound!" The eagle is known as the fastest bird and the king of birds. The eagle represents a swift messenger carrying an important edict which is to be published everywhere. David described Saul and Jonathan as being "swifter than eagles" (II Sam. 1 : 23).

The eagle was used by the Assyrians on their emblem to symbolize the spread of their empire and omnipresence of their emperors who were worshiped as deities.

Red denotes bloodshed, famine and suffering which every tragedy leaves behind.

EAT THE BOOK

And I went unto the angel, and said unto him, Give me the little book. And he said unto me, Take it, and eat it up; and it shall make thy belly bitter, but it shall be in thy mouth sweet as honey.
And I took the little book out of the angel's hand, and ate it up; and it was in my mouth sweet as honey: and as soon as I had eaten it, my belly was bitter.
Rev. 10 : 9–10.

The book represents mysteries concerning coming events which are ready to be revealed (verse 11). The book being eaten and digested like food is symbolic of the prophet receiving God's message and making it a part of his very life. The prophet Ezekiel was told in his vision to eat a scroll. "Eat this scroll, and go speak unto the house of Israel . . . Then did I eat it; and it was in my mouth as honey for sweetness" (Ezek. 3 : 1–4). (Compare also Ezek. 2 : 8–9.)

Honey is symbolical of temporary joy, which is followed by bitterness and sorrow. The taste of sweets last but a short while. "Thy words were found, and I did eat them; and thy word was unto me the joy and rejoicing of mine heart" (Jer. 15 : 16). Various writers describe God's words as "sweeter than honey" (Psa. 119 : 103).

The apostle was glad to be worthy to receive the revelation of the mysteries of God, but their predictions of destruction to come upon the earth made him sad and sorrowful. Bitterness denotes immediate action. In the East, when a man has a secret that he cannot keep any longer, he says, "My belly is sore."

STAFF OF REED

And there was given me a reed like unto a rod: and the angel stood, saying, Rise, and measure the temple of God, and the altar, and them that worship therein. Rev. 11 : 1.

The Eastern text reads: "Arise, and anoint the temple of God, and the altar, and those who worship therein." The Aramaic word *meshakh* means "to anoint" and "to measure." The two words are written and pronounced the same, so that the reader and the translator must be guided by the context. When the Aramaic text was translated into Greek the word for "rod" was interpreted as meaning "measuring rod," and thus the Aramaic word *meshakh* was thought to mean "measure" instead of "anoint." The angel of God spoke to John in his own native tongue, which was Aramaic.

The reed was a staff which bishops carried to lean on during services. Even today some of the elderly bishops and priests of churches in the East lean on a staff during prayers. In Western churches they are used only by bishops and other high ecclesiastical authorities. They

THE REVELATION 577

are also used by travelers. When Jacob blessed both the sons of Joseph, he worshiped, leaning upon the top of his staff.

Moses had a rod when he was a shepherd. Later he wrought many wonders by it in the land of Egypt (Exod. 4 : 2–5). Aaron's rod was kept in the ark of the covenant. Rods and staffs are symbolical of protection, strength and power. Shepherds carry rods and staffs for protection. "Thy rod and thy staff they comfort me" (Psa. 23 : 4). "The Lord shall send the rod of thy strength out of Zion" (Psa. 110 : 2). "And he shall rule them with a rod of iron" (Rev. 2 : 27). Jesus told his disciples not to carry a staff on their journeys. They were to rely on God for protection. Some staffs are made of thick reeds.

In a vision the angel of the Lord gave John a rod made of reed and told him to arise, and anoint the temple of God, and the altar, and those who worship there. The reed is symbolical of weakness. When the commander of the Assyrian armies delivered the ultimatum to Hezekiah, he warned him not to put his trust in Egypt. "Now, behold, thou trustest upon the staff of this bruised reed, even upon Egypt" (II Kings 18 : 21). Staffs and rods are generally made of strong wood.

Jerusalem was to be taken and portions of the Temple defiled, but the inner court (the holy of holies) was to be spared. This portion of the Temple, and other remnants which had been anointed, were to be spared destruction and defilement.

In the East, land is measured by feet, rods, and ropes. Cloth is measured by the arm. The new Jerusalem was measured with a golden reed. "And he that talked with me had a golden reed to measure the city, and the gates thereof, and the wall thereof" (Rev. 21 : 15). That is the measuring line of which the prophet Zechariah speaks: "I lifted up mine eyes again, and looked, and behold a man with a measuring line in his hand. . . . To measure Jerusalem, to see what is the breadth thereof, and what is the length thereof" (Zech. 2 : 1–2). But nowhere in the East are *people* measured with rods, as the King James Version of this verse suggests.

The vision of John was fulfilled when Jerusalem was besieged and destroyed and the Temple defiled by the Romans under Titus.

CLOTHED IN SUN

And there appeared a great wonder in heaven; a woman clothed with the sun, and the moon under her feet, and upon her head a crown of twelve stars:
And she being with child cried, travailing in birth, and pained to be delivered. Rev. 12 : 1–2.

The woman in this vision is symbolical of the Jewish religion. The sun means deity, truth and light. Centuries ago, the sun was worshiped as a god. The moon represents the things of the earth—glory and worldly power—which were to be conquered by the spirit and truth. The twelve stars represent the Twelve Apostles.

Judaism for many ages shone like a flickering light in the midst of a world dominated by hatred, darkness and ignorance. After many centuries of persecution, struggles and travail, however, Judaism gave birth to Christianity.

When Jesus was conceived, Mary was clothed with the Holy Spirit and the light of the truth (the sun) which descended upon her. Christ was born into a world dominated by evil forces, hatred and greed. The child miraculously escaped from being destroyed by King Herod. The dragon (opposition) was ready to destroy the child and smother the light of the truth.

The Twelve Apostles shine like stars in the skies. They are like costly jewels in a great crown. The number twelve is the sign of the Zodiac. It suggests here the completeness of the Christian gospel.

VIRGIN MARY

And she brought forth a man child, who was to rule all nations with a rod of iron: and her child was caught up unto God, and to his throne. Rev. 12 : 5.

The woman is the Virgin Mary, and the child is Jesus Christ. Jesus was destined spiritually to rule over all nations and establish the kingdom of God on earth. Had the people received him, the reign of God would have been established long before this and he would have ruled the world and fulfilled the Messianic prophecies. But the world knew him not; it crucified him. But God received him and clothed him in glory and honor. God's reign and his righteousness will be established in due time.

Jesus died as a young man, leaving his work to his disciples. His followers were persecuted, and they fled from place to place, but the guiding hand of God helped and preserved them even when everything seemed dark and hopeless. The evil forces did their utmost to destroy Christian teachings, but at last they were defeated and the truth emerged victorious.

THE DRAGON

And when the dragon saw that he was cast unto the earth, he persecuted the woman which brought forth the man child.

And to the woman were given two wings of a great eagle, that she might fly into the wilderness, into her place, where she is nourished for a time, and times, and half a time, from the face of the serpent.

And the serpent cast out of his mouth water as a flood after the woman, that he might cause her to be carried away of the flood. Rev. 12 : 13–15.

The dragon is symbolical of earthly power, opposition and enmity. Pagan rulers from the very beginning were cognizant of the growth of the Christian church and its influence on their people. The pagan religions, over which the kings presided, were losing power and giving way to a hidden force which was fermenting the Empire just as leaven ferments dough.

Pagan rulers tried to stamp out Christianity and destroy the Church. Christians fled and took refuge in deserts and other regions beyond the boundaries of the Empire.

The first persecution started under King Agrippa I, in which James the son of Zebedee was slain. Christian converts fled into Syria and the Arabian Desert.

Wings are symbolical of omnipresence and divine protection. The Church, even though harassed from all sides, survived through the guidance of the Holy Spirit. The flood means charges and accusations. Christians were denounced as the enemies of mankind and of the Empire.

Other persecutions, much more severe in nature, started under Nero, A.D. 69, and lasted until the conversion of Constantine I, in 318.

BEAST WITH TEN HORNS

> . . . *and saw a beast rise up out of the sea, having seven heads and ten horns, and upon his horns ten crowns, and upon his heads the name of blasphemy.*
> *And the beast which I saw was like unto a leopard, and his feet were as the feet of a bear, and his mouth as the mouth of a lion: and the dragon gave him his power, and his seat, and great authority.*   Rev. 13 : 1–2.

The vision is similar to that seen by Daniel, relative to the four kingdoms: Babylon, Persia, Greece and Rome (Dan. 7 : 3–8). The fourth beast, (Rome) is described as being dreadful and terrible. It had great iron teeth and ten horns (Dan. 7 : 7). The seven heads are seven imperial wizards. The ten horns are the ten kings. "The name of blasphemy" is the divine title by which the emperor was called.

The dragon is the anti-Christ, heresy, deception and devil. The dragon gave power to the beast (emperor) who had authority over the people, to suppress the truth of the gospel of Jesus Christ, supplant it with pagan doctrines, and clothe them with worldly power. Rome lost its political power over the world. The city was replaced by Constantinople as the capital of the world empire. Indeed, the Imperial City for a time was stripped of power and glory. But the wounds were healed. Rome once more regained its political influence over the world. The Church was constantly threatened with heresies, schisms and rivalries. Some of the popes misused their power and authority, and most of those who stood and fought for the truth were powerless.

WOUND HEALED

And I saw one of his heads as it were wounded to death; and his deadly wound was healed: and all the world wondered after the beast. Rev. 13 : 3.

When Constantine I changed the capital of the Roman Empire and made Constantinople the Imperial City, Rome for a time lost its prominence and influence. After the death of Constantine, the Empire was divided among his three sons: Constantine II, Constantius and Constans. Constantine II ruled in the West.

Years after, the severe wound which Constantine had inflicted upon Rome was healed, and the city once more regained its prestige. In the fifth century, when Constantinople was slipping, Rome was gradually becoming the center of the Empire again. The city was ruled by both kings and popes. The latter, at times, exercised both spiritual and temporal powers over the citizens of the western portion of the Empire.

After the death of the Emperor Jovian, in 364, the Empire was split in two—eastern and western. Rome gradually became free from Constantinople. In 492 Pope Gelasius I advanced his claims to political authority.

In the year 800 Roman and Greek Christianity were divided. Greek Christianity remained as the official church of the Byzantine Empire. The pope became the supreme authority in the West. Papal influence continued to gain in succeeding years. The prestige and political authority of the popes were restored. The kings of the small countries in Europe derived their authorities from Rome.

THE NUMBER OF THE BEAST

And that no man might buy or sell, save he that had the mark, or the name of the beast, or the number of his name. Here is wisdom. Let him that hath understanding count the number of the beast: for it is the number of a man; and his number is Six hundred threescore and six.
Rev. 13 : 17–18.

Every letter in the Aramaic and Hebrew alphabets is also a numeral. For instance, the letter *alep* is equivalent to the number one, *beth* to two, *gammel* to three, *dalet* to four, *yoth* to ten, *kap* to twenty, *lameth* to thirty, *mem* to forty, *koop* to one hundred, *resh* to two hundred, and *taw* to four hundred.

Code writing was common in biblical days, just as it is today. The name of any person can be written in figures instead of letters. The reader deciphers the numerals and reduces it into letters. For example, *semket* is equivalent to sixty and, with a dot over it, becomes six hundred. *Semket* with the dot and another *semket* and the letter *waw* (six) following becomes six hundred and sixty-six. The reader must find a name which corresponds exactly to these figures.

Nero Caesar in Aramaic is NRON KSR. Vowels are interpolated for English use. Aramaic letters have numerical values as follows:

N	50
R	200
O	6
N	50
K	100
S	60
R	200
	666

Which is the number of the beast or Nero.

In Hebrew, the figure would be 676. This is because Hebrew has an extra *yoth,* equivalent to ten. But Hebrew was not spoken at this time. It had been superseded by Aramaic after the Babylonian captivity.

John had seen this vision many years before it was written. This prophecy was fulfilled during the severe persecutions beginning with the reign of Nero, and continued for three centuries. Thousands of Christians lost their lives. (The visions were written on separate scrolls.)

The beast mentioned here is called *khaywat shina* in Aramaic, meaning "a wild or vicious beast." *Shina* is used to distinguish it from other beasts, such as the four beasts or living creatures. This beast is the power which is to oppose the teaching of Christ and persecute his followers. *Shina* in Aramaic means "teeth." The beast is dreadful and terrible, like a tiger, ready to tear and destroy. (Compare Dan. 7 : 7.)

The beast is a symbol for a temporal ruler disguised in religious garments, who blasphemes against the teaching of Christ and forces men to accept pagan teachings which are contrary to the word of God.

When the apostle John saw this vision, the Roman Empire was ruled by an emperor, who presided over numerous kings whom he had appointed to rule on his behalf over various parts of the Empire. The beast is the symbol of great authority and power. The seven heads are the seven authorities or emperors who were to become the persecutors of the Church. The ten horns are the ten small kings who were to rule, and the authority of the emperor's crown means absolute power. The emperor is to bestow unlimited authority on those who rule under him and persecute the Church.

Some biblical authorities believe that the beast referred to here is the papacy. It is true that many of the popes were more temporal than spiritual, and that they exercised tremendous political authority over the people. Some of them were notoriously evil, and persecuted those who challenged their political power and corrupt practices. Nevertheless, not all of the popes were bad. The majority of them were good. All Christian difficulties cannot be blamed on Rome. Heresies started first in Alexandria and Constantinople long before Rome regained its influence.

When John saw this vision there were no popes in Rome. The few Christian Jews in Rome were harassed and insignificant. But the Empire which ruled the world from a city surrounded by seas saw the danger of the growth and spread of Christianity, and devised means to destroy it. Then again, John received his vision in Aramaic, his native language. The secret number which he gave does not correspond with the name of any pope. It is the number of Nero Caesar. But it could mean any beastly, temporal or ecclesiastical authority who acts like Nero Caesar and suppresses the truth.

Imperial Rome, or the fourth and terrible beast, like the realms of Babylon, Persia and Greece, has now passed away, but small kings have continued to rise and rule. The truth of Christ is still suppressed and his followers are persecuted.

LAMB

And I looked, and, lo, a Lamb stood on the mount Sion, and with him an hundred forty and four thousand, having his Father's name written in their foreheads. Rev. 14 : 1.

The "Lamb" is Christ. "Behold the Lamb of God, which taketh away the sin of the world" (John 1 : 29).

In olden days lambs were considered the most acceptable offerings to the Deity. This is because lambs are gentle and meek. When Easterners visit a ruler or a chief of a tribe, they take a lamb with them as a gift of reconciliation. Abel brought some of the firstlings of his flock as an offering to God, and the Lord was pleased with his offering (Gen. 4 : 4).

One hundred and forty-four thousand is the number of those who are favored by God, twelve thousand from each of the Twelve Tribes. The figure is used collectively.

The number of Christians at that time might have been a hundred and forty-four thousand.

BABYLON SYMBOL OF WORLDLY POWER

And there followed another angel, saying, Babylon is fallen, is fallen, that great city, because she made all nations drink of the wine of the wrath of her fornication.
Rev. 14 : 8.

The reference here is to the words of the prophet Jeremiah. "Babylon hath been a golden cup in the Lord's hand, that made all the earth drunken: the nations have drunken of her wine; therefore the nations are mad" (Jer. 51 : 7).

Babylon was condemned by God and its doom predicted by the Hebrew prophets. Nevertheless, Babylon was not destroyed when Cyrus, king of Persia, conquered it in 539 B.C. The city remained for many years a center of beauty, culture and commerce.

In the year 311 B.C., Babylon was taken by Alexander the Great, and for a short period became the capital of the world-wide Greek Empire. After the death of Alexander, one of his generals, Seleucus, built a new city not very far from the environs of Babylon and called it Seleucia. This city became the capital of the Seleucian Empire, and later of the Sassanid Persian dynasty.

We do not know how Babylon was destroyed. Some authorities believe the city was destroyed by a flood, which is very possible. Some parts of the ancient city are buried under many feet of mud. But, regardless of how it was destroyed, the city is now in ruins. The words of prophets were fulfilled.

Like Sodom and Gomorrah, Babylon has been a warning to other great cities. The city of Babylon is used here symbolically, of course. Constantinople and Rome, like Babylon, were the center of luxuries, greed and corrupt politics.

THE WINEPRESS

And the winepress was trodden without the city, and blood came out of the winepress, even unto the horse bridles, by the space of a thousand and six hundred furlongs.   Rev. 14 : 20.

An Eastern winepress is about ten feet in diameter and two and a half to three feet deep, constructed of bricks and inlaid with cement or clay. Grapes are put in it and trodden under the feet of men. The juice drains out through a narrow passage and is caught in earthen jars or skin containers.

In the vision, the winepress was so large that the grapes were trodden under the feet of horses, just as oxen are used in threshing wheat. The winepress was a thousand and six hundred furlongs. The Eastern text speaks of juice instead of blood.

Wine is symbolical of drunkenness and destruction. When damage is done during wars and revolutions, it is said, "The people are drunk with wrath and revenge."

The apostle points out that in the latter days the people would be drunk with pride and hatred, and that, as a result, suffering and destruction would prevail everywhere. The upheaval would be wrought by men themselves. The world would be drunk with human pride, selfishness, and other evils that are distasteful in the sight of God, and which result in destruction and human suffering. The term "wrath of God" is used because God hates evil, and his attributes (love, harmony, and justice) are utterly opposed to it.

SONG OF MOSES

And they sing the song of Moses the servant of God, and the song of the Lamb, saying, Great and marvellous are thy works, Lord God Almighty; just and true are thy ways, thou King of saints. Rev. 15 : 3.

The Song of Moses" is a psalm sung in celebration of the Hebrew victory over the Egyptian army when the Israelites crossed the Red Sea. "Then sang Moses and the children of Israel this song unto the LORD, and spake, saying, I will sing unto the LORD, for he hath triumphed gloriously: the horse and his rider hath he thrown into the sea. The LORD is my strength and song, and he is become my salvation: he is my God, and I will prepare him an habitation; my father's God, and I will exalt him. The LORD is a man of war: the LORD is his name" (Exod. 15 : 1–4).

"The song of the Lamb" is a song which the Hebrews sang when they left Egypt. It is the song of deliverance and triumph over Egypt. It was always sung when the Jews ate the passover.

"The Lamb" here means Jesus Christ, who was slain for the sins of the world and who now lives in heaven.

SEVERE PUNISHMENT

For they have shed the blood of saints and prophets, and thou hast given them blood to drink; for they are worthy. Rev. 16 : 6.

One of the cruelest punishments which one may inflict on his enemies is to compel them to drink the blood of their children or relatives. It is often said: "I will drink his blood," or "I will make him drink the blood of his people." It often happens that when the chief of a tribe or any ruler is defeated, a severe judgment is passed against him by his adversary. His children and relatives are killed in his presence.

When the captain of Nebuchadnezzar's army captured Jerusalem, he took King Zedekiah and brought him before the King of Babylon; and when the judgment was passed upon him, they slew his sons in his presence and then put out his eyes (II Kings 25 : 6–7).

This was in accordance with the law of Moses—an eye for an eye, and a tooth for a tooth. These men had shed the blood of saints and prophets, and they had received a just judgment.

THE KINGS OF THE EAST

And the sixth angel poured out his vial upon the great river Euphrates; and the water thereof was dried up, that the way of the kings of the east might be prepared.
Rev. 16 : 12.

For many centuries the Euphrates River has served as a natural boundary between the East and the West. In the past, many great battles were fought between the kings of the East and those of the West, for supremacy over the rich provinces in Mesopotamia. In the thirteenth century the Mongols, under the Emperor Kublai Khan and his brother Hulagu, captured and destroyed Bagdad. Their armies, after crossing the Euphrates River, occupied Syria and menaced Palestine, but at last they were defeated and Jerusalem was spared.

No one can foretell what events are to take place in the Near East, or when the armies of the kings of the East may succeed in crossing the Euphrates River.

"The water thereof was dried up" is an Eastern saying which means that the armies were large and powerful. When a large and thirsty army encamps by a stream or a river, it uses a great quantity of water. Then again, when the campaigns of a successful general are related, it is said that the rivers dried up before him.

The kings of the East are the Chinese and Japanese. In Aramaic, they are called *malkey demadnakhi shimsha,* "the kings of the rising sun." According to this prophecy, the world's last battle, the battle of Armageddon, will be a racial battle. It will be a conflict between the armies of the East and those of the West. (See Armageddon, Rev. 16 : 16.)

ARMAGEDDON

And he gathered them together into a place called in the Hebrew tongue Armageddon. Rev. 16 : 16.

Armageddon is a place in the large plain of Esdraelon, west of the river Jordan. In biblical times the place was called Megiddo; the famous battlefield in northern Palestine where the Egyptian, Assyrian and Babylonian armies fought over the supremacy in Palestine and Syria. Josiah, king of Judea, was slain at Megiddo by Pharaoh-Nechoh, king of Egypt, when the former went to the help of Assyria, against Egypt (II Kings 23 : 29–30). Armageddon, or, as it is called in Hebrew, Har-Megiddo, was the meeting place of the rival armies.

Armageddon is chosen as the battlefield for the final struggle between the forces of good and the forces of evil. In ancient times the place was noted for battles; it was a familiar battleground and the gateway to Syria and the Euphrates valley. The battle is symbolical of the great contest between the forces of good and those of evil. The good will ultimately triumph and the blood of the saints will be avenged.

GENTILE RULE

And the great city was divided into three parts, and the cities of the nations fell: and great Babylon came in remembrance before God, to give unto her the cup of the wine of the fierceness of his wrath. Rev. 16 : 19.

Babylon" is used allegorically, meaning "the Gentile world." Babylon was noted for its wealth, luxuries, corruption and worldliness. The great city is depicted as the center of corruption and mother of harlots (Rev. 17 : 5). This is because the period of the Gentile powers began with the destruction of Jerusalem by the Chaldean army, and the Babylonian captivity. Jerusalem, the holy city of God, became subject to pagan Babylonian kings and later to Persians, Greeks, Romans, Arabs and Turks. The Temple was destroyed and the worship was interrupted for a long period.

When the Lord comes in glory, this period will come to an end. The Gentile rule will be overthrown, and a new Jerusalem will rise in place of the old. The true religion will be restored and the Holy City will once more become the center of worship.

Political Israel came to an end with the Babylonian captivity, but the spiritual Israel was crushed under the Roman rule, when the Temple was destroyed by Titus in A.D. 70. Jesus had predicted the destruction of the Holy City and the Temple: "And Jerusalem shall be trodden down of the Gentiles, until the time of the Gentiles is fulfilled" (Luke 21 : 24). The days of the Gentiles are numbered. They will come to an end.

The remnant, or the spiritual Israel, will be restored by the Messiah, who in due time will establish the kingdom of God and his righteousness on earth. The Jews will return to their homeland. The scattered remnant of Israel will be gathered. The glory of God will once more shine from Jerusalem.

MANY WATERS

And there came one of the seven angels which had the seven vials, and talked with me, saying unto me, Come hither; I will shew unto thee the judgment of the great whore that sitteth upon many waters: Rev. 17 : 1.

Babylon was built at the junction of two great rivers, the Tigris and the Euphrates. The two historic rivers, in olden times, were considered the two great bodies of water. In those days, other rivers were unknown. "Babylon" is often used by prophets figuratively, meaning corruption and political power. The methods of conquest, deportation and destruction employed by the kings of Babylon became the pattern for later conquerors who were drunk with worldly power.

The Aramaic and Hebrew word for Babylon is *Babel,* "confusion." Thus the name of the great city is used symbolically, to indicate political chaos and confusion, which will remain until the Gentile rule comes to an end and spiritual Israel (the true religion) is once more restored.

The great destruction which befell Babylon is typical of the destruction which is to come upon the Gentile kingdoms and apostate churches.

WOMAN IN SCARLET

So he carried me away in the spirit into the wilderness: and I saw a woman sit upon a scarlet coloured beast, full of names of blasphemy, having seven heads and ten horns.

And the woman was arrayed in purple and scarlet colour, and decked with gold and precious stones and pearls, having a golden cup in her hand full of abominations and filthiness of her fornication: Rev. 17 : 3–4.

The woman symbolically arrayed in costly garments here is apostate Christendom, beginning with the Emperor Constantine. The woman sitting upon the scarlet beast, full of names of blasphemy, and having seven heads and ten horns, is symbolical of conspiracy between the Church and the State. Scarlet denotes earthly power. Kings and emperors wore scarlet robes. The woman is the Church; the scarlet beast is the State, which induced the woman, by means of power, luxuries and material things, to sit upon it, so that it might be carried to its destruction. After the confederacy between the Church and the State, Western bishops arrayed themselves in scarlet robes.

Note:—Constantinople is surrounded by many waters and built on the hills. From this metropolis one can see the waters of the Black Sea, the Bosporus and the Sea of Marmara.

When Constantinople replaced Jerusalem and Antioch as the seat of Christendom, heresies and political corruption crept in, which split the Christian church asunder. New doctrines contrary to the teaching of Jesus and his apostles were introduced. Bishops and patriarchs sold out to the Byzantine emperors. Easy living and luxuries took the place of martyrdoms and the Christian life.

Many Protestant commentators believe that Babylon in this case is the symbol of the ecclesiastical world, that is, the Roman Catholic Church and the papacy. But we must not forget that when the Church merged with the State under Constantine in A.D. 325, Roman Christianity was secondary. Constantinople became the ecclesiastical seat of Christendom. The emperors dictated to the bishops whom they had appointed. The Church gradually adapted itself to the political and economic policy of the Empire. The great issues pertaining to the doctrines and creeds were determined by emperors and their military advisers. On the other hand, controversies over church doctrines were between Antioch in Syria and the new ecclesiastical capital, Constantinople. Rome was not in the picture at this time, nor had the pope any political power.

This prophecy nevertheless can be interpreted to mean any great city where corruption, greed and tyranny dominates and where the truth is repressed. It is true that Rome in the middle ages resembled Babylon in many respects. Some of its popes were as bad as some of the Byzantine emperors. Rome replaced Constantinople as the center of political and ecclesiastical power. Both cities have exerted tremendous influence over the kings of the world.

Constantinople was conquered by the Turks in the year 1454, and soon lost its prominence as a center of shipping and commerce. Its loss was lamented by all the kings and merchantmen of Europe. Rome has never been a great commercial center. (See Rev. 18 : 3–20.)

When the Gentile power ends, the Church will be free from political power, heresies will be renounced and the true teaching of Christ restored.

BABYLON MYSTERY

And upon her forehead was a name written, MYSTERY, BABYLON THE GREAT, THE MOTHER OF HARLOTS AND ABOMINATIONS OF THE EARTH. Rev. 17 : 5.

The reference to Babylon is symbolical. Babylon fell before the Persian armies about 539 B.C. The prophets had predicted its eternal doom. Isaiah states that Babylon shall never be inhabited. "And Babylon, the glory of kingdoms, the beauty of the Chaldees' excellency, shall be as when God overthrew Sodom and Gomorrah. It shall never be inhabited, neither shall it be dwelt in from generation to generation; neither shall the Arabian pitch tent there; neither shall the shepherds make their fold there" (Isa. 13 : 19–20).

After its occupation by the Persian armies, Babylon lost its imperial glory, splendor and wealth. How much of Babylon escaped the fury of the invading forces is a mystery. The city was occupied by the Grecian army about 311 B.C. When the prophecy was fulfilled and Babylon's fate as a great city was sealed, we do not know. One thing we do know is that when John saw his mysterious vision, Babylon was not an imperial capital. At the time, the capital of the Persian or Median Empire was Agbatana (Hamadan).

Then again, Babylon was built on the plains at the junction of the rivers Tigris and Euphrates. At that point there are no mountains as described in the book: "The seven heads are seven mountains, on which the woman (city) sitteth" (Rev. 17 : 9). The Euphrates River was known as a great body of water (Jer. 51 : 13), but a city built on a river can hardly compare with Constantinople, which is built on hills and surrounded by the waters of two seas, or Rome which is close to the sea and built on seven hills and the river Tiber. Be that as it may, the vision is similar to that which was seen by the prophet Nahum concerning the fall of Nineveh. The latter was also called a harlot (Nahum 3 : 4–6).

Babylon is symbolically used, as Sodom and Gomorrah.

The Hebrew prophets and poets denounced her in bitter words: "The nations have drunken of her wine; therefore the nations are mad" (Jer. 51 : 7). No doubt the city which the apostle had in mind, and which he likens to Babylon, is either Constantinople or Rome. At this time, the great Babylonian, Persian and Grecian empires had become part of history.

Rome was the world power when John saw his vision, and many small kingdoms were under its protection. Its emperor was the king of kings and the lord of lords who was worshiped as the god of the Empire. Persecutions against the Christian religion were just beginning. The beast and the kings who were under him were soon to persecute the church. Some commentators state that the city is ecclesiastical Rome and the beast is the pope. But this does not correspond with the number of the beast, 666, which is Nero Caesar (Rev. 13 : 18).

The Byzantine emperors also persecuted Christianity and suppressed the truth. The patriarchs and other high ecclesiastical authorities were directly under the emperors. The latter declared themselves as the "heads of the church." This act was a blasphemy. Moreover, image worship and many pagan rites were restored.

HORN

And the ten horns which thou sawest are ten kings, which have received no kingdom as yet; but receive power as kings one hour with the beast. Rev. 17 : 12.

The horn is symbolical of temporal power. Alexander the Great was said to have had a golden horn, meaning that his rule was crowned with glories. Nebuchadnezzar was called "the head of gold" (Dan. 2 : 38). Thus a horn is symbolical of a kingdom.

The vision is similar to that of the great and terrible image seen by Nebuchadnezzar. "This image's head was of fine gold, his breast and his arms of silver, his belly and his thighs of brass, his legs of iron, his feet part of iron and part of clay" (Dan. 2 : 32-33). The four metals in the image were symbolical of the four great empires. Gold was the glorious Babylonian Empire, brass the powerful Grecian Empire, and iron the durable Roman Empire. The four mighty empires were broken to pieces by the stone cut without hands. The stone is the Messianic kingdom which triumphed by the power of God. The iron and clay feet are the Eastern and Western empires under Rome.

The ten horns correspond to the vision of the four winds and the four great beasts—a lion, a bear, a leopard, and the beast with iron teeth and ten horns (Dan. 7 : 1-7). The ten horns are part of the fourth beast, and hence they symbolize the ten small kingdoms ruled by the ten kings after the fall of the Roman Empire, which is the iron kingdom. These kings are defeated by the Lamb which is Christ. One hour means a brief reign. After centuries of struggle Christianity triumphed over the kings and rulers of the world.

When Christianity triumphed over the Roman Empire, the rule of the four great realms ended. From the days of Constantine the Great, A.D. 318, to the present time, the rulers of the European nations have been known as "The Defenders of the Faith." In other words, they are servants of Christ on earth. Then again, since the fifteenth century the world, to some extent, has been governed by Christian laws and teachings. Christ has been the Supreme Ruler in most parts of the earth. Hitherto, both the political and moral power had been invested in the person of the emperor who ruled over the realm. With the defeat of the ten kings, the moral power triumphed over the political power. Thus the realm of the Gentiles still remains, but is subject to the laws of the Church of Jesus Christ. The political power of the Gentile kings will end at the second coming of Christ (Luke 21 : 24).

CONSTANTINOPLE

And the merchants of the earth shall weep and mourn over her; for no man buyeth their merchandise any more:
Rev. 18 : 11.

Not until the rise of the British power in the seventeenth century was Constantinople rivaled as a great center of commerce. Since its foundation in the fourth century it had been the world's market. Its shops and warehouses were filled with diverse merchandise which was brought on the backs of camels and on ships. It replaced Babylon, Damascus and other ancient cities as a market for cloth, jewelry, spices and delicacies. The city, under Byzantine emperors, was noted for its luxuries.

Rome has never been a great commercial city. The Italians, instead of exporting, import much food, clothing, gold and silver (verses 16–17). But Rome is not a shipping center.

Constantinople, as a great commercial city, was replaced by London. The latter has every resemblance to the former. It is situated on the water and thrives on shipping and commerce. It has been the world's chief market for gold, jewelry, spices, pearls and other merchandise, but lacks the ecclesiastical domination which characterized Constantinople and Rome. London has never been an ecclesiastical center. Moreover, London even though built on the river Thames is not founded on seven hills.

THE FOUR CREATURES

And the four and twenty elders and the four beasts fell down and worshipped God that sat on the throne, saying, Amen; Alleluia.
Rev. 19 : 4.

The four beasts here are the four living creatures (angels). They should not be confused with *khewat shina,* the wild beast which is often mentioned in the book of Revelation. In Aramaic, the beast is called a vicious

THE REVELATION

beast, to distinguish it from other beasts. "Thou that dwellest between the cherubims" (Psa. 80 : 1; Ezek. 10 : 2; Num. 7 : 89).

The four and twenty elders are the twelve representatives of the Old Testament and the twelve of the New Testament.

The angelic order and the sons of men unite in worshiping God and saying "Amen, Alleluiah."

LAMB'S WIFE

Let us be glad and rejoice, and give honour to him: for the marriage of the Lamb is come, and his wife hath made herself ready. Rev. 19 : 7.

The term "Lamb" means Christ, that is, the Lamb of God. This name was given to Jesus by John. "The next day John seeth Jesus coming unto him, and saith, Behold the Lamb of God, which taketh away the sin of the world" (John 1 : 29). A lamb is symbolical of gentleness, meekness and purity. Lambs are always preferred for gifts and for offerings.

The wife of the Lamb is the Church of Christ, which he has purchased with his blood (Acts 20 : 28). The Church is likened to a bride. This is because in the East men pay large dowries for their brides. In the prayer book of the Church of the East, we read: "The Church is the spouse of Christ, for he has purchased her from deception."

Hosea spoke of Israel as an unfaithful and estranged wife because she had gone after other gods. She had been rejected and then restored. "And I will betroth thee unto me for ever; yea, I will betroth thee unto me in righteousness, and in judgment, and in lovingkindness, and in mercies" (Hosea 2 : 19).

MARRIAGE OF THE LAMB

Let us be glad and rejoice, and give honour to him: for the marriage of the Lamb is come, and his wife hath made herself ready. Rev. 19 : 7.

Marriage of the Lamb and his wife is symbolical of union of Christ with the true Church. The garments of fine linen denote chastity and purity. Before this marriage will take place the Church must purge itself of evil and become righteous and worthy to be called the wife of Christ, who purchased her with his blood. The whiteness of the linen represents holiness. Angels are portrayed in white garments, and the priests wore white linen when ministering in the Temple of God. (See Rev. 21 : 9.)

WHITE HORSE

And I saw heaven opened, and behold a white horse; and he that sat upon him was called Faithful and True, and in righteousness he doth judge and make war. Rev. 19 : 11.

White is a color that Easterners admire and love. When a person accomplishes a deed of merit, it is often said, "His face is white." On the other hand, when a man fails in his mission or does something bad, it is said, "His face is black." During conversations one often hears people saying to each other, "May God whiten your face and the face of your father." Likewise, good women are always spoken of as having "white faces."

A white horse is symbolical of purity, sincerity and the triumph of truth over evil.

Red horses are very common in Arabia and Syria. White horses are very scarce and they are generally used by kings, princes and noblemen.

DIVINE JUSTICE

And out of his mouth goeth a sharp sword, that with it he should smite the nations: and he shall rule them with a rod of iron: and he treadeth the winepress of the fierceness and wrath of Almighty God. Rev. 19 : 15.

The Eastern text reads: "And out of his mouth came a sharp two-edged sword."

In ancient days, swords were made in many styles. Each nation fashioned its own swords; some were short, others long, some two-edged and others single-edged. The Aramaic term for "edge" is *poma,* "mouth." The phrase above literally means, therefore, "a sword with two mouths." This type of sword is still found in Arabia.

The sword is symbolical of speech, sharpness and decision. We often say, "His tongue is like a sword," which means that his words are well chosen, or that he is a good speaker. Sharpness is a symbol of prompt decision. The two-edged sword symbolizes justice. The two-edged blade cuts forward and backward, just as justice, when thoroughly executed, cuts both ways. A single-edged sword, when used in war, may be caught by the adversary and taken away from its holder, just as justice can be perverted and purchased. But no warrior would dare to seize a two-edged sword with bare hands. Divine justice cannot be perverted, prevented or purchased.

STANDING IN THE SUN

And I saw an angel standing in the sun; and he cried with a loud voice, saying to all the fowls that fly in the midst of heaven, Come and gather yourselves together unto the supper of the great God; Rev. 19 : 17.

The angel symbolizes the Word of God conveyed to men. "Standing in the sun," means that the words will be spoken openly and the hidden secrets will be revealed. The sun is a symbol of God, light and truth.

The reference is to the battle of Armageddon. The forces of evil will be utterly destroyed. The supper of the Great God is symbolical of complete victory over the enemy, whose dead body will be given to the fowls of the air.

The remnant of the Church which has stood loyal to the teaching of God will be delivered from oppression and persecution and the power of evil forces, which are represented by the wild beast and the prophet. Christians will be free to speak the truth. Mysteries and false doctrines will be exposed under the light of God which will shine on the true believers. (See Rev. 16 : 14.)

DESTRUCTION OF THE VICIOUS BEAST

And the beast was taken, and with him the false prophet that wrought miracles before him, with which he deceived them that had received the mark of the beast, and them that worshipped his image. These both were cast alive into a lake of fire burning with brimstone.

And the remnant were slain with the sword of him that sat upon the horse, which sword proceeded out of his mouth: and all the fowls were filled with their flesh.

Rev. 19 : 20–21.

The destruction of the vicious beast and his host is symbolical of the destruction of the earthly powers. The prophet represents false doctrines of dictatorship under the guise of religion. The false prophets for a long time succeeded in deceiving the people and induced them to accept the mark (authority) of the vicious beast and his political power. When the false prophet and his teaching is brought to an end, political corruption, materialism and earthly powers will give way to the reign of the kingdom of God and his Christ.

Vicious beasts and false prophets have existed from the very beginning. Their reign will continue until the coming of the reign of Christ, which, according to the Scriptures, will be preceded by many great events and signs, wars, famine, revolutions, false teachings and false Christs

(Matt. 24). Not until all of these things are fulfilled will the reign of justice come.

The burning of the vicious beast and the false prophet is symbolical of their sudden fall and the end of their power forever. The others who will fall with sword are the political and ecclesiastical authorities who had left the truth and were in league with the vicious beast and the prophet. The sword proceeding out of his mouth means that the truth will destroy the error. That is, the powers of darkness will be exposed and put to shame.

MILLENNIUM

And I saw an angel come down from heaven, having the key of the bottomless pit and a great chain in his hand. And he laid hold on the dragon, that old serpent, which is the Devil, and Satan, and bound him a thousand years,
Rev. 20 : 1–2.

The Jews, having suffered under many foreign rulers, expected a period of peace and prosperity. This was to be the Messianic kingdom. The pagan rulers were to be overthrown and God's rule restored. The work of restoration was entrusted to the Messiah who was expected to re-establish the realm of David and gather the scattered people of Israel. Since the destruction of the Temple by Titus in A.D. 70 the Jews have dreamed of a third Jewish commonwealth.

Easterners, when persecuted and misruled, dream of God's rule and his righteousness. Indeed, this dream of restoration and rehabilitation sustained the faith of every Jew, and strengthened them when everything seemed dark and hopeless. They also believed that injustices will finally be righted and the wicked punished, and consequently those who are persecuted and crushed will rise again to power and see their enemies suffer. The Jews look forward to what they call "the day of the Lord," that is, the day of reckoning when every person will be rewarded according to his deeds.

The Hebrew prophets, at the outset, predicted the destruction of the wicked Gentile realms, and the restoration of Israel through a small remnant. Later they predicted the destruction of the wicked in general. That is, both the wicked Jews and the Gentiles. "The Lord maketh the earth empty, and maketh it waste, and turneth it upside down, and scattereth abroad the inhabitants thereof. The land shall be utterly emptied, and utterly spoiled: for the Lord hath spoken this word" (Isa. 24 : 1, 3).

The destruction is to be followed by the period of restoration and God's rule. "And the Lord shall be king over all the earth: in that day shall there be one Lord, and his name one" (Zech. 14 : 9). Other prophets also predicted such a period of tribulation to be followed by a bright and hopeful future, a period of peace and prosperity. "They shall not hurt nor destroy in all my holy mountain: for the earth shall be full of the knowledge of the Lord, as the waters cover the sea (Isa. 11 : 9). The righteous will see the carcases of the wicked who have transgressed against the Lord" (Isa. 66 : 24).

The author of the book of Revelation was born and reared in the Jewish religion. Like other Jews, he believed in the eventual restoration of Israel and the punishment of their enemies. Thus, the millennium period, even though it is not mentioned in the Four Gospels, was predicted by the Hebrew prophets and expected by the people throughout the centuries. This is one reason why the Church of the East refused to consider the book of Revelation as a scriptural authority equal to the Four Gospels. However, though it is never read in the church, yet it is read and admired by the public.

The angel mentioned here represents God's command at the battle of Armageddon, resulting in the defeat of the forces of evil and the beginning of the reign of peace. The dragon is the material world of deception, ruled by the forces which, from the very beginning, have disputed God's authority and suppressed the truth. The evil will be brought under subjugation and ultimate destruction; that is, spiritual understanding and the light of the truth will fill the earth and darkness will disappear.

The great victory will herald the beginning of the thousand years of peace and tranquillity, the millennium. During these years the forces of evil will be inoperative and those who have suffered for the sake of justice will enter upon a new life.

The Aramaic word *alep,* "thousand," is the same as the letter *aleph* in the alphabet, which signifies God. During these thousand years God's truth and his authority will be supreme, the gospel will be preached in all parts of the world for a witness unto all nations. Every individual will have an opportunity to know God and his truth. Nevertheless, some people will reject the word of God and rebel against his authority. The good and evil will remain until the last coming of the Lord, where the good and the wicked will be separated like a shepherd who separates the sheep from the goats (Matt. 25 : 31–34).

FIRST RESURRECTION

But the rest of the dead lived not again until the thousand years were finished. This is the first resurrection.
Blessed and holy is he that hath part in the first resurrection: on such the second death hath no power, but they shall be priests of God and of Christ, and shall reign with him a thousand years. Rev. 20 : 5–6.

According to the Gospel of Matthew, only one resurrection will take place at the second coming of Christ. This resurrection will be preceded by wars, revolutions, famine, earthquakes and other tribulations. Jesus' coming will be like that of a thief at night. No one will know the day and the hour. After the great signs and tribulations, the sun shall be darkened and the moon shall not give her light, and the whole system of the heavenly bodies will be destroyed. Then the Son of man will appear "in the clouds of heaven with power and great glory" (Matt. 24 : 29–31). According to the Gospels, all men will rise, the good and the bad, but the righteous will receive the reward of everlasting life, while the wicked will rise to receive judgment and punishment.

Jesus told his disciples and followers that when the hour cometh, all who are in graves "shall hear his voice, and shall come forth; they that have done good, unto the resurrection of life; and they that have done evil, unto the resurrection of damnation" (John 5 : 28–29).

The teaching about the thousand years between the first and second resurrection is found only in the book of Revelation. There we are told that those who will participate in the first resurrection will not taste a second death. They will pass into eternal life, but the wicked will be destroyed.

The thousand years between the first and second resurrections is a period of peace and tranquillity which will be enjoyed by the righteous who were persecuted and deprived of joys while they were on this earth, living among the wicked. This period is similar to the Messianic reign which will precede the kingdom of God. The church of Christ, the truth, will finally triumph over the forces of evil. Pride and worldly ambition will cease for a long time. "Satan shall be bound" means that the forces of evil will become inoperative at least for a period of a thousand years. The thousand years of peace are symbolical of the everlasting peace which will take place after the resurrection.

SATAN LOOSED

And when the thousand years are expired, Satan shall be loosed out of his prison,   Rev. 20 : 7.

I saw Satan loosed" is an Eastern way of saying, "I saw evils prevailing." "Satan tied up or chained" means that evil has been conquered and truth established. The chain is symbolical of truth and power, which restrains deception and violence.

Easterners in their conversations often say, "He has been a Satan to me," which means that he caused me to err or that he misled me. "Satan has entered into him," means that he has been influenced or dominated by evil thoughts. Iron is symbolical of power, because all other metals may be hammered with it. When truth and understanding dominate, evil is destroyed; and when evil prevails, the chain is broken and the wicked flourish.

The thousand years of peace and tranquillity will be once more disturbed by the forces of evil. The righteous will be given a trial. Many men will be misled, but at last, the devil (deceiver) and the false prophet will be utterly destroyed. These events will be followed by the final resurrection (verses 13–15).

MONGOLIA AND CHINA

And shall go out to deceive the nations which are in the four quarters of the earth, Gog and Magog, to gather them together to battle: the number of whom is as the sand of the sea.

And they went up on the breadth of the earth, and compassed the camp of the saints about, and the beloved city: and fire came down from God out of heaven and devoured them. Rev. 20 : 8–9.

Gog and Magog" (in Aramaic) mean "Mongolia and Manchuria" (Gen. 10 : 2; Ezek. 38 : 2–15). In the thirteenth century the Mongol khans overthrew the Arabian Empire and invaded the Holy Land. Indeed, the whole world at that time was threatened by the armies of Kublai Khan, Holakhu and Genghis Khan. Their armies penetrated Europe as far as Hungary.

He will gather his army from the utmost corners of the world and even from Gog and Magog, means from China, Japan and Mongolia. These lands were supposed to be at the utmost ends of the world. Semites thought the earth was flat, stretching over the water.

China and Japan were not known to the Western world until the thirteenth century, when Marco Polo made his famous visit to the Great Khan. On the other hand, China and Japan, being closer to Mesopotamia, Persia, and India were known centuries before the Christian era. Assyrian and Persian colonies were established in India. Their culture and commerce were widely spread throughout Asia. Mongolia is called in Aramaic the land of Magog. China, Mongolia and Japan always had a large population—"as the sand of the sea," which means "countless."

OPENS BOOK

And I saw the dead, small and great, stand before God; and the books were opened: and another book was opened, which is the book of life: and the dead were judged out of those things which were written in the books, according to their works. Rev. 20 : 12.

In primitive countries, where lawyers and jurists are unknown, judges are elected temporarily from among pious and unbiased men. Cases are tried under the laws which are contained in books or oral statutes handed down from one generation to another. When a man is on trial the judge opens the book in the presence of the parties concerned, determines the guilt, and prescribes the punishment. When judges are illiterate, a scribe is selected to open and read the book. Every punishment and liability is prescribed. The guilty are punished and the innocent rewarded accordingly.

The first book is the book of the law which prescribes the punishment for crimes and the rewards for gallantry and good deeds.

There is another book, the book of deeds and records, where every man's acts are written down, just as in the case of Mordecai (Esther 6 : 1–11). These books are kept very carefully and are brought out only on special occasions, when difficult cases are tried. Some judges commit the statutes to memory, especially in regions where books are rare and writing is unknown. Others are guided by the precedents.

NEW JERUSALEM

And I John saw the holy city, new Jerusalem, coming down from God out of heaven, prepared as a bride adorned for her husband.

And I heard a great voice out of heaven saying, Behold, the tabernacle of God is with men, and he will dwell with them, and they shall be his people, and God himself shall be with them, and be their God. Rev. 21 : 2–3.

Throughout the Scriptures, Jerusalem is used by the prophets and New Testament writers in a symbolic sense. Just as Babylon is typical of worldly power, whoredom and confusion, Jerusalem is typical of peace, righteousness and holiness. The name of the city in Hebrew and Aramaic means "a place of peace."

Jerusalem is the place which God chose from which to reveal himself to his children. The city is often denounced and condemned as a rebellious city. Jesus charged it with being the murderer of the prophets and men of God. He predicted its doom and the destruction of its holy Temple.

Even though Jerusalem is known as the City of God, the prophets and apostles stated that God does not dwell in temples made by the hands of men. Jesus told the Samaritan woman that the hour was coming when God would not be worshiped in Mount Gerizim or in Jerusalem. "God is a spirit: and they that worship him must worship him in spirit and in truth" (John 4 : 24).

Just as the tabernacle and the Temple were symbolical of the true worship and were temporal, the earthly Jerusalem is the pattern of the heavenly Jerusalem. And when this material pattern is removed, the new Jerusalem, which means peace and harmony, will be revealed and the kingdom of God and his throne will be established on earth just as they are in heaven. Tears will be wiped away, sorrows and sickness removed, and the presence of God and his glory felt everywhere.

JASPER STONE

Having the glory of God: and her light was like unto a stone most precious, even like a jasper stone, clear as crystal;
Rev. 21 : 11.

"Jasper," a beautiful, bright and precious stone, was one of the stones used in the ephod (Exod. 39 : 13). "Clear as crystal" signifies that the pattern of the new city is different from that of the old. That is, everything will be open and free from evil.

Hebrew worship was shrouded with mysteries. The inner court of the Temple, the holy of holies, was entered only once a year, when the high priest offered the sin offering. Because of the presence of God, the high priest covered his head. Sinful men could not see the face of God and live. Not even Elijah, the great Hebrew prophet, could see God's face (I Kings 19 : 13). Even the seraphims covered their faces when they praised the Lord (Isa. 6 : 2).

The veil which separated the holy of holies from the rest of the Temple will be removed—all mysteries will disappear. For the glory of God will shine through the walls of the new city and his throne will be seen by those who worship him and stand in his presence (Rev. 22 : 4). Evil forces will be destroyed and sin will no longer be a barrier between man and his Creator. God will become a loving Father to all men, his children. (See verse 18.)

TWELVE FOUNDATIONS

And the wall of the city had twelve foundations, and in them the names of the twelve apostles of the Lamb.
Rev. 21 : 14.

Each foundation represents the work and teaching of an apostle. This does not mean twelve different teachings or church foundations, but twelve builders. In the East, the name of the builders is always associated with the building, and sometimes is inscribed on one of the foundation stones.

The teaching of the apostles is the cornerstone of the Christian church. The church, like a large city, has many gates, but all lead into the city. The twelve foundations are symbolical of apostolic churches which were built on the teaching of Jesus Christ. The apostles preached the gospel in different parts of the world, where they converted people of diverse races and colors. Each apostle became a gate which led to the great and unseen temple which is Christ's church on earth.

TWELVE FURLONGS

And the city lieth foursquare, and the length is as large as the breadth: and he measured the city with the reed, twelve thousand furlongs. The length and the breadth and the height of it are equal. Rev. 21 : 16.

The area of the city, according to the Eastern text, is about twelve furlongs—twelve thousand paces—which is in accordance with the area which the city of Jerusalem now occupies. The city could hardly have been twelve *thousand* furlongs! That would cover an area many times larger than that of any city in the world. Since a furlong is one eighth of a mile, the area indicated here would be 900,000 square miles! No doubt this error is due to mistranslation. The ancient Jerusalem, that is, the city within the walls, or as it is called, the City of David, is small, occupying only a few square miles. The ancient city is built on a small plateau on Mount Zion. The original city is still intact. The narrow streets, bazaars and some of the historic sites remain to the present day.

MEASURE OF THE ANGEL

And he measured the wall thereof, an hundred and forty and four cubits, according to the measure of a man, that is, of the angel.   Rev. 21 : 17.

In the East, dry goods and other articles are measured by the arm. Land is measured with ropes, but the rope itself is measured in terms of cubits. "The measure of a man" is either the length of his arm from the tips of his fingers to the shoulder joint, or from the tips of the fingers to the nose.

The Aramaic word *malakha,* "angel," is pronounced exactly the same as the Aramaic word *malakha,* "sailor," but the written characters are different. I believe that the scribe who wrote down John's vision took it for granted that the apostle meant "angel." Such errors are unavoidable in dictation. I believe that what the author of Revelation meant to infer is that the measurement was based on nautical measure and not on land measure. There is a difference even today between land measure and sea measure. For instance, our nautical mile is considerably longer than the statute mile. In addition the apostle would not have used the word "angel" because he would have known that angels are spirits and have no bodies. Therefore, any measurement based on arms would have been impossible.

TWELVE PRECIOUS STONES

And the foundations of the wall of the city were garnished with all manner of precious stones. The first foundation was jasper; the second, sapphire; the third, a chalcedony; the fourth, an emerald;

The fifth, sardonyx; the sixth, sardius; the seventh, chrysolyte; the eighth, beryl; the ninth, a topaz; the tenth, a chrysoprasus; the eleventh, a jacinth; the twelfth, an amethyst.   Rev. 21 : 19–20.

The twelve foundation stones of the wall of the city symbolize the Twelve Apostles. (See verse 14.) The names of the apostles were engraved on the precious foundation stones, just as the names of the Twelve Tribes of Israel were engraved on the twelve precious stones which were set in the ephod. The names of the stones on the ephod are sardius, topaz, carbuncle, emerald, sapphire, diamond, ligure, agate, amethyst, beryl, onyx and jasper (Exod. 39 : 10–15). The precious stones were set in pure gold and mounted on blue linen.

The ephod that the high priest wore during services was the sign of purity and holiness. God's glory shone like the precious stones. (See also urim and thummim, Exod. 28 : 29–38.)

The work of every apostle shone like a precious stone. The Twelve Apostles preached in different parts of the ancient world. The work of each one of them was like a foundation stone in the great and living temple of God.

The precious stones and pure gold are symbolical of the fullness of God's revelation and his glory. The different colors represent the different races and peoples who were to embrace Christianity. God will no longer be hidden from his children, nor will he be worshiped in temples enclosed within walls. His glory will shine like the sun over all the peoples and colors. The light of truth will replace the light of the heavenly bodies (verses 22–23).

RIVER OF LIFE

And he shewed me a pure river of water of life, clear as crystal, proceeding out of the throne of God and of the Lamb. Rev. 22 : 1.

In the ancient book of dreams and visions, water is a symbol of abundance. Clear water means peace and harmony. Muddy and turbulent water signifies hardships, and strife.

The river of water "clear as a crystal" represents the truth which will pour out of the throne of God and of Jesus Christ. The present teachings and philosophies by which humanity is guided will come to an end. Prophecies will cease, and secrets and mysteries will be fully revealed.

TREE OF LIFE

In the midst of the street of it, and on either side of the river, was there the tree of life, which bare twelve manner of fruits, and yielded her fruit every month: and the leaves of the tree were for the healing of the nations. Rev. 22 : 2.

Man is often portrayed as a garden, and God as the husbandman. (Compare the parable of the vineyard. Luke 20 : 9–10.) The psalmist says, "And he shall be like a tree planted by the rivers of water" (Psa. 1 : 3). Wisdom likewise is pictured as a tree. "She is a tree of life to them that lay hold upon her" (Prov. 3 : 18). Jesus also illustrated some of his sayings by speaking of good trees and bad trees (Matt. 3 : 10). (Compare also the tree of life, Gen. 3 : 22.)

The tree of life is symbolic of perfect man, which in the beginning was created in the image and likeness of God. Man will at last be restored to his original self. His life will be eternal like the life of his Creator. The number twelve is symbolical of the Twelve Apostles and the twelve foundations (Rev. 21 : 14). The "twelve manner of fruits" are the twelve blessings which came out of the teaching of the apostles. Leaves suggest healing and protection. In the East, where the sun is hot, the sick and weary seek relief and cures under the shadows of the trees. The leaves of some trees that are frequently visited by the sick and suffering are considered sacred. Then again, certain leaves are used for medicine.

I COME QUICKLY

Behold, I come quickly: blessed is he that keepeth the sayings of the prophecy of this book. Rev. 22 : 7.

"Behold, I come quickly" means, "I will come when I am not expected." Jesus told his disciples of his second and sudden coming. He assured them that he would be with them to the end of the world. Some of his sayings were taken literally and therefore the Christians in the first century expected the return of Jesus momentarily, especially the Christians in Asia Minor, whom Paul warned in his epistles. Jesus did not set the hour and the time of his return. But his coming will be like a flash of light.

Time has no meaning in divine terms. A thousand years are like a day with God.

THE SECOND COMING

He that is unjust, let him be unjust still: and he which is filthy, let him be filthy still: and he that is righteous, let him be righteous still: and he that is holy, let him be holy still. Rev. 22 : 11.

When the end will come, everyone will be caught up as he is. The unjust will be unjust, the filthy will be filthy, and the holy will be holy. That is to say, the end will come like a twinkle of the eye. The writer of Revelation does not mean that the wicked ought to continue in their wickedness. What he means is that everyone will be caught unawares, as he is. The people will have no time to repent of their evil works.

The righteous and the holy are those who are set aside or separated from the evil ones. The Aramaic word *kadesha* means "sanctified." That is, set aside to serve God. Righteous are those who are noted for their good works and hospitality.

The coming of Christ will be so sudden that no one will have a chance to repent. He will come as a thief at night when no one expects him (Rev. 16 : 15). This is why the apostles admonish their followers to keep alert and be ready.

ETERNITY

I am Alpha and Omega, the beginning and the end, the first and the last. Rev. 22 : 13.

I am Alpha and Omega" is a literal translation of Aramaic into Greek: *ena na aleph otau,* "I am the A and Z," the beginning and the end. *Aleph* is the first letter and *taw* the last in the Semitic alphabet. The first two letters in *aleph* are the first two letters in *Alaha,* "God."

Describing God as "the beginning and the end" is an attempt to describe eternity in terms of time. But actually God has no beginning and therefore he has no end.

DOGS

For without are dogs, and sorcerers, and whoremongers, and murderers, and idolaters, and whosoever loveth and maketh a lie. Rev. 22 : 15.

Dogs" here means "vicious men." In the East, heretics, vicious men and gossipers are called dogs. Jesus once used the term "dogs" in referring to pagans when he said to the Syrian woman: "For it is not meet to take the children's bread, and to cast it unto the dogs" (Mark 7 : 26–28).

Paul in his epistle also warns the faithful to "beware of dogs," that is, "heretics and troublemakers." (See *Gospel Light,* page 187.)

WARNING AGAINST FORGERIES

And if any man shall take away from the words of the book of this prophecy, God shall take away his part out of the book of life, and out of the holy city, and from the things which are written in this book. Rev. 22 : 19.

Many Aramaic manuscripts of the Holy Scriptures, liturgies and other sacred writings contain warnings against forgeries. The scribe, in order to prevent forgeries and protect the sacred writings, puts the reader or anyone in whose possession the manuscript may fall, under curses. This is why Easterners have never dared to tamper with their sacred literature. The people believe in the words of the Scriptures and the warning they contain. When a sacred manuscript is copied, the work is examined and re-examined before it is dedicated.

Forgery has been very common in some countries. Altering the word of God to suit new theological doctrines is an old practice. Apostolic letters were forged. Paul warned against this evil practice. To forge manuscripts is an easy task. The removal of a single dot or the change of a letter will alter the meaning. A number of manuscripts which have been purchased by European and American collectors and institutions of learning were forged before they were sold. The dates of some of them have been reduced one thousand years.

INDEX

A

	PAGE
Abba, Father	200
Abounded, sin	194
Abraham, our father	51
Abraham, believed	186
Abraham, seed of	312
Abraham, by faith	478
Abraham, met	466
Absence, in my	361
Accord, with one	27
Account, on my	449
Adorn, women	407
Adultress	197
Affections, inordinate	378
Afflictions, my	365
Afflictions, bonds and	148
Age, flower of	253
Aleph, I am	614
Alexander	406
Alive, behold I am	551
Almighty, Lord	303
Alpha, I am	546
Altar, an	127
Altar, under the	567
Altar, and the	576
Amen, say	280
Amen, saith the	558
Amen, saying	596
Anathema	290
Angel, by his	543
Angel, his	91
Angel, measure of the	610
Angel, the sixth	588
Angels, one of the	590
Angels, four	569
Angels, spared not	512
Angels, elect	421
Angels, better than the	453
Angels, spoken by	454
Angels, lower than	455
Angels, I saw the seven	574
Angels, entertained	484
Angry, be ye	349
Antichrist, spirit of	523
Antioch, unto	86
Antioch, sailed to	105
Antioch, in	109
Apollos, I am	238
Apostle, am I not	259
Apostles, chiefest	315
Apostles, names of the	608
Apostles, before the	48
Apostleship, seal of mine	259
Apparel, modest	407
Appii, forum	173
Aprons	136
Aquila	133
Arabia, into	323
Archangel, the	537
Areopagus	125
Armageddon	589
Arts, curious	140
Asia, whom all	141
Asia, in	545
Asleep, fallen	283
Assunder, he burst	12
Athenians	125
Athens, men of	126
Athens, waited for them at	124
Authority, usurp	408
Authority, with	169
Authority, he had	70
Away, shall pass	489
Azotus, found at	66

B

Babylon, great	589
Babylon, church that is at	507

	PAGE		PAGE
Babylon, saying	585	Body, one	270
Balaam, the way of	514	Boldly, spoke	73
Balaam, the doctrine of	554	Bondage, spirit of	200
Balak	554	Book	563
Balances, a pair of	565	Book, written in this	615
Baptism, by	195	Book, words of the	615
Baptism, with him in	374	Book, prophecy of this	613
Baptized, she was	117	Book, the little	575
Barak	481	Book, another	606
Barbarian	379	Book, volume of the	476
Bar-Jesus	96	Books, brought	140
Barnabas	36	Books, the	606
Barnabas, me and	327	Books, the	436
Barnabas, Paul and	97	Bosor, the son of	514
Barnabas, called for	96	Bought, ye are	247
Basket, in a	72	Bound, I go	148
Bastards, are ye	483	Bowels, your own	303
Bear, feet of a	580	Bowels, in the	359
Beast, a scarlet coloured	591	Bowels, gushed out	12
Beast, number of	582	Branches, natural	211
Beast, mark of the	600	Branches, the	211
Beast, name of	582	Brass, as	277
Beast, first	562	Brass, like unto fine	549
Beasts, four	562	Bread, from house to house	27
Beasts, fought with	285	Bread, breaking of	24
Beasts, the four	596	Bread, break	144
Bellies, slow	442	Bread, unleavened	245
Benjamin, tribe of the	364	Bread, are one	270
Bishop, office of	410	Brethern, saluted the	153
Bishoprick	13	Brethern, five hundred	283
Bithynia, into	114	Brethern, unto his	457
Bitter, thy belly	575	Brethern, greet all the	395
Black, sun became	568	Bridles, unto the horse	586
Blasphemy	580	Briers, thorn and	464
Blinded, were	209	Brother, the Lord's	324
Blood, water and	523	Burden, his own	341
Blood, moon became as	568		
Blood, without	475	C	
Blood, his own	149		
Blood, of one	128	Caesarea, came to	66
Blood, your	131	Caesarea, came unto	153
Blood, the field of	13	Caesarea, certain man in	75
Blot, will not	557	Calf, like a	562
Bodies, busy	419	Calves, the blood of	475
Body, giveth it	286	Candace	61
Body, out of the	313	Candlestick, the	473
Body, members of	353	Candlesticks, seven golden	546
Body, keep under my	265	Candlesticks, seven golden	552

	PAGE		PAGE
Candlesticks, seven	547	Clothes, cast off their	163
Captain, the chief	164	Clothes, rent off their	121
Captain, chief	158	Clothing, the gay	493
Captive, captivity	348	Cloud, received him	6
Carriages, our	154	Coals, heap	215
Carpus, with	436	Colony, a	116
Castle, into the	158	Commandments, after the	377
Castle, into the	164	Common, that is	80
Cenchrea	133	Common, all things	25
Censer, golden	474	Common, all things	34
Centurion, the	173	Confesseth, spirit that	523
Centurion, a	75	Confirmation, an oath for	465
Cephas	260	Contentment, with	424
Cephas, seen of	283	Corinthians, O ye	303
Chain, a great	601	Cornelius	75
Chains, two	90	Cornelius, from	81
Chamber, the upper	145	Cornelius, saying unto him	76
Chariot, to this	62	Corner, of the	31
Charitably, not	221	Corners, standing on the four	569
Charity, have not	277	Corruptible, this	287
Charran, in	51	Counsel, determined	23
Chastisement, be without	483	Covenant, the ark of the	474
Child, a man	579	Covenant, the first	472
Children, adoption of	346	Covenant, my	471
Christ, the day of	399	Craft, of the same	129
Christ, faith of	330	Craft, this our	141
Christ, love of	301	Creature, a new	301
Christ, be in	301	Crete, in	441
Christ, ministers of	312	Cretians, the	442
Christ, rock was	265	Cross, preaching of the	230
Christ, life in	199	Cross, blood of his	371
Christ, truth in	203	Crown, receive a	507
Christ, gospel of	179	Crowns, upon his horns ten	580
Christ, name of Jesus	120	Crucified, Christ	233
Christians, called	86	Cup, a golden	591
Church, head of the	352	Curse, from the	334
Churches, seven	545	Customs, expert in all	168
Churches, I robbed other	309	Cymbal, tinkling	277
Cilicia	109	Cyprus, the country of	36
Cilicia, Syria and	112	Cyprus, to	94
Cilicia, a city in	160		
Circumcised, being	250		
Circumcision, sign of	188	**D**	
Circumcision, we are the	363		
City, every	441	Damascus, went to	169
City, that great	585	Damascus, unto	323
Cloke, the	436	Darkness, things of	242
Clothes, rent their	103	Darkness, not in	391

	PAGE		PAGE
Darkness, chains of	512	Drink, or in	376
Darts, fiery	354	Drink, nor	69
Daughters, four	154	Drink, give him	215
David, saith	210	Drink, spiritual	265
David, days of	54	Drunken, are	393
Dawn, the day	511	Drunken, are not	22
Day, regardeth	219	Dust, threw	163
Day, as one	516		
Day, fell in one	269	**E**	
Day, spoken of another	459		
Day, the eighth	364	Eagle, wings of a great	579
Deacons, the	412	Eagle, like a flying	562
Dead, husband be	197	Ear, nor	237
Dead, thou livest and art	556	Ear, he that hath	553
Dead, and was	551	Earth, taken from the	65
Dead, received their	482	Earth, hurt not	570
Dead, good as	480	Earthquake, a great	568
Death, abolished	432	East, the kings of the	588
Death, should not see	477	Edification	279
Death, suffering of	456	Egypt, land of	471
Death, wounded to	581	Egyptians, wisdom of the	52
Death, not unto	524	Elder, the	529
Death, the second	554	Elders, four and twenty	561
Death, keys of hell and of	551	Elders, ordained them	104
Death, that sat on him was	567	Elders, ordain	441
Death, ministration of	296	Elders, let the	419
Death, by man came	285	Elect	503
Death, the second	603	Emerald, like unto an	560
Derbe, to	113	Enemy, thine	215
Destruction, sudden	392	Enoch, by faith	477
Devil, place to the	350	Ephesians	143
Devils, doctrines of	413	Ephesians, city of the	143
Diana, great is	143	Ephesus, angel of the church	
Diana, goddess	140	of	552
Diana, great goddess	143	Ephesus, men of	143
Disciples, the number of the	49	Ephesus, at	285
Dishonour, some to	333	Epistle, this	225
Divination, of	118	Esaias	207
Doctrine, in the apostles'	24	Esaias	223
Doctrine, form of	196	Esaias, the prophet	64
Dogs, beware of	362	Esteemeth, one man	218
Dogs, without are	614	Eternal, are	300
Door, an open	557	Ethiopia, a man of	61
Door, I stand at the	560	Eunuch	61
Door, open the	560	Euphrates, the great river	588
Door, a	295	Eutychus, named	146
Dragon, laid hold on the	601	Eve	308
Dragon, the	579	Evil, with	490

INDEX

	PAGE		PAGE
Eyes, anoint thy	559	Flesh, one	353
Eyesalve	559	Flesh, come in the	523
		Flesh, after the	301
F		Flesh, in the	364
		Flesh, in my	372
Fables, give heed to	405	Flesh, a thorn in the	314
Face, over his	297	Flock, the	149
Faith, shield of	354	Flood, water as a	579
Faith, proportion of	212	Flying, an angel	575
Faith, depart from the	413	Flux, a bloody	172
Faith, justified by	191	Fool, a	315
Faith, weak in	218	Foolish, the	235
Faith, spirit of	299	Foolishness	230
Faith, through	333	Fools, we are	243
Faith, not by	495	Foot, down to the	547
Faith, justified by	336	Footstool, under my	493
Faithful, the Lord is	401	Forehead, in their	570
Faithful, was	458	Foreheads, in their	584
Faithful, merciful and	457	Foreknowledge, of God	23
Faithful, was called	598	Forgetful, be not	484
Faithful, to be	117	Fornication, to avoid	248
Farewell	317	Fornication, from	107
Fashion, grace of the	489	Fornications, wrath of her	585
Fasting, prayed with	104	Forty days	3
Father, glory of the	195	Foundation, this	240
Father, without	466	Foundations, twelve	608
Father, leave his	353	Fountains, living	573
Fatherless, visit the	492	Free, am I not	259
Fathers, unto the	222	Free, made me	199
Fault, finding	471	Fruits, twelve manner of	612
Faults, confess your	500	Furlongs, twelve thousand	609
Fear, in	236	Furnace, burned in a	549
Feet, at the	37		
Feet, from thy	53	**G**	
Felix, governor	167		
Fever, of a	172	Galatia	503
Field, of blood	13	Galatians, foolish	332
Fields, reaped down your	499	Galilaeans, which speak	19
Figure, in a	480	Galilee, ye men of	9
Filthy, which is	613	Galilee, from	82
Fire, as a flame of	547	Gamaliel	44
Fire, a little	497	Gamaliel, feet of	160
Fire, on the	171	Garlands	102
Fire, revealed by	240	Garment, clothed with	547
Fire, coals of	215	Gate, before the	81
Fire, tongue is a	497	Gate, suffered without the	485
First, Jews	179	Gaza	60
Firstborn, be the	201	Genealogies, endless	405

	PAGE
Generation, his	65
Gentiles, manner of	329
Gentiles, over the	223
Gentiles, of the	185
Gentiles, possession of the	54
Gentleness, meekness and	306
Ghost, gave up the	93
Gideon	481
Gift, stir up the	431
Gift, free	194
Gifts, gave	348
Gifts, to offer	470
Girdle, golden	547
Glass, face in a	491
Glass, a sea of	562
Glory, partaker of the	505
Glory, crown of	507
Glory, nothing to	263
Goats, of	475
God, against	50
God, angel of	76
God, church of	273
God, churches of	388
God, the church of	149
God, caught up unto	579
God, form of	360
God, hid in	347
God, the gift of	431
God, most high	466
God, judgment of	399
God, ordained of	216
God, servants of our	570
God, sons of	177
God, tempted of God	490
God, power of	316
God, word of	461
God, wisdom of	232
God, people of	460
God, the unknown	127
Goddess, the great	141
Godliness, form of	434
Gold, crowns of	561
Gold, silver or	150
Gold, vessels of	433
Gomorrah, unto	207
Gospel, truth of the	329
Gospel, in the	178
Gospel, furtherance of the	359

	PAGE
Gospel, light through the	432
Grass, flower of the	489
Great, Babylon the	593
Greater, by the	465
Grecians, against the	73
Grecians, of the	46
Greek, a	113
Greek, to the	179
Greek, speak	158
Greeks, to the	147
Greeks, Jews and	233
Greek, neither	379
Greek, a	325
Greeks, the devout	123
Greeks, of the	98
Ground, holy	53

H

Habitation, of their	128
Hair, broided	407
Hand, on the right	55
Hand, Mine own	402
Hand, on his	171
Hand, in his right	552
Hand, mine own	449
Handkerchiefs	136
Hands, palms in their	571
Hands, they laid their	48
Hands, putting on my	431
Hands, lay	421
Hands, holy	406
Hard, joined	132
Harlot, Rahab the	496
Harlots, the mother of	593
Head, become the	31
Heads, your own	131
Heads, seven	580
Healing, the gift of	275
Heart, of one	34
Heart, of the	182
Hearts, counsels of the	242
Heat, nor any	572
Heat, a burning	489
Heathen, justify the	333
Heaven, towards	8
Heaven, third	313
Heaven, gazing up into	9

	PAGE		PAGE
Heaven, midst of	575	Ignorant, being	208
Heavens, higher than the	469	Image, to the	201
Hebrew, in	159	Image, not the very	476
Hebrews, against the	46	Immortality, put on	287
Hebrew, an	364	Immortality, life and	432
Hebrews, are they	312	Infirmities, our	462
Heir, the	338	Inheritance, an	478
Hell, set on fire of	497	Ink, with	533
Hell, down to	512	Interpretation, private	511
Heretick, a man	445	Iron, a rod of	579
Herod, the king	88	Israel, of the children of	571
Hidden, the	242	Israel, the kingdom to	4
High, ascended up on	348	Italian, called the	75
Holiday, an	376		
Holiness, spirit of	177	J	
Holy, he that is	613		
Honey, sweet as	575	Jambres	435
Honour, glory and	455	James, save	324
Honour, some to	433	James, killed	89
Hope, rejoice in	191	James, unto	92
Hope, believed in	190	Jannes	435
Horns, ten	580	Jasper, like a	560
Horns, the ten	594	Jasper, was	611
Horse, a white	598	Jasper, like a	608
Horse, a black	565	Jephthae	481
Horse, another	564	Jerusalem, from	10
Horse, pale	567	Jerusalem, in	5
Hospitality	213	Jerusalem, multiplied in	49
Hour, the ninth	76	Jerusalem, went up to	154
Hour, sixth	77	Jerusalem, holy city	607
Hour, third	22	Jerusalem, unto	10
House, Simon's	81	Jerusalem, dwellers at	13
Household, of Caesar's	366	Jerusalem, dwelling at	16
Housetop, upon the	77	Jesse, root of	223
Husband, her own	248	Jesus, I am	67
Husbands, your own	381	Jesus, this same	9
		Jesus, (Joshua)	54
I		Jesus, the name of	45
		Jesus, this	122
Iconium, in	98	Jesus, received Christ	373
Idle, learn to be	419	Jew, being a	329
Idol, things offered unto an	258	Jew, nor	379
Idol, conscience of the	258	Jew, am a	160
Idol, offered to	101	Jewess, was a	113
Idolaters, neither be	268	Jews, land of the	83
Idolatry, given to	124	John, I	607
Idols, unto	256	John, Cephas and	327
Ignorant, and unlearned	33	John, his servant	543

	PAGE		PAGE
John, and Peter	33	Law, bound by the	256
John, the baptism of	135	Law, offered by the	476
Journey, Sabbath day's	10	Leaven, the old	245
Judaea, all	82	Leaven, a little	339
Judaea, ye men of	21	Leopard, like unto a	580
Judah, house of	471	Letter, not of the	295
Judgment, going before to	424	Letter, wrote a	167
Jupiter	101	Letter, not in the	182
Jupiter, priest of	102	Letters, wrote	109
Jupiter, from	143	Lie, maketh a	614
Justified, a man is	495	Life, river of water of	612
Justus, named	132	Life, the tree of	612
Justus, is called	383	Life, the book of	606
		Life, newness of	195
K		Life, the book of	557
Kingdom, worthy of the	399	Life, spirit giveth	295
Kingdom, restore again	4	Light, give thee	351
Kingdom, pertaining to the	3	Light, God is	521
Kings, ten	594	Light, bring to	242
Kings, reigned as	242	Light, angel of	310
Kinsmen, my	204	Lights, many	145
Kiss, an holy	395	Lion, mouth of a	580
Kiss, holy	290	Lips, other	280
Knowledge, word of	275	Little, gathered	305
		Live, now we	390
L		Loft, third	146
		Lord, brethern of the	260
Labourers, the hire of the	499	Lord, the day of the	517
Lack, no	305	Lord, seek after the	106
Lady, the elect	529	Lord, revelations of the	313
Lamb, the marriage of the	597	Lord, the terror of the	301
Lamb, the song of the	587	Lord, prisoner of the	347
Lamb, and before the	571	Lord, Angel of the	60
Lamb, lo, a	584	Lord, the day of the	391
Language, speak in his own	17	Lord, way of the	135
Laodicea	384	Lot, fell upon	14
Laodiceans, the church of the	558	Lots, their	14
Last, first and the	550	Love, God of	317
Law, a doctor of the	44	Lucre, filthy	412
Law, without	180	Lukewarm, thou art	558
Law, in the	180	Lump, the whole	339
Law, boast of the	181	Lump, new	245
Law, free from that	197	Lysias, Claudias	167
Law, end of the	208	Lystria	113
Law, under the	336		
Law, curse of the	334	**M**	
Law, works of the	330	Macedonia	115
		Macedonia, departed from	365

INDEX 625

	PAGE		PAGE
Macedonia, part of	116	Mortify	378
Macedonia, came from	13	Moses, books of	108
Magistrates, the	121	Moses, against	50
Magog, Gog and	605	Moses, was learned	52
Male, neither	338	Moses, in the law of	262
Man, a good	192	Moses, face of	296
Man, a righteous	192	Moses, the body of	537
Man, what is	455	Moses, the song of	587
Manna, the hidden	555	Moses, as also	458
Maranatha	290	Moses, withstood	435
Marcus	507	Mother, without	466
Mark, the	582	Mourn, weep and	596
Mark, received the	600	Mouth, by the	30
Marriage, giveth her in	255	Much, gathered	305
Marrow, joint and	461	Muzzle	262
Marry, forbidding to	413	Mysia, to	114
Mars' hill	126	Mysteries, he speaketh	278
Marvelled, amazed and	19	Mystery	593
Master, ye also have a	382	Mystery, a	282
Masters	382	Mystery, followship of the	347
Masters, their own	444		
Matthias	14	## N	
Measure, a	566		
Measure, according to the	610	Name, excellent	453
Meat, not with	237	Nations, many	190
Meat, thy	221	Nations, of all	571
Meat, judge you in	376	Nations, in thee shall all	333
Meats, abstain from	413	Nations, to rule all	579
Meats, abstain from	111	Nature, the course of	497
Melchisedec, order of	463	Nazareth, Jesus Christ of	28
Melchisedec, this	466	Necks, their own	224
Member, a little	497	Nephews, children or	417
Men, doctrines of	377	Nicolaitanes	553
Men, wicked	401	Nicolas, a proselyte	47
Merchants, the	596	Night, thief in the	391
Mercurius, and Paul	101	Night, sleep in the	393
Mesopotamia	51	Night, thief in the	517
Michael	537	Number, of the	307
Milk, with	237	Nurse, as a	388
Mind, be of one	317	Nymphas	384
Minister, was a	222		
Ministers, able	295	## O	
Miracles, working of	276		
Miracles, that wrought	600	Offence, rock of	208
Money, he offered them	58	Offering, sacrifice and	476
Money, brought the	37	Old, three score years	418
Moon, the new	376	Olive, wild	211
Mortal, this	287		

	PAGE		PAGE
Olivet, called	10	Play, rose up to	268
Omega, Aleph and	614	Pontus	503
Omega, Alpha and	546	Poor, say to the	493
Ordained, was	198	Poor, despised the	494
Osee	206	Poor, became	304
Overseers, made you	149	Pot, golden	474
Ox, the	419	Poulus, Sargius	96
Ox, the mouth of the	262	Powers, higher	216
Oxen, bought	102	Prayer, fasting and	249
		Prayer, fervent	500
		Preaching, foolishness of	232
P		Pricks, the	67
		Priest, an high	462
Palsies, with	57	Priest, such an high	469
Paphos, unto	96	Priest, abideth a	466
Paps, about the	547	Priest, thou art	463
Parchments	436	Priest, such an high	470
Passion, after is	3	Priest, high	166
Passover, Christ our	245	Priests, company of the	49
Paul, I am of	238	Priests, the chief	70
Peace, God of	494	Principalities	347
Peace, king of	466	Principalities, spoiled	375
Peace, having made	371	Priscilla	133
Pearls, or	407	Prison, sent to the	43
Penny, for a	566	Prison, spirits in	505
Pentecost, the day of	15	Prison, loosed out of his	604
Perfect, be	317	Prison, cast us into	121
Peter, and other apostles	11	Prison, out of the	92
Peter, boldness of	33	Prochorus	47
Peter, she saw	74	Prophecy, word of	511
Pharaoh, saith unto	205	Prophesy, let us	212
Pharisee, a	364	Prophet, a false	96
Phenice, far as	85	Prophets, their own	388
Phenicia, unto	152	Prophets, spirits of the	281
Philip	47	Prophets, subject to the	281
Philip	60	Prophets, his holy	30
Philip, run thither	64	Prophets, false	522
Philip, said unto	62	Prophets, saints and	587
Philip, he desired	64	Prudent, of the	231
Philip, caught away	66	Psalms, the book of	13
Philip, house of	153	Psalms, in	380
Philippi	116	Ptolemais, came to	153
Philippians, ye	365	Publius, father of	172
Piety, to show	417	Published, was	82
Pillars	327	Purchased, a field	12
Pit, bottomless	601	Pure, keep thyself	419
Pit, key of the	601	Purification, days of	157
Place, into one	273	Purple, arrayed in	591

INDEX

R

	PAGE
Rahab	496
Raiment, shook his	131
Raiment, clothed in	557
Rainbow, there was a	560
Reading, attendance to	415
Reap, he also	342
Reconciliation, to make	457
Record, God is my	359
Red, that was	564
Redemption, the	183
Reed, a	576
Religion, pure	492
Resurrection, a better	482
Resurrection, the first	603
Rest, a	460
Rest, into my	458
Restitution, times of	30
Revelation, the	543
Revelation, by the	321
Revived, sin	198
Reward, own	239
Rich, ye are	242
Rich, was	304
Righteousness, by the	194
Righteousness, for	187
Righteousness, king of	466
River, a pure	612
Robbery, not	360
Rock, spiritual	265
Rod, Aaron's	474
Rod, like a	576
Rod, rule them with a	599
Romans, being	121
Rome, came to	173
Root, a	223
Root, of the	211
Ruler, the	166

S

	PAGE
Sabaoth, the Lord of	499
Sabaoth, Lord of	207
Sabath, of the	376
Sabbath day's journey	10
Sacrifice, offered in	256
Safety, peace and	392
Saint, salute every	366
Saints, necessity of	213
Saints, blood of	587
Salamis, at	94
Salem, king of	466
Salutation, the	402
Salute, all the Saints	366
Samson	481
Samuel	481
Samaria, and	5
Sanctuary, a minister of the	470
Sanctuary, a worldly	472
Sand, upon the	580
Sand, as the	480
Sandals, bind on thy	90
Sapphire, the second	611
Sardis, the church in	556
Satan, messenger of	314
Saul, Barnabas and	96
Saviour, appearing of our	432
School, daily in the	136
Science, opposition of	426
Scripture, the	186
Scripture, prophecy of the	511
Scripture, the	333
Scriptures, the other	518
Scythian	379
Sea, sand of the	605
Seal, a	188
Seal, the sixth	568
Seal, fifth	567
Seal, the third	565
Seal, the seventh	574
Sealed, which were	571
Seals, seven	563
Seats, judgment	494
Seats, four and twenty	561
Seed, thy	190
Seed, to every	286
Seek, Greeks	233
Seleucia, unto	94
Sell, buy and	498
Senate, all the	43
Serpent, that old	601
Serpent, the	308
Servants, exhort	444

	PAGE		PAGE
Shadow, having a	476	Soweth, a man	342
Shaven, shorn or	271	Sparingly, soweth	305
Sheep, counted as	202	Speaker, chief	101
Sheet, a great	79	Spirit, not every	522
Shepherd, the chief	507	Spirit, law of the	199
Shewbread, the	473	Spirit, soul and	461
Ship, finding a	152	Spirit, lead by the	340
Shod, feet	354	Spirit, in the	182
Shoes, put off thy	53	Spirit, I was in the	560
Shorn, having	133	Spirit, the evil	139
Shorn, be	271	Spirit, said to the	120
Sight, without	69	Spirit, with a	118
Sight, received	71	Spirits, unclean	57
Sign, a	233	Spirits, the evil	136
Silas, and Timotheus	131	Spirits, discerning of	276
Silence, a great	159	Spirits, from the seven	545
Silence, be in	408	Spirits, preached unto the	505
Silence, learn in	408	Spirits, father of	483
Silver, pieces of	140	Spue, I will	558
Silver, no man's	150	Stairs, on the	159
Simon, the magician	58	Star, the day	511
Sin, servants of	196	Stars, a crown of twelve	578
Sin, death by	192	Stars, seven	550
Sin, by one man	192	Stars, as the	480
Sin, made him to be	302	Steal, him that stole	350
Sin, without	462	Stephen, chose	47
Sins, some men's	424	Stephen, about	85
Sion, I lay in	208	Stewards, required in	241
Sion, the mount	584	Sticks, bundle of	171
Sister, a	260	Stomach, thy	423
Sister, thy elect	530	Stone, give him a white	555
Sky, stars of the	480	Stone, a living	504
Slain, crucified and	23	Stones, engraven on	296
Sleep, not all	282	Stones, precious	611
Sleep, and many	274	Store, in	289
Slumber, spirit of	209	Strangers, Athenians and	125
Snare, a	210	Strangers, to entertain	484
Snow, white as	547	Strangled, things	107
Sodoma, as	207	Stumblingblock, a	233
Soldiers, between two	90	Subjection, into	265
Son, my	433	Subjection, be in	483
Songs, spiritual	380	Subjection, with all	408
Sons, my	303	Submit, wives	381
Soothsaying, gain by	118	Suffering, my	372
Sorcerer, certain	96	Sun, clothed with	578
Sorcerers	614	Sun, standing in the	599
Soul, of one	34	Sun, let not the	349
Soul, spirit and	394	Superstitious, ye are too	126

INDEX

	PAGE		PAGE
Supper, his own	273	Throne, out of the	612
Supper, Lord's	273	Throne, one sat on the	560
Supper, into the	599	Time, born out of due	284
Synagogue, hard to the	132	Times, latter	413
Synagogues, read in	108	Timotheus, and Silas	131
Syria, through	112	Timotheus, named	113
Syria, into	133	Timothy, O	426
Swear, men verily	465	Tithes, receive	468
Sword, with the	89	Titus	325
Sword, a sharp	599	Tongue, the	497
Sword, sharp two-edged	550	Tongue, in their proper	13
Sword, a great	564	Tongue, an unknown	278
		Tongues, of other	280
T		Tongues, interpretation of	276
		Touch, not to	247
Tabernacle	470	Trance, into a	77
Tabernacle, there was a	473	Trance, in a	163
Tabitha	74	Translation, before his	477
Table, the	473	Treasure, we have this	298
Table, their	210	Treatise, the former	2
Tarsus, born in	160	Tree, leaves of the	612
Tattlers	419	Tree, on a	83
Taverns, three	173	Tree, olive	211
Teach, apt to	410	Tree, hangeth on a	334
Tears, wipe away all	573	Tribute, to whom	217
Temple, prayed in	163	Troas	436
Temple, into the	157	Troas, came to	295
Temple, speak in the	43	True, faithful and	598
Temple, measure the	576	Trumpet, sound of the	575
Temporal, are	300	Trumpets, seven	574
Tentmakers	129	Trust, thy	426
Tertius, I	225	Truth, love in the	529
Testament, new	295	Truth, sincerity and	245
Testament, blood of the	475	Truth, I say the	203
Testament, the first	475	Truth, obey the	339
Thanks, giveth God	219	Truth, spirit is	523
Theophilus	2	Twelve, of the	283
Thief, as a	391	Tyrannus, the school of	136
Thirst, neither	572	Tyre, from	153
Thorn, a	314		
Thorns, beareth	464	**U**	
Thousand, fifty	140		
Thousand, three and twenty	269	Uncircumcised, to men	84
Thousand, hundred and forty		Uncircumcision	252
and four	571	Unclean, or	80
Thousand, as a	516	Unjust, before the	245
Throne, a	560	Unjust, let him be	613
Throne, midst of	562	Unlearned, are	518
		Upper room	11

INDEX

V

	PAGE
Vagabond, the	138
Veil, put a	297
Vessel, a certain	79
Vessels, earthen	298
Vials, seven	590
Viper, came a	171
Virgin, his	253
Virgin, keep his	255
Virgins, daughters	154
Vision, he saw a	76
Vision, seen in the	115
Vision, this	81
Voice, a loud	55
Voice, hearing a	68
Vow, have a	155
Vow, he had a	133

W

	PAGE
Wages, taking	309
Wall, by the	72
Wall, thou whited	165
Water, came by	523
Waters, fountains of	573
Waters, many	590
Waters, sound of many	549
Weak, the	151
Weak, that is	218
Weak, became I as	264
Weak, many are	274
Weakness, through	316
Weakness, in	236
Wealth	271
Week, of the	289
Wells, are	515
Wheat, a measure of	566
White, apparel	8
Whore, the great	590
Widows, fatherless and	492
Widows, their	46
Wife, husband of one	410
Wife, a	260
Wife, head of the	352
Wilderness, fly into the	579
Will, of his	346
Window, sat in a	146
Winds, holding the four	569
Wine, not given to much	412
Wine, a little	423
Wine, given to much	443
Wine, oil and the	566
Wine, drink of the	585
Wine, new	19
Winepress, the	586
Wisdom, the word of	275
Wisdom, in all	380
Wisdom, the	231
Wisdom, after	233
Wise, ye are	243
Wise, the	235
Wise, wisdom of the	231
Wise, are not	307
Witness, God is a	387
Witness, God is my	178
Witnesses, the	56
Witnesses, shall be	5
Wivies, Old	414
Wivies, love their	353
Woe, woe, woe	575
Woe, is unto me	263
Woman, travail upon a	391
Women, the aged	443
Women, the chief	123
Wonder, a great	578
Wool, white like	547
Wool, scarlet	475
Word, hearer of the	491
Words, remember the	151
Works, without	187
Works, by	495
Works, justified by	496
Worms, eaten of	93
Worthy, counted	458
Worthy, labourer is	419
Wound, deadly	581
Wrath, sware in my	458
Wrath, fierceness of his	589
Wrath, worketh	189

Y

	PAGE
Years, thousand	601
Years, as a thousand	516
Years, bound him thousand	601